# MAYBE THE WHOLE OCEAN

Exploring New Metaphors
for Navigating Feelings and Relationships

Brian R. K. B. Lim

MAYBE THE WHOLE OCEAN
Exploring New Metaphors for Navigating Feelings and Relationships
Brian R. K. B. Lim
Editor: Joan Phillips
Cover: NX Arts and Zoe K. Lim

Third Edition published February 2022
Copyright © 2018, 2021, 2022 by Brian R. K. B. Lim

Published by Paradigm Hawai`i Publishing
a division of Paradigm Hawai`i Counseling, Inc.
970 N. Kalaheo Avenue, Suite A-216
Kailua, Hawai`i 96734
www.maybethewholeocean.com

Printed in the United States of America

# Contents

# Prologue: Horizons

*Little things console us because little things afflict us.*
*Blaise Pascal*

*Twenty years from now you will be more disappointed by the*
*things that you didn't do than by the ones you did do.*
*So, throw off the bowlines.*
*Sail away from the safe harbor.*
*Catch the trade winds in your sails.*
*Explore. Dream. Discover.*
*Mark Twain*

*Most* of life does not *have* to be difficult.

This is a risky statement. If it is not true, this book will have no credibility. If it is true, then the content of the following pages could change lives.

There are additional risks. First, I risk originality. Many readers will recognize that my opening line sounds almost identical to the timeless words of M. Scott Peck in his pioneer work, *The Road Less Traveled*. There, he begins with the "great truth" that "life is difficult."[1] And so it may sound as though I am either plagiarizing or contradicting him when I assert that this does not *have* to be the case. To the contrary, I have been quite influenced by Peck's writings. Further, while I do hope to make a unique contribution with my writing, I believe I am the proverbial small person standing on the shoulders of giants and much of what I share is a repackaging of lessons I have learned from others much more seasoned than I.

---

1   Peck, M. S. (1978). The road less traveled: A new psychology of love, traditional values, and spiritual growth. New York, NY: Simon & Schuster, p. 1.

Second, I risk integrity. Even as I write, I ask myself if I will be true to my own words. It is one thing to make a bold claim but another to live up to it or to live by it. This, of course, is where the difficulty comes in. My firm belief is that much of life can be easier than it often is, but to get there does take work. I confess that I can be, and indeed often am, hypocritical. Perhaps this is a risk for anybody who aspires to write a book about personal change. Even Peck once said of himself, "I'm a prophet, not a saint."[2]

Third, I risk faith. Any assertion about life has implications for ultimate reality. And so, my claims need to take seriously deep issues like pain and suffering, evil and good, and God. In this case, I will write out of my own experiences as a follower of Jesus. I will do my best to show why I believe what I have written is consistent with my faith, simultaneously doing my utmost to respect and to not impose. And, if my writing happens to influence even one reader to what I believe is truly good news, then I will be thankful and consider the risk well-taken.

Fourth, I risk truth. On one hand, this claim might seem *too good* to be true, wishful thinking perhaps. A quick look around, especially a survey of our current health, economic and geopolitical landscape, reveals hardship and uncertainty are all around us, often threatening to worsen. To say then that most difficulties do not have to be experienced could seem ludicrous. On the other hand, this statement may not be so unfamiliar. Anybody who claims that they have a say in their quality of life, anybody who believes that success is a personal choice, would probably agree.

So, there are risks either way. Risks, however, are among those things that make the world go 'round, and some risks are worth taking. And the risk of my opening statement might be the first step toward a new "ocean" of possibility.

## Moving Forward

*Oceanspeak*
Throughout this book, let us think of the ocean as a double

---

2  Billen, Andrew (2005, May 10). Gin, cigarettes, women: I'm a prophet not a saint. The Sunday Times. Retrieved from http://www.thetimes.co.uk/tto/life/article1722240.ece

metaphor for relationships and emotions. Collectively, think of the major oceans (Atlantic, Pacific, Indian, Arctic, and Antarctic) as the World Ocean, which will serve as our primary metaphor for relationships. Let us treat relationships as any purposeful interaction or connection between two or more individuals.

Covering nearly three-fourths of the earth's surface, the World Ocean is the single-most dominant feature of our planet. And like the World Ocean, relationships comprise most of life as most know it. So, throughout this book let us also use "ocean of relationships" to creatively refer to "most of life."

So, saying "most of life does not have to be difficult" is another way of saying that *relationships do not have to be hard*. We all want better relationships, and this book addresses that desire.

*Revolution*
The ways we interact with others—work together, play together, live together, fight, laugh, cry, lament, and celebrate together—are essential to existence. Relationships with ourselves, our neighbors, and our Creator cover the surface area of most of our lives. Similarly, relationships can range in intensity and meaning, paralleling both the protected shallows and the unfathomable depths of the ocean.

We can find ourselves caught in all sorts of places on the ocean of relationships that may be less than ideal, to say the least. For some, relationships can be an exercise in frustration, like sailors working against a strong current or windless waters. For others, relationships are like a nasty gale which beats on their vessel with other-worldly force. Still others are content to stay in the shallow water, perhaps not even getting off the shore, because the threats of waves, winds, and the depths in general are too terrifying. Often, this latter, land-bound position is held by those who have tried relationships and found them sorely lacking or too painful. And for many, past experiences and current fears are instrumental in discouraging or preventing even the possibility of exploration.

Imagine sitting on the shore and looking out at the expanse of blue beyond the sand. Watching the way the waters meet the sky in a horizontal line, it is easy to see why mariners of old believed that the earth was flat. Who could blame them for fearing that their ships would drop off the edge into some chasm or abyss? Indeed, the visible ocean was just a large body of water that literally stood between the beach and the end of the world.

Common sense suggests that it might be folly to embark on a journey at all. Just stay on shore, where it is safe, dry, and solid. This, of course, makes sense if what is seen is what is; if perception equals reality. The world *looks* flat, so therefore it *is* flat.

Much like the early sailors who opted for exploration, we need a shift in perspective when it comes to the ocean of relationships. We need to consider that this ocean is more than meets the eye and, in fact, wraps around the globe of our lives. Our world is not flat.

Once this is considered, there is reason to venture out onto the waves and toward the convergence of sea and sky. And as we do so, perhaps we will even find that the horizontal line widens until it completely encircles our craft, yielding broader horizons and further still, new shores and other beautiful lands.

Just a shift. At the outset, it might seem like a grain of sand, so small and tiny it could hardly mean anything—a "drop in the bucket." And yet for some, this granule, this droplet, might be just a beginning. And it might be a certain kind of beginning— one that continues to grow and expand until one day it fills to overflowing the bucket itself and then possibly much, much, much more. It's neither new nor rocket science but for some it might represent a complete turnaround. Just a drop in the bucket and then . . . maybe the whole ocean.

# Chapter 1: Water

*Counsel in a person's heart is like deep water,
but an understanding person draws it out.*
*Proverbs 20:5*[1]

If relationships are the ocean, let us think of emotions as the water. Emotions, in both a real and figurative sense, make up the heart of relationships. They give form and dimension, substance and body, to the ways in which people experience life together. Whether positive or negative, emotions make relationships personal.

This personal influence is also a primary reason people approach interpersonal dynamics the way they do, whether those dynamics constitute pursuit or distance, depth or superficiality, entries or exits, or various gradations between. Emotions, for many, also represent risk.

## Venturing Out

*The Plunge*
Risk is a complex concept. It involves vulnerability and potential costs, and almost by definition, it excludes the comfort of a guarantee. For many, emotions seem all too complicated and uncertain, and so the concept of taking emotional risks can be daunting as well. Should I tell a person how I feel? Will I open my heart? Be transparent? What if they get angry with me? Or hurt? What if I am rejected? Such are the questions that can surface when people consider whether to venture further out onto an emotional limb.

1   NET Bible®

This, again, is why the ocean of relationships can often seem stormy or even treacherous at times. Better to stay close to shore, where life is more stable. Or, alternatively, if one is already on the water (as in a relationship which contains risk), certainly avoid "rocking the boat."

Stepping out into the risk of relationships can seem like stepping off a ledge or walking the plank. A leap of faith. Taking the plunge. Either way, many people have mixed feelings about the risk of opening themselves up to the sensations that accompany this step.

In one sense, when it comes to risk in relationships, the primary feeling in question is love. Love is the most desired and, simultaneously, often the most difficult emotion to give and to receive. Love may be considered the ultimate emotion, because it is more than emotion. Love is action. Elsewhere it has been described as a language and as a verb. And therefore, love, more than any feeling, carries the most risk.

C. S. Lewis, an author who had many profound insights into relationships among both children and adults, once wrote the following:

> To love at all is to be vulnerable. Love anything, and your heart will be wrung and possibly broken. If you want to make sure of keeping it intact, you must give it to no one, not even to an animal. Wrap it carefully 'round with hobbies and little luxuries; avoid all entanglements . . .

Lewis goes on to point out that to refrain from love, to avoid the risk of love, is to risk selfishness and tragedy, even using the language of loss and death to describe what occurs when one protects oneself from love. The quotation above continues:

> Lock it up safe in the casket or coffin of your selfishness. But in that casket, safe, dark, motionless, airless, it will change. It will not be broken; it will become unbreakable, impenetrable, irredeemable. The alternative to tragedy, or at least to the risk of tragedy, is damnation. The only place outside Heaven where you can be perfectly safe

*from all the dangers and perturbations of love is Hell.*[2]

Risk therefore is on both sides of love, and by extension, on both sides of emotion. This book, however, is about risks and the modest proposal that *most* of life does not *have* to be difficult. The bigger issues, then, revolve around which risks will be taken.

In this case, let us also risk the idea that emotions do not have to be complex; they might be simpler than we realize. With respect to Lewis, maybe even "the dangers and perturbations of love" can be minimized.

Oliver Wendell Holmes is credited with saying, "I would not give a fig for the simplicity this side of complexity, but I would give my life for the simplicity on the other side of complexity."[3] The suggestion that emotions are not necessarily as complex as we make them out to be aspires to the simplicity on complexity's other side. Furthermore, if, as Lewis suggests, the risk of not loving or feeling is death, then might opening ourselves to love and emotions in general, be a pathway to life? This, of course, is the audacious claim of this book.

*The Punchline*
We begin with what I would like to call two relationally strategic moves, namely, the Rational Shift and the Motivational Shift. Specifically, the **Rational Shift** is this: *where relationships are concerned, thoughts determine feelings.* And later, we will see that the second, **Motivational Shift** pertains to how *distinguishing between needs and wants empowers conscious choices.*

The Rational Shift is the punchline of this chapter. In oceanspeak, this is both the line in the sand that marks a decision about how we will approach relationships and the bottom line to this book. It is an appeal for us to seriously consider what we believe about ourselves and others and to take a first step, as it

2  Martindale, W. & Root, J. (Eds.). (1989). The quotable Lewis. Wheaton, IL: Tyndale House Publishers, p. 403.

3  Oliver Wendell Holmes quotes. (n.d). In Thinkexist. Retrieved November 26, 2017, from http://thinkexist.com/quotation/i_would_not_give_a_fig_for_the_simplicity_this/217651.html

were, away from the beach and toward the water.

It is important to emphasize that this certainly is not a new concept. The Stoic philosophers of ancient Greece were committed to this notion. For example, one of the founders, Epictetus, was known to have said about negative emotions, "Men are disturbed not by things but by the view which they take of them."[4] In certain spiritual traditions, belief is regarded as the source of emotion, and in a very real sense, the source of identity. For example, Buddha taught, "All experience is preceded by mind, led by mind, made by mind."[5] Similarly, the Christian apostle Paul told the early believers in Rome to "be transformed by the renewal of your mind."[6] Paul also encouraged the Christians in the city of Philippi to have a certain perspective on life, saying, "have the same *mindset* as Christ Jesus . . ."[7] Much of modern psychology has also been heavily influenced by the role of the mind in the management of emotions overall, and this has been especially central to the theories of seminal clinicians such as Albert Ellis (Rational Emotive Behavioral Therapy), Aaron Beck (Cognitive Therapy/Cognitive Behavioral Therapy), and Donald Meichenbaum (Stress Inoculation Training). Thinking, therefore, has long been identified as the determinant of emotional experience, and I gratefully acknowledge all the above authors and more as key influences upon the ideas proposed in this book.

At the same time, for many people the hypothesis that thoughts determine feelings has little to no impact upon experience. Frankly, in my experience, when I suggest that this principle might revolutionize relationships, people often seem quite disappointed. And if we are honest, this idea can sound hollow, anticlimactic, or even irrelevant. Caught in the throes of interpersonal upheavals such as the pain and tragedy of betrayal or the threat of divorce, people are initially more discouraged than encouraged to hear that their thinking might be the very place to focus their energy and their interventions. Why is this?

4   Beck, A. T., Rush, A. J., Shaw, B. F., & Emery, G. (1979). Cognitive therapy of depression. New York, NY: Guilford Press, p. 8.

5   Dhammapada (Gil Fronsdal translation), Chapter 1, verse 1. (2011, March). In New-Buddhist. Retrieved November 26, 2017, from http://newbuddhist.com/discussion/10027/all-that-i-am-is-the-result-of-all-that-i-have-thought-buddha

6   Romans 12:2

7   Philippians 2:5, New International Version® (NIV®), italics added

At least three responses come to mind: nature, human nature, and forces of habit. Simply put, there are important intrinsic and extrinsic reasons for us to believe that emotions and therefore, relationships, are highly complex. The irony, however, is that our potential to adapt can paradoxically become maladaptive. Life all too easily becomes unnecessarily difficult, and all too often we find ourselves hurting those we love or being hurt by them. We naturally find it too simple to say our feelings are more influenced by our thinking than we might realize. And often when this happens, we will likely take one of two routes to address relationship difficulties: active resistance or passive resignation.

To illustrate, consider a couple, Amy and Bob, caught up in an argument. Bob is frustrated because Amy does not listen to him, and Amy is frustrated because Bob does not hear her. Both are thinking about how the situation could be so much better if *the other* would just cooperate, budge on the issues, or take the time to see from another perspective. There may be elevated tones, exaggerated words, indirect or direct criticisms, and ultimately, division. After some time of trying to get through to the other, the result is for both to either push back or back off, pursue or distance, or maybe even pretend the conflict never happened.

This admittedly negative description of an argument shows how natural it can be for either person to regard the resulting feeling, in this case, frustration, as a complex state that is generated by not being listened to. Bob might think that his frustration is due to Amy's stubbornness, and Amy might attribute her frustration to Bob's selfishness. If they are particularly ambitious, each might also be overwhelmed by other factors such as the other's personality, upbringing, the nature of the dispute itself, and any number of extenuating circumstances, e.g., lack of sleep, a "bad day," influence of a substance, time crunches, a previous unresolved argument, etc.

Into this fray might come the suggestion for this couple to seek the help of a counselor or some other third party. If they decide to attend, the counselor might propose that each could manage the situation more effectively by monitoring his or her own perceptions and thoughts. And in the face of such a proposal, it would not be surprising if the couple were to rather quickly dismiss the suggestion as a futile "mind game" or a "psychological trick."

One aim of counseling is to facilitate a process where each person discovers that attending to their own mind can expose very convincing *self*-defeating tricks and thereby show that this endeavor is neither futile nor a game. At the same time, the counselor will do well to recognize that from where the couple is sitting, suspicion and even opposition to oversimplified and seemingly tedious techniques are highly understandable. Interestingly, the validity of each person's views introduces additional potential for emotions, and the stage is set for either another standoff or a new understanding; a recapitulation of old patterns or a new and hopefully therapeutic experience. Again, since the complexities can seem overwhelming, a certain kind of innovative simplicity might be particularly helpful.[8]

---

## "Stepping out into the risk of relationships can seem like stepping off a ledge or walking the plank."

---

### Two Models

*Emotion Chemistry*
Again, thoughts determine emotions. And just as there are always two sides to risk, it may be useful to think of our topic from two angles. In this case, let us think further about the nature of water, namely its chemical formula: $H_2O$.

Water is made up of two elements: hydrogen and oxygen. Similarly, emotions involve two general "ingredients": 1) a situation and 2) its meaning (or interpretation). And as we shall see, just as the proportion of hydrogen to oxygen is critical

---

8   This book emphasizes a predominantly intrapersonal approach to optimizing relationships, largely inspired and informed by a cognitive understanding of emotions. Two particularly powerful and effective approaches to relationships that are evidence-based and more interpersonal and experiential (especially in their emphasis on attachment and bonding) are Leslie Greenberg's Emotion-Focused Therapy and Sue Johnson's Emotionally Focused Therapy.

for water chemistry, so the differential emphasis given to a situation or its interpretation is vital for our understanding of how emotions are experienced.

We can use an acronym to depict the differential emphasis we give to the situation and its interpretation. It has been said that a picture is worth a thousand words. We might also say, "a word is worth a thousand pictures," and in many ways, the versatility of words is an integral part of this book.[9] So, to illustrate, and hopefully have a little more fun, let us consider the word and acronym: FIT.

Each of the letters in FIT point to one of three components of any emotional experience: feelings (F), incidents (I), and thoughts (T). Moreover, let us begin by thinking of these as forming a simple equation:

***Feelings = Incidents + Thoughts***
or
$$F = I + T$$

It is important to give some operational definitions to each of these terms as they will be returned to repeatedly throughout the course of this discussion. For our purposes, let us generally use the word **incident** to refer to a situation and **thought** to refer to the meaning or interpretation of a situation. So, an incident will again refer to any situation, event, environment, or circumstance that occurs at any given time. Likewise, a thought will refer to any cognitive activity that happens relative to an incident, including beliefs, expectations, perceptions, assumptions, or values. Finally, a **feeling** will refer to any emotional state (such as happiness or sadness) that arises whenever an incident and thought(s) about the incident occur together. In this case, at the risk of oversimplifying, we will use the words "feeling" and "emotion" interchangeably. Furthermore, it will be useful to generally define incidents as external or "outside" of a person and thoughts as internal or "inside" of a person.

---

9  I affectionately think of the theoretical approach I am here trying to articulate as "Literal Therapy."

To summarize:

**Incident:**
any (external) situation, event, environment,
or circumstance that occurs at any given time.

**Thought:**
any (internal) cognitive activity that happens
relative to an incident.

**Feeling:**
any emotional state that arises
whenever an incident and thought occur together

In the equation above, it appears that a feeling is the sum of an incident and a thought. However, the plus sign simply signifies that feelings occur when incidents and thoughts combine, and it is probably more accurate to say that a feeling is the *product* of an incident and a thought. Thus, incidents and thoughts are factors, which can differentially impact the intensity of an emotion or feeling. A better summary might be:

*Feelings* = *Incidents* x *Thoughts*
or
$F = I \times T$

Two possible approaches to this concept emerge, depending on whether one gives incidents or thoughts more weight in the creation of a feeling. So, if feelings are analogous to water and if incidents and thoughts correspond to the hydrogen and oxygen molecules, then emotional experience will vary according to which factor (incident or thought) is regarded as "hydrogen."

However, to compare an incident or thought to hydrogen does not mean that the differential impact of one factor is always "double" that of the other factor. Rather, we can think of which factor gets the majority or deciding "vote" on the feeling itself, e.g., which factor, incident or thought, is seen as having roughly 51% (or higher) of the vote and which is assigned 49% (or lower). For future reference and to illustrate this, we can show which factor has the most influence by capitalizing and putting in bold its corresponding letter in our acronym. So, if we attribute at least 51% of the influence on a feeling to the incident factor, we can write it like this:

$fIt$

Likewise, if we attribute at least 51% of the influence on a feeling to the thought factor, we can write it like this:

$fiT$

Finally, let us refer to the general idea that feelings are influenced by both incidents and thoughts as the FIT model.

## The Default Model

*Survival*

The first ($fIt$) understanding of relationships and emotions is one that emphasizes the incident. This is the dominant or default understanding of emotion at work in most of society. Before going further, it is important to understand the believability of this model and the reasons for how it has become the majority approach.

The single, most powerful reason for saying that feelings are caused by the incidents in our lives is *survival*. Of course, survival is an all-important consideration. Where survival is in question, the emotions we experience are built-in warning systems that help us to navigate our world. In many respects, if we do not make an immediate or direct connection between what we feel and what is happening outside of us, we may do so to our peril.

This approach to our world, therefore, is natural and works nicely with a Darwinian understanding of natural selection[10] as well as what Herbert Spencer referred to as the "survival of the fittest,"[11] and so the parallel to our FIT acronym is intentional. People are the most highly evolved species because people have been best able to adapt. Adaptation involves our ability to defend against hostile environments. To borrow from Lord

---

10   Darwin, C. (1859). The origin of the species by means of natural selection, or preservation of favoured races in the struggle for life. London, United Kingdom: John Murray.

11   Spencer, H. (1864). The principles of biology. London: Williams and Norgate.

Alfred Tennyson, we have been able to overcome "nature, red in tooth and claw."[12]

Feelings, in this way, are instinctive and rather physiological. We can see this in the way we are literally "wired," with a significant aspect of our nervous system being devoted to the sympathetic response, also known as the "fight-or-flight" system. Biological urges to move away from pain are important aspects of our physical survival as well.

On one hand, this is good, and there is no denying the remarkable ways in which we, the human race, have overcome adversity after adversity. There is something inherently exciting and exhilarating about the accomplishments brought about by our ability to continually develop and adapt. Survival is certainly something to aspire to and reflects something noble and glorious within us.

> **"Where survival is in question, the emotions we experience are built-in warning systems that help us to navigate our world."**

*Competition*

This ability to overcome, to achieve dominance, and to triumph is necessary for survival against the elements and the wilds of nature. It is also at the heart of being able to enjoy a game or contest. Thus, in addition to being recreational, competitive activities, like sports, are valuable ways of experiencing something very fundamental to life. The human spirit is drawn to the thrill and rush of competition, where the events themselves evoke strong feelings. Take, for instance, the way the world comes together every two years to celebrate the extraordinary gifts and talents of exceptional athletes during the Olympic Games.

Feelings associated with sports and competition connect to the innate desires we have to survive and to win. Indeed,

---

12 Tennyson, A. (1850, 2013). In Memoriam A. H. H., Canto 56. Cambridge: Cambridge University Press.

these desires ultimately connect us to our Maker, the one who designed us with a will to strive, to overcome, and to endure. Borrowing again from an analogy to the Olympics, a classic example of this may be found in the movie *Chariots of Fire*, where runner Eric Liddle (played by Ian Charleson) says of his love for the sport, "...(God) made me fast, and when I run, I feel His pleasure."[13] Here again, strong emotion is immediately and directly connected to the event (i.e., incident) at hand.

## Battle

The "will to survive" and the "thrill of the games," so to speak, are two very powerful ways in which emotions seem to be inextricably driven by the situations or incidents that are occurring at any given time. When survival and competition combine on local, national, or international levels, a third, formidable experience results in emotions tracing directly back to surrounding events: battle. "Wars and rumors of wars"[14] bring fear, excitement, anxiety, and sorrow. Perhaps no other experience runs as deep with adrenaline, blood, and fight-flight energy as facing off with an enemy who is bent on killing or capturing another. In this life-threatening context, emotions run high and in streams that seem directly imposed by the conflict between the warring parties. There is no ocean of relationships between adversaries—just liquid hatred and the philosophy of drown or be drowned, kill or be killed.

Taken together, the dynamics of survival, competition, and battle are very persuasive arguments for the belief that emotions are determined *directly* by the externals in our lives. In such situations, it follows that what we feel is a function of the environment itself. One thus feels fear when encountering a beast in the wild, joy in winning a championship, or rage or fear when confronted by an enemy.

In each of these areas, we can see the sympathetic system hard at work. This is nature at its fittest, and it works to say events determine emotions. When survival is at stake or when survival mechanisms like the fight-flight system are involved,

13 From Chariots of Fire (1981), original screenplay written by Colin Welland, directed by Hugh Hudson, and produced by Twentieth-Century Fox, Allied Stars, and An Enigma Production.

14 Matthew 24:6

we literally *need* to feel the things we feel or else risk losing life itself. Our biology requires certain emotions, and when the above incidents are involved, our environment essentially has a very compelling and direct impact.

*Positive, Direct Feelings*

So far, our focus has been on ways external incidents drive emotions such as fear, anger, or happiness upon winning a competition. Additional examples can be seen when biological factors are involved. For example, certain events such as eating, drinking, elimination, sex, and sleep can, in and of themselves, generate strong positive emotions. Although temporary, a very real sense of fulfillment can be experienced when such events occur. Therefore, we can say that food and drink can "satisfy," people "relieve" themselves, a couple can "pleasure" one another, and sleep can "refresh." And, conversely, negative emotions will likely be felt to the extent that these events are not experienced.

In these situations, emotions quite legitimately function as verbs. Perhaps this is one reason why the feelings associated with these basic events are called "drives." The early developmental nature of the overlap between emotions and behaviors is captured by the Swiss scientist, Jean Piaget, who referred to infancy as a period characterized by "sensorimotor" experience.[15] Behaviors combine with physiology, and there is direct correspondence between these activities and feelings. In this way, our awareness of the persuasive nature of the first type of FIT model begins from a very early age. We learn to equate our emotions with the things we do and to say that experiences themselves "make" us feel certain ways.

## Emotional Reactivity and Responsiveness

*Actual and Perceived Problems*

When incidents pose actual threats, the feelings that result can be considered problematic. There is essentially no need to distinguish between the discomfort of the feelings and the danger of the situation. Indeed, to do so could risk creating more danger. However, this is not the same as saying the emotions

---

15   Piaget, J. (1930). The child's conception of physical causality. London, UK: Routledge and Kegan Paul.

themselves are always dangerous. They are just problematic in that they necessarily signal that something in one's environment should change.

Problems, by definition, need to be solved, answered, or fixed. The original Greek word *próblēma* indicates something that is thrown, in the way, a hindrance, or an obstacle.[16] When threats are involved, uncomfortable feelings signify that something is not right or is "broken," and these feelings function as a necessary tool for fixing the damage, a map for navigating away from the danger. When "life is on the line," it makes sense to attribute emotions to events. However, the ocean of life's relationships is rarely an *actual* battleground, and casualties are usually avoidable. So, the stage for an unnecessary difficulty is set when survival is not at stake and two conditions co-occur: 1) emotions are externalized and 2) negative emotions are assumed to be problematic. Of course, by definition, unnecessary difficulties can be averted or at least minimized. Again, *most* of life does not *have* to be difficult.

When emotions are attributed to external factors, they feel imposed upon from without. People learn to be on guard against such feelings, especially negative ones such as anger or fear. Just as walls are constructed to keep intruders out of a city, strategies are developed for coping with negative feelings that seem to come at us from the outside.

Take, for instance, a situation where a man and a woman are dealing with financial issues. In this case, let's say the man thinks that the woman is a spendthrift, and the woman thinks that the man is a miser. Let's call the woman Lucy and the man Miles. Lucy believes that all her contributions to the relationship have earned her an occasional shopping spree. Miles believes that "frugalness is next to godliness." So, when Miles learns of an unexpected purchase on Lucy's part, his anger leads him to criticize the spending and scold her as the spender. Feeling treated like a child, she justifies herself and labels him "selfish." For each, the other represents a threat, a dispenser of something that seems against peace and happiness.

---

16  problem. (n. d.). In dictionary.com. Retrieved February 5, 2018, from http://www.dictionary.com/browse/problem?s=t

When this happens, an interesting phenomenon occurs. The emotion, apparently externally generated, is doubly unwanted. It is unwanted first because it comes from outside and second, because it is uncomfortable to not have one's way. It is a kind of foreign discomfort. Returning to our example, Miles wants Lucy to spend less, and Lucy wants Miles to allow her to spend more. This "double dose" of foreign discomfort so to speak, makes it seem like the emotions are problems, obstacles to be eliminated. And while this makes sense, it is one step closer to concluding that the other person is the problem. And most of the time, *if we think another person is a problem, that, in itself, is a problem.*

There are two basic reasons it is problematic to view a person as a problem. First, problems call for fixing or some sort of removal, and second, people generally do not want to be fixed or removed. Even more importantly, if we must change a person to fix a situation, then that situation will hardly be conducive to a relationship.

> **"Good motivations in a relationship can be missed when reactive approaches to emotions are at work."**

In this sense, externalized or incident-focused emotions naturally lead to reactive strategies. By contrast, internally driven or thought-focused emotions lead to responsive strategies. So, for our purposes, an emotional **reaction** occurs when the source of the unwanted emotion is external to a person and when negative emotions are treated as problems in that we assume they ought not be felt.[17] Alternatively, an emotional **response** occurs when emotions are primarily driven by a person's thoughts rather than by incidents. As such, negative emotions, while uncomfortable, are not treated as problematic

---

17    This model I am proposing is similar to Steven Covey's understanding of reactivity and proactivity (see Covey, S. R. (1989). The seven habits of highly effective people: Restoring the character ethic. New York, NY: Simon & Schuster, Inc., p. 70). At the same time, I trust that developing the emotional nuances of reaction and response will be one of the unique contributions of this book.

per se (see Table 1 for a summary of these differences).[18]

| REACTION $f\,\mathbf{I}\,t$ | RESPONSE $f\,i\,\mathbf{T}$ |
|---|---|
| *survival* context | *non-survival/thriving* context |
| *incident*-focused | *thought*-focused |
| emphasis on *situation* as primary reason for emotion | emphasis on *interpretation* as primary reason for emotion |
| negative emotions are *outsourced and "problematized"* | negative emotions are *insourced and "utilized"* |
| focus on *facts* | focus on *opinions/beliefs* |
| acting often precedes thinking | thinking often precedes acting |
| relationships tend to be more competitive (biased towards *emotionally "fittest"*) | relationships tend to be more cooperative (biased towards *emotional "fitness"*) |

Table 1:
Differences between Reaction and Response as
Two Distinct Approaches to Addressing Emotion

## Quality of Relationship, Quality of Life

According to the FIT equation, emotional reactivity simply means that, when an uncomfortable feeling is felt, one's first move is to directly intervene at the level of the unwanted incident as opposed to changing one's thoughts. While this makes sense if there is actual danger or if survival is in question, it generally does not work for the goal of being in a relationship with another person.

18  The Latin phrase per se (literally, "by itself") can often be used when discussing the category of experience that we are calling the "situation" (the facts, circumstances, incidents, and external/environmental details that are distinguished from opinions, interpretations, and other more internal/cognitive factors). Since this distinction (between situation and interpretation is so central to our discussion of emotion, I will also intentionally use this phrase (per se) from time to time throughout this book.

In this way, reactivity involves acting before thinking (again, changing the incident factor of the equation before changing the thought factor). Of course, acting without thinking is an important reflex, but in a relationship, it can lead to a vicious cycle. To return to our example earlier, Lucy contradicts Miles and then Miles scolds Lucy. Both are well-intentioned, and both are most likely trying to improve the relationship (save money, have nice possessions), but ironically, these intentions to help are probably the last motivations that will be heard. Reactivity is characterized by acting on impulse, and because this impulse is essentially directed at a perceived imposition, it most often takes the form of aggression or defensiveness.

Good motivations in a relationship can be missed when reactive approaches to emotions are at work. Further, when good motivations are missed in a relationship, we have *unnecessary problems*. And, when unnecessary problems accumulate, there is a proportional decrease in the quality of relationships which further translates into a decrease in quality of life. By the same token, quality of life will also significantly increase to the extent that we can reduce or minimize unnecessary problems. This brings us to the second approach to emotions, which will be the focus of our next chapter.

# Chapter 2: Eagles and Dolphins

*Once you have tasted flight, you will forever walk the earth
with your eyes turned upward, for there you have been
and there you will always long to return.*

*Leonardo da Vinci*

I once attended an inspirational conference where a speaker, who was originally from another country, shared about how his first encounter with Americans led him to see amazing opportunities for motivational speaking. He recounted how, after a brief amount of time in the States, he called his wife and excitedly told her something to the effect of, "Honey, we're going to make it big here. These people think *they* have problems!" In comparison to the poverty and other injustices he had witnessed in his country, American issues seemed to him to be quite trivial. Ironically, this meant Americans would be a very willing audience for his motivational techniques. I resonated with both this speaker's humor and his message. His joke underscored the way we can tend to see problems as outside of ourselves, and paradoxically, how amenable most of our problems are to internal, motivational interventions. Moreover, his statement pointed to how certain thought patterns can be a central factor in suffering. Stephen Covey puts it so well: "The way we see the problem *is* the problem."[1]

## Shifting Perspective

*Eagles*
Let us think now of a second approach to the FIT equation.

---

1   Covey, S. R. (1989). The seven habits of highly effective people: Restoring the character ethic. New York, NY: Simon & Schuster, Inc., p. 40.

Rather than emphasizing the incidents in our lives as the direct source of our emotions ($f\ I\ t$), let us focus on the idea that our feelings are more determined by our thoughts ($f\ i\ T$). This is again an appeal for us to make the Rational Shift in our understanding of how feelings operate in relationships. If we consider, and ultimately if we commit to, the idea that feelings are more a product of thinking than of the situation itself, how might this change the emotional landscape, or in our case, seascape, of our relationships?

In a word, it will change our understanding of freedom. One of the best ways to illustrate this is a now popular story that I believe was first told by Ted Engstrom in his book, *The Pursuit of Excellence.*[2] In the story, a young Native American finds the egg of an eagle but is unable to return it to the eagle's nest. Instead, he places it in a more accessible home, the nest of a prairie chicken. The baby eagle hatches and imprints upon the mother hen of the prairie chicken clan. In this way, it starts its life believing that it is a prairie chicken. It grows up scratching in the dirt, scrounging and scraping for insects, and even imitating its adoptive relatives by only flying a few feet off the ground. One day, after the eaglet has matured to a full-fledged adult it looks up into the sky and sees a great bird soaring majestically above. Fascinated, it asks a prairie chicken family member, "What is that?" The prairie chicken replies, "That's an eagle, chief of the birds, but we'll never be like him—we're just prairie chickens." And so, the story concludes with the eagle living the rest of its days on the ground, believing that it is a lowly prairie chicken.

This is a beautiful but tragic story. Its beauty creatively illustrates the possibilities of living an ordinary or extraordinary life. The tragedy of the story is its unnecessary ending!

Actually, when I tell my clients or my children the story, I confess I change the ending. When we get to the point where the young eagle looks up into the sky, I say that it sees several majestic birds above. And when the curious raptor asks its older prairie chicken companion, "What are they?", I usually have the older prairie chicken reply, "Why, that's actually your family. We've been glad to have you with us, but that's where you

2 Engstrom, T. W. (1982). The Pursuit of Excellence. Grand Rapids, MI: Zondervan.

belong. You're an eagle, and you were made to fly."

In my opinion, this story has the potential to be a powerful parable of freedom. And perhaps nothing epitomizes the experience of freedom quite like the image of eagles catching thermal drafts in a wide-open sky.

## Inside Job

Freedom of any kind ultimately implies options. Whether the circumstances involve what we eat, where we live, or whom we spend our lives with, having a sense of choice is the key to being free. In relationships, this concept is crucial because, without freedom, interactions with others become stifled or devoid of life. When there is no space to move about freely in a relationship, there is very little, if any, space for genuine care, sacrifice, or love. The result is that we operate as automatons or robots, essentially going through the motions and missing out on the heart of the relationship itself.

In relationships, *the way to prevent ourselves from merely going through the motions is to have a thoughtful approach to emotions.* And, as we mentioned earlier, emotions are at the heart of any relationship. To use the popular saying, "the heart of the matter is the matter of the heart."

The writer of the book of the Bible known as Proverbs teaches, "above all else, guard your heart, for everything you do flows from it."[3] These are strong words referring to the extreme priority of protecting and cherishing our deepest desires, longings, and beliefs. They suggest that the extent to which we understand and manage our inner lives will determine the quality of the rest of our experiences.

Of course, this concept, that our external experiences flow out of our internal experiences (and not primarily the other way around) is also the heart of this book. I believe this teaching was particularly important to the teachings and mission of Jesus. It was He who exhorted people (particularly the religious leaders of his day) to first clean the inside of a vessel before cleaning the outside.[4] In fact, the implication was that focusing exclusively

3   Proverbs 4:23 (NIV)
4   Matthew 23:26; Luke 11:39

on outward appearances without attending to internal affairs would be pointless and unhealthy. Ironically, while this seems a simple principle and even a wildly popular approach for many counselors, clergy, and motivational speakers, we, as a society, largely miss out on its power. The FIT equation is one attempt to contribute to our understanding of this phenomenon and to inspire a kind of freedom in relationships that can all too often seem elusive.

> **"...the way to prevent ourselves from merely going through the motions is to have a thoughtful approach to emotions."**

*Big Ideas*

A brief review will be helpful here. Recall that the FIT equation refers to the general elements that make up an emotional experience: feelings, incidents, and thoughts. In addition, recall that this equation is best thought of as a multiplication problem, where incidents and thoughts are factors in the generation of feelings, such that:

### Feelings = Incidents x Thoughts

In the first chapter, we saw how certain contexts such as survival, physiology, competition, or early concrete thinking mean the incidents factor is the controlling variable in the equation. This then is the "default setting" that we all begin life with, the world we are born into.

We also introduced the idea that this default setting leads to predominantly *reactive*, "acting-before-thinking" behaviors such as impulsivity, aggression, and defensiveness. Implied in these behaviors are the assumptions that negative feelings are problematic and that feelings in general are largely externally caused.

## The Second Approach

*Changing Settings*

Let us now consider the implications for the second approach to the equation, one where thoughts are assumed to be the controlling variable (*f i T*). A metaphor from computer technology is useful. For example, if prioritizing incidents is the default setting, then prioritizing thoughts can be considered the "custom setting." This implies that new preferences are set from those which were originally programmed. Of course, once these preferences are selected, the custom setting becomes the new default setting.

Changing settings can involve some anxiety. Depending on one's knowledge of computers and the importance of having the computer function well, tooling around with the internal modes and controls can be quite uncomfortable. I am not as knowledgeable about computers as I would like to be, and it can be quite daunting to consider the amount of information I have yet to learn. Admittedly, when it comes to technology, I hesitate to change arrangements that already seem to work, even when such changes can lead to improvements.

For example, some years ago, I asked a family member to assist me with reconfiguring the settings on my computer. While he was there, he asked me if I would be interested in having a router installed to make the move to a wireless internet connection. Thinking about how it is crucial for me to always have access to the internet, I was initially hesitant because the wireless option seemed to me, for some reason, less reliable. Fortunately, I was persuaded to go with his suggestion, and I am so glad that I did! Not only can I now use the wi-fi with my phone or tablet, I have a much cleaner workspace, I can utilize more multimedia options (such as video teleconference calls or streaming audio background music), and I have the option of allowing others access to the internet as well. I am struck, however, by how my commitment to a particular method nearly prevented me from enjoying all of these possibilities!

Just as a wireless connection can provide more freedom, emphasizing the role of thoughts in emotional experience can open new vistas on relationships. Once again, this is because we essentially have more options, and options are central to freedom.

## Fittest or Fitness?

In keeping with the topic of freedom, let us consider some additional wordplay. If we apply our computer metaphor to our feelings equation, the customized setting becomes the customized FIT. Broadly speaking, this yields two different kinds of ways of being fit.

Incident-focused emotions are related to being "fit" in the areas of survival and basic physical/biological needs. Incident-focused emotions are also about competition or being the "fittest." By contrast, thought-focused emotions, point to being fit in terms of healthy living and overall well-being.

Thought-focused emotions are about cooperation, "goodness of fit," and "fitness." Thus, they are here proposed to be the pathway to more satisfaction and fulfillment in life, particularly via a new understanding of the role emotions play in relationships. Furthermore, the idea of having a customized fit nicely captures a sense of comfort which is related to the idea of minimizing and even eliminating *unnecessary* stresses, burdens, and problems. Therefore, whereas we might say that incident-focused emotions pertain to *surviving*, thought-focused emotions are especially relevant to *thriving*.

## Dolphins

Before closing this chapter, one more analogy may be useful. We have discussed two different approaches to what we assume to be the cause of emotions: a focus on either incidents or thoughts. Building upon our ocean theme, we can look at another familiar and well-loved creature: the dolphin. It is interesting to consider that there are two different categories of dolphin.

The first and probably less well-known is a "cold-blooded" fish, often called a *dorado* or dolphinfish. In Hawai`i, where I live, it is more popularly called the *mahi mahi*. A powerful creature, it is a prize catch among deep sea anglers because of its great ability to fight, its vibrant colors, and its delicious taste.

I will use the shortened form, *mahi*, in subsequent references (incidentally, in Hawaiian, the word *mahi* can mean strong and powerful, as in the case of a worker or a warrior).[5]

The second is of course the one that we might call the "true" dolphin, a "warm-blooded" mammal like a porpoise such as the Pacific bottle-nose or the spinner dolphin. Particularly powerful, it also has a reputation for being playful, intelligent, friendly, and even a symbol of peace. To keep things clear, I will be referring to this second, true dolphin in subsequent uses of the word.

We might say we practice "*mahi*" behavior when we emphasize the role of incidents in emotions and "dolphin" behavior when we emphasize thoughts. Both are important, but one is more conducive to our enjoyment of the ocean of relationships.

Related to this, we can consider a parallel between thermal and emotional regulation. *Mahi*, being cold-blooded, are generally "ectothermic" in that they rely on outside sources of heat for regulating their body temperatures. Dolphins, on the other hand, being warm-blooded, are "endothermic" in that they rely on their own bodies, their internal resources, for thermal regulation. In fact, two terms can be used to refer to similar processes emotionally: *ectothymic* (meaning emotions or moods that rely on external sources) and *endothymic* (meaning emotions or moods that rely on internal sources).[6]

Eagles and Dolphins. Customized fits. Endothymic responses. Additional concepts that could easily sound like gibberish or psychobabble, just more words from another psychologist trying to label and analyze. And I do not blame those who might

5  Pukui, M. K. & Elbert, S. H. (1986). Hawaiian dictionary: English-Hawaiian Hawaiian-English. Honolulu, HI: University of Hawaii Press.

6  American psychologist James Hillman refers to the internal implications of emotions as "endothymic" in his discussion of German psychologist Philipp Lersch's concept of "endothymic ground" (see Hillman, J. (1960). Emotion: A comprehensive phenomenology of theories and their meanings for therapy. London, United Kingdom: Routledge, p. 91. Retrieved August 25, 2018, from https://books.google.com/books?id=C1ZgmmVlkPsC&p-g=PA91&lpg=PA91&dq=endothymic&source=bl&ots=go7GBE_b5-&sig=RH6RkAD7xro-ylEzSsTONF5YjrCw&hl=en&sa=X&ved=2ahUKEwjBveTa34ndAhVB6Z8KHXCRCEsQ6A-EwAHoECAMQAQ#v=onepage&q=endothymic&f=false
To my knowledge, the term "ectothymic" is unique to our present discussion.

think this way. I continue to have my share of these kinds of thoughts as well.

My own reservations notwithstanding, I also believe each of these concepts represent small shifts that could lead to huge changes. In this case, we might transition to another metaphor—that of plate tectonics, where seemingly imperceptible vibrations in the ocean floor move slowly but persistently toward transformations on a continental or even global scale. And where these vibrations form faultlines, we have the makings of additional oceanic phenomena like earthquakes, tsunamis, undersea volcanoes, mountain ranges, and vast, deep, oceanic chasms—the next topic of our exploration.

# Chapter 3: Chasms

*Deep calls to deep ...*
*Psalms 42:7*

Challenger Deep is the name of the lowest known point of the ocean. Located at the southern tip of the Mariana Trench in the western part of the Pacific Ocean (near Guam) and measuring a depth of nearly 36,000 feet (almost 7 miles), it is believed to be the absolute bottom of the ocean's floor.[1] An abyss and a chasm, it is an apt introduction to our next topic of discussion.

## Needless Suffering

*The Hollow Sting of Misery*
Again, *most* of life does not *have* to be difficult.

Unnecessary difficulty. Just the sound of it is unappealing, harsh, even grating. Like nails on a chalkboard or biting down hard on metal. "Gnashing of teeth," perhaps.

Many would argue that the worst kinds of suffering are those that are unnecessary because there is no point, no meaning. Viktor Frankl, Holocaust survivor and author of *Man's Search for Meaning*, distinguishes between suffering that can be meaningful and suffering that can be avoided, saying:

> *Is this to say that suffering is indispensable to the discovery of meaning? In no way. I only insist that*

---

1 Retrieved January 18, 2020, from http://www.deepseachallenge.com/the-expedition/mariana-trench/

*meaning is available in spite of—nay, even through, suffering, provided...that the suffering is unavoidable. If it is avoidable the meaningful thing to do is to remove its cause, for unnecessary suffering is masochistic rather than heroic. If, on the other hand, one cannot change a situation that causes his suffering, he can still choose his attitude.*[2]

Whether self-inflicted and masochistic or coerced and sadistic, unnecessary hardship and meaningless suffering are key contributors to experiences most would regard as torture because they ultimately combine the sting of suffering with the hollow ring of futility. Chasms again come to mind.

Before long, futility becomes the ground of tragedy. When futility pervades daily living, which can happen in surprisingly common ways, we call it insanity. Thus, "crazy" behaviors are popularly characterized as "doing the same thing while expecting different results." Furthermore, when futility becomes interminable, we have the makings of hell. Again, gnashing of teeth.

From insanity to damnation, the essence of all needless suffering is misery. A glimpse of this may be seen in the story of Sisyphus, a king in Greek mythology forever condemned to the mundane and yet grueling task of endlessly rolling a stone up a mountain, only to watch it fall hopelessly back down.

## Parallel Canyons

### Image-Bearers

The depths can refer not only to the outer and utter ranges of futility but also to the foundations of personhood. And there is something about futility that is not just tragic; it is also profoundly opposed to what it means to be human. Here, it seems important to mention two basic beliefs about humanity (in this case, from my perspective as a follower of Jesus). And so, let us consider two chasms that run like parallel canyons in the chambers of the human heart.

2 Frankl, V. E. (1984). Man's search for meaning. New York, NY: Simon & Schuster, p. 172.

First, people are made in the image of God.[3] This is the first chasm, and like a deep well it feeds and supplies life to all we do. This concept, also known as the *imago Dei*, points to the idea that we were fashioned by a designer who patterned us after His own nature, person, image. More accurately, according to the earliest creeds, this designer is a Trinity, a perfect family comprised of Father, Son, and Spirit. And so, patterned after this same community of love, we too are designed and destined for relationship.

While we are neither original nor identical, we are directly derived from the Original and our identity is inseparable as a result. We are penultimate, but our lineage traces back to the Ultimate. To borrow a wonderful phrase from C. S. Lewis and put it into a new context, this is the "deeper magic from before the dawn of time" that lies at the core of what it means to be the Trinity's image-bearers.[4] To reference the metaphors described earlier, this same "magic" is integral to eagle DNA and dolphin behavior. It is our raw material, our native fuel.

This is admittedly uncomfortable and potentially even divisive or dangerous anthropology. It requires that we begin even further back, with a certain *theology* or belief about God, about the Trinity. Our concept of humanity, then, flows forth from our concept of God. We are made in His, in Their, image, and not the other way around.[5]

If God is limited in power or love, then, even with God's help, people, as God's image-bearers, are likewise limited in their ability to exert power or love. However, if God is perfect in that nothing can be added to His nature to improve upon it, then He

3  see Genesis 1:26-27

4  see Lewis, C. S. (1950, 1994). The Lion, the Witch, and the Wardrobe. New York, NY: HarperCollins, chapter 15.

5  The simultaneous use of singular and plural pronouns is intentional but can be confusing. I employ it here to reinforce the Christian belief that God is one being in three persons. Going forward, to keep things as simple as possible, I will primarily use the capitalized, singular pronouns "He" and "His" when referring to God (or just repeat the word "God" when this does not sound too redundant). This is my way of affirming two particular tenets of faith (monotheism and Jesus' identification with and representation of humanity as the Last Adam) even as it unintentionally favors a singular, masculine understanding of God and admittedly and unfortunately misses out on the communal and feminine implications of the imago Dei (e.g., "Then God said, 'Let us make man in our image, after our likeness" (Genesis 1:26); "So God created man in His own image...male and female He created them" (Genesis 1:27), italics added).

is complete and whole; and the source and epitome of all that is good, true, beautiful, powerful, just, gracious, and loving. This assumption changes the whole complexion of the matter. For, if I am made after this latter pattern, then the more that I return to God and the more that I grow to resemble His nature, character, and image, the more I will experience goodness, truth, beauty, power, justice, grace, and love.

So, if God is the unlimited source of power and love, this has profound implications for what it means for us to be persons, to be selves. Among other things, we need not see self-care (or perhaps it would be better to say the appropriate care of the *imago Dei*) as a problem or a threat. Rather, it will be more problematic and precarious to neglect self-care precisely because such neglect jeopardizes both truth about ourselves and truth about God.

### Image-Distorters

Second, people fall short. This is the second chasm, and, like a great void it saps and alienates us from all that is energizing and life-giving. We sin. And sin depletes and kills. The apostle Paul in his letter to the church in Rome writes, "there is no distinction, for all have sinned and fall short of the glory of God..."[6]

This is exceedingly unpleasant to acknowledge, and yet there is something deeply important, even intuitive, about stating it as a reality. Once again, we live in a world of hurt. We are bruised, bent, and broken, and we are all too familiar with bruising, bending, and breaking—especially those we love the most. We have fallen, and we continue to fall. Desperately short. Of perfection. Of goodness. Of God's standards which ultimately are pure love. To deny the obvious and serious nature of this predicament is to risk missing the truth about ourselves, and again, the truth about God.

Again, theology precedes and determines anthropology. If we shrink from the awful, and it is indeed awful, bankruptcy of our ability to measure up to God's love, then we will diminish our understanding and experience of that love.

---

6   Romans 3:23

Our tendency to fall short, to sin, is much more than a behavioral pattern; it is simultaneously a virus and tumor—of the heart, the soul. It is a canyon, a cancer. If we are honest, we deeply resist and, simultaneously, desperately need, this diagnosis. The disease itself is deceptive and opposes itself and us to the only antidote that can counter it—our Creator, God. The apostle Paul writes of humanity, "For although they knew God, they did not honor him as God or give thanks to him, but they became futile in their thinking and their foolish hearts were darkened."[7]

Here again, the specter of futility looms large, and in fact, it is part and parcel of the condition of our heart. Acknowledging just how deeply our hearts are affected, even infected and infested, with this virus and cancer is crucial for any hope of recovery, survival, or salvation.

Of course, the implications of the *imago Dei* for sin and of sin for the *imago Dei* have been debated for centuries by great leaders of faith, and I want to carefully state my position here. I call sin a virus and a cancer because its effects permeate our entire being and there is no part of us that is left untouched— just as a virus overcomes a whole body with fever and just as certain cancer cells can circulate throughout the bloodstream and metastasize to the entire body.

And just as the sure effect of such spread is death, I believe we are fundamentally cut off from our true, native life by the disease of sin. The apostle Paul, emphasizing and setting the framework for the good news of Jesus, says "The wages of sin is death..."[8] Further, because sin is a moral issue in that it involves a fundamental attitude of opposition to our Creator, the fever and metastasis it produces also have profound moral consequences. I here identify myself with those who say we, as a race, bear guilt as individual and collective hosts of our disease. The double meaning of the word "host" here is intentional. We host our disease as both carriers and, tragically, as welcomers and entertainers, of it.

---

7  Romans 1:21

8  Romans 6:23

*Spelunker and Organ Donor*

This is bad, bad news. And yet, there is a personal, and I daresay universal, opportunity here. For our willingness to grapple with the "bad news" of our predicament will set the stage for any hope of healing and hearing of "good news." And to be sure, I believe there is much good news! The canyon, virus, and cancer of sin in my heart are insidious and terminal, and my only hope of rescue hinges on a radical surgery and transplant.

As a follower of Jesus Christ, I believe that the good, indeed exceedingly good news includes the following: 1) as a passionate spelunker, Jesus, through His perfect humanity and crucifixion descended into the deepest darkness of our chasm, decisively addressing every malignancy and completely cleansing us from the inside-out and 2) through His resurrection and ascension, He has given us His heart and His perfect, undying health, vanquishing sin and death, restoring us to the triune family, forever confirming His loving supremacy over all. He is thus also the ultimate organ donor who takes our "heart of stone" in exchange for His life-giving "heart of flesh."[9] The only move, so to speak, on our part is to believe that we now have the gift of His life. Since these things have already been accomplished, believing is the principal way of receiving what we have already been given.[10] This is all gift, totally unearned and totally undeserved; grace in its purest form.

> ## "It is crucial to begin with the *imago Dei* because this emphasizes that sin is not native to us as a species."

Here is the more complete version of the previously mentioned teaching of the apostle Paul: "... for all have sinned and fall short of the glory of God, *and are justified by his grace as a gift, through the redemption that is in Christ Jesus...*" And

---

9 See Ezekiel 26:36

10 Another analogy worth considering here is that of a monetary inheritance that has already been deposited into our account where no amount of arguing, denying, or explaining otherwise will remove the fortune from our possession. We have only to believe the riches are ours, and we will experience all we have been afforded. Still, although the riches were imparted at immeasurable cost, our Benefactor is so patient and wise that we are actually free to not experience the gift if we so choose.

similarly, "For the wages of sin is death, *but the free gift of God is eternal life in Christ Jesus our Lord.*"[11] This is the secret of the Gospel. The mystery of faith. The "deeper magic from before the dawn of time."

All this to say that the good news is God Himself. Through Jesus, and specifically through His living, dying, rising from death, and ascension, God has given humanity an antidote to the problem of death itself. The more we return to Him, the more we will recover and discover everything He has to offer, everything He is—goodness, truth, beauty, justice, power, grace, love, life. And this brings us again to the *imago Dei*, His image in us. This is critically important because it underscores the idea that our original design is good because God is good.

I hope that my brief description of the heinous and severe nature of sin leaves no room for doubt that it stands as both a gaping gulf and a formidable corruption between us and life. We are fundamentally affected and riddled with its disease. We are victims of its systemic effects, we victimize one another, and we bear the responsibility for our respective roles in this *tragic* drama of our race.

At the same time, our story is ultimately about deliverance and ransom and rescue, a *comedy*, in that it has the potential for an exquisitely happy ending. Jesus, through the gift of His life and the power of His resurrection victory, has abolished the power of sin and removed the sting of death.[12] He is thus the deliverer, the way, the initiator and true first responder who goes into the full depths of our chasm and ascends victorious, bringing us with Him. Once we embrace His life, we can experience the fullness He created us to enjoy.

It is crucial to begin with the *imago Dei* because this emphasizes that sin is not native to us as a species. It was not part of our original design, and so it neither suits nor "fits" us. It is an aberration of the highest order and is fundamentally alien to us. Whenever we experience good things in life, then, we essentially come full circle. We return to the God who made us and to His image in us.

11  Romans 3:23-24 and Romans 6:23 (italics added)
12  2 Timothy 1:10; 2 Corinthians 15:55

This is done ultimately through His empowerment because sin wholly robs and depletes us. We have no "purchasing power" when it comes to anything that can be done to heal or redeem ourselves. By the same token, the image of God in us is still very much a reality, and so all of the countless beautiful and meaningful things we do as a species are essentially some combination of our potential for good and the actualizing power of God. When good things happen, God and the *imago Dei* are both at work in concert, accomplishing a union and reunion which trace back to the beginning of humanity, even to God's intention from before the beginning of time.[13] This cooperation is our natural element and made possible by God's benevolent, "common grace" over the whole of creation.[14]

## The Whole Earth and Beyond

*Fit for Life*

This concept of God's common grace is directly related to the thrust of this book, that most of life does not have to be difficult. This is the ocean, as it were, of possibility in relationships, that I believe anybody can experience since we all bear the image of God and since we need not miss out on God's work in our lives.

Having said this, it is important to notice that while the ocean is massive and covers most of the globe, it is not the whole earth. This book, therefore, is intentionally limited in scope. It is not intended as a panacea (or "pan-*ocea*" as the case may be). It does not claim to solve all the problems of our world or even of our individual lives. That, I am convinced, is the province of another Book and the Author of life Himself. This is a conviction that I readily acknowledge even as this book is intended for a broad audience. Because the psychological principles I am here discussing are informed by a certain theology, namely that found in my understanding of the Judeo-Christian scriptures, I have and will continue to refer to various biblical passages. In this way, even more than common grace, the saving work of God through Jesus and the present reality of His kingdom and reign are even larger driving forces behind the thesis of this book.

---

13   see Ephesians 1:4-6

14   see Matthew 5:44-45

And so, at the risk of being pedantic or even overbearing here, I will briefly venture one more approach to the customized "FIT" metaphor I introduced earlier. In this case, to be fit can also mean to be prepared and ready. Jesus had much to say about readiness for His kingdom. In His words, "Why would people gain the whole world but lose their lives? What will people give in exchange for their lives?"[15]

On one hand, this is a stark reminder of the deceptive and depriving nature of sin as a deep void, a virus, and a cancer. On the other hand, there is good news, even great news, and once it grips us, it cannot possibly be overstated: *"For God so loved the world that he gave his only Son, that whoever believes in him, should not perish but have eternal life."*[16]

This concept is so important to the gospel of the apostle John, that He seems to repeat it in his closing explanation for why he wrote the book in the first place: "But these are written so that you may believe that Jesus is the Christ, the Son of God, and that by believing you may have life in His name."[17]

It is instructive and profound to consider that the way for us to be fit, to be prepared, for life in the kingdom of God is to believe and take a certain, ultimate thought to heart: that God has provided a way back to Himself through Jesus who has overcome and done away with death, the "last enemy" and the primary incident that haunts our lives. Indeed, when we do this by faith, we essentially remind ourselves that a new, more permanent incident has been established, namely, resurrection. What's more, as we meditate on this all-important thought and the myriad implications it has for our futures as children of a reportedly Risen King, we will experience equally ultimate feelings: joy, peace, and blessing.[18]

---

15  Mark 8:36 (Common English Bible® (CEB®))

16  John 3:16

17  John 20:31

18  I am particularly grateful for Dallas Willard's definition of joy as "a pervasive and constant sense of well-being." Dallas further notes that from a specifically Christian perspective such joy is is also compatible with suffering. See, for example, http://www.dwillard.org/resources/WillardWords.asp

*Full Circle*

This is the promise of salvation and the hope of recovering our lives in their entirety—the whole earth and even universe, so to speak, which certainly include, but are not limited to, the ocean of our relationships. Again, we come full circle to our Creator and see Him in a new light—not just as the one who patterned us after Himself and gave us His image, but as theologian Paul Tillich puts it, the one who is the ultimate "ground" and "power" of being.[19]

This full circle return to God is the essence of worship, an overwhelming awareness of God and His creative, sustaining, redeeming, and saving nature. In the beautiful words of the extraordinary poet, T. S. Eliot, "We shall not cease from exploration, and the end of all our exploring will be to arrive where we started and know the place for the first time."[20]

These trenches, these deep arteries that go far into the reaches of our hearts and souls, are the reason I care so much about the ideas in this book. They are why I make such a big, dramatic deal about the importance of cognitions and beliefs, and why I think overstatement is impossible. On the other hand, healthy, fulfilling relationships are entirely possible. We have access to power over our emotions through our thinking, and this is directly related to a life-transforming thought: that, because of Jesus, no incident other than God's triumph over death and darkness ever has to have the "last word." An ocean of possibility ultimately exists because He is the hope of the whole world.

19  Tillich, P. (1951). Systematic Theology, volume 1: Reason and revelation being and God. Chicago, IL: University of Chicago Press, p. 21.

20  Eliot, T. S. (1942). Little gidding. In Columbia.edu. Retrieved November 27, 2017, from http://www.columbia.edu/itc/history/winter/w3206/edit/tseliotlittlegidding.html

# Chapter 4: Wind and Air

*I have seen everything that is done under the sun,*
*and behold, all is vanity and a striving after wind.*
Ecclesiastes 1:14

*This is the air I breathe...*
Michael W. Smith

From birth to death, we are on a journey, on a quest, in a story. We are going somewhere. And, as noted, frustration is ever present, like looming clouds that increasingly permeate our atmosphere. As the apostle Paul writes in Romans, "For the creation was subjected to futility..."[1]

If we are honest, we live in a world of hurt. A world where "hurt people hurt people." A world shot through with pain, disappointment, and suffering. A world groaning in protest. A world where futility and tragedy are, for many, a baseline way of life. And a world where, interestingly and ironically, we all *add* unnecessary difficulties to the mix.

With all these challenges, keeping perspective is the best hope we have for steering and persevering, for finding a way through the clouds, for anticipating and envisioning birth on the other side of the agony. Understanding the nature of futility and the way in which it interacts with our human nature is the first vital step to minimizing its grip on our lives. Again, bad news can strangely enhance good news. Futility can be the counterpoint to hope.

---

1  Romans 8:20

## Designed for Freedom

*The Human Race*

We are the only species in the animal kingdom who have the capacity to plot out our course with knowledge and with wisdom. We call ourselves *homo sapiens* or "knowing, wise persons." Wisdom, then, is the virtue we constantly need to discern how to live—like a map for negotiating the twists and turns of a maze. Or a nautical chart for navigating an ocean. Again, the assumption is that we are headed in a direction, driven toward a purpose.

The author of Ecclesiastes, who is simply called the Teacher, writes of a curious convergence between how God has created us and how we find fulfillment:

*"I have observed the task that God has given human beings. God has made everything fitting in its time, but has also placed eternity in their hearts, without enabling them to discover what God has done from beginning to end. I know that there's nothing better for them but to enjoy themselves and do what's good while they live. Moreover, this is the gift of God: that all people should eat, drink, and enjoy the results of their hard work."[2]*

Interestingly, this description is tucked into a book which is largely about how futility is very much a part of life "under the sun." We have within us an innate desire, perhaps need, for happiness and satisfaction, and it is inextricably linked to the blueprint God has placed in our hearts. It is a blueprint with His fingerprint, His "touch ID," His signature, as the eternal Creator. His image.

And, according to the writer of Proverbs, Wisdom was herself God's apprentice in the creative and happy enterprise of fashioning the world and humanity: "I was beside him as a master of crafts. I was having fun, smiling before him all the time, frolicking with his inhabited earth and delighting in the human race."[3] Since Wisdom comes from God and from an accurate understanding of Him, we can expect that, as we return

---

2   Ecclesiastes 3:10-13 (CEB)

3   Proverbs 8:30-31(CEB)

to Him, we will find this same abiding joy.

Perhaps this innate desire to be free and happy is the ultimate inspiration for that place in the United States' *Declaration of Independence* where the authors affirm, "We hold these truths to be self-evident, that all men are created equal, that they are endowed by their Creator with certain inalienable rights, that among these are life, liberty, and the pursuit of happiness."[4] There is something about the "American dream" that transcends our United States—it applies to "all men"—to all people and to all nations.

Of course, *how* we conduct our pursuit of happiness makes all the difference. If we pursue happiness in illegitimate ways, then the happiness itself will be illegitimate. Among other things, a legitimate pursuit of happiness must take into consideration others' rights to pursue happiness. This seems like a simple enough principle, and yet we seem to repeatedly encroach upon one another. It is as if our journey as people is also a massive struggle where we are constantly running into and over each other. It is like a universal speedway with individual drivers constantly vying for the lead; where careening and crashing are just part of the game. The human *race*.

And on one hand, there is something about this race that indeed makes it very *human*. As mentioned earlier, we love to go toe-to-toe and head-to- head with others, to contend for a prize, to compete. It brings a rush, sometimes an unbelievable thrill. Winning, even for a little while, feels so good. Made in God's image, we resonate with having a sense of control, of power, of dominion. In this atmosphere, we feel truly happy and free, and there is something very right and good about this experience.

**"We are the only species in the animal kingdom who have the capacity to plot out our course with knowledge and with wisdom."**

---

4  U. S. Declaration of Independence. Paragraph 2 (1776).

Still, made in God's image, there is also something about our "human *race*" that simultaneously can quickly degenerate into pseudo-happiness and false freedom. This is what the Teacher seems to refer to as "a striving after wind." It is either a forceful rush or it feels light and breezy, but in the end, it has no substance. This is because when we top and trounce one another, we undermine relationship. Dominion morphs into domination, and *this* latter kind of power is at odds with God's image.[5]

*Chasing Wind, Breathing Air*

This idea, that power through domination is antithetical to God's image is another concept that cannot be overstated. C. S. Lewis develops this theme with extraordinary creativity in the *Screwtape Letters*, a remarkable exploration of how people are deceived, in this case via an imagined correspondence between a senior devil teaching a junior devil the "art of temptation." Consider the following excerpt from the alleged author of the *Letters*, Uncle Screwtape:

> *The whole philosophy of Hell rests on recognition of the axiom that one thing is not another thing, and, specially, that one self is not another self. My good is my good and your good is yours. What one gains another loses. Even an inanimate object is what it is by excluding all other objects from the space it occupies; if it expands, it does so by thrusting other objects aside or by absorbing them. A self does the same. With beasts the absorption takes the form of eating; for us, it means the sucking of will and freedom out of a weaker self into a stronger. "To be" means "to be in competition."[6]*

Of course, Screwtape's diabolical philosophy is diametrically opposed to the idea that human selves are made in the image of God. And, as mentioned, an important part of what it means to bear the *imago Dei* is to have the capacity for relationship, for community, and for unity amid diversity. Again, as the author of

---

5    For a more in-depth treatment of how original goodness is distorted, especially between men and women, see Van Leeuwen, M. S. (1990). Gender and grace: Women and men in a changing world. Leicester, United Kingdom: Inter-Varsity Press.

6    Lewis, C. S. (1958). The Screwtape Letters. New York, NY: The MacMillan Company, p. 92.

Genesis notes, "Then God said, 'Let us make man in our image, after our likeness.'"[7]

As previously mentioned, Christian tradition historically identifies this verse as key to the doctrine of the Trinity, of God's unity amid the plurality of three persons. And Lewis goes on to point out that this unity is inseparable from God's loving nature. Thus, Uncle Screwtape continues, again from a reversed perspective where God is regarded as the "Enemy":

*Now the Enemy's philosophy is nothing more nor less than one continued attempt to evade this very obvious truth. He aims at a contradiction. Things are to be many, yet somehow also one. The good of one self is to be the good of another. This impossibility He calls love, and this same monotonous panacea can be detected under all He does and even all He is—or claims to be. Thus, He is not content even Himself, to be a sheer arithmetical unity; He claims to be three as well as one, in order that this nonsense about Love may find a foothold in His own nature. At the other end of the scale, He introduces into matter that obscene invention the organism, in which the parts are perverted from their natural destiny of competition and made to cooperate.*"[8]

Lewis' insights again have profound implications for our understanding of relationships. Screwtape's words may drip with sarcasm, but we need only consider the supposed source: hell. Rather than being a "monotonous panacea," love is oxygen for our souls. And understanding this concept is like a compass for navigating relationships. "Panocean" navigation, so to speak. Apart from relationship, we are out of our natural element, like fish out of water, birds without sky. Left to ourselves, we struggle to breathe, because the one who breathed life into us, exists in the perpetual, ecstatic atmosphere of perfect, unbroken relationship.

If the reader will indulge me, there is another interesting parallel in Hawaiian culture here. *Aloha*, the versatile word for love and salutation, derives from the way Native Hawaiians

---

7   Genesis 1:26 (CEB). Italics added.

8   Lewis, C. S. (1958), p. 92-93.

would share a greeting by facing each other (*alo*) and breathe the breath of life or *ha* into one another. In old Hawai`i, where culture revolved largely around the local community, this was an everyday, accepted practice. Though this beautiful and literally life-breathing act is less common in the islands today, the spirit of *Aloha* remains. This is yet another reminder of how the fate of relationships relies on an "about-face," a move away from facing off with one another, a move away from being strongest and fastest and "*fittest.*" And it involves a move in the direction of facing one another and toward health and wellness, through mutuality and emotional *fitness*.

True happiness and true freedom require something more than chasing, and being chased by, the winds of competition. Because, in relationships, following the competitive "winds" leads all-too-often to only fleeting or illusory "wins."

These wins are, inevitably, hard to hold, hard to catch, hard to capture. They involve and become games we play, stunts we pull, masks we wear. Hard to get. Often entertaining, nevertheless frustrating, and never fully satisfying. Again, like trying to grasp the wind.

Wind, in this context, reminds us of something that is good and powerful but futile as a pursuit. Just as wind slips through our fingers, intimacy cannot be achieved through games, stunts, and masks.

It bears repeating that it is counterproductive to *base* relationships on competition. While relationships move toward closeness and mutuality, competing invariably ends in winners and losers. The sum is zero. Chasing this kind of *win* is a form of chasing the *wind*.

We can come to the arena, shake hands, put on our game face, and experience a great, even titanic, clash of will and strength, skill and sport, thrill and surge, the glory of battle. Still, at the end of it all, there is one up and one down, one ahead and one behind, one with and one without. So, after all the action, all of the drama, all of the excitement, and even all of the fun, we still go home, as it were, in separate vehicles. We don't stay together.

Togetherness, of course, is not all there is to relationships. Healthy separateness and interpersonal boundaries are very important as well. The point of this discussion is not so much to be anti-competition as it is to be pro-relationship, and relationships truly win when all parties benefit.

As image-bearers of the Trinity, we have this in our genetic code. Metaphorically, this is eagle DNA—where freedom and joy are the nucleotides, the two strands that form the cellular backbone of how we operate. And this code promotes dolphin behavior, where friendship and peace are part of our nature, and cooperation and unity mark our relationships.

The problem, of course, is that we imprint onto prairie chicken models and attach to *mahi* struggles. We learn to react rather than respond. We get our way at another's expense. It feels like a score, and it resembles a win. Or we put up walls. We stay inside. Withdraw. It feels like safety and resembles a refuge. But it's all second best. Even free combatants are prisoners of war, and refugees are displaced, home away from home.

And so, the multi-directional "win/win" is so valuable and in the words of Steven Covey, "a total philosophy of human interaction."[9] Anything else risks settling. Nevertheless, sometimes, many times, even this noble aspiration—this search for the win/win—can seem so elusive in relationships.

This "air" is vital to the ocean of relationships. And ultimately again, as King Solomon notes, its life-giving potential resides in a well-tended heart: "Above all else, guard your heart, for everything you do flows from it."[10] As we have seen, the heart of the matter is the matter of the heart. And, in relationships, let us consider that caring for the heart is directly related to caring for the *mind*.

---

9  For an excellent, in-depth discussion of this topic, see Chapter 4 of Covey, S. R. (1989). The seven habits of highly effective people: Restoring the character ethic. New York, NY: Simon & Schuster, Inc., p. 205.

10  Proverbs 4:23 (NIV)

## Freedom from, Freedom to

*Release*

Healthy thinking is integral to the recovery and preservation of freedom and joy in relationships. And healthy thinking will inevitably lead to healthy actions. The two are inseparable and synergistic. When speaking with the people who believed in Him, Jesus affirmed, "If you abide in my word, you are truly my disciples, and you will know the truth, and the truth will set you free."[11]

Jesus goes on to imply that sin is what people need to be set free from[12], so the knowledge of the truth He speaks of has moral and spiritual dimensions. Freedom from sin, in this context, is necessary for a healthy relationship with God. And again, Jesus is the antidote and answer to the virus, the cancer, the crevasse that stands between us and God. This is evident in His own self-identification as "the way, and the truth, and the life,"[13] and it is clear in the proclamation of an angel who announced His coming birth, "... *you shall call his name Jesus, for he will save his people from their sins.*"[14]

*Overflow*

Of course, freedom *from* is only one aspect of freedom in relationships. Jesus provides the ultimate way out of and away from the formidable powers of sin and futility. This is accomplished through the power of His name, precisely because His name stands for His nature, His character, and the way He lived, died, and overpowered death. And, thankfully, this is only the beginning.

Not only does He offer power over death in the final sense of the word; He also gives power over death in the day-to-day sense of the word, over the things that steal joy, kill dreams, and destroy hope. This includes the power to live and experience a very real fullness, even amid the challenges of sin and futility; the power to "taste and see" the goodness of God, in His original

---

11  John 8:31-32

12  see John 8:34-36

13  John 14:6

14  Matthew 1:21

design for relationships;[15] the call to feast on the richest of fare at His banquet table and drink deeply from His spring of living water; and the invitation to experience additional helpings, if you will, seconds, thirds, and more, feeling increasingly satisfied while never full. He offers this, His overflow, to all who ask, seek, and knock at His door.

In Jesus, we have the extraordinarily happy pairing of freedom *from* and freedom *to*. Freedom from death and freedom to live. Both are necessary to be truly free, truly happy, truly joyful. Both are central to our DNA. The first paves the way for the second, and the second gives purpose to the first. In Jesus, we are afforded the way for both to be accomplished.

Again, in relationships, the place where we are most aware of our choices is more internal and within us than external and outside of us. Previously, we discussed how our defaults make it quite easy for us to forget this. We explored how changing our thinking, specifically how changing our thinking about our feelings, is the first step toward a new, expanded understanding of what is possible in relationships. We saw that this Rational Shift is the first step across a line in the sand which signifies a decision to move off of the beach and toward the water. This sets the stage for the second Shift, which moves us from how we think about emotions to how we think about motivation.

15  Psalm 34:8

# Chapter 5: Billows and Blades

*Like a small boat on the ocean, sending big waves into motion.*
*Like how a single word can make a heart open*
*I might only have one match, but I can make an explosion...*
Rachel Platten

People are "the who, the where, and the when" of relationships. Any time two or more persons are present, we have the potential for a relationship to occur. We have the makings of an ocean.

We began this book with an attempt to explore a major, perhaps primary, "what" on this ocean, the water—emotions. Moreover, we considered the idea that for relationships to flourish, a shift in our understanding of emotions is necessary. Emotion is psychological "energy in motion," and the first Rational Shift involves a closer look at our understanding of what factors set the energy in motion in the first place: incidents or thoughts. When we consider that thoughts determine, and even drive, emotions, we have the makings of a punchline, a line in the sand that identifies our decision to move away from the beach and toward the ocean.

If people are the "who, where, and when" and emotions are the "what" of relationships, then motivation is the "why." And as we understand our own reasons for what we do in relationships, we will have a better sense of how to navigate the ocean.

## Two Primary Motivations

*Along for a Ride*
We live life according to two primary motivations: wants and

needs. We do things, all sorts of things, because we either *feel like* doing them or because we *have to* do them. Often, these are the explanations given for the decisions we make, whether positive or negative. We do "this" because we want to. We don't do "that" because we don't want to. We go "here" because we have to. We don't go "there" because we don't have to. These two motivations are like two great rivers that feed into the ocean of relationships. Once these two rivers merge with the ocean itself, they become the currents and the waves that carry us along.

According to this metaphor, relationships are a matter of bringing wants and needs together in such a way that they take us somewhere. We therefore find people whose wants and needs line up with ours and off we go. With the flow. And into the "wide blue yonder." There is a sense of excitement and adventure here. Being carried along, with like-minded people, can feel great.

My family and I once vacationed at a hotel with a huge indoor waterpark, and we had a grand time. Without question, the highlight of the park was a ride named after a tornado: a ride which involved four people sitting in an inflatable clover-leaf raft and riding down a flume containing a nearly ninety-degree drop into a checker-boarded funnel that eventually opened into a wide pool. We all agreed it was exhilarating, well worth the initial climb and the subsequent wait. We laughed, screamed, even howled the entire way down, especially during the free fall. Some of us even closed our eyes or tried to go down backwards because this added to the fear factor, which, in turn, added to the experience. We were at its mercy, carried along, with like-minded people, because we wanted to and because, after a certain point, we needed to. In the words of Jessalyn, my then eight-year-old daughter, "It was exquisite!"

This type of up and down, often unpredictable, activity frequently characterizes our relationships. It can seem like we are along for a ride. Again, when we're with people we know, our interpersonal experiences can be enhanced by having some sense of shared purpose and direction and a certain amount of like-mindedness and trust. At the same time, if it continues for very long, this sense of excitement and drama, of being carried along by highs and lows, even with those we love, can become overwhelming. Perhaps this is the reason so many of us are not necessarily happy when we compare our relationships to a "roller coaster." In oceanspeak, when waves and currents collide enough, it is easy to become seasick.

### Collision and Conversion

Just as waves and currents do collide, so do wants and needs. And when these two primary motivations are at odds with each other, we have the potential for difficulty. Whitewater and whitecaps. A crash of foam and froth and sea spray. How do we deal with such conditions?

First, don't be surprised by the collision. Wants and needs are both important and integral to relationships. It is nice when they line up in our lives; when what you want to do corresponds with what I want to do or vice versa. When this occurs, *we* are happy, and *we* have some semblance of a win/win. Conversely, it is very easy for what I want to seem at odds with what you need, and it is easy for what I need to appear contrary to what you want. This, in a word, is disagreement, and as we know, it happens in relationships quite frequently.

A second step is to consider that one of the reasons we find ourselves in the whitewater is because of what we might call a kind of *conversion*, where we make our wants into our needs. This occurs all too easily and may seem like mere semantics. Still, identifying it is central to being aware of what motivations guide our relationships, so let us examine this process in a little more depth.

### Ice Cream and Apples

What we want can quickly morph into what we need. I call this the "ice cream parlor" phenomenon. One particular ice cream parlor, Cold Stone Creamery®, offers delightful, "super-premium" ice cream. Patrons make their own "creations" by combining various ice cream flavors with "mix-in" toppings. The first step to the order is to select from three sizes, cleverly named, in order of smallest to largest, "Like It™," "Love It™," and "Gotta Have It™." These are more than just size designations; they are ingenious marketing strategies that lead customers to associate servings with positive feelings *and* to believe that a natural progression exists between wants and needs (with the latter corresponding nicely to the largest and most expensive quantity). In my experience, the strategies are successful. At the mercy of both delicious taste and persuasive labeling, I almost always find myself telling the server, "Gotta Have It™!"

With all due respect (and appreciation) to Cold Stone Creamery®, this phenomenon seems to reflect an almost identical process that occurred at the dawn of humanity. In one poetic account, our first progenitors, Adam and Eve, yielded to temptation and ate that fateful fruit, the notorious "apple," from that forbidden tree "whose mortal taste brought death into the world, and all our woe..."[1] As the book of Genesis says,

*"So, when the woman saw that the tree was good for food, and that it was a delight to the eyes, and that the tree was to be desired to make one wise, she took of its fruit and ate, and she also gave some to her husband who was with her, and he ate."*[2]

Delightful. Desired. Taken.
Like It™. Love It™. Gotta Have It.™

The beginning of Genesis is one account of the origin of human problems. Could it be that, even today, mistaking wants for needs is also at the root of unnecessary problems in relationships? Could this still be a primary deception for us?

---

**"Nevertheless, being made in God's image, we will surely help our relationships as we deepen our understanding of intimacy with God."**

---

1   Milton, J., Fenton, E., Barrow, S., Johnson, S., & Marvell, A. (1821). Paradise lost. London: W. Wilson, p.3.

2   Genesis 3:6

## Wants and Needs

*One Necessary Thing*

Interestingly, certain phrases in the English language lend themselves to this phenomenon. For example, whereas a "want" points to something that is desired, the expression, "to be in want" points to not having what one needs. One of the most beloved texts in Judeo-Christian scripture, Psalm 23, opens with the confident words, "The Lord is my shepherd, I shall not want."[3] This phrase is ironic because it seems that the author, Israel's King David, is acknowledging that he has all that he needs even if he may not necessarily have everything that he wants.

The body of the psalm points to this when David refers to experiences that are clearly unwanted such as walking through the "valley of the shadow of death" and being in the "presence of [his] enemies." Further, he implies that he is like a sheep who needs to be led, perhaps even away from the things that he wants. Elsewhere, for example, sheep in scripture are known to have a nature of going "astray."[4] At the same time, by calling God his shepherd, David affirms his reliance, as a sheep, upon his shepherd's care and guidance. And then there are the references to things that sheep require for sustenance and strength—"green pastures," and "still waters." At the finale of the poem, David describes "dwelling in the house of the Lord forever." All point again to the notion that, for David, not being in want means having what he needs. His survival is guaranteed.

And, by extension, perhaps this psalm also demonstrates how a right understanding of needs leads to the fulfillment of our wants. In this case, the Lord's presence might be considered the primary need. Fast-forward approximately a thousand years, and we hear David's descendant, Jesus, telling his friend, Martha, that only "one thing is necessary," and this is apparently to simply sit at Jesus' feet.[5] This is especially interesting and compelling if we take seriously the claim that Jesus is God incarnate.

---

3   Psalm 23:1. I gratefully acknowledge my mom, Diana Lim, for teaching my siblings and me this precious, life-giving Psalm, which she, in turn, learned as a young girl from her father and my grandfather, Russell Bill.

4   Isaiah 53:6

5   see Luke 10:38-42

All of the positive notes of hope and renewal in the psalm seem to have their source in David's opening statement—"The Lord is my shepherd." Restoration, righteousness, comfort, overflow, goodness, mercy . . . the house of the Lord forever. "For you are with me." The trajectory of this hymn of the king is heading in a certain direction—quality of life, desire, satisfaction, fulfillment. It is more than just surviving; it is thriving.

This Psalm is about David's relationship with God, so I am again venturing outside the original scope of this book—since this book is about *most* of life, the *ocean* of relationships, while the story of God is really about the hope of the whole *earth, indeed, universe.* Nevertheless, being made in God's image, we will surely help our relationships as we deepen our understanding of intimacy with God.

This Psalm, with its references to flourishing even amid apparent trials, can remind us of our second relationally strategic move—the Motivational Shift. And the first step is to realize that equating wants with needs contributes to many unnecessary problems.

*Convergence and Overlap*

Default approaches to emotions and motivation converge and overlap with each other. When I experience a negative emotion that seems caused by a situation, I essentially go into "survival mode"—I assume that a change in the situation is the key to feeling differently. The emotion is unwanted, and it seems like a problem. Because this is an external problem, I experience it as foreign and a threat. Therefore, it seems logical to escape or avoid the situation that ostensibly caused the feeling in the first place. In survival mode, it is highly likely that the *unwanted* emotion is felt as something I *need* to avoid or to eliminate. There is hardly any room for anything but removing myself from the situation, and if the situation is the relationship, then my default move is to step away from the relationship.

It is critical to note here that safety is essential, so it may be necessary to step away from certain people (e.g., especially those who are violent or dangerous). As long as safety is established, we can define relationships as a non-survival context and explore the options that result when thoughts rather than incidents are the primary reasons for emotions.

Let's consider a simple example. Tim tells John that he will pick him up for the game at noon. However, Tim stops to help another friend, and as a result, is late for John. Now John is upset with Tim for not being respectful of John's time. John tells this to Tim and then Tim, also feeling upset, tells John to just go on his own next time. Tim adds that John needs to relax, and John calls Tim unreliable.

What is occurring between each of these two men? If we allow for some oversimplification, the primary problem is the negative emotion of feeling upset, because, according to a default, survival-based model, negative emotions are impositions. Then, because "upset" feelings are abstract, they are attributed to certain incidents, namely tardiness and critical remarks. Finally, because tardiness and criticism cannot occur without people, Tim and John essentially become each other's problem, respectively. Ironically, although there are very well-intentioned efforts to address the upset feelings, it is very doubtful that either man will leave feeling closer to the other. And at this rate, the stage seems set for the best outcome to be that only one of the men prevails and in only a one-sided way.

> **"Choice is the exercise of will in a certain direction. Choice is moving according to a careful and intentional thought process. Choice is engaging with a sense of purpose and cause."**

*Maybe Two*
Default settings. Ectothymic reactions. Prairie chickens and *mahi mahis*. Winners and losers. Ultimately, more reasons to stay on the shore and away from deeper experiences with the ocean of relationships. The results can be summarized in one word, maybe two: unnecessary (problems).

The reason is that our default approaches to emotion and

motivation work best when we find ourselves facing actual threats. We resort to attack or defense because these are the primary ways to change our situations. Either/or. Fight or flight. Again, basic instincts that are necessary for survival.

When situations are marked by either/or predicaments, we might liken them to a pond or a lake. Bodies of water sometimes fed by a river but with little or no outlet. Only so much space. One form of access, or again, at best, maybe two.

This expression—"maybe two"—may prove to be increasingly useful as we continue with our exploration. It can be a reminder of what we can call a "dual reality" or a duality. First, it points to a risk of dichotomizing and, second, to the value of seeking out additional alternatives.[6]

On one hand, suggesting "two" involves risk, because if the best we can do is come up with one way or another, we are essentially caught between two extremes. Good or bad. Fight or flight. No in-between. Yes or no.

On the other hand, suggesting "two" can also imply a combination, a coupling. "Two" can point to *at least* "both" sides of a matter.

And so, "maybe two" can remind us of a risk *and* of the value of searching for something more. After all, we are concerned not with ponds and lakes but with the ocean. Maybe. The. Whole. Ocean. Maybe t.w.o.

## Choices

*A Third Option*

Once we decide to move away from the beach, and once we determine that we quite possibly are embarking on the whole ocean, how do we enter the water? How do we take the plunge?

---

6   I distinguish here between this specific duality and a more general dualism. The former points to a "both/and" arrangement where there are a minimum of two options to consider. The latter suggests an "either/or" dichotomy where options are limited to a maximum of two. Due to our focus on themes such as freedom and thriving, this book tends to favor duality and presupposes that dualism is often a factor in life's unnecessary problems. I am particularly grateful to the work of theologian Dr. Jeff McSwain for his thinking on these distinctions.

In a word, we recall the one ability more central to motivation than even wants or needs—*choice.*

Choice is the exercise of will in a certain direction. Choice is moving according to a careful and intentional thought process. Choice is engaging with a sense of purpose and cause.

The focus here is not so much on our ability to choose as it is on our *awareness* of this ability. Again, we bring to mind this unique quality. We remind ourselves that whatever is before us is somehow, and in some way, up to us. It may be small, almost imperceptible, but if we can identify even a modicum of "say" in a matter, we will have retained our voice and with it our sense of what it means to be human. And this, of course, is essential to relationship.

This again is the second major move, the Motivational Shift. If the Rational Shift (thoughts determine feelings) is the *punchline* of this book, then the Motivational Shift (distinguishing between wants and needs empowers conscious choices) is the *plunge line*—the point of entry into the ocean of relationships, where we leave the shore and make contact with the water.

*Ability and Option*

In both my personal and professional relationships, I am struck by how people, myself included, can be almost oblivious to the availability of choice as an alternative form of motivation. Again, this lack of awareness is preceded by a certain gravitation towards either/or thinking, which, in turn, is usually influenced by an almost unconscious use of certain words and phrases.

One example of this, again from the local culture in Hawai`i that I am most familiar with, can be seen in an expression that has recently gained a fair amount of popularity. When faced with a certain opportunity or decision, many people including me, will say something to the effect of, "if it can be done, we'll do it; if it can't be done, we won't" or to quote the actual phrase that we use in Hawai`i, *"if can, can; if no can, no can."*

It is important to acknowledge that this statement reflects the culturally rich heritage that helps to make Hawai`i the paradise that it is, including a curious balance between an openness to doing what is possible and a relaxed, laid-back approach to life, coupled with the delightful economy of words that is so much a part of the "pidgin-English" way of communicating. Furthermore, as with most cultural idioms, it would be a mistake to take it too literally. Nevertheless, to the extent that this expression captures a typical approach to decision-making, it provides a useful opportunity for exploring the ramifications of certain patterns of thinking.

If can, can; if no can, no can. On one hand, this is a clever, benign phrase and quite handy for actual situations where our ability or lack thereof are deciding factors in whether certain courses of action are pursued or not.

However, dividing up decisions into the possible and impossible can create the illusion of a dichotomy between two alternatives, when more than two solutions might be possible. This has the same effect as equating wants with needs, since a sense of obligation is created wherein the opportunity to choose is less obvious. If I really am not able to do something, I have no choice in the matter, and I am obligated to do something else. Furthermore, if we are honest with ourselves, if we categorize things according to what can and cannot be done, we will find that, most of the time, the things we are considering are actually possible. As another saying goes, "where there's a will, there's a way." This, among other things, also puts us at risk for unnecessary problems, including a sense of burnout since there is a cumulative effect to assuming that whatever is possible should be done.

In a way, when we tell ourselves, "if can, can; if no can, no can" we overlook the option of, "if can, choose not to." I suspect (and have observed) that many people will experience a bit of a double take upon hearing this. It is as if the very thought of "opting out" is a foreign concept. And, in some ways, if we have learned to live out of a philosophy that assumes we should say "yes" to everything that is possible, it will feel like learning another language to consider using the word, "no." It takes practice. Moreover, depending upon what we have learned to believe about opting out, the word "no" might even seem inappropriate or wrong. When this happens, we will most likely feel... guilt.

Is this not ironic? People overextending themselves out of a genuine sense of commitment to what is possible and then feeling badly when they discover, and even honor, their limitations? For all intents and purposes, such people, who subscribe to the "if can, can" mindset often have a strong work ethic that easily translates into doing things for others at personal expense. Such people are responsible, even to a "fault." So, for all their giving, sacrifice, and diligence, they deserve commendation, not censure. Still, too often, such well-meaning folk live with a gnawing sense of being "not good enough" that can subtly but insidiously seep into their relationships.

*Two Spellings*

As a cognitive counselor, I am persuaded that language can unlock a significant percentage of life's unnecessary problems. So, when I talk with people who experience this paradoxical blend of hard work and guilt, I recommend... "wordplay."

This involves experimenting with new ways of thinking, talking, and sometimes, even spelling. For these individuals, *responsibility* is not lacking, so working harder or being more careful will only risk more burnout. Instead, we might say that what can be improved on is a sense of *"response-ability."*[7]

Response-ability. Again, this is marked by the power to make conscious choices, including the possibility of opting out of perceived obligations. As mentioned earlier, due to certain, ingrained patterns of thinking, we often don't experience our own sense of choice—the awareness of our ability to say "yes," "no," or even "maybe" without fear of consequences. When this awareness is present, we experience responsiveness rather than reactivity. Furthermore, we can choose which routes to take because we recognize that, when it comes to relationships, talking freely about what we are thinking is a viable and very important option.

Thus, we might say there is a bidirectional dynamic between emotions and motivations. When emotions are determined by thoughts (the Rational Shift), then we can think before we act and this, in turn, enhances our sense of choice (the

7   Covey, S. R. (1989). The seven habits of highly effective people: Restoring the character ethic. New York, NY: Simon & Schuster, Inc., p. 71.

Motivational Shift). Likewise, when we affirm that we are free to act without fear of recrimination (Motivational Shift), we reinforce the kind of thinking that allows for healthy emotional awareness (Rational Shift). Thus, we might say that we have the proverbial chicken-and-egg dynamic where each contributes to the other. Or, to return to another metaphor and continue with constructive wordplay, perhaps we could call it an eagle-and-egg dynamic! And in this dynamic, both shifts, Rational and Motivational, contribute to new beginnings, wider horizons, and increasing freedoms.

*Decisions*
We can also posit a difference between choices and decisions. Awareness of "choice" in relationships allows for multiple alternatives and makes thinking outside the box a very viable alternative. However, true "decisions" call for selecting sides and relinquishing the comfort of being able to "eat my cake and have it, too." As the influential existential therapist, Irvin Yalom, points out, "the root of the word *decide* means 'slay,' as in homicide or suicide."[8] So whereas choices can involve "both-and" arrangements, true decisions are characterized by something more like "either-or" scenarios, where saying yes to one alternative means saying no to another. And, for our purposes, saying no to one option is akin to rejecting or killing that option off. Since all death, actual or figurative, involves some element of pain, all true decisions can then be regarded as containing some inherent difficulty. Moreover, because decisions are an inevitable part of living responsibly, the difficulties inherent in them may be considered *necessary suffering*.

Acknowledging and engaging this sort of necessary suffering is crucial to our goal of decreasing unnecessary suffering. The point of this book is to consider the ways that relationships, as the overall context and goal of our lives, do not have to be filled with suffering. This premise, however, calls for significant courage, because having what we want in relationships often involves opting out of what we want as individuals.

8 Yalom, Irvin D. (1989). Love's executioner and other tales of psychotherapy. "Prologue." New York: Basic Books. Retrieved from https://books.google.com/books?id=anRSNigZ8bIC&printsec=frontcover#v=onepage&q&f=false

Pain and difficulty are inevitable. It is just a matter of time until we experience them. Choosing what may seem the "easy" way often leads to pain in the long-run, and choosing what is difficult in the short-run feels initially painful but often leads to long-term rewards. These are again essentially either/or choices, and so they are true decisions. In fact, when it comes to these kinds of true either/or arrangements, not choosing is itself a choice and one that often leads to unnecessary difficulties.

> **"Since all death, actual or figurative, involves some element of pain, all true decisions can then be regarded as containing some inherent difficulty."**

So, awareness of choice as a third motivation includes the process of discerning when to treat certain arrangements as true decisions. When to relinquish. When to release. When to leave and let go.

Life is full of such decisions. Will I go left or right? Will I wear this or that? Will I stay or go? Will I commit or not? These are decisions where the middle ground may not be an option. These are decisions where there is an actual fork in the road and trying to take both paths eventually has its limits. As Judith Viorst notes in the conclusion to her brilliant book *Necessary Losses*:

> *As for our losses and gains, we have seen how often they are inextricably mixed. There is plenty we have to give up in order to grow. For we cannot deeply love anything without becoming vulnerable to loss. And we cannot become separate people, responsible people, connected people, reflective people without some losing and leaving and letting go.*[9]

Either way, the power to choose and to make decisions

---

9  Viorst, Judith. (1986). Necessary losses: The loves, illusions, dependencies, and impossible expectations that all of us have to give up in order to grow. New York, NY: Fawcett Gold Medal, p. 368.

is exactly that—power. The ability to act upon our world and, somehow, to influence our destiny, is integral to our understanding of what it means to be persons. And, because we are relational beings, our individual destinies overlap with the destinies of others.

This is remarkable if we think about it. Our capacity for agency means we do not ever have a passive role, wherever we are. We may choose to either seize or forgo certain opportunities, but whether we do something or do nothing, there will still be consequences for our relationships with ourselves, each other, and our Creator.

*Ripples and Inches*
And so, our choices and decisions go out from us like ripples on the ocean. These set us apart. For, if animals or rocks or trees do nothing, nothing usually happens. However, if we as people do nothing, *something* will still happen. To borrow a popular phrase, "we are "human beings, not human doings." Our existence is meaningful. We bear the image of our Creator, and our freedom to reflect this image may be the noblest reason for our existence and deepest source of all meaning.

The image of God is fundamentally a *spiritual* phenomenon in that it is intangible and invisible and yet essential, powerful, and life-giving. Like breath. And, in the Scriptures, the word for spirit is the word for breath: *pneuma*. The apostle Paul speaks of the whole of scripture as *God-breathed* or *inspired*.[10] In the same way, we as image bearers of God have the capacity to make choices, life-giving or life-taking, with every breath we are afforded. Either way, such choices are life-altering. Once again, power. And it comes primarily, or at least initially, through the conscious use of our minds.

Dallas Willard explains this unseen, spiritual power as the "ultimate" power, which forms the basis for other forms of physical, visible power. He writes:

> *To consider the simplest of cases, once again, if you are now seated in a room probably everything you see around you owes its existence, or at least its presence*

---

10   2 Timothy 3:16

*there, to the feelings, ideas, and willings of one or more persons. Again, when you look up and see an airplane flying overhead, you are looking at something that owes its existence to the spiritual reality, the mind and will, of the human beings. Airplanes do not grow on trees.*[11]

When we are convinced of this, of our capacity to choose and thereby shape both our present reality and our future, this is when we are particularly positioned to embrace our humanity. The ability to look ahead and take the next brave step, no matter how small, is always our option, regardless of our circumstances.

A powerful depiction of this may be seen in the movie *V for Vendetta*. Thrown into a prison cell, a woman (played by Natalie Portman) discovers notes written by a previous inmate (Valerie) on scraps of toilet tissue. In one scene, Valerie compares the ability to choose to "an inch," saying, "Our integrity sells for so little, but it's all we have. Just an inch, but within that inch we are free."[12] These scrawlings become a lifeline for Portman's character, something to look forward to after daily deprivations and tortures. A powerful contrast is created as this captive woman with shaved head and orange jumpsuit defies her captor's attempt to strip her of her identity and extort information, all as she is reminded of the saving strength of one concept, one hope, one word. One inch.

Of course, the themes that play out in these prison scenes have a long history. The power to choose something about our destiny is central to that quality of human spirit perhaps best described as *indomitable*. One ancient example may be seen in the biblical narrative of the book of Judges. Near the end of the story, Samson, the Hebrew judge, known for his long hair and phenomenal strength, has been captured by his Philistine enemies who have shaved his head, blinded him, and forced him to work as a slave grinding grain. The day comes when the

11  Willard, D. (1998). The divine conspiracy: Rediscovering our hidden life in God. New York, NY: HarperSanFrancisco, pp. 79-80

12  From V for Vendetta (2005), based on DC comics (1988) by David Lloyd and Alan Moore (uncredited), screenplay by Lilly and Lana Wachowski, directed by James McTeigue, and produced by Warner Bros., Virtual Studios, Silver Pictures, Anarchos Productions, Studio Babelsberg, Medienboard Berlin-Brandenburg, DC Comics (Vertigo), and Wonder Works Studios Entertainment Group.

Philistines, as a way of celebrating their religious festival, decide to display Samson in their temple as a trophy and symbol of their victory over the Israelites. Little do they consider, however, that Samson's hair has been growing back, once again conferring upon him his divinely empowered, superhuman strength. And in a final show of defiance, he asks a servant to guide him between two pillars, prays to God for strength, and proceeds to topple the temple on himself and the thousands of Philistines who had gathered to ridicule him. Even in his death, Samson found a way to have the final word, and the account reads, "thus, he killed many more while he died than while he lived."[13]

*Please understand that my inclusion of this story is certainly not intended as an endorsement of either revenge or suicide. Indeed, I would put both into the category of unnecessary and deeply tragic problems.* I mention the story of Samson here to illustrate how people will exercise the last vestiges of their volition in remarkable ways regardless of how adversarial their environment may be.

Perhaps the most well-known modern champion of this concept is Victor Frankl, an Austrian neurologist and psychiatrist who survived the Holocaust and described his observations in his landmark work, *Man's Search for Meaning*. For example, he writes of the other Holocaust survivors who found a way to endure the dehumanization of the concentration camps:

*They may have been few in number, but they offer sufficient proof that everything can be taken away from a man but one thing: the last of the human freedoms—to choose one's attitude in any given set of circumstances, to choose one's way. The way in which a man accepts his fate and all the suffering it entails, the way in which he takes up his cross, gives him ample opportunity—even in the most difficult circumstances—to add a deeper meaning to life.[14]*

This "attitude" that Frankl refers to is not subject to the actions or intentions of others. It is the exclusive property of

---

13  Judges 16:23-30

14  Frankl, V. E. (1946, 1984). Man's search for meaning. New York, NY: Simon & Schuster, p. 86.

the self. Again, invisible and intangible, it can never be captured apart from its own involvement in the surrender. And it can be so subtle and unassuming. So small, yet so packed with potential—like atomic energy.

Just inches. Just increments, and then quite possibly, over time, an exponential leap forward. Just a drop in the bucket, maybe two, and then maybe the whole ocean. And it all flows from an awareness of options at any given time, a shift in our understanding of both emotions and motivations. The ability to exercise decisions over circumstances, to voluntarily move in certain directions. A "living will" that allows for living well. Choice.

> **"...we are designed and destined for untold horizons and depths of life in and through relationship..."**

In oceanspeak, choice is that part of the vessel that both propels and steers it along its course. It is a sail, a paddle, a motor, a rudder. A canvas that catches the billows of the wind or a blade that cuts the water, both of which set the craft in motion. These mechanisms underscore the difference between the waves and the vessel itself, between driftwood and a canoe, between something "blown and tossed"[15] and something that has a purposeful trajectory. In the words of the Reverend Martin Luther King Jr., upon his acceptance of the Nobel Peace Prize, we are not "mere flotsam and jetsam in the river of life."[16] Instead, we are designed and destined for untold horizons and depths of life in and through relationship—with ourselves, with others, with creation, and with our Creator—and the freedom to choose is quite possibly our greatest resource.

---

15  James 1:6 (NIV)

16  Retrieved February 27, 2021 from Acceptance Address for the Nobel Peace Prize | The Martin Luther King, Jr., Research and Education Institute (stanford.edu)

# Chapter 6: The Sweet Sound

*Have you been half asleep? And have you heard voices?*
*I've heard them calling my name.*
*Is this the sweet sound that calls the young sailors?*
*The voice might be one and the same . . .*
Paul Williams and Kenneth Ascher

*If grace is an ocean, we're all sinking . . .*
John Mark McMillan

Just as knowledge of wind and wave patterns can greatly assist a sailor, once we resolve to move off the beach and into the water, our efforts to relate to one another will be enhanced as we return to the logic behind these two Rational and Motivational Shifts. Understanding certain points of reference is also vital to charting a course, and this especially applies to mapping out a journey where freedom is our ultimate destination. Again, let us consider the ways freedom is a part of our larger story as a people "endowed by their Creator" with the gift of free will as well as our Creator's sovereign ability to remedy the fallout once the gift became a curse.

## The Coordinates of Grace

*Life Above Both Baselines*
Picture our relationship experience on a simple graph divided into quadrants, with two axes, $x$ and $y$ (see Figure 1). Suppose the horizontal $x$ *axis* represents our relationship with ourselves and with fellow people (*human*) and the $y$ *axis* represents our relationship with God (*divine*). The coordinates $(0,0)$ represent our origin, and for the sake of simplicity, let's treat the number 1 as symbolic of our status at any given time in either relationship dimension. Intended for glory in both dimensions, we, through

our first ancestors, Adam and Eve, briefly experienced (+1, +1): life above both baselines, undisturbed harmony with God and with one another. Sin entered the picture early on, however, and in an almost preemptive strike, plummeted us into that region of conflict with God, ourselves, and one another, symbolized by (-1, -1). These are the Coordinates of Futility, where negativity and deficit characterize relationships. We can and do function here, but our experiences are suboptimal, below our original design.

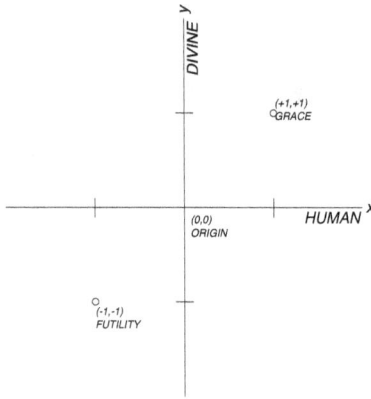

*Figure 1:*
*The Coordinates of Grace*

In contrast to futility, the freedom to choose makes healing and growth possible, and it remains love's greatest risk. This is the backstory to our relational problems and even more broadly to the tragedy of sin in the first place. We, as a race, opted away from and against God's instruction, and in so doing, opted out of His life-giving boundaries. These boundaries were necessary for harmony in relationships and for peace. Or to borrow from two other cultures, these were boundaries that made possible a sense of all things being what native Hawaiians call *pono*[1] and what the Hebrew people call *shalom*.[2]

And we continue to opt away from, against, and out of the

---

1    Other expressions that relate to this concept of pono are goodness, uprightness, morality, or "perfect order." Retrieved December 3, 2017, from http://wehewehe.org/gsdl2.85/cgi-bin/hdict?e=d-11000-00—-off-0hdict—00-1——0-10-0—-0—-0direct-10-ED—4———-0-1lp0—11-en-Zz-1—-Zz-1-home-pono—00-3-1-00-0—4——0-0-11-00-0utfZz-8-00&d=D18537&l=haw

2    Other expressions that relate to this concept of shalom are completeness, wholeness, health, and peace. Retrieved December 3, 2017, https://www.therefinersfire.org/meaning_of_shalom.htm

pattern we were made from and for. Nevertheless, every time we deviate from the original design, in an ironic and mysterious way, we affirm the endless love and grace of God. In this case, we affirm love and grace that prize the possibility of relationship even above the great pain of rejection. And we affirm love and grace that allow us to participate in His life despite our ambivalence and resistance. And herein lies the rub. For apart from these potential costs, it would hardly be love, something other than grace. Vulnerability is the lifeblood of love and the open door to grace.

Vulnerability implies we can be hurt. Still, the possibility, even likelihood, of hurt does not mean the inevitability of hurt. As a gift, choice is what allows for hurts to occur, and it can also be used to prevent needless hurts from happening. To the extent that we experience relationships where the benefits of choice include the option of freely engaging in and making decisions that minimize pain and hurt, we will experience the "best of both worlds." When this happens, we again have ourselves a win/win. The challenge is getting to that place where we are aware of our own choices in any given matter.

Jesus embodies this best-of-both-worlds and epitomizes the win/win. He is victory personified. Perhaps this is one reason why His saving accomplishment is called, in Latin, *Christus Victor*.[3] Fully divine and fully human, He satisfies all requirements of justice and love. He thus is our exemplar and much, much more, since it is *through* Him that we can experience the redemption, healing, and restoration of our freedom and of our very souls. As the apostle Paul notes, "in Him, we live, and move, and have our being."[4] And, because He chose to live and give His life on our behalf, we can now find our own lives in the paradoxical acts of giving and sacrifice. In the words of missionary Jim Elliot, a man killed by people he was seeking to serve, "He is no fool who gives what he cannot keep to gain what he cannot lose."[5]

So, a major implication of this is that God's provision in

3   Thompson, M. M. (n. d.). In Fullerstudio. Retrieved December 3, 2017, from https://fullerstudio.fuller.edu/christus-victor-the-salvation-of-god-and-the-cross-of-christ/

4   Acts 17:28

5   Elliot, E. (1957, 1996). Through gates of splendor. Peabody, MA: Hendrickson Publishers Marketing, LLC, p. 173.

His son makes settling for the coordinates of Futility and ultimately of death *unnecessary*. It is possible to live truly free and truly joyful, though this opportunity comes to us at an incomprehensible cost. Something was *necessary* for the Coordinates of Futility and death to be made unnecessary: Jesus' gift of His life on our behalf.

Thus, the apostle Luke records Jesus saying, "Was it not *necessary* that the Christ should suffer these things and enter into his glory?"[6] This was the ultimate exchange, where our losses and deficiencies were replaced with His gains and life. This was the ultimate reversal where all negativity was turned on its head. This was the ultimate act of both necessity and sufficiency. It was and still is an act that was *crucial*, in all senses of the word, for it was severe, decisive, and involved a literal cross. To return to our coordinate system, there is a beautiful though ironic symbolism in how plus signs resemble crosses.

Jesus permanently undoes the effects of sin, futility, and death, and makes possible life above both baselines. He alone can move us up the vertical axis, so to speak, into restored relationship with God, and likewise all horizontal experience is also empowered by Him. This again is the hope of the whole earth, indeed of the whole universe. If we do not acknowledge this vertical dimension of our experience, it seems our "best life" is somewhere between the coordinates of (*-1, -1*) and (*+1, -1*). To be sure, this is a very important space, because it implies progress in the human dimension. At the same time, the progress is still suboptimal and below the truly life-giving baseline.

The use of this coordinate model admittedly shows my conviction that life above the life-giving baseline is not possible without vertical movement. Or put another way, the quality of our relationship with God has profound implications for our relationships with one another. The sacred, in this sense, can literally and figuratively elevate the secular. Then again, perhaps there really is no such thing as secular in the strictest sense of the word. Our humanity, after all, consists in the very life of God and derives from the very image of God.

So, when this elevation along the vertical takes place, it is

---

6   Luke 24:26 (italics added)

fundamentally a return to our permeating source and our original design, the ultimate way to recover what it means to be human, and an opportunity to live again above both baselines. Since life above both baselines is made possible only through God's most generous gift of Jesus, we might call (+1, +1) the Coordinates of Grace, and these are the coordinates where we are most free (see again Figure 1).

> **"It is possible to live truly free and truly joyful, though this opportunity comes to us at an incomprehensible cost."**

*One Letter*

Made in the image of a triune and transcendent Creator, we too are meant to transcend, to live above our circumstances, to rise above the status quo. We are intended to experience what the psalmist calls, the "goodness of the Lord in the land of the living."[7] And again, Jesus makes this possible by releasing us from bondage to sin, futility, and death, *and* by inviting us to share in a new kind of life—a life where grace is the pulse; the gravity behind the tides and the rise and fall of the ocean itself. This is freedom to truly live by embracing the freedom to truly love. In the soaring words of the apostle Paul, "for by grace you have been saved..."[8]

This salvation is a provision for our souls; we are not left to ourselves—we have an advocate who stands between us and hell. The ramifications are eternal and point us to a great hope in the hereafter. For the whole earth, for the universe, and beyond. And, at the same time, this salvation, the very gift that we are offered in Jesus, has direct potential for how we live now. Jesus, upon reading from the book of Isaiah and announcing that He was God's promised "anointed" one, declared, "*Today* this scripture has been fulfilled in your hearing."[9] This is, to quote Jesus (and Isaiah), good news indeed! We need not wait

---

7   Psalm 27:13

8   Ephesians 2:8

9   Luke 4:21 (italics added)

any longer to experience the life-changing power that God now provides. We can begin with our present-day, everyday relationships. The dynamics of saving grace have profound and immediate implications for the whole ocean of relationships as well.

It has been said that good things come in small packages, and this is especially true of grace. If we will only look for it, we will see this gift on all hands, especially in life's details. It is there in the delicate beauty of a flower; in microscopic organisms and majestic beasts; in the fragrant aroma of a freshly brewed beverage; in the familiar sound of a loved one's voice; in the warmth of the sun; in music and art and song and dance; in color and in light; in the act of breathing itself, and on and on. And to be sure, it is present in our very words and language.

Theologian and pastor John Piper begins his *Desiring God*, his paradigm-shifting treatise on "Christian hedonism," with a reference to the saving power of words, saying, "You might turn the world on its head by changing one word in your creed."[10] And in many ways, reading his development of this idea did turn my world, at least my thought life, on its head. For this, I am deeply grateful. So, it is with great respect that I venture to add another dimension to Reverend Piper's thought-provoking idea. That is, perhaps we might also turn everything upside down by changing even just one *letter*.

For example, it has been said that Christianity is a matter of moving from "got to" to "get to." Through the power of Jesus' sinless and love-filled life, sacrificial death, and victorious resurrection and ascension, we are afforded liberation from the universal demands and obligations of moral law. And so, we are no longer "slaves" to this exacting taskmaster; no longer subject to an impossible standard. There is *nothing* we've "got to" do! Grace is unearned. Unmerited. Undeserved. And, insofar as its recipients are concerned, unconditional. It does not depend on us.

---

10 Piper, J. (1986, 2011). Desiring God: Meditations of a Christian hedonist. Colorado Springs, CO: Multnomah Books, p. 17.

## Mercy and Favor

*Better Way*

This is the first half of the good news, and it is further evident when we think about what our predicament would have been apart from Jesus. Consider the full weight of the burden we would have had to carry. The burden, in this case, of our perfection—total, complete, unmitigated perfection. An impossible standard, to be sure. No margin for error. Zero tolerance. The thinnest of tightropes with no semblance or sign of a safety net. The most stringent of tests with no hope of a grading curve. Swimming the ocean with no assistance.

However, in Jesus, we are released from this crushing requirement and likewise from the consequences we would undoubtedly have faced on the day we inevitably buckled beneath the pressure. Because, in truth, no person can withstand such pressure. Sooner or later we all fall short, and, once we do, the consequences are dire. But thanks be to God for His great clemency! For He has released us from the sentence pronounced upon even the slightest deviation from perfection. The sentence that reverberates like cannon blasts in every mortal person's ears and heart. Guilt. Punishment. Death. Hell.

These, again, are the natural effects of breaking moral law and the exacting ramifications of a universal justice system where even the smallest infractions are a violation of God's design for Life. And these are the effects we've no longer "got to" experience! Now, because of Jesus, we are happily in the clear. We are no longer obligated to pay. We need not face our Maker with fear. This first half of grace is mercy. As the psalmist says, "He does not deal with us according to our sins, nor repay us according to our iniquities."[11]

And this very happy beginning only gets better. For not being treated as our sins deserve is not limited to escaping the downside of our sin. There is a very real upside as well. With the psalmist we can also pray, "Bless the Lord, O my soul, and forget not all his *benefits*."[12] Not only are we not held to the interminable weight of our own brokenness and its grave consequences, but

---

11   Psalm 103:10

12   Psalm 103:2 (italics added)

we are also given incomparable, immeasurable *favor*.

Profound, abiding, life-giving favor. Another chance. A second wind. A do-over. Redemption. An invitation to participate in everything our Maker is bringing about in the universe. The opportunity of a lifetime. And a lifetime of opportunity. We now "get to" join in the Story that is so supernatural, so staggering, and so sacred, that our very lives become acts of worship and prayer to this Maker who made the ultimate sacrifice to bring everything back together.

This intimate connection between grace and its tendency to look for redemptive opportunities is at the heart of the good news about God and His plan for relationships. I am struck by the opening lines of singer Michael Card's song, "That's What Faith Must Be" where he writes: "When the universe fell from His fingertips, He decided He wanted some fellowship, but the man and the woman would not submit, so He made a better way." [13]

A *better* way. [14] This is God's signature. His call sign. His *modus operandi*. The shape and size of His imagination. Taking the shards and chips of broken situations and shattered lives and transforming them into a mosaic that surpasses even the original and "very good" ceramic. Seeing the diamonds in the rough. The roses among the thorns. Perceiving what *could* be and bringing forth new, improved realities. Turning obligation into freedom. Freedom from and freedom to. From the realm of "got to" into the realm of "get to." From *o* to *e*. One vowel. One letter.

### The Still Point

Grace can come in the smallest of packages and yet it permeates the whole cosmos and all of eternity. In the words of author Philip Yancey, "It contains the essence of the gospels as

---

13   Card, M. (1981). That's what faith must be. [Recorded by M. Card]. On Present reality [CD]. Nashville, TN: Sparrow.

14   Here I would distinguish between a "better way" and what we might call a "Plan B," in that God's intervention was a part of His original Plan A all along. And perhaps a good summary of this Plan A can be found in Paul's words when he says, "In love He predestined us for adoption to himself as sons through Jesus Christ, according to the purpose of His will, to the praise of His glorious grace, with which He has blessed us in the Beloved" (Ephesians 1:5-6).

a drop of water can contain the image of the sun."[15]

With one such droplet, we might turn the entire ocean around. This is the good news for relationships. Hope embedded in a shift. A shift that itself is motivated by grace and a grace that flows from the freedom to choose. Indeed, it is a grace that begins with a Creator who chose to turn the shambles of our choices into love's highest opportunity, and in so doing, turned the whole universe around.

In the *Four Quartets*, TS Eliot writes about the mysterious convergence of past, present, and future time, referring on one occasion to the "still point of the turning world."[16] While scholars continue to debate how to best interpret Eliot's meaning, I believe this phrase captures the essence of grace and its saving, sustaining, and life-stirring work in our world at any given time and indeed, at all times.

Even before the beginning of time, this grace has been the pulse behind our Creator's loving way of keeping all of life in its delicate orbit. This is the story of His supreme confidence and competence to rescue, redeem, and restore His creation. It is not without its severity and suffering. In fact, the transformation often comes through the crucible of shock and pain, for that is the cryptic and strangely beautiful way in which He works to bring lasting change and life and hope.

From the dawn of history to the fullness of time. From speaking light into existence to breathing His spirit into one man and fashioning from his rib one woman; from the moment He saw this first couple hiding in the garden to the day he spread his covenant-colored banner over a family he preserved from a flood; from the promise fulfilled of a son well after child-bearing years to the protection of that son from obedience unto death; from the family feud where deceit won the battle but blessing won the war to the lasting nature of that feud and the even more resilient power of faith and forgiveness; from the drawing of a boy *from* the waters of a river to the passing of this man and

15   Yancey, P. D. (1997). What's so amazing about grace. [EPub]. In Chapter 1 "The last best word." Retrieved from https://books.google.com/books/about/What_s_So_Amazing_About_Grace.html?id=YoiM82U_X-AC

16   Eliot, T. S. (1942). Burnt Norton. In davidgorman.com. Retrieved December 3, 2017, from http://www.davidgorman.com/4Quartets/1-norton.htm

a million others *through* the waters of a sea. And on and on through the rules of judges and the corruptions of kings; through the pleas of prophets and the saving plea of one courageous queen. It is the grand, master story of God continuously raising and providing His promised deliverance, which persists and perseveres until finally it culminates in the modest yet time-splitting, earth-shattering arrival of Jesus, the Son. "God from God, Light from Light, true God from true God."[17]

From the very beginning of His earthly mission, conceived by the Holy Spirit and born of the virgin Mary, He took into and upon Himself all of humanity. "Full of grace and truth,"[18] He would teach and live out the perfect logic of both, winning the trust of the people while threatening the ways of the powerful, taking His place as the only person who could fully satisfy the eternal requirements of God, who loves both justice and mercy at the same time, all the time. And ultimately positioning, indeed giving Himself, through death, as the only completely perfect and innocent mediator between God and humanity . . . on a cross. Though brutal and heinous with all of its place and significance in history, the cross of Christ could be considered the "still point" between all of heaven and earth, because the cross held the Blessed Hope and Hero of all humanity. For it was on this Roman device of torture and death that grace and love rushed to their climax—the tragic, *still point* for which they had been building their momentum from time immemorial. And true to form, God would use that day and the raw severity of suffering to fulfill His *better way*, indeed His best and only way. The day when it would seem all of life and all the cosmos stood deathly still. The curtain call where eternity hung in the balance and all creation waited with desperate, bated breath. The still point of all of existence itself, because the one suspended for all was God's one and only Son, who, while holding the world together with His very word, would give Himself over to it and for it, that it might be saved.

And, once accomplished, it was only a matter of time before crucifixion, death, and hell would give way to resurrection and triumph, ascension and glory. Shortly after the cross carried out its—indeed *our* awful work—on day three, time itself would essentially be reversed and the world would begin to turn again, though this time in such a way that death and darkness would never again speak the final word. For even the grave could not thwart grace. And fear could not prevail over love. Perfectly divine and perfectly human, Jesus would be raised from death to life, never to die again. Like a relentless torrent, the grace and truth and love that filled and overflowed His being could not be stopped, and these continue to pour from Him as their eternal source, and so much more so, now that the permanent power of death has been removed. The sting no more. The venom neutralized. The ultimate oppressor vanquished.

So, now, even amid life's vicissitudes and fragilities, people everywhere can have hope of living without fear. We can live without concern for irreversible or permanent damage. Instead, there is freedom to embrace and savor and revel in a grace-infused, truth-adorned, love-driven world. A gift. A lifetime of opportunity. A rhythm and rhyme; a new song of celebration conducted by God, who, with infinite wisdom, orchestrates and incorporates every move of creation into His sovereign score. God, of whom it was once said, "The Lord your God is with you, He is mighty to save. He will take great delight in you; He will quiet you with His love, He will rejoice over you with singing."[19]

And so, life in God has been understandably conceived of as a romance, where Jesus is the Lover of Souls and the Lord of the Dance. Considering this, perhaps it is even more compelling to say that He *Himself* is the "*still point* of the turning world." Perhaps in this way, we can say with TS Eliot, "Except for the still point, there would be no dance, and there is only the dance."[20]

The dance. A picture of personal, beautiful, energetic, creative, cooperative movement, with music and rhythm, tempo and groove, where all participate and all are free. Where will and body and heart and mind are joined, and the result is art and flow. Where enjoyment is mutual; giver and receiver are one, and good is shared. He is Lord of all of this, and He invites us to the floor. To simply take His hands in ours, trust Him to lead the way, and move in time with Him.

19  Zephaniah 3:17

20  Eliot, T. S. (1942). Burnt Norton. In davidgorman.com. Retrieved December 3, 2017, from http://www.davidgorman.com/4Quartets/1-norton.htm

*The Sweet Sound*

If we will take the time to look, God's choreography pervades the "turning world" we continue to inhabit. All around creation pulsates with life and vitality, and every moment brings opportunity to step in and take part in this dance that, in the end, is what relationships with God and people and creation are all about. The stage is set, and it's an ocean of opportunity, made possible ultimately by Jesus, the Lord of the Dance Himself. Indeed, this Jesus as the hope of the whole earth, and even the whole universe, is certainly also the good news for the whole ocean of relationships as well. Here we have, in the wonderful words of Paul Williams and Kenny Ascher, the probable magic, the voice from beyond the rainbow, "the sweet sound that calls the young sailors."[21] Thus, this call to dream, to sail, and to dance is the larger cause for shifting from the shore and towards the water, from the sand into the sea.

I am convinced that this good news is the same power that makes both Rational and Motivational Shifts such viable options for turning relationships in better, more fulfilling directions. I believe that this is the same power that coursed through Jesus as His hands held children and healed disease, as He touched untouchables and washed His followers' feet. This is the same power that sustained Him as He shouldered the cross, hung on Calvary's hill, and yielded His spirit. It is the same power that simultaneously gathered strength and released captives as He lay entombed, bursting the cords of death on that glorious third day.

Even now, at every turn, He *chooses* to give. For full of love and grace and truth, His heart is set on giving, on blessing. Indeed, His heart cannot help but bless, like springs of the deep that flow from a continual, overflowing fount. Just as wide as it is deep, this blessing spans God's vast redemption across time, for all of creation, culminating in the matchless gift of the life, death, and victory of His Son, and continuing through His abiding presence that remains with all who accept the invitation to join the dance.

---

21 The song "Rainbow Connection" was originally written by Paul Williams and Kenneth Ascher and first performed by Jim Henson (as Kermit the Frog), who first recorded it for the 1979 film The Muppets. Retrieved January 18, 2020 from https://www.billboard.com/articles/news/awards/8543796/rainbow-connection-appreciation

*Overflow and Transformation*

This concludes the first portion of this exploration and my attempt, through the primary metaphor of the ocean, to lay the groundwork for what I believe are definitive steps: two often subtle shifts that, though small, might make all the difference in bringing new life to relationships. These are steps and shifts for which I am particularly passionate, because they trace directly to Jesus as the reason for hope that *the better* and *the best* are yet to come. And while I readily own my excitement, my intention is not to convert people to a specific religion, but rather to show how my understanding of the Christian gospel is also patently good news for relationships. It is good news because through God's gift of Jesus and Jesus' gift of His life, the *necessary* suffering for restoration of relationship has already taken place, making most problems in relationships today largely *unnecessary*. And it is good news because, if it is true, then relationships can have significant potential to experience actual resurrection power.

Of course, this power can seem to start utterly small and inconsequential, like a droplet of seawater is hardly noticed in a bucket waiting to be filled. Nevertheless, drip by drip and drop by drop, this power, once released, tends to accumulate. Drip by drip and drop by drop, this power tends to build and to overflow.

And the overflow continues until one day something shifts altogether and the container itself is transformed from something that used to hold the water, into something that is now held *by* the water. It is transformed from receptacle into reservoir.

This transformation continues until one day the sweet sound that quietly beckoned has become a soaring, sacred song that guides and empowers, even becoming the journey itself.

And so, as we consider our own longings to experience this transformation in our own relationships and to be lifted, as it were, by the music of the sea, let us turn our attention to some of the practical ways in which we can continue to move from just a drop in the bucket to . . . the whole ocean.

# Chapter 7: Salt

*Great communication begins with connection.*
*Oprah Winfrey*

Jesus used an interesting metaphor to describe the way His followers would impact their world. He called them the "salt of the earth." Salt can be used to preserve and to enhance what is good. It can protect perishable foods from decaying and spoiling, and it can improve taste, adding flavor and seasoning and zest. In these ways, salt can simultaneously be necessary and optional, depending on the context. The same might be said of communication. Communication is required for relationships to function, and when used skillfully, communication can also bring relationships to higher, deeper, and closer levels. On the ocean of relationships, if emotions are analogous to water, then communication is the "salt of the sea."

## Necessary and Optional

*Keeping it Simple*
Of course, the topic of communication is a field of study in itself, and veritable libraries have been written on the subject. The purpose of this chapter is to explore how the two shifts proposed earlier might lead to a simple model of communication that establishes and enhances relationship quality. We will consider strategies that flow out of the notion that thoughts determine feelings as well as the idea that choice is always a third form of motivation.

For our purposes, communication is the process of two or more parties sending and receiving verbal or nonverbal messages to and from one another. It is a transaction where symbols, gestures, and expressions become progressively meaningful to those involved. And, just as salt is a necessary condition for life in the sea, so communication is vital to interpersonal relationships at just about any level.

There is an irony here in how something so important can so easily and so often seem so complicated. And not surprisingly, the risk of complexity appears to increase when emotions are involved. The reader will recognize that the operative word here is "appears," because, in fact, the potential for excessive complexity does not have to be realized, even when emotions are involved. Again, the Rational Shift calls for a simpler rather than more complex understanding of emotions, and when this shift is made, we have already begun the process of minimizing unnecessary problems in communication.

Simplifying emotions is a strategy for improving communication by moving away from unnecessary extremes and achieving more balance in how we relate to others. This is not to say that emotions themselves are simple phenomena. On the contrary, emotions, as experiences that give form and depth to relationships are profoundly deep and intricate, so much so that the prospect of comprehending or even just sitting with our own emotions can be mysterious and daunting. With practice and skill, however, balance can be achieved, even amid complexity, precisely when the most important matters are kept simple.

*Fun with Percentages*
In ocean life, just as saltwater itself is necessary for survival, so the balance between the salt and water is also crucial. Understanding the basics of communication is integral to interpersonal life.

This chapter explores this understanding via a deeper look at the building blocks of communication, namely, words. We can return to our preliminary use of wordplay to help with this process. So, to use an oxymoron—as a "strictly fun" observation, consider the popular notion that most communication is nonverbal. This notion can be traced to a popular study on communication conducted during the 1960s which suggested the following percentages were relevant to explaining "liking" in communication of feelings and attitudes: 55 percent to body language, 38 percent to tone of voice; and 7 percent to words.[1] And, while it is surely just a curious coincidence, a similar breakdown might be found to pertain to "salt" in that the concentrations of various salt ions in seawater roughly correspond to the following percentages: 55 percent (chloride), 39 percent (sodium and sulfate), and 6 percent other (e.g., magnesium, calcium, potassium)![2] On one hand, this probably just depicts how numbers can be manipulated to defend any argument. On the other, we might see it as a playful form of oceanspeak in which we again are reminded of communication as the salt of the sea.

## A Manner of Speaking

*Word and Words*

On the ocean of relationships, the default model of emotions (where incidents are given more weight than thoughts in the development of feelings) works well for survival and for the early years of life. However, as soon as a child begins to understand language, this initial model begins to change. The infant who cries because they are hungry gives way to the toddler who is taught to say "please." Common courtesy means encouraging a respectful stance and discouraging a demanding quality. "Please," in this regard, is quite truly a "magic" word, for it is one of the first steps toward a more mature relationship.

We teach our children that manners are a *requirement* for precisely this reason. This is ironic, of course, since ultimately relationships derive their power from the realm of choice.

This is how we develop. We begin with certain rules, obligations, and necessities, but they are only meant as means to a greater end. And if we stop with just the rules, we will most likely be settling for something second-best at best. Freedom and joy are our destiny especially as we learn to embrace the

1 Thompson, J. (2011, September 30). Is non-verbal communication a numbers game? In Psychologytoday.com. Retrieved May 24, 2020 from https://www.psychologytoday.com/us/blog/beyond-words/201109/is-nonverbal-communication-numbers-game

2 Castro, P. & Huber, M. E. (n.d.). Marine biology. Retrieved December 3, 2017, from https://www.fws.gov/uploadedFiles/Sea%20water%20composition%20chart.pdf

principles behind them.

Of course, as a race, we have established a tendency to leave off, to make the rules the end of the story and to literally and figuratively seek second-rate, second-best forms of freedom and happiness. And so, as we have seen, we need grace. Theologically, this means we need God, the author of true freedom and joy and creator of these two strands in our common DNA. It also means that, left to ourselves, we will perish under our obligations. Psychologically, grace means that we must recover both reason and choice, lest we also fall into the grip of forced interactions that also leave us feeling imprisoned in relationship. And, in both cases, communication represents the opportunity for such grace. The Word and the words can free us, but will we receive what are offered?

This book, primarily geared toward the psychological dimensions of horizontal relationships, simultaneously acknowledges a theological conviction that God, in the person of Jesus Christ, is the hope of the whole earth, who lays the ultimate foundation for change in any form. Our serious approach to words therefore is premised on the belief that "the Word became flesh and dwelt among us."[3] He is the ultimate communication event, "full of grace and truth."[4]

## "...feelings are simply words."

And so, words, as small as they may seem, return us to our common humanity and our great potential for being and doing good. Indeed, even Jesus taught that we will not live by bread alone but by the very words of God. Words, in this regard, might be considered among our basic needs. In the wonderful language of philosopher Robert Roberts, we, as people are, "verbivorous."[5]

Metaphorically speaking then, our conscious use of words is

---

3  John 1:14a

4  John 1:14b

5  Roberts, Robert C. (1993). Taking the word to heart: Self and other in an age of therapies. Grand Rapids, MI: William B. Eerdsmans, p 34.

again like stepping away from the beach and toward the water. This prepares us for the shifts that will bring us from off the sand, into the ocean, and beyond.

*The Key*

Let us consider specifically how emotions can be a resource for better communication and thus better relationships. And, let us not be surprised if this endeavor leads us to strategies that, at the outset, might seem all too basic or too simple. After all, we are trying to improve the quality of our lives by minimizing unnecessary complexities, which themselves create problems. And as one more reminder, let us be aware that our very attempts to simplify might seem like unnecessary complexities since we've likely grown accustomed to certain ways of relating to one another.

So, to unlock the communication potential of emotions, here is the key: *feelings are simply words.*

I can almost hear the questions now, "Really, Brian? That's all you've got? What does that even mean?"

> ## "Emotions are clearly multifaceted and mysterious aspects of our experience..."

Or, put another way, I suspect this "key" will be frustrating or disappointing to some readers, despite the above caveats, i.e., what we have noted about how our conclusions will likely seem too basic or simple and the notion that these conclusions themselves might reflect the pervasiveness of old patterns. In fact, I have asked myself questions similar to the ones above. I struggle with the idea I have just proposed and still sometimes wonder if I am being intellectually honest with myself. I think of the many times I have felt overwhelmed by certain strong emotions, emotions that seem to almost come from out of nowhere and that seem to defy any short-term intervention. These are times when I feel a sense of doubt about the very theories I am here trying to explain. I do not fault for one second the person who questions, criticizes, or dismisses me. Instead, I think that questions and reservations are natural and important. At the same time, when I try to work out the principles alongside my own doubts, I am helped. So, let us see if I can demonstrate this concept a bit further.

## Emotions *for* People

If I am honest, I am using a pragmatic approach that relies on a simplification of emotions, because it seems to work as opposed to saying that this simplified definition of emotions is, in and of itself, true. Emotions are clearly multifaceted and mysterious aspects of our experience, and they can exist in very mixed states. So, in this sense it is not true per se to essentially equate feelings with words. Having said this, I choose my language very carefully when I say that to unlock the communication potential of emotions, the key is to regard feelings as "simply words." The context is again the way in which emotions can be used to improve communication, essentially utilizing them for our benefit.

We might draw a parallel here between both the "default" and "customized" approaches to emotion and the ways Jesus approached certain widely accepted cultural practices of His day. For example, the religious leaders He interacted with were convinced that it was wrong to do any work on the Sabbath day, including healing. Jesus, however, saw the importance of the day in the context of people's well-being, so He performed controversial healings, teaching that "the Sabbath was made for people, not people for the Sabbath."[6] Keeping with the spirit of this teaching, we can also say that when it comes to interpersonal communication, "emotions are made for people, and not people for emotions."

That is, emotions are resources for us to use rather than experiences that essentially use us. And, again, we will best be able to tap into our emotions (rather than have them tap into us, so to speak) to the extent that we directly attribute them to our thoughts instead of to the incidents in our lives. When we do this, we will have an increased sense of control over our emotions and thereby be more "fit" for traversing the ocean of our relationships.

This, then, is something that I find worthwhile when it *seems* like the interpersonal incidents I am facing are emotionally overwhelming and when doubts about this very theory settle in. In this case, the apparent ability for interpersonal incidents to single-handedly create overwhelming feelings is itself a "widely accepted cultural practice" of our day (akin to the assumptions about the Sabbath in Jesus' day), and it easily leads to the idea that if our situations do not change, we will be emotionally stuck. However, if I am to practice careful communication, I believe I will be best served (and the relationship will be most enhanced) to the extent that I can identify my thoughts on the matter and their relationship to the feelings I am experiencing. This is when I can be more responsive than reactive and benefit from approaching my emotions as a resource designed for me rather than the other way around.

At this point, I hope that I am demonstrating what I mean by the "communication potential" of emotions and how it is consistent with the first Rational Shift that allows us to engage relationships more fully. Against this backdrop, we can explore the second side of the key to unlocking this potential, namely the notion that "feelings are simply words."

## "...feelings are vital information about *oneself*."

Here I am also very purposeful in my reference to simplicity. This is significantly different from other similar ways I could have described this concept. For example, I might have said, "feelings are only words" or "feelings are merely words." However, such language would likely diminish and undermine my point, since it is my opinion that "mere words" is a contradiction. Instead, my intent is to imply and preserve the power of both simplicity and of words. Again, I want to do this because words and wordplay are at the heart of this book and because words, as the building blocks of communication and relationship, are a quintessentially human endeavor. Moreover, words are a gift from God who Himself is the Word. To borrow another phrase, "words create worlds."[7] Somewhat paradoxically, the goal is to develop a simple way of using our emotions to better navigate the often complex depths of our interpersonal, oceanic world. And I believe that treating our feelings as words is a first step to doing just this.[8]

## Single-Word Messages

*General Feelings, Specific Thoughts*
An important corollary to the strategy of treating feelings as words is to go one step further and limit each feeling to one word, as much as possible.[9] The purpose of this is to distinguish feelings from thoughts as much as possible, essentially by making feelings general and thoughts specific. So, if we slightly rephrase our customized FIT equation, it becomes:

**F** (a feeling) = **I** (an incident) × **T** (a thought)

Alternatively, we can also turn the equation into the following formulaic statement:

*I **feel** one word to identify feeling because I **think** a particular thought.*

At the outset, this will likely seem elementary and confining and perhaps, at the same time, somewhat familiar. One reason for the familiarity could be another popular formula which can be found in communication strategies which usually takes the following form:

*"When you do X, it makes me feel Y, and I do Z."*

While they may seem similar, these two approaches are

7  I am grateful to two particular people for this phrase: author and motivational speaker, Rob Bell, and my mentor and dear friend, Rob Paris.

8  I will generally use the words "feeling" and "emotion" interchangeably, and I will use the capitalized word "Feeling" whenever I am also noting implications for what we have previously identified as the "FIT" equation. Whereas I treat "feeling" and "emotion" as fairly synonymous, I think it is interesting to consider that there are different connotations when these words are used as verbs (e.g., to "feel" implies a more internal experience, whereas to "emote' implies expression of such an experience).

9  My first introduction to this strategy was Patricia Resick's Cognitive Processing Therapy, and I readily acknowledge the influence of this approach on the thinking I am here outlining in this book. For additional information, see https://cptforptsd.com/.

significantly different. The latter "XYZ" formula directly connects one person's feelings to another's *behavior*, which is akin to what we have identified as a default, incident-focused way of understanding emotions. This runs the risk of a more reactive (vs. responsive) outcome and essentially keeps us unnecessarily in survival mode. Conversely, when we directly connect our feelings to the *thoughts* we have *about* various incidents in our lives (including the behaviors of others), we can make our emotions work for us rather than against, increasing the chances of having our relationships experience what we might call a "thriving (rather than surviving) mode."

*Four Fundamental Feelings*

While there are many ways to group and categorize emotions, this discussion will focus on one aspect—the identification of four basic feelings and, therefore, four basic words: anger, sadness, happiness, and fear. One way to remember these four basic feeling words is to consider that the first three can be made to rhyme (mad, sad, glad, and scared).[10]

When listed this way, they create the acronym, MSGS, which can be regarded as the abbreviation for "messages." In this case, the concept of feelings as messages "fits" nicely with the topic at hand, since feelings essentially represent information that can enhance communication and thereby, connection as well. In an incident-focused approach to feelings, feelings indicate what is going on in the environment. However, from a thought-focused approach, feelings are vital information about *oneself*. Thus, anger, sadness, happiness, and fear become very important resources for an individual to understand their own perspectives on any given situation, especially where relationships are concerned.

For the most part, we talk about feelings very rapidly, and we often use multiple words to explain ourselves. And, frequently, this works fine. For example, suppose we are listening in on a conversation between person A and person B:

*A:* *I feel like you really helped me recently.*
*B:* *Thank you. It was my privilege.*

---

10 Selecting and rhyming these feeling words are two strategies I first learned from Patricia Resick's (2005) approach to Cognitive Processing Therapy..

**A:** I'd like to show my appreciation by taking you to lunch.
**B:** Sure. That's very kind of you.

Talking about feelings in detail in this scenario works because, in general, the feelings are positive and can probably fit into the category of happiness or gladness. When both parties are on good terms, the use of more complex feeling language does not usually pose a problem because even though the feelings could sound like they are incident-focused, the positive nature of the incidents means that people are generally content and not looking for ways to change how they feel.

*Subtle Complexities*
However, complex feelings can be difficult to sort through when less positive emotions are involved. For example, in a conflict we might hear the following interchange:

**A:** I feel like you don't care about me anymore.
**B:** I can't believe you said that. Of course, I care about you.
**A:** Well, if you cared about me, you would take me more seriously.
**B:** You're too sensitive. I am taking you seriously; you just don't see it.

There are several things that make this brief interaction difficult, such as the way in which neither party appears to be hearing the other and both seem to be on edge and critical in their tone. For our purposes, the primary point is that this interchange represents a highly reactive, incident-focused approach to emotions that ultimately leads to a communication breakdown. Of course, we don't know what the context of the conversation is, but that is likely to be secondary, since the context of the interaction *is the incident,* and we are trying to move away from having the external incidents we experience dictate how we feel. Again, the goal is to find a way to treat our feelings like a window into our thoughts, so we can more effectively engage others.

Imagine if the above conversation were to take the following turn:

**A:**  *I feel like you don't care about me anymore.*
**B:**  *There is something I have done to offend you.*
**A:**  *Well, I wish you would take me more seriously.*
**B:**  *Do you feel I am not taking you seriously now?*

Here the two parties seem to be more in step with each other. Interestingly, the dialogue started off the same way but ended quite differently. In the first interchange, we hear person A express doubt that person B cares, and we hear B say that they think A is too sensitive. In the second interchange, B seems genuinely open to what A may be feeling.

The point of limiting feelings to words (and single words if possible) is again to keep feelings general and thoughts specific. Of course, we usually do not talk this way, so it can help to start with whatever is expressed as a feeling and work backward. For example, let us return to A in the above interchange:

**A:**  *I feel like you don't care about me anymore.*

We probably all know what it is like to feel as though another person does not care for us anymore. This is a painful feeling that we commonly protest. It is in the same family of emotions as feeling rejected, excluded, or forgotten. And it is difficult to know how to respond to somebody when they share such feelings.

> **"...when it comes to clear communication, translation often involves moving from the figurative to the literal."**

When a person says, "I feel like you don't care about me anymore," the complexity of the emotion makes prioritizing the relationship difficult for at least two reasons. First, the listener most likely hears that they (as listener) are the focus of the emotion. Second, the speaker more easily believes that to feel better, the listener needs to change. Though often not intended, the result of these two dynamics is that both parties frequently experience such conversations as contests or competitions. As such, most of the awareness of relationship as a cooperative enterprise is lost.

One explanation for this is that the complexity of the emotion makes it difficult for both parties to know how to interact with each other. As indicated above, the listener is "felt" by both to be the focus of the uncaring feeling, even though the speaker is talking about their own feeling. This has the effect of turning the feeling into a problem because the assumed cause is located outside of the person who experiences it. Since it makes sense to "fix" a problem, an attempt is made to essentially change the person who has just expressed that they feel uncared for. This, in turn, has the impact of sending a message that the person should not feel what they are in fact feeling. The result is that a new sort of problem is created, a problem which most likely could have been circumvented.

Another way of looking at this is to consider what would occur if the listener did *not* care about the speaker. It would seem they would say something like, "You're right. I don't care about you anymore," (unless they were trying to be deceptive, which would undermine the conversation altogether) at which point the speaker might wonder what the point of the communication is in the first place. Ironically, agreement here means the two will most likely go their separate ways. So, it seems that when a person shares that they do not feel cared for in a relationship, it is because they do care about the other person as well as because they ultimately believe the other person will consider what they have to say. The irony again is that often such conversations end up with one party or both feeling the other is not taking them seriously.

*Strategic Translating*
The solution can be found in a process of translation. If either the speaker or the listener engages in this process, the communication is likely to be clearer and more productive.

Translation here refers to taking specific steps to focus on one's respective role in the conversation to better utilize the information at hand. Thus, the speaker more carefully articulates their position, and the listener focuses on interpreting what is shared with equal care and consideration. Hopefully, both will experience a deeper sense of understanding, regardless of what was initially expressed or confided.

So, let's look again at how this might be done with an initial feeling of not being cared for. How can such a feeling be better communicated?

At this point, it will not surprise us to consider that the best translation strategy will draw from our FIT equation and the key reminder that feelings are simply words. Therefore, we translate the feeling of not being cared for into a format that keeps feelings general and thoughts specific.

Again, while it is initially undoubtedly more comfortable to use default expressions (such as "I feel like you don't care about me." or "I feel as if you don't care about me."), we can now see how these expressions risk potential problems. As mentioned, this type of sharing makes it easy to shift the focus of the feeling to the listener which essentially sets up an emphasis on external factors that typify survival situations where feelings are treated as problems to be fixed. Moreover, sharing that we "feel like" or how we "feel that" such and such means a translation process is inevitable since the speaker is essentially comparing their feeling to another experience, which can itself be a complex expression. Grammatically speaking, the use of an analogy or of a simile calls for a certain degree of abstract thinking ability. And since feelings are abstract to begin with, it will be useful to find a way to make them less abstract. Therefore, when it comes to clear communication, translation often involves moving from the figurative to the literal.

*Delivery Systems*
The feeling that, for our purposes, is best limited to one word, might be considered a sort of casing or skin that contains a thought. Consider, for example, a medication capsule where the outer gelatin casing "delivers" the inner liquid substance of the medication itself. Here the casing would be analogous to the feeling and the liquid would be analogous to the thought. This does not mean that the feeling is unimportant or unsubstantial. Instead, it is to emphasize that the purpose of feelings is to help us identify our thoughts. And when our feelings function in this

way, they also bring form, dimension, and depth to life. They add spice to life, just like salt.

Let us consider what we might experience if we risk becoming simple, even concrete, in our approach to emotions. Here, the strategy is to use at least one of the four basic feeling words—mad, sad, glad, scared—and convert the original, complex feeling into the "causal" thought. Thus, our speaker might say:

**A:** *I feel (sad) because **I think** (you don't care about me).*

There are at least two reasons why this is important. First, the feeling is acknowledged; there is nothing wrong with a person feeling sad. In fact, it is completely understandable and logical for a person to feel the emotion of sadness if they are telling themselves that another person does not care about them. Essentially, the feeling of sadness is experienced when there is a perceived loss or when something is missed or longed for. Put another way, if I tell myself that somebody does not care about me, I am identifying a loss of being cared for, and the reasonable feeling to follow is sadness.

Second, if I do not want to feel sad, I can do something about this. However, the intervention is not focused on another person who is caring or not caring for me. Rather, the strategy for feeling differently is to modify my thinking. Thus, I might say "I feel (sad) because I think (you don't care about me), *but I could be mistaken*," or "*I just might not be seeing how you care right now.*"

This does not have to be a mind game. I can sincerely remind myself of the way in which my thoughts can be inaccurate if I want to have a different emotional experience. In this case, the sadness will most likely not go away entirely, and this is okay, because sadness per se is neither bad nor wrong. However, with every modification to my thinking that mitigates messages of loss, I can expect to gradually dial down the feeling and hopefully bring it into more alignment with what is occurring. The more realistic the thinking, the more useful my emotion will be. And, again, as my emotion draws my attention to my thinking and I achieve a more accurate perception of the situation, I am on my way to potentially experiencing deeper relationships.

*Freedom to Feel and to Fly*

With the above example, we have touched upon the idea that each emotion corresponds to a *certain way* of thinking. At the risk of being simplistic, we might use the following pairings as springboards for incorporating emotional content into various relationships. In this case, we have another possible acronym— FLGT—an abbreviated version of the word "flight." Here, flight does not refer to fleeing a danger (as in "fight or flight") but rather to the possibility of freedom, of soaring to new heights, of taking relationships to greater levels (again, we are interested, metaphorically speaking, in eagle DNA and dolphin behavior):

| | |
|---|---|
| **M (mad):** | **F (fairness)** |
| **S (sad):** | **L (loss)** |
| **G (glad):** | **G (gain)** |
| **S (scared):** | **T (threat)** |

Accordingly, anger results when we think that fairness is compromised; sadness results when we think something has been lost; happiness results when we think something has been gained; and fear results when we think that a threat exists. If we trust this process of linking general feelings with specific thoughts, we can extrapolate to other feelings by considering other variations on the same themes.

For example, let's take another common emotion such as frustration. Let us say that I am frustrated because a friend seems to interrupt me while I am talking to them. At this point, it should be clear that if left in this form, e.g., "I am frustrated because you keep interrupting me," the other person will likely take offense, since I am essentially telling him that he is the reason for my frustration. Therefore, the strategy is to take the rather specific emotion of frustration and convert it into a specific thought that is in turn linked to a general feeling.

Of the four general feelings, it seems reasonable to say that frustration is most related to anger and the perception that something is unfair. Thus, I might begin with:

*I feel angry because I think this conversation is frustrating.*

This seems awkward at first, especially since we often

reserve anger for more intense situations. However, since anger is simply a word and we believe it is appropriate to share our opinions or thoughts at any given time, anger simply becomes a pathway to deeper and hopefully better communication.

When this happens, we might have an exchange like this (assuming both parties are working with the same approach to emotions):

**A:** *I feel angry because I think this conversation is frustrating.*
**B:** *It's so frustrating you care enough to tell me.*
**A:** *Yes, it seems to me that when I talk, I do not have the opportunity to finish my thoughts because you start talking, and I don't think that is very fair to me.*
**B:** *I've been interrupting you.*
**A:** *Yes, it seems like that to me.*
**B:** *Well, thank you for telling me this. That would be frustrating for me too. I'll try to be more patient and let you finish.*
**A:** *Thank you. I think you're being patient right now.*

For many people, this way of talking might seem way too tedious and not very true to reality. While these concerns are certainly understandable, the focus here is not so much to prescribe specific wording as it is to illustrate the principle of using general feelings attributed to specific thoughts. As another example, we might look at how two different people talk about a similar incident (i.e., frustration with interruptions) using different points but the same themes.

**A:** *I get mad when it seems like the same thing happens over and over.*
**B:** *You're trying to do something about it by telling me.*
**A:** *Yeah, seems like you keep talking when I'm talking.*
**B:** *So I'm interrupting you.*
**A:** *Yeah.*
**B:** *Am I doing it right now?*
**A:** *Actually, right now, no.*
**B:** *That's good to hear. I'm sorry for my interruptions earlier.*
**A:** *That's okay. I appreciate you talking with me now.*

Again, this could seem very unrealistic, and at some level, any attempt to illustrate the "ideal" conversation will seem too good to be true. However, as mentioned earlier, the audacious claim of this book is that such conversations are possible, especially as we learn to use our emotions as information about both *ourselves* and *how we see our situations*. As this process guides our communication, we will better tap the full potential of the relationships that are important to us. And when this happens, we will experience more vitality in our interactions, in much the same way salt sustains life in the ocean.

# Chapter 8: The Polar Seas

*Controlling your temper is better than being a hero*
*who captures a city.*
*Proverbs 16:32[1]*

As we continue our exploration of the ocean of relationships, we can think of each major category of emotion as an integral part of the World Ocean itself. And we begin this portion of our journey with the deep, icy waters of the Arctic and Antarctic as we consider our first emotion: anger.

Assigning anger to the freezing oceans of the North and South Poles is meant to pair anger with especially formidable waters, though it is not intended to create a negative connotation per se. We are likely more familiar with how anger can become dangerous and hostile and less acquainted with how anger can be useful and even relationship-promoting. This chapter aims to specifically address this latter consideration.

As we embark on this next phase of our exploration, let us continue to be mindful of our FLGT acronym, looking at each of the four basic feelings in more depth. Let us particularly consider how becoming more aware of each feeling can continue to move us away from our default, prairie chicken and *mahi* tendencies and into the freedoms that eagles and dolphins enjoy.

## Breaking the Ice: Problem or Resource?

*The Importance of Anger*
Anger (shortened to *mad* in MSGS), is again produced by a belief that fairness (represented by the F in FLGT) has

1   The Holy Bible (Contemporary English Version, Second Edition (CEV))

been violated. Thus, anger appeals to our sense of justice. There is something in all of us that wants life to be fair, and we rightly protest when fairness is missing or lacking. In the words of theologian Cornelius Plantinga, Jr., anger is a feeling of "passionate againstness."[2] Therefore, while anger can range in intensity, from mild irritation to intense rage or fury, this element of protesting or opposing something that is perceived as not right is central to the experience of it.

Because of this characteristic, anger is often regarded as a problem in and of itself, and it often feels uncomfortable. However, if we take seriously the notion that anger is about injustice, we will see that it is very important to retain anger as an integral part of the moral compass we use to navigate the ocean of relationships. Thus, while anger seems to have a negative "charge" to it, it is neither immoral nor wrong to feel it. In fact, it seems better to think of each of these basic four emotions as morally neutral and of the moral value of the emotion as primarily determined by how we act upon it.

This is again an unconventional approach to anger. Often, anger is treated as a problem to be fixed. For example, when resolving certain disagreements, it is not uncommon for one person to reassure another by saying, "I am not angry." If we think about it, this is an interesting thing to do: to say what we are not or to say what we do not feel. And it begs the question, "Why?" Why does one tell another what they do *not* feel?

It seems this usually reflects an assumption that it is somehow bad or wrong to be angry or that it is good to avoid being angry. And there is some truth to this in that life is undoubtedly better if anger is kept to a minimum, and many significant problems (and many crimes in particular) would certainly go away or at least go down in frequency if anger were eliminated.[3]

However, the fact is anger does exist, and managing it is a necessary life skill. When situations are even remotely unfair or unjust to us, we will feel some level of anger, and denying this

2   Plantinga, C. Jr. (1995). Not the way it's supposed to be: A breviary of sin. Grand Rapids, MI: William B. Eerdmans Publishing Company, p. 165.

3   Willard, D. (1998). The divine conspiracy: Rediscovering our hidden life in God. New York, NY: HarperSanFrancisco.

will risk creating even more problems. The popular expression, "don't get mad, get even" comes to mind. In this case, denial of anger becomes a rationale for revenge. Of course, the irony in the expression is that revenge can hardly exist apart from anger, especially if we consider that both anger and revenge are about perceived injustices. Revenge itself can be considered an expression of aggressive anger.

## Aggression

For our purposes, aggression is that extreme form of anger in which one person tries to win by somehow making the other person lose. When aggression is involved, survival mode is at work, and so a change in an external stimulus is required for the anger to change. This is because, in survival mode, anger means an actual problem exists. The incident component of the FIT equation is emphasized, and we retaliate in one way or another. In a word, we fight. This again works in athletic competition or in battle, but it is rarely conducive to relationships.

## Defensiveness

Another extreme form of anger is defensiveness. In defensiveness, we do our best to keep from appearing to lose. Here, the external incident is also the focus and the target of the anger, however, the person withdraws from whatever is occurring and does whatever necessary to protect themself from accusation. Such protection includes refusing to acknowledge any involvement in the situation that might implicate them in the problem. The unfairness they are trying to avoid is any suggestion that they are in the wrong. Whereas aggression involves fighting, defensiveness involves fleeing. And, while this is again not wrong per se, where defensiveness is concerned, when one party avoids another party to avoid experiencing a sense of defeat, both parties lose (especially if such avoidance was unnecessary to begin with).

Taken together, aggression and defensiveness comprise the fight-flight reaction. Interestingly, as we have seen, this corresponds physiologically to the sympathetic nervous system activity commonly known as the fight-flight *response*. For our purposes, however, since reactivity is more characteristic of survival mode and responsiveness is more characteristic of thriving, let us refer to the fight-flight *reaction* rather than the fight-flight *response*.

Often aggression and defensiveness overlap, and so there can be outright attempts to attack and ward off the other at the same time. The bottom line is that neither is very useful in an interpersonal context. On one hand, since both aggression and defensiveness seek to correct a perceived wrong, they are understandable and good in intention. However, as the saying goes, "The road to hell is paved with good intentions." This is all too often a description of the havoc that misguided anger can cause. Whether the goal is to win or whether the goal is to not lose, the relationship suffers if another person is made to lose. One party survives but at the other's expense.

True relationship is characterized by thriving, and thriving requires us to find win/win scenarios. In relationships, win/ wins are best identified as we look *within* to identify how feelings such as anger can be best utilized. As is suggested by our FLGT acronym, when this happens, our relationships will really start to "take off."

### A Few Mad Men: Destructive and Constructive Anger

*A Pivotal Question*

In my opinion, the film *A Few Good Men* expertly illustrates anger's negative and positive potential. The story opens with the controversial death of a Marine, Private William Santiago (played by Michael DeLorenzo), at the hands of two other Marines (Lance Corporal Harold Dawson (Wolfgang Bodison) and Private Louden Downey (James Marshall)) who are following an unofficial order known as a "Code Red." The Code Red ultimately comes from Colonel Nathan Jessup (Jack Nicholson) as an attempt to intimidate his soldiers into better performance. As the plot unfolds, we learn that Jessup tends to be very aggressive with his anger, and the death of Santiago tragically illustrates the extreme and irreversible damage that results from such anger.

Into this situation come three Navy attorneys (Lieutenant Daniel Kaffee (Tom Cruise), Lieutenant Sam Weinberg (Kevin

Pollak), and Lieutenant Commander Joanne Galloway (Demi Moore)) who are responsible for defending the Marines who were following the order. The film intensifies when the team suddenly loses a key witness and then Galloway suggests that they take the risk of summoning Jessup to testify as to whether the Code Red was actually issued. Kaffee, already anxious about the case and under the influence of alcohol, becomes livid with Galloway and launches into a tirade about the risks of a court martial. Galloway in turn leaves the meeting, and Kaffee and Weinberg begin to talk.

This talk is the turning point in the movie. Weinberg begins to share with Kaffee about Kaffee's father, Lionel, who was a renowned trial lawyer. At this point, Kaffee begins to ask Weinberg if he thinks his (Kaffee's) father would put Jessup on the stand and further if Weinberg would do it. Seizing the opportunity, Weinberg creatively puts the question back to Kaffee, saying,

*"With the evidence we got, not in a million years. But here's the thing. Neither Lionel Kaffee nor Sam Weinberg are lead counsel in the case of Santiago vs Dawson and Downey. So, the real question is . . . what would you do?"*[4]

Again, in my opinion, everything in the film pivots on Weinberg's question and specifically, his ability to redirect Kaffee back to himself. What follows are first an apology and then a reconciliation between Kaffee and Galloway. After these, the team begins to plan out their strategy which ultimately works by *turning Jessup's anger against Jessup*. And in a climactic finish, one man skillfully uses anger to his utter advantage, while another man finds his anger to be his tragic flaw and ruin.

This film, with its depiction of the double-edged nature of anger, underscores the dominant themes of this book. When we approach it as a personal responsibility (instead of it being the responsibility of something or someone outside of ourselves), anger can function as a *resource* that enhances our relationships

4  From A Few Good Men (1992), written by Aaron Sorkin (who also wrote the 1989 play by the same name), directed by Rob Reiner, and produced by Columbia Pictures and Castlerock Entertainment.

rather than as a problem for our relationships that needs to be fixed.


## Anger as an Ally

*Breaking Company to Befriend*
This approach is unconventional for most of us, myself included. Many times, long-standing problems with anger seem very deep and complex. And no doubt, when a person has been wounded by others over and over, there is much cause for anger and legitimate pain. Abuse, abandonment, assault, insult, and betrayal are all profound forms of injustice. For certain people, these experiences have become the "story of their lives," and it makes sense for their anger to become almost second nature. In fact, if anger were not felt, there could very well be a disconnection or an unhealthy denial of past wounds. When anger is this familiar, it might feel more like a long-time companion rather than a problem to fix.

> **"Indeed, much is at stake when we make ourselves emotionally vulnerable with one another."**

However, the challenge of keeping lingering company with anger is that it is difficult to feel connected to an angry person. Often anger is a secondary emotion, and the more primary emotions are feelings like hurt, frustration, and fear. These feelings often correspond to events in the person's past, present, and future, respectively[5]. Connecting to these primary emotions often takes less effort because of the way in which each contains an element of vulnerability. Ironically, the person who feels these primary feelings may have difficulty sharing them because expressing vulnerability can be so uncomfortable.

In relationships, when vulnerability is regarded as weakness or something to be avoided, this can be a sign that survival mode is at work. On the ocean of relationships, vulnerability is like a dolphin and, in fact, is a form of dolphin behavior.

5 Stoop, D. (1982, 2005). You are what you think. Grand Rapids, MI: Fleming H. Revell.

However, because expressing a feeling like hurt or fear can be uncomfortable and seem threatening, such a feeling may look and feel more like a shark than a dolphin. Nonetheless, talking about a vulnerable feeling is a way of allowing another person to come closer.

We will benefit to the extent that we can share from our hearts with each other as we discover that what seem like sharks are actually dolphins. This is difficult to do, however, when our hearts are in pain and when we attribute our pain to each other—when it not only seems like there are sharks in the water but also seems like they have bitten us. The operative word, again, is *seems*. And the point of this chapter is that as we break company with past ways of equating our pain with others' actions and recognize the roles our perceptions play in our experiences, we will be able to befriend our anger long enough to access the underlying vulnerable emotions that are more amenable to connecting with one another.

*The Risk of Criticism*
This is not to say that vulnerability does not pose any risk. Indeed, much is at stake when we make ourselves emotionally vulnerable with one another. One such risk is that either party will move backward, from thriving back to surviving mode. And once this happens, it can be very difficult to return to vulnerability as a resource for the relationship.

Consider the person who tries to communicate something potentially sensitive to another person to better the relationship. She may tell the other that she feels offended or say something about the other's appearance or express something that she wishes the other would do differently. If the other person feels criticized, the well-intended comment can become a wedge in the relationship. In fact, if this becomes a pattern, a progressive gap between the two people can result.

This is particularly evident in the research of psychologist and marriage expert Dr. John Gottman and colleagues, who have identified a phenomenon known as "The Four Horsemen of the Apocalypse"—a warning pattern that signifies that a relationship is in distress—beginning with Criticism and then moving to Defensiveness, Contempt, and finally Stonewalling.[6]

In these steps identified by Gottman and his team, we see alternating expressions of aggressive and defensive forms of anger. And while it is easy to imagine how these "horsemen" can quickly ride into a relationship and bring destruction, it is also important to note that this progression is very unnecessary. For example, Gottman indicates that whereas ordinary complaining is a common feature of relationships overall, Criticism becomes the first "horseman" by allowing personal blame to enter an interaction. Thus, he writes,

> *You will always have some complaints about the person you live with. But there's a world of difference between a complaint and a criticism. A complaint only addresses the specific action at which your spouse failed. A criticism is more global—it adds on some negative words about your mate's character or personality.*[7]

Criticism is certainly difficult to hear. When people tell us that they think we are somehow "not measuring up," we take issue with this. And often taking issue is warranted. Criticisms feel like attacks, and it makes sense to become defensive. At the same time, let us remember that analogies and similes call for translation. When something "feels like" an attack, this is an analogy and a simile. What happens, however, if we translate this using the "custom FIT" approach? For example, "I feel angry, because I *think* I'm being attacked." This may seem too simple, and it may even look like the change is so subtle that it hardly matters. The difference, however, is that now I can both own my feelings *and* use them constructively—much like taking away the first horseman's sword and using it to protect the relationship. The change is therefore potentially very consequential.

## Anger and Wisdom

*Silver and Gold*
Considering some of the presuppositions I stated at the

6 Gottman, J. M., & Silver, N. (1999). The seven principles for making marriage work. New York, NY: Three Rivers Press, pp. 27-34.

7 Gottman, J. M., & Silver, N. (1999), p.27.

beginning of this book, it seems important here to consider how this theory on emotions lines up with the Bible. Interestingly, the Bible generally appears to have been written with the assumption that one person can actually *make* another person angry. For example, the apostle Paul writes, "Fathers, do not provoke your children to anger, but bring them up in the discipline and instruction of the Lord."[8] Provocation often implies the direct impact of one person on another. This could easily contradict the dominant themes in this book. After all, our thesis is that one's own thoughts determine one's own feelings, including anger.

However, there are several things to keep in mind. First, because the books of the Bible were written during a certain period, many of the apparent discrepancies between then and now could reflect artifacts of time and culture. So, for example, frequent references to the *heart* as the emotional center of a person parallel the beliefs of that day. In the same way, when certain Bible authors talk about emotions as if they are externally caused, perhaps this is more of a reflection on the thinking of that day than a way of saying that this is how emotions work per se.

The Bible, then, is not primarily a textbook on science or history but rather an account of God's redemptive work beginning in the lives of a specific people (the nation of Israel), and culminating in a specific person (Jesus of Nazareth) for the redemption of the world itself.

As such, the Bible is full of wisdom regarding the impact this redemption has on our experience of day-to-day relationships with others. The principles in this book attempt to tap into this wisdom as a deep and endless source of knowledge, much the way a miner looks for a vein of precious metal beneath the surface of the earth.

> ## "Provocation often implies the direct impact of one person on another."

---

8   Ephesians 6:4

Interestingly, recent discoveries suggest that there are places deep at the bottom of the ocean where gold and silver have been found.[9] Perhaps we could say that Biblical wisdom is like oceanic gold and psychological principles are like oceanic silver. When discrepancies seem apparent, we can especially consider interpretations that allow for both the priority of ancient wisdom and the practicality of contemporary application. To use a familiar saying in a new context, we can "make new friends and keep the old, one is silver and the other is gold."

*Whose Words?*

Let us explore this kind of synthesis between old and new in more depth. The writer of the book of Proverbs writes, "A soft answer turns away wrath, but a harsh word stirs up anger."[10] This is classic advice for potentially difficult situations where anger is likely. Speak softly and respectfully with one another and the chances of interpersonal conflict will decrease dramatically. This, no doubt, is one way of tapping into the "gold" of this passage. Still, in addition to this, what if we consider the influence of looking for the "silver" as well. For example, the concepts of a "gentle answer" or a "harsh word" could refer just as much to how a person *thinks* about the situation. And if so, an *intrapersonal* interpretation could be equally important to understanding the wisdom of this passage.

For example, consider a situation where person A is trying to talk with person B and B does not seem interested in the conversation. It would be understandable for A to become upset and feel anger towards B because B is ignoring A. In this case, A might approach B and gently talk with B about how A wants B to be more attentive. Again, this could work very well.

We will notice, however, that in this scenario, if B is not responsive, A is still stuck with anger because it is attributed to B *ignoring* A. Anger, in this situation, is a function of how B treats A. Therefore, because this anger is directly connected to an *external* source, i.e., person B, it is essentially a problem imposed from without. Moreover, we have all probably had

9 Harris, H. (2012, April 2). Gold miners dig deep—to the ocean floor. In Npr.org. Retrieved December 4, 2017, from http://www.npr.org/2012/04/02/149838302/seafloor-becomes-next-frontier-for-gold-diggers

10 Proverbs 15:1

experiences of trying to speak softly or gently with another person only to have the person persist in their anger towards us. The fact is there are no guarantees if we are concerned with interpersonal results, which is ultimately a good thing, since guarantees would imply we can control others, and this would, in turn, undermine relationships.

So, how might an *intrapersonal* approach to a gentle answer address this situation? To begin with, A would attribute A's anger to the *perception* that B is ignoring A. While this may seem like mere semantics, it is one possible first step toward a "gentle answer"—toward the ocean, so to speak.

Conversely, if A labels B's behavior as "ignoring" A, this is a possible first step toward the "harsh word" that will lead to anger. This is because anger logically follows from situations that are regarded as unfair. And, for the most part, it is healthy and understandable to say that being ignored by another person is not fair. So, if B were trying to ignore A, then A would have good reason to feel angry. In such a case, it would be accurate to say that B was being unfair to A.

In either case (whether the ignoring is intentional or not), what would be the best thing for A to do with A's anger? The answer to this begins with the importance of recognizing that the context of the whole interaction is a *relationship*. Therefore, the emotion of anger (whether the initial unfairness is intended or not) is both understandable and *utilizable*. It is a resource to be accessed rather than a problem to be solved. It is information about *oneself* that allows for increased self-control which could, in turn, constructively influence the relationship.

The opposite approach to this (seeing anger as a problem that comes from outside of oneself) would involve A somehow targeting B and attempting to right the wrong by changing B, e.g., through direct confrontation (such as a scolding), through reciprocal behavior (such as also ignoring B), or through withdrawing altogether, all of which would be variations on fight-flight reactions. The difficulty with this, however, is that B will most likely be opposed to being fought or being fled, and so escalation of some sort might easily occur.

Again, this all can be mitigated and even circumvented to the extent that the anger is attributed to A's *perception* of B. When this is done, A has an opportunity to partial out B's *behavior* from *who* B is as a person, which is a subtle but powerful return to awareness of the relationship. This awareness of being in the presence of another *person* is essential for the "gentle word" that turns away anger.

## The Gentle Path

So, let's imagine how A might further utilize his anger. First, since this is a relational context and anger does not have to be a problem per se, we can say that accessing anger's utility simply starts with acknowledging the anger in the first place. Let's look at how A might "customize" A's thought process for more emotional fitness in the relationship:

*A:*  *I feel angry because I think that B is ignoring me.*

Again, this is simply a logical statement. Once A recognizes this, the emotion can be utilized:

**A's thought process:** *It is a good thing to not want to be ignored. It is a good thing for me to want to be treated fairly. How can I treat B with the kind of fairness that I wish B would give me? Well, to begin with, I can be fair by not assuming that this is intentional on B's part. Even if it is, that does not have to represent a threat to me. It would just mean that my anger is more justified. Nevertheless, because this is **a relationship** between two adults (and therefore not an actual survival-oriented situation), the "cause" of my anger is still predominantly within me (through what I think about the situation) rather than outside of me. Therefore, if I do not want to be angry, the primary way for me to do this is to see B's actions as something other than unfair to me.*

This is of course a lot of internal dialogue, and it may seem convoluted to some people. However, thinking is, in many ways, a continuous process, and so we experience a lot of internal dialogue on a daily, even moment-to-moment basis. The difference here is that A is making the dialogue very explicit, and A is repeatedly returning to the principles of emotional fitness and emotional responsiveness as reference points. In addition, to be this explicit and specific will likely take more time and therefore slow down A's approach. So, another difference is that this approach could seem tedious and time-consuming. When it comes to anger, however, slowing down is often a risk worth taking, since the step of slowing down is essentially required for people to be more responsive. In most cases, it seems more will be risked if a person does the opposite and acts impulsively.

So, let us explore some of the options that A might have if A is interested in continuing to pursue the "gentle" path. If anger exists, two possible scenarios emerge: either B is primarily perceived as ignoring A or B is actually ignoring A. How does A work with these two scenarios? Let us begin with the first:

*Perceived Unfairness*
Suppose A starts out A's thinking by putting an emphasis on the way it could *seem* like B is ignoring A:

**A's thought process:** *I feel angry because I think that B is ignoring me. But just because I think this is what B is doing does not necessarily mean that this is what B is doing. Are there other ways to see this? Could B be distracted or preoccupied? If so, then this would be different from ignoring me. In fact, B might be frustrated with B for not being able to pay more attention to what I have to say. Maybe there is something that I can do to make it easier for B to hear what I have to say. Maybe I should find out first if this is a good time for B to talk.*

Since A begins with awareness of A's perception, A identifies how this perception directly influences anger at B. Once this awareness is in place, A has the space to consider alternate explanations. This, in turn, leads A to consider what B might be feeling and begins to give B the benefit of the doubt. The result is that A is then able to think about what A might do to influence B in a more positive way.

*Actual Unfairness*
Alternatively, B might be trying to ignore A, in which case A might process it this way:

*A's thought process:* I feel angry because B just told me B is actively trying to ignore me. It is not right for B to treat me this way, and that's exactly why I am so angry. I want to do something to hurt B back. It seems like if I give B a piece of my mind or tune B out, I will be getting even, and that will probably feel good.

*But even if this does feel good, it probably won't really solve the situation. I doubt that me getting back at B will make B want to listen more carefully to what I have to say. I mean if I oppose B for treating me wrongly, am I really any better if I behave the same way toward B?*

*No, two wrongs don't make a right. So, what will?*

*Well, if B is really trying to ignore me, maybe there is something that I did that makes B think I deserve to be ignored. Again, it's hardly ever right to ignore another person, so if B is trying to get me back then B is probably seeing me as the cause of B's feelings. I wonder if there is anything I can do to help B to see that the only way that B will feel better is if B sees me differently. Right now, B thinks B will feel better if B ignores me. And there was a time I used to think this way too (in fact, I came close to this just a little while ago). Maybe I can give B some space from me for a while and that might tell B that I've learned my lesson. Then maybe B will feel more able to hear what I have to say.*

In this situation, the task of being gentle is more difficult since A has apparently heard directly from B that B is intending to ignore A. Thus, A goes through an initial process of validating A's own anger and then contemplates revenge. Revenge, in this case, would be more understandable for A because B has explicitly stated B's motive. However, while it might be understandable, revenge would still be unnecessary precisely because of the interpersonal context. And once A is able to recognize that it would be inconsistent to treat B unfairly just because B is treating A unfairly, A becomes aware of the needless nature of any type of retaliation. Further, A realizes that such inconsistency will likely not increase the chances of B responding differently to A. As a result, A again can consider how "actual unfairness" could still be seen as making sense to B, and this, in turn, becomes a springboard for A to think about how to willingly enter into B's logic and move into a possible solution.

In either situation, anger is the logical outcome precisely because A is on the receiving end of unfairness, whether perceived or actual. And, in both situations, anger can be addressed by considering ways to move away from hearing unfairness as the last word. In this regard, "gentle answers" and "harsh words" can differentially impact anger, even when offenses are intentional. To fully maximize this principle, however, it also seems important to consider *whose words* are ultimately influencing the anger. If the words are coming from another person, then that person can essentially bring on my anger or turn it away, and either way, I am at their mercy. If, however, the gentle or harsh words are my own, I have the final say on whether anger is experienced, and then it can be of service to both me and the relationship.

## Anger and Relationship

*Anger and Wrongdoing*
The very first reference to anger in the Bible (in the story of Cain and Abel) is closely followed by a warning that sin is not far behind. And the first time God mentions anger directly, it is in the form of a question: "Then the Lord said to Cain, "Why are you angry?"[11] As the story unfolds, it points to how a right understanding of why we get angry is directly related to right living and protection from sin. What might be the significance of these first references for our current discussion?

The context of this story is that of two brothers, Cain and Abel, bringing offerings before God. God views Abel's offering ("of the firstborn of his flock and of their fat portions") with favor but does not view Cain's offering ("of the fruit of the ground") with favor. As a result, Cain becomes "very angry" and his "face (falls)."[12]

---

11  Genesis 4:6
12  Genesis 4:3-5, parenthetical clarification added

If we think about this story through the categories suggested in this book, it seems Cain becomes angry because of the situation, namely God looking with favor on his brother instead of with favor on him. Perhaps Cain is seeing Abel, God, or both as the direct cause of his anger. His way of dealing with his anger, i.e., aggression in the form of attacking and killing Abel, confirms this. Cain sees his anger as a problem imposed from an outside circumstance, and thus he takes steps to alter the circumstance directly and permanently to "solve" the problem, which, of course, only makes the situation worse. It does not cause God to look with favor on Cain's offering but rather to issue a curse on Cain.[13]

God's warning is profound for our understanding of anger and how it can work for or against us. He asks Cain, "Why are you angry, and why has your face fallen? If you do well, will you not be accepted?" And then He says, "And if you do not do well, sin is crouching at the door. Its desire is contrary to you, but you must rule over it."[14]

The line of questioning that God uses with Cain is thought-provoking if we consider it as a way of understanding God's perspective on anger. He asks two open-ended questions, then a third closed question, and then issues a cautionary statement. The tone overall is characterized by concern and exhortation, and the outcome seems to hinge on Cain "ruling" sin by doing "well."

Mastering anger is therefore very important to God. And so, here are some personal thoughts on how anger might serve us (rather than vice versa) based upon God's words to Cain.

First, mastering anger requires acknowledging anger. When God asks why Cain is angry, I do not think God is evaluating Cain's anger as good or bad, healthy or unhealthy. Neither do I think He is saying that Cain should or should not be angry. Nor is He asking Cain for information that He does not have. Rather, it seems God is asking Cain about the reason for his anger so that Cain can become more aware of what is at stake for him and for Abel.

13  Genesis 4:11-12

14  Genesis 4:6-7

Second, mastering anger involves not equating it with sin. God certainly draws a close connection between anger and sin, but He does not explicitly say that they are one and the same. Recognizing that anger and sin are not interchangeable is key for managing both. If anger is initially denied or denounced, the person experiencing it is more at risk for not knowing how it functions. The risk includes not only a sort of blindness to anger's effects but also a similar blindness to its potential utility. If anger is always sinful, then it stands to reason that anger is always a problem, and problems call for solutions rather than acknowledgement.

God does prescribe a solution, but it is not for anger; it is for sin. The solution is to "do well" which in turn will lead to acceptance from God and mastery over anger and sin. This intimate relationship between anger, sin, and doing well brings about a certain precariousness for Cain. It seems God is communicating a sense of urgency to Cain—perhaps sternly warning him, using the equivalent of a raised voice or a harsh tone. Or perhaps God is pleading with Cain, imploring him to consider each next step before moving forward.

Interestingly, God tells Cain he "must" master sin, employing the language of a conditional obligation. That is, if Cain does not master sin, it (sin) will fulfill its desire to have Cain. The connotation seems to be that of a predator waiting to pounce upon its prey. So, sin itself is separate from Cain and not yet a part of Cain's experience. By contrast, anger is something that is a part of Cain's experience and somehow makes Cain vulnerable to being attacked. If sin is the beast, anger is the energy within Cain that could motivate him to step into the beast's path, outside of what God calls Cain's "door."

> **"We may try to talk about our emotions as objectively as possible and still struggle to not have our tone, volume, or facial expressions "show" how we feel."**

*Show or Tell*

We can consider God's reference to Cain's face being downcast as another sign of the risk of the type of anger Cain is experiencing. On one hand, it is natural and important that we utilize facial expressions to show various emotions, including anger. In fact, anger is perhaps the feeling that lends itself most to outward expression. However, because anger traces back to a perceived unfairness, outward communication of it, even via facial expressions, moves us into the realm of an outward attempt to address it. And when this happens, we have the potential for anger to take either an aggressive or passive form, neither of which is very conducive to relationship.

So, when it comes to anger and other negative emotions, we do well to "tell" about how we are feeling instead of "show" how we are feeling. This, however, is not easily done. First, it is not easy because reactive, survival-based approaches to anger argue against this. If we are *actually* being treated unfairly, it makes sense to either protect ourselves or to withdraw, to fight or to flee. The situations or incidents at hand call for direct intervention, and the *meaning* of our situation (our thoughts about it, interpretations) can seem essentially irrelevant, since, by definition, the unfairness is actual.

However, in a relationship, the other person is the "situation" being interpreted. Therefore, a second reason it is difficult to talk about anger is that even though the offense is "perceived" instead of actual, it is felt as very *personal*. Moreover, we do not have very good options when it comes to the language at our disposal. Because we are not accustomed to doing this, it will feel and sound odd. For example, a way to talk about strong anger is to say, "I feel furious" or "I feel very, very, very angry" and attribute the feeling to attendant thoughts about what seems unfair. To do this calmly and carefully is especially challenging in the heat of the moment. We may try to talk about our emotions as objectively as possible and still struggle to not have our tone, volume, or facial expressions "show" how we feel.

The point here is not that we should never show our anger. Rather, the point is to be aware that when we do "show" how we feel, we are at risk for somehow escalating the situation. This is precisely because showing how we feel implies that we are attributing our feelings to an external source, leading to the likelihood of reactivity rather than responsiveness. This again may be behind God's purpose in initially asking Cain, "*Why* are you angry?" (emphasis mine). If Cain can identify the reasons for his anger, which I propose would be found in his thoughts and beliefs about Abel and God—especially since apparently neither Abel nor God are being unfair to Cain in any way, then, it would seem, he would be more equipped to manage his anger well.

In this regard, it is again interesting to consider God's instruction to Cain to "do well." God indicates to Cain that if he does well, he will be "accepted," and this would then represent a protection from the threat of sin. There are at least two things about this instruction that seem worth noting for our current discussion.

First, if our theory is true, why does God instruct Cain to "do" what is right instead of to "think" or "believe" what is right? Some obvious responses that come to mind (but that do not necessarily answer the question) are again that the purpose of the passage is primarily to recount a story rather than to teach or illustrate certain psychological principles overall. Or we might say that "thinking" and "believing" more accurately are forms of "doing" well.

These possibilities notwithstanding, it seems when God is telling Cain to do well and thereby be accepted, he is addressing the situation itself, namely that Cain's sacrifice was not acceptable to Him. Cain's anger is then essentially a reaction to an actual rejection from God *of Cain's actions, though not of his feelings or even more, not of Cain as a person* (the fact that God continues to talk with Cain, admonish and advise him seems partial evidence of this). For God, Cain's anger is not so much a problem as is Cain's misguided way of making an offering (apparently because it was not as costly or sacrificial as Abel's offering). Therefore, for God, there is a problem that does need to be remedied, and even if Cain changes his perspective to modify his anger (and therefore, the risk of sin), this problem will remain.

The second important point is that because I believe God's

perspective is itself objective reality, even though our emotions are often matters of perception and interpretation, the final analysis must take God's perspective into serious account. This divine perspective is what I have metaphorically referred to as the "whole earth and universe" of our lives, and the domain of this book (being relationships and how we interpret them) is what I am referring to as the ocean. Suffice it to say that this account of the first biblical record of anger is important for understanding both the nature of anger (ocean) and the larger priority of understanding God's perspective on life (earth and universe) and what makes for lasting fulfillment, including the experience of having our actions "accepted" by Him.

*Anger and Doing Well*

Once we learn to distinguish anger from both the situations that seem to engender it and the thoughts that do themselves fuel it, then we can utilize it and experience it enhancing our relationships. To the extent that we are interested, we can increase our insights into this emotion by mining the "gold" that is to be found in the Bible. For example, in parallel with the story of God and Cain, we can see just how the apostle Paul can instruct the people at Ephesus, "be angry and do not sin."[15] Or we can see the example God sets for us in being "slow to anger, abounding in love" which is echoed by the apostle James in his recommendation to be "quick to hear, slow to speak, slow to anger."[16]

Interestingly, this latter instruction from James is followed by the notion that "an angry person doesn't produce God's righteousness."[17] However, while anger itself does not bring about righteousness, it seems it can be harnessed as a form of energy for doing what is right. Ultimately, Jesus seems to incorporate and even utilize His anger in His ministry. Thus, He drives moneychangers and vendors out of the temple when He defines their actions as inappropriate, even employing anger in an aggressive form.[18]

And finally, anger appears to be part of Jesus' healing of

15  Ephesians 4:26
16  James 1:19
17  James 1:20 (CEB)
18  Matthew 21:12; Mark 11:15; John 2:15

others. Concerning a man Jesus encountered in the synagogue with a withered hand, the apostle Mark writes of Jesus' interaction with the religious leaders,

> *And he (Jesus) said to the man with the withered hand, 'Come here.' And he said to them, 'Is it lawful on the Sabbath to do good or to do harm, to save life or to kill?' But they were silent. And he looked around at them with anger, grieved at their hardness of heart, and said to the man, 'Stretch out your hand.' He stretched it out, and his hand was restored.*[19]

In both the account of the temple and the synagogue, it seems Jesus' biographers are describing His *practice* of the emotion of anger in purposeful ways. To the extent that we see Jesus as an exemplar of how to live (and indeed much more if we aspire to locate the very meaning of life in Him), then His approach to anger in these ways demonstrates both the legitimacy and the utility of this powerful emotion.

Maybe the secret to how He does this is embedded in the question He Himself poses regarding how to approach the institution of the Sabbath—to do good or to do evil, to save life or to kill. We have considered that emotions, like the Sabbath, are intended for the service of people and not the other way around (i.e., people are neither intended to serve the Sabbath nor emotions). In the same way, then, we can regard Jesus' principles of doing good and saving life as guidelines for understanding when we too are legitimately utilizing anger.

### Anger, Goodness, and Life

*Creative and Constructive*

These principles of "doing good" and "saving life" can particularly inform creativity. We can think of anger and all emotion as energy. And just as the second law of thermodynamics tells us that energy is neither created nor destroyed, emotional energy, so to speak, can be either constructive or destructive. Creative emotions lead us and our relationships to deeper levels of goodness and life.

---

19  Mark 3:3-5, parenthetical clarification added

What does creative anger look like?

On an individual, person-to-person scale, it can take the shape of something as simple as an intentional conversation. A friend once told me a story that illustrates one such way anger was managed in a constructive manner. This friend, whom I will call Alex, recounted how, after starting a new job, he made a mistake that cost his company some money, to the tune of about $2,000. Upon realizing this, Alex's boss, Jeff, clearly upset, scheduled a meeting with Alex later that same day.

Between the time that Alex heard that Jeff wanted to meet and the time of the meeting itself, Alex began to brace himself for bad news and even to consider what he would do if his employment was terminated. When the time for the meeting came, Jeff puzzled Alex when he sat with him and discussed the mistake with him. Jeff specifically noted the amount of the loss, asked Alex various questions about his decision process, and pointed out alternatives that might have been considered along the way. Alex did his best to answer the questions and found himself seeing the situation from Jeff's perspective.

At the end of this interview, Alex, still expecting bad news and thinking that Jeff was prolonging the inevitable, proceeded to ask Jeff if he should pack his belongings, adding, "Aren't you going to fire me?" After a pause, Jeff looked intently at Alex and responded, "Why would I fire you? I just spent $2,000 training you!" Alex added that these words from his boss stayed with him throughout the duration of his employment, he never made the same mistake again, and in fact he went on to make valuable contributions to the company overall.

On a larger scale, we can look to events such as the nonviolent protests of the Civil Rights Movement. At the heart of this movement were people coming together in sustained, coordinated, and passionate opposition to injustice, in the name of freedom and an unwavering commitment to common humanity and dignity. The passionate opposition fueling the movement was, in a word, anger. And the use of *nonviolence* to combat *actual attacks* on people's fundamental value and safety called for a special kind of courage and innovative thinking.

Such conscious courage and strategic responsiveness are exemplified in the life and work of the Reverend Dr. Martin Luther King, Jr., who, noting his intention to never "adjust" to society's inequities, once proposed the development of "The International Association for the Advancement of Creative Maladjustment." To the extent that "maladjustment" represents "passionate againstness," I believe we can say anger (at society's inequities) is implied. And if anything, the subtlety in Reverend Dr. King's words seem due to the powerful and gentle effect of another quality, namely . . . love.[20] Consider the transformational good will that permeates his words in the following description of his philosophy of "creative maladjustment" and nonviolence:

*So, in many instances, we have been able to stand before the most violent opponents and say in substance, we will meet your capacity to inflict suffering by our capacity to endure suffering. We will meet your physical force with soul force. We cannot in all good conscience obey your unjust laws because non-cooperation with evil is just as much moral obligation as is cooperation with good, and so throw us in jail and we will still love you. Threaten our children and bomb our homes and our churches and as difficult as it is, we will still love you. Send your hooded perpetrators of violence into our communities at the midnight hours and drag us out on some wayside road and beat us and leave us half-dead, and as difficult as that is, we will still love you. But be assured that we will wear you down by our capacity to suffer and one day we will win our freedom. We will not only win freedom for ourselves, we will so appeal to your heart and your conscience that we will win you in the process and our victory will be a double victory. This is a nonviolent message."[21]*

---

20   By love, Dr. King is referring to the biblical concept of "agape" love, and he specifically says that this is not "emotional bosh" or "affection." Rather, he notes, "Agape is more than romantic or aesthetic love. Agape is more than friendship. Agape is creative, understanding, redemptive goodwill for all men. It is an overflowing love that seeks nothing in return. Theologians would say that this is the love of God operating in the human heart. When one rises to love on this level, he loves every man. He rises to the point of loving the person who does the evil deed while hating the deed that the person does."

21   Rev. Dr. Martin Luther King, Jr.'s 1963 speech to the faculty and students of Western Michigan University on December 18, 1963 as reproduced at https://libguides.wmich.edu/mlkatwmu/speech, retrieved December 16, 2019.

*Outside of the Box*

If we are honest, these kinds of real-life examples of constructive, creative anger are fairly few and far between. Often, we hear stories of negative approaches to offenses—criticisms, retaliations, withdrawals, losses of temper, or even outright attacks. There may also be a part of each of one of us that identifies with Alex preparing himself for some sort of punishment. We automatically understand that when money is lost, bosses get angry, and when bosses are angry, employees suffer. Some might even call this intuition, like knowing a basic law of nature. So, whether it is business or friendship, if the mistake is big enough, people can expect to get "fired." Still, if this type of punitive dynamic does make automatic or intuitive sense to us, it likely shows just how compelled we are by a reactive, default understanding of emotion and of anger especially.

The prevalence of this default approach is the reason we take note of people like Jeff or Dr. King, who think outside the box. The "box" here might be the assumption that anger is bad and therefore a feeling to be either avoided or voided as quickly as possible. Or the "box" might turn people into problems to be fixed so others can feel better. This same "box" would have ultimately motivated Jeff to punish rather than restore Alex or would have led Dr. King to base his leadership on more violent principles. Where actual survival is concerned, this box is invaluable, like a protective covering that keeps us from being harmed. However, when people are not actually or physically endangered, this box can become an altar where important relationships are sacrificed to preserve individual interests. And, in the case of the Civil Rights Movement, as Dr. King so eloquently expressed, even when physical harm is a very real possibility, thinking outside the box can still prove to be superior.

> **"When the bigger picture is considered, anger can be a vital catalyst for love."**

I believe we resonate with people like Jeff and Dr. King because deep down we know that our longing to thrive in community is even more essential than our need to survive individually. If so, then perhaps this points to an even deeper intuition we have which recognizes that without community, individuality can degenerate into loneliness which, when prolonged, does jeopardize actual survival. At the same time, the health of our relationships will correspond directly to our health as individuals.

Is it possible to frame injustices as opportunities to bless—in Jesus' words, to do good and to preserve life? People like Jeff and the Reverend Dr. Martin Luther King, Jr. are compelling examples that such blessing is indeed an option. When the bigger picture is considered, anger can be a vital catalyst for love.

In closing, just as the polar waters of our earth are both unbearably cold and yet teeming with life, anger is an emotion that presents us with unique opportunities to balance our individual and interpersonal values. The challenge is finding those combinations of imagination and self-restraint that allow us to utilize anger constructively and in the service of relationship. To the extent that we invest time and thought into this sort of creativity, we can expect to see our relationships improve and flourish.

And, again, like so many opportunities, this sort of creativity begins with a multifaceted understanding of ourselves and of the deepest reaches of our hearts. And so, keeping these things in mind, let us turn to the next emotion on our journey: sadness.

# Chapter 9: Atlantic

*Every lament is a love song.*[1]
Nicholas Wolterstorff

*I can use this for life . . .*[2]
Russell Wilson

The Atlantic Ocean is named after Atlas, a Greek Titan who was believed to have been sentenced to stand between the sky and the earth, keeping them separate and preventing the one from collapsing into the other. As a result, Atlas was thought to be responsible for supporting the heavens, and over time, he has come to be depicted as a person, hunched over, bearing the weight of the world. Like Atlas' great burden, sadness can feel like the weight of the world. In this way and others, it seems the Atlantic is an appropriate metaphor for exploring this category of emotion.

## "If anger is energizing, sadness is wearisome."

Sadness. The term itself can catch us off guard, creating a curious mixture of vulnerability and seriousness. Like a bitter cocktail, this mixture leaves us feeling unsettled and disoriented. Deep down, no matter what form it takes or how accustomed we

---

1  Wolterstorff, N. (1987). Lament for a son. Grand Rapids, MI: Wm. B. Eerdmans Publishing Company, p. 6.

2  Seattle Seahawks quarterback, reflecting upon his opportunity to continue to grow as an athlete and person after the team's painful loss of Superbowl XLIX to the New England Patriots. Retrieved June 2, 2018, from http://www.peaksports.com/sports-psychology-blog/how-this-nfl-qb-learns-and-grows-from-setbacks/

may become to its effects, sadness has a foreign quality to it.

## Objective and Subjective Sadness

*The Ironic Heaviness of Loss*
On one hand, the brokenness of our world means sadness is ever with us. And at the same time, at an even more fundamental level, when we are sad, we are out of our element. We were designed for freedom and joy, and so sadness is an add-on, so to speak, to our original DNA.

This additional, non-native nature of sadness is why, perhaps more than anything, it leaves a person feeling various shades of being "down." Let down. Brought down. Weighed, pulled, and sometimes even dragged down. With Atlas, we experience burden and restriction. If anger is characterized by a sense of opposition, then sadness is marked by a sense of heaviness. If anger is energizing, sadness is wearisome. Maybe it could be said of sadness, more than any other emotion, both that "less is more and more is less."

The reader will recognize an irony here. The acronyms that we have been using (i.e., MSGS and FLGT) connect *sadness* with *loss*. So, how is it that when we lose, miss, or long for something, we feel heavy, burdened, and weighed down?

The answer to this question might lie in identifying what kind of loss is occurring at any given moment. Thus, we can ask a second question: what is the nature of the object that is being lost, missed, or longed for?

The extent to which the loss relates to something that we might regard as *necessary* is the extent to which the loss will be accompanied by the "heavy" feeling of sadness. Similarly, sadness is felt when we experience the *weight* of unnecessary suffering. Or, alternatively, sadness is felt when we experience the *loss* of what feels comfortable, pleasant, or desired.

Consider an experience like that of being diagnosed with a terminal illness. At a minimum, we can immediately call this a painfully difficult and challenging occasion. Illness, by definition, is abnormal and foreign. Because of the ways in which illness can detract and subtract from what we regard as "normal" living, even to the point of complete extraction of life, it represents significant potential loss. A life-threatening illness is therefore an extreme example of how the *presence* of something can lead to loss and sadness, because its very presence represents the actual or potential absence of something essential to life. This characteristic, what we might call "present absence," is the reason sadness brings a heavy feeling even as it represents loss.

*Objective Sadness*

To the extent that a condition such as a terminal illness means life is being diminished or taken away, we can say that the diagnosis actually causes sadness. When life is endangered, our emotional experiences can be regarded as matters of survival. If we return to our FIT equation, the incident (in this case, terminal illness) has a controlling influence upon the feeling (sadness). And because the diagnosis represents varying levels of objective loss (whether of health, comfort, physical functioning, or life itself), modifying our thoughts will not alter the fact that serious, fundamental changes have taken place.

> **"As we come to terms with this terrible truth, that all death is sad, we immediately widen our perspective on life."**

One way of describing actual losses is to call them deaths, and any death is objectively sad. The question is to what extent the loss can be identified as an actual loss. This suggests that subjective (thought-generated) and objective (incident-generated) forms of sadness can exist simultaneously. Thus, it is equally true to say that even amid the actual or objectively sad nature of a terminal illness, one can experience an increased sense of purpose, meaning, and even hope. When this happens, the intensity of the sadness attached to the diagnosis itself is lessened even in the face of the very real possibility of death.

Perhaps the clearest example of how death objectively causes sadness can be seen in the gospel account of Jesus' response to the death of a friend. In this case, we can find a very deep truth in yet another small package, a single verse, John 11:35. Traditionally, this is regarded as the shortest verse in the entire Bible, but it speaks volumes to us about the nature of sadness and, ultimately, comfort.

One word. Maybe two: *"Jesus wept."*

The person who has died is Lazarus. He had two sisters, Martha and Mary. Several times in the passage, the relationship between Lazarus and Jesus is characterized by love. In fact, the author, the apostle John, explicitly states, "Jesus loved Martha and her sister and Lazarus."[3] This love seems intricately related to the sadness Jesus feels upon losing Lazarus. Immediately after Jesus is described as weeping, John writes, "Then the Jews said, 'See how he loved him!'"[4]

On one hand, Jesus' love for His friend explains His tears. On the other hand, however, there is another feature of the story that makes His tears seem very strange. That is, the larger context of the story reveals that Jesus had no need for sorrow. Jesus seems sure that the loss of Lazarus is only for a time, and Jesus Himself determines the parameters of the timing. Upon hearing that Lazarus is sick, He says, "This illness does not lead to death,"[5] and later, He refers to Lazarus' death as mere "sleep."[6] He seems to take His time with any sort of attempt to visit Lazarus, waiting two days before changing His travel plans. Moreover, upon meeting Martha in her grief, Jesus, announces to her, "your brother will rise again."[7] And finally, in a display of unprecedented authority and power, He commands Lazarus to come out of the tomb, and Lazarus responds accordingly!

But Jesus weeps *before* He raises Lazarus.

He has every reason to not be sad, and yet He, who tells

3   John 11:5
4   John 11:36
5   John 11:4
6   John 11:11
7   John 11:23

Martha that He is "the resurrection and the life,"[8] sheds tears for her brother. He repeatedly announces that things are not as they seem, but ultimately allows Himself to be "deeply moved in his spirit and greatly troubled."[9] Even as He repeatedly hints at future hope, He enters the pain of the present moment, a moment in which the actual absence of Lazarus is still the reality. And so, He weeps—*before* He raises Lazarus.

How do we explain this apparent discrepancy? How do we understand the coexistence of sorrow and confidence, tears and hope, weeping and resurrection? Initially, we might return to love and say that Jesus was simply showing His solidarity with those who were grieving. It seems He expresses His tears shortly after meeting Mary and seeing her weeping along with others who have come to grieve.

While solidarity is certainly a factor and it is appropriate to "weep with those who weep,"[10] I believe this story illustrates something even more profound: the objective sadness of death.

Despite all the ways Jesus demonstrated that sorrow was not necessary at the beginning of the story, He still experiences it when confronted with the fact that His friend has been placed in a tomb. And I imagine that, in that moment, He laments the pervasive, unrelenting reality of mortality. I picture His tears falling not just for Lazarus and his sisters, but for all of humanity. I hear His cries protesting death as the ultimate anomaly to life.

As a pastor friend once shared during my friend's mother's funeral, this story affirms that death is "not the way it's supposed to be." We, too, can cry when a loved one dies. We, too, can weep when a life is ended. We, too, can mourn without shame.

As we come to terms with this terrible truth, that all death is sad, we immediately widen our perspective on life. Perhaps it might even be argued that Jesus' weeping was itself a part of the process of preparing to raise Lazarus. For the broken condition of our world is such that healing and restoration only come after first entering into pain and suffering. Joy comes in the morning,

8   John 11:25
9   John 11:33
10   Romans 12:15

after the weeping that lasts for a night.[11]

Interestingly, shortly after Jesus raises Lazarus, John records Jesus as teaching: "Truly, truly, I say to you, unless a grain of wheat falls into the earth and dies, it remains alone; but if it dies, it bears much fruit."[12] Jesus is speaking of how He will offer His own life for the sake of the world, and He is also affirming a great principle: Growth requires sacrifice. Moreover, since all sacrifice involves loss, all growth brings the potential for sadness.

Jesus' tears at the tomb of His friend speak further to this, conveying the objective, unrelenting, and unforgiving way in which death results in sadness. Similarly, His miraculous raising of Lazarus *after* weeping for him reveals the vital role sorrow plays in meaningful living. Again, an accurate understanding of true life begins with an honest appraisal of the tragic, mysterious, and objectively sad reality of death.

*Standstill*
This awareness, indeed acceptance, of the objective sadness of death is the first step in the immense and often complex task of navigating the losses of life. This acceptance is important when people we love or things we hold dear change and are, in some way or another, never the same. This acceptance is useful when someone or something goes away for a while or passes away forever. In the words of one beloved hymn, this acceptance is necessary, "when sorrows like sea billows roll."[13] Whatever the loss, remembering that any death is itself sad can help shed light on the heaviness we feel and even help to lighten the load itself. Consider the following hypothetical examples:

A man is dying and asks to see his family before it is too late. The man sends word to his son who has been estranged from

11  Psalm 30:5

12  John 12:24

13  From the hymn, It is Well with My Soul, written in 1873, by Horatio G. Spafford, when he was told that his ship was crossing the place on the Atlantic Ocean where his four daughters drowned after their ship the Ville du Harve collided with a Scottish ship called the Loch Earn. Horatio's wife, Anna was his only family member who survived and was later quoted as saying, "God gave me four daughters. Now they have been taken from me. Someday I will understand why." From Terry, L. (2014, October 16). "Story behind the song: It is well with my soul." Staugustine.com. Retrieved December 8, 207, from (http://staugustine.com/living/religion/2014-10-16/story-behind-song-it-well-my-soul).

him for many years. The son comes to his father's side and is at a loss for words. Years ago, there was an argument that led to a separation which grew into a rift. The man can count on his hands the number of times he has seen his father in his lifetime, and even then the interactions were brief and superficial. Now, the topic they initially argued about is long-forgotten though the words that divided them are seared into each one's memory. "You are not my son." "You are hardly a dad." Now, the father, on the brink of eternity, utters a faint, "Thank you for coming. I'm sorry for everything." And the son, who has been waiting all his adult life for an apology, suddenly does not know what to say.

Or a woman has just been told the baby she's been carrying for eight months no longer has a heartbeat. For as long as she can remember, she has wanted to be a mom. She practiced with dolls and played house. She took good care of various pets. She worked hard in school and all throughout, looking forward to passing on the things she was learning to her own child. In due time, she met and married the man of her dreams, and they waited exactly two years to start a family. The timing moved like clockwork, and they rejoiced upon learning of the pregnancy. The ultrasound indicated that they would have a girl, and pink quickly became the new black. They thought of a name and imagined who she would look and sound like. And now, they have come to the examining room only to hear the awful news. Their daughter must be delivered but she will not move. They will call her name, but she will make no sound. They will tremble, and she will be still. Black will be the new pink. And this woman who has waited all her life for the chance to be a mom, suddenly will not know what to say.

In both situations, the sense of loss is actual because death is the very present reality, and so sadness is not only expected, it is also profoundly appropriate. With survival being a central concern, the incidents themselves, i.e., the physical illness of the father or the stillbirth of the daughter, are enough to determine the feelings. In this way, any attempt to feel differently by thinking differently will be painfully limited. Moreover, because of the actual life-and-death nature of these scenarios, there is more room for stating things objectively and more space for the language of obligation. The actual losses *must* be acknowledged—

to try and deny them is to live apart from reality. Sadness *needs* to be felt. The situations facing the father, the son, and the two bereft parents *should* be taken seriously. To say otherwise is to practice unhealthy denial. No matter what angle is taken, when death touches us, it leaves a lasting impression.

These are just two examples, admittedly extreme, of loss and losing. And we can probably think of a million variations. Life is finite, but it seems there are an infinite number of ways it can end. And each time life ends, words fall short.

We observe private and public "moments of silence" because all loss, whether it be a missed opportunity, a stillbirth, or an international tragedy, carries a sort of speechlessness. We don't know what to say. The heaviness catches us off guard. We struggle to comfort others and to be comforted, and our language borders on inadequate. In my own experience, if words are to be adequate, they must acknowledge the overwhelming power incidents of death have to give pause to even our best thinking. When a dear family member of mine died, a friend wrote just two words to me in a card: "*mysterium tremendum.*" Years later, I still find strange solace in what he wrote.

Death halts us; it causes us to cease and desist and come to a standstill. This standstill is sadness. The dense weightiness of this sadness is perhaps the reason we refer to situations—where the stakes are high, where something or someone could die—as having a certain "gravity" to them. It is why the saddest place of all, where the standstill hits with the most force, is an actual grave.

But just as gravity connects us to this earth, so acknowledging the sadness of the grave can also keep us grounded. The Atlantic is named after a Titan whose unenviable fate was inextricably bound up in his strength and endurance. And so, like the Atlantic, sadness is a deep and vital resource for the ocean of relationships. Sadness, after all, can lead not only to recognizing the value of what once "was" but also to affirming and appreciating what still "is." And often, in relationships, losses can be more like illusions than actual disappearances.

## Subjective Sadness

Why spend so much time on the story of Jesus and Lazarus? Why make such a big deal about objective sadness? I have chosen these beginning points because once we come to terms with the objective sadness of death, then we can entertain the equally important concept of subjective sadness in other situations. But the order is critical. We cannot fully understand the second without the first. We cannot see sadness as an ally until we first realize how it functions as a foe. We cannot experience the blessing before we first taste the curse.

> **"...death is a profoundly unsettling topic and we trivialize it to our own peril."**

Let us return to our example of the man whose father is dying. Objectively speaking, there is much for both men to be sad about. Years of missed opportunities. Time that could have been spent together. Conversations that never occurred. Kindnesses and memories and loving words left unexpressed, uncreated, and unheard. And over all the history of things undone looms the awful shadow of impending death. So, loss and absence and emptiness are very real. A thousand figurative deaths and more shroud the hospital room in a heaviness which itself could possibly hasten the final blow.

And, at the same time, the man has been called to his father's bedside. Why? What reason or reasons could possess the father to do such a thing? Why risk yet another disappointment?

While a host of guesses could be made about why a dying father summons an estranged son, perhaps a general observation can be made: *there is still time.* And this, maybe more than any other statement, is how we can retain subjective sadness as an option, even amid the stark, objective sadness of death.

And so, the father, racked by the pangs of death and the terrible awareness of what never was, can still reach out and risk and possibly redeem the pain. And the son, also saddled with the burden of decades of disconnection, can do the same. There is still time. Even with silence and standstill appearing to insist that nothing can be done, the fact that they are in the same room means something different, even new, could still happen.

And so, the father apologizes, thanks his boy, now a man, for coming. He takes the risk that leads to the awkward but incredibly important pause. The pause that is awkward precisely because it means one has now spoken to the other. And now the slightest gesture of goodwill, the smallest move toward, rather than away from, each other, could be the deciding factor in the possibility of some type of recovery, some shred of reconciliation. Though everything leading up to this point may suggest otherwise, all is not lost.

Or return to the second scenario. The loss of a long-awaited child. Years of preparation, prayers, and anticipation. Culminating now in bitter, unthinkable news and heartache. An actual death. Objective, indisputable, permanent loss. It would seem a terrible insult to tell the young couple, "There is still time."

And yet, it is still curiously true. Time confronts the couple, and all of us, as an undeniable, incontrovertible fact. The sinking awareness that someone will no longer be around never completely goes away. And the existence of this awareness means that precisely when everything of significance seems to have gone away, one thing remains: time. For some, this is a crushing sentence, an interminable pronouncement, or an enduring curse. For others, the passage of time can become a gift and a doorway to healing. Either way, when death thrusts us into the awful awareness of time without another, we simultaneously experience the dual realities of objective and subjective sadness.

These are admittedly tricky waters. In oceanspeak, we have two streams that can make the Atlantic very daunting indeed. How do we balance the pain of an actual loss with the fact that some things remain? How do we honor the seriousness of death itself without losing sight of the bigger picture of what continues about life? These questions are difficult to answer, not only because physical death is so formidable, but also because we routinely face countless additional, nonphysical deaths. And when death is nonphysical, the process of discerning what is lost and what remains is itself less clear.

Referring to death as a routine, almost commonplace experience may sound rather strong or even harsh. Or worse, the concept of "nonphysical death" may seem excessive or insensitive, like an unhealthy fixation on morbidity or mortality that is counterproductive to our ultimate goal of more joy and freedom in relationships. Such reservations should be taken seriously since death is a profoundly unsettling topic and we trivialize it to our own peril. Still, let us remember that to understand sadness we must understand both its objective and subjective causes, including figurative, nonphysical deaths. The more we understand the physical and nonphysical dimensions of death the more we will be able to effectively utilize sadness and "cross the Atlantic." The following are several concepts that are especially important to traversing these waters.[14]

## Objective and Subjective Loss

*Limitations*
We can begin with a closer look at what it means to balance objective and subjective losses. Again, as we think about this task, let us revisit the concept of a nonphysical death. A return to a previous discussion may shed some light on this.

Earlier, we noted that the word "decide" is a word that implies something must die, indeed be slain, whenever one is faced with choosing between two options.[15] Decisions, then, qualify as nonphysical deaths and are daily reminders of our own limitations because they confront us with the fact that sometimes we cannot have it both ways. Sometimes we must give up one thing to have another. Sometimes it is just not possible to, as the saying goes, "eat our cake and have 'it' too."

---

14  In addition to the process of discerning between actual and perceived changes we experience at any given time, some people experience the profound challenge of "ambiguous loss," where they live with simultaneously having and not having a loved one in their lives (e.g., due to situations where a person may go missing or when a person may be bodily present but not cognitively or emotionally present). For more on this, see Boss, P. (1999). Ambiguous loss: Learning to live with unresolved grief. Cambridge, MA: Harvard University Press. And for a very compelling and helpful personal account, see McLeod, P. & McLeod, T., with Ruchti, C. (2019). Hit hard: One family's journey of letting go of what was and learning to live well with what is. Carol Stream, IL: Tyndale House Publishers.

15  Yalom, I. D. (1989). Love's executioner and other tales of psychotherapy. New York, NY: HarperCollins.

Simply put, decisions involve loss, so decisions, big or small, involve sadness.

This is not usually how we think. We are more inclined to think of decisions as frustrating or stressful than we are to think of them as sad. But this, I believe, is a carryover from our default, survival-oriented approach to emotions, which moves us away from any experience of feeling vulnerable.

Vulnerability is inevitable in sadness because losses leave us feeling exposed. When something or someone good goes away, our sense of security is affected. As such, sadness is often mistaken for weakness. But weakness is only dangerous if survival is in question. And in adult relationships, feelings, including sadness, can function more as opportunities for thriving and enjoying life than survival per se.

So, sacrifice is built into every true decision. This is more than just a comment on etymology. Rather, this is about *ontology*, about the way our world is and about who we are. Our world is an incredibly rich and complex place, full of opportunities, and such opportunities often come at a price. As people, we are deeply self-directed, and we naturally desire to shape our own destinies. At the same time, we are finite and unable to exert total control over any given circumstance. This means that, despite our best efforts, we will ultimately have our limitations. To effectively seize the opportunities life affords us, we must both acknowledge these limitations and accept them, along with all of their implications.

*Acceptance*
Acceptance, which essentially involves an openness to both limits and losses, is integral to a healthy understanding of how we make decisions. When we recognize that all true decisions cost something, we can be more honest with ourselves and prepare for whatever difficulties are natural to the opportunities at hand.

We allow for a certain amount of difficulty to exist because we recognize the sadness inherent in not being able to have something both ways. By allowing for such difficulty, we minimize the unnecessary hardships that can come with trying to have the situation be easier than it is. This, in turn, allows for more balance and therefore more clarity—balance of the objective and subjective dimensions of the decision and clarity on what our options truly are. And as the situations we face become more balanced and clearer, we can live more in line with reality.

These might be considered the ABCs of decision-making: authenticity, balance, and clarity. We achieve the former as we experience the latter two. And, common to all three is an openness to sadness.

*Change*

Life involves change. Things and people simply do not stay the same. We are constantly in a state of flux. Thus, the ancient Greek philosopher Heraclitus speaks of how one "could not step twice into the same river."[16] Thus, a cornerstone of most, if not all, spiritual teachings is the notion of life's "impermanence."[17] Thus, the prophet Isaiah declares, "all flesh is grass, and all its beauty is like the flower of the field."[18] Thus, the poet Robert Frost, in speaking of the relentless cycle of the seasons and the persistent passage of time, reminds us how "nothing gold can stay."[19]

Everything we do is, at the very least, bounded by time, by space, and ultimately, by our own mortality. We are, therefore, constantly moving, aging, *becoming*. On one hand, this is good news because it allows for growth, improvement, and progress. On another, it can imply other less comfortable things: uncertainty, instability, stress, and anxiety.

Either way, change is the one constant that consistently marks our lives, and it requires us to acknowledge our limits. To do

16  Graham, D. W. (February, 2007). "Heraclitus." E. N. Zalta (Ed.). The Stanford Encyclopedia of Philosophy. Retrieved March 10, 2018, from https://plato.stanford.edu/entries/heraclitus/

17  An example of this might be seen in a letter titled "White Ashes" by Rennyo Shonin, 15th century Jodo Shinshu Buddhist priest. This letter, often read at Buddhist funeral services, contemplates the "winds of impermanence" that ultimately point to human fragility and finitude. The full letter can be found here: www.nishihongwanji-la.org/teachings/readings/white-ashes/, retrieved December 8, 2017.

18  Isaiah 40:6

19  Frost, R. (October, 1923). "Nothing Gold Can Stay." Yale Review.

otherwise, is to live inauthentically, and to live inauthentically, is to miss what is possible. Ironically, we gain more when we sincerely acknowledge our actual losses.

This, in a word, is the process of *grief*. This is the task of utilizing our sadness to accept our limits and losses, which in turn, allows for more authentic living. As author and motivational speaker Shane Hipps puts it, "grief is the process of moving from resignation to acceptance."

As simple as this sounds, this transition from resignation to acceptance can be grueling. Or on another level, it can seem foolish, even self-defeating. Nevertheless, these difficulties are paradoxical. And so, far from being harmful, they are vital for healthy living. To repeat a phrase from another context, as author and martyred missionary Jim Elliot once affirmed, "He is no fool who gives what he cannot keep to gain what he cannot lose."

Grief involves letting go. It involves letting go of that which we cannot keep. And at the same time, it involves letting go of that which unnecessarily keeps us . . . stuck, bound, and weighed down. In the end, grief involves letting go of those things that prevent true freedom.

## Letting Go

*To be Caught*
Imagine a trapeze artist preparing to move from the platform or the bar, through the air, to the waiting arms and hands of his partner. This move requires a release—from relative safety to the unknown danger of the free fall, and toward the possibility of either spectacular success or tragic failure.

In his book, *Writings*, the gentle and influential author and Dutch Catholic priest, Henri Nouwen, shares a conversation he had with his friend Rodleigh. In fact, Rodleigh is a professional trapezist with the trapeze troupe, The Flying Rodleighs. And, true to the name of the troupe, Rodleigh is the "flyer" and his friend Joe is the "catcher." Nouwen retells the point in the conversation when Rodleigh reveals the "secret" to successful flying:

> *"How does it work?" I asked. "The secret," Rodleigh said, "is that the flyer does nothing and the catcher does everything. When I fly to Joe, I have simply to stretch out my arms and hands and wait for him to catch me and pull me safely over the apron behind the catchbar."*[20]

The "flyer" must only hold his arms out and be still. In so doing, he will allow himself to be caught. To do otherwise will be to risk failure—distracting the process and introducing too many variables. Success relies upon stillness, waiting, and ultimately, trusting the "catcher" to come through. The letting go leads, in the end, to being caught, delivered, and held.

## To be Released

As a young child, I remember my father telling my siblings and me about various ways he would catch different animals. He seemed to especially take pride in relaying the clever tricks he and his brothers would employ right from their own backyard in a small neighborhood in Singapore. With a twinkle in his eye, he described how he would make a noose from bamboo and horsehair to snag geckoes or put glue on branches to catch birds. My favorite story, though he never claimed personal experience with it, was the way in which hunters would catch monkeys. He told me of how they would take a vessel with a small opening, such as a jar or a coconut, and fill it with some sort of food or shiny object. Next the hunters would tie the vessel to a tree or a stake in the ground, and then they would simply wait. In time, a monkey would notice the food or the shiny object in the vessel, put its hand in the narrow opening, and grab the "bait." As long as the monkey continued to hold onto its prize, it would not be able to remove its hand from the vessel since its closed fist would not fit through the vessel's narrow opening. And, of course, this meant that the monkey was now attached to the tree or stake, making it easy prey for the waiting hunters.

By now, this analogy may be quite familiar (I have heard several pastors refer to it as an example of how temptation

20  Nouwen, H. J. M. (1998). Henri Nouwen: Writings. (Robert A. Jonas, Ed.). The University of Michigan: Orbis Books. Retrieved December 8, 2017, from http://www.spiritualityand-practice.com/books/reviews/excerpts/view/17109

can lead to destruction). If so, perhaps we can regard it as a classic example of how we can hold onto various "things" in life unnecessarily and how letting such things go can lead to freedom and release.

For the trappings of this life can glitter and shine in such compelling ways. And it can seem like having and grasping are *necessary* for being free. But true freedom is found precisely in releasing this need to possess the things that we cannot keep. And this usually begins with an openness to the sadness inherent in the "losses," while simultaneously recognizing the subjective implications of our own ways of defining our circumstances and their meanings.

*To be Freed*

As a final metaphor for this concept, I recall a conversation with a person who was telling me about how he was learning to operate a high-powered jet ski. In this case, he as the driver of the ski was wearing a life vest that was equipped with a cord that activated a "kill switch" on the ski's engine. In the event of an emergency or any situation in which he as driver was separated from the ski, the ski would automatically shut off for safety purposes. He added that he was able to enjoy riding the ski even as he took it to breakneck speeds because he would remind himself, "if I let go, I can get off." In this case, letting go was not only related to freedom but adventure and confidence as well.

So, letting go can mean many things. Deliverance. Escape. Freedom. But these rewards require something in exchange. They call for a kind of mindset, a specific way of believing that ultimately becomes a certain way of trusting. This mindset trusts that, in the end, relinquishing will pay off. This mindset trusts that the potential of what is not yet experienced will somehow be worth, and will somehow be even better than, the relative security of what currently is. And, finally, it trusts that loss can somehow lead to gain. For, it makes no sense to drop unless something or somebody catches us. There is no point in surrendering life's charms unless a greater treasure is available. And it does no good to stop the ride unless something greater than the ride exists.

## Misdirected Sadness

*Letting Go*

Letting go ultimately requires trust and faith, since in the end there is only the promise of a possibility and no guarantee. The question is whether deliverance, escape, and freedom are worth the cost of stepping beyond our usual comfort zones.

We encounter discomfort, because, again, we are opening ourselves to releasing or *not having* certain things. And letting go is first about allowing ourselves to acknowledge the sadness of such losses. To quote a popular saying, "the way out is through."

Moving *through* the sadness is necessary for being able to move on *from* the loss. This, again, is not easy. Part of the difficulty is due to our discomfort with sadness, which, in turn, suggests that we are all too familiar with treating our negative emotions as problems to be fixed instead of as resources to be utilized. When this discomfort interferes with interpersonal matters, it is usually unnecessary and unfortunate since sadness is especially valuable for the process of navigating relationships.

Another reason for the difficulty is that sadness itself is painful. Whether the loss is actual or just perceived as actual are secondary issues. The pain of loss is always real, and we instinctively avoid pain. The question is whether the avoidance in general is conducive to health.

> ## "Moving *through* the sadness is necessary for being able to move on *from* the loss."

There are several ways we can make our experiences with grief more difficult than they need to be, and we can collectively call these experiences different expressions of "misdirected sadness." The following are four common ways in which this can occur, seen again through the lens of personal responsibility for emotions.

*Blame*

The common denominator in all forms of misdirected sadness is blame. This is not surprising when we consider personal responsibility as the chief goal of all emotions, including sadness, since blame is usually an *attempt* at taking personal responsibility. Indeed, blame and responsibility are often used synonymously, though they are in fact quite different. Where sadness calls for honest and accurate acceptance of a loss, blame summons an entirely different reaction: harshness. This harshness is characterized by a sense of personalized fault-finding that ultimately requires some sort of punishment. Another way of describing the harsh tone of blame is to say that the person feels a sense of opposition or "againstness" to the assumed cause of the loss. The reader will recall that this terminology has previously been applied to the emotion of anger. As such, we might say that blame misdirects sadness to the extent that anger is felt when a loss is experienced.

This is not to say that we should refrain altogether from anger when we lose something for anger may be very warranted. For example, if a person burglarizes my home, I will most certainly feel sad *and* angry. Both emotions are especially reasonable to the situation at hand since a burglary means I have experienced actual loss *and* injustice.

The issue, however, is how both emotions can best serve their purposes. To the extent that I am focused on the *facts* of the situation (that I was burglarized and no longer have certain possessions), my anger and sadness will be best treated as problems to be solved. Therefore, the details of the incident in question (in this case, burglary) will need to be directly addressed. To not feel sad or angry, I must either recover or replace my possessions or see the burglar(s) brought to justice. Other than the passage of time, anything short of these things will not do much for the *actual* reasons for my emotions. And, because these are legitimate options, treating my feelings as problematic is itself strategic—there is no need for me to view either the loss or the injustice as positive per se. It is unnecessary for me to find a way to feel something other than sadness and/or anger.

Questions remain, however, such as, what if my possessions

are not recovered or replaced? Or what if the burglar is never found and prosecuted? Or, what if the recovery, replacement, or prosecution for that matter, are only partial? In these instances, my primary option for dealing with the loss is grief. This may appear simple, still how we unpack it can make all the difference.

For where grief is necessary, blame becomes a liability. Anger must eventually give way to sadness. And when this happens, harshness yields to something more forgiving and more gentle (since sadness reminds us of our limitations and can *seem* weak). Ultimately, the semblance of weakness shows us that when grief is called for, our subjective appraisals become equally as important as the objective facts of the situation. So, though it sounds strange, as I stare my losses in the face, I acknowledge the reality that my losses are not *total*.

There is always another way to look at the situation. The challenge of grief is to preserve the meaningfulness of this last statement. This will involve an ability to look upon my limits, call them what they are, and equally importantly, to not call them what they are not.

For, suppose the burglar steals a television, a significant amount of jewelry, and cash. Grief would recognize the loss of these items and at the same time refrain from thinking of the situation as if it were the proverbial "end of the world." Televisions and money are replaceable. Jewelry may be less so, but my survival per se is not in jeopardy. Still, we can become so attached that losses can seem overwhelming. This is logical to the extent that the losses are thought of as total. The challenge, again, is to refrain from saying the losses *are* total.

In fact, if I find myself treating the losses as if they are all-encompassing, then I am essentially in survival mode with my own approach to emotions. My situation directly impacts what I am feeling, and *it* must change for me to feel differently.

As alluded to earlier, in survival mode, blame is not far away. The situation is the culprit, and whether I realize it or not, harshness is at work. It is harshness by both commission and omission. Either way, the harshness is subtle, often more like remaining in an open prison cell as opposed to outright punishment, though punishment is always the ultimate trajectory of blame.

Psychologically, I inflict harshness to the extent that I subject myself to extreme thinking. For example, if I say the loss is total ("I've lost everything" or "this is terrible" or some similar reaction), there is no recourse—I am stuck with my raw circumstances. The facts themselves become grounds for despair.

I will be particularly empowered, however, as I allow myself to see the opportunities embedded in the difficulties. To put it another way, psychologically I expose myself to harshness to the extent that I prevent myself from experiencing potential opportunities to see the situation differently. In the case of a burglary, I can be grateful to still have the things that were not stolen. Or, if I am really ambitious, I can find the value in the suffering itself—the motivation it might provide me to experience any number of "lessons" (learn more about myself and my approach to my own emotion management; possibly make my house more secure; make a change such as get a dog, start a neighborhood watch or some other humanitarian effort; or even learn to live more simply, considering the priority of having less tangible or less material things).

To miss out on these possibilities would be to again experience unnecessary harshness because these possibilities could ultimately be good for me. And if I deprive myself of something that is possibly good (that does not harm others), then I am at risk for further doing unto myself what the burglar has already done to me (i.e., harming myself). What's more, by both acknowledging the actual loss and recognizing these possibilities (whether in the form of nuancing my thinking or entertaining some redemptive action), I help myself to move on. I accept my situation rather than resign myself to it, and in so doing, I grieve. I refrain from blaming the incidents in my life and prevent them from having the last word. I acknowledge my anger and simultaneously honor the sadness by assessing the loss as accurately as possible. In a word, I take *responsibility* where I have it, and in two words, I free myself up for *response ability*. In so doing, I might even convert the loss into a form of achievement. As this happens, my grieving is further facilitated, since letting go works best when the loss is exchanged for something even greater.

Similar things might be said of interpersonal loss. Suppose instead of a physical burglary, I experience something akin to being "robbed" in a relationship. A classic example might be the "losing" of a partner through an extramarital affair. Something very real and very personal has been taken away, even stolen. And at the same time just what has changed may be challenging to pinpoint. Perhaps it is trust or loyalty or confidence. Whatever it is, the recovery may seem irreparable. Still, to the extent that it is defined this way alone, it will be very difficult to grieve and move on. What is necessary is a balance between a brutal honesty about the pain and the sadness that I feel and a recognition that again all is likely not lost.

## Betrayal

The loss of trust in what was earlier thought to be a committed relationship can seem as devastating as a physical tornado or explosion. Perhaps we could even argue that matters of life and death are at stake if it is possible to die of a "broken heart," or more practically, if a divorce ensues which leaves the injured party less financially, physically, or emotionally stable (though these very serious outcomes might be evidence themselves of a survival-oriented approach to emotions to begin with).

Overall, however, even infidelity itself has derivative power. And so, my spouse's affair will threaten me to the extent that I label it dangerous. This will no doubt sound ridiculous to many.

Many will argue that the infidelity is itself betrayal and betrayal is itself a danger and therefore a threat. Indeed, relationships require trust, and betrayal shoots trust to pieces. Still, violations of trust do not in themselves have to be fatal. If anything, the *relationship* may be in jeopardy, but the individual (offender or offended) does not have to follow suit. Of course, to the extent that the individual is dependent upon the relationship, the affair would represent a very real threat. Again, if this were the case, a survival approach to emotions would be at work, since that which is depended upon is, by definition, necessary for survival. Nonetheless, this would also be ironic since relationships represent, for all intents and purposes, a non-survival context. And so, while there are certainly exceptions, affairs generally epitomize the concept of "unnecessary problems" in relationships.

This discussion of some of the dynamics involved in affairs is admittedly very brief and primarily aimed at illustrating how less-tangible losses are also amenable to principles of personal responsibility in emotional processing. Even the most unnecessary of problems are important to grieve. As with physical thefts, the strategy for healing wounds due to affairs is to move *through* the anger (which certainly is warranted) *to* the sadness. Moreover, the sadness will best be utilized to the extent that I accurately identify what has been lost, which more than likely will mean refraining from calling it total ("no trust" will probably only be warranted if I cease all communication with my former partner completely, for all time). In so doing, I will move away from harshness (putting all the power on the situation itself, depriving myself of methods of nuancing my feelings) and towards more kindness (ultimately, finding ways to dial down the personal nature of the offense since the affair probably reflects my partner's insecurity and survival-based morality more than anything). And as this transition is made, blame will give way to responsibility, thus creating space for the painful release that characterizes grief.

*Regret*
   "Of all sad words of tongue and pen, the saddest are these, 'it might have been.'" Thus wrote poet and abolitionist John Greanleaf Whittier in his poem lamenting a marriage that never took place. And another poet, Francis Bret Harte, later wittily parodied this poem by suggesting that if the marriage had occurred, the couple would have grown tired with each other and ultimately said, "more sad than these we daily see: it is but hadn't ought to be."[21] These lines poignantly capture our second particular form of misdirected sadness and the first specific form of blame: regret.

   I once watched a session of a television fill-in-the-blank

---

21   Whittier's poem is titled "Maud Muller," and Harte's poem is titled "Mrs. Judge Jenkins." Retrieved January 18, 2020, from https://www.newenglandhistoricalsociety.com/john-greenleaf-whittier-real-maud-muller/

game show[22] where I was so sure of the solution to the puzzle but still answered incorrectly. In this case, the category of the puzzle was "Before and After" and there were only a few blanks to complete such that the puzzle looked like the following:

$$F\_S\_\quad FOOD\quad FOR\quad T\_OUG\_T$$

In the privacy of my own home, I quickly ventured, "Fast Food for Thought." And shortly thereafter, the puzzle was solved when the winning contestant answered, "Fish Food for Thought."

I think I initially took note of this episode because I was in the middle of writing a chapter for this book, and ocean themes were on my mind. In addition, it seemed to me a perfect example of a stage set for regret since I was so sure of my answer, and if I were on the show, I would have missed out on the prize money.

Regret is a master manipulator and a convincing illusionist. It appears to have our best interest in mind, but in the end, leaves us feeling sorely disappointed, wishing for something else. Nevertheless, it fails to acknowledge that something *could never be*. Its signature comes in the form of the classic, "would've, could've, should've, didn't" sort of conclusions that haunt indefinitely. But this logic quite literally represents what researchers call, "counterfactual thinking."[23] Or from another angle, grammatically, it can be characterized as operating in the "past *unreal*" forms of language.[24] So, as persuasive as it can be, regret is fundamentally illogical and anything but real.

Still, the pain that regret causes is very real and compelling. When we find ourselves saying, "if only..." we really believe that we have fallen short and have missed out on something that surely would have been better. In the game show example above, I was vulnerable to this. I can be quite competitive in my own way, and I'm pretty sure that I thought something like, "If only I had taken the time to see that the letter "T" had already been used, I would have guessed differently." Such a conclusion

---

22  Wheel of Fortune®, Episode #5107, November 3, 2009. Retrieved March 19, 2018, from https://andynwof.wordpress.com/2013/09/25/wof-retro-recap-november-3-2009/

23  Roese, N. J., & Olson, J. M. (1995). Counterfactual thinking: A critical overview. In N. J. Roese & J. M. Olson (Eds.), What might have been: The social psychology of counterfactual thinking. Mahwah, NJ: Lawrence Erlbaum Associates.

24  I am grateful to my good friend and linguist, Damian Wyman, for this observation.

seems very sensible, and I can just as easily imagine myself falling into harsher self-criticisms—lamenting my "foolishness" or "impatience" or "hastiness" or any number of other epithets that would add pain to an already painful situation.

## "Regret is a master manipulator and a convincing illusionist."

And yet, this is how regret works its sleight of hand. For though the deed or misdeed is already in the past, the effect of regret is to make us think *blame* is still warranted. Indicting ourselves in this way, however, is unnecessary, and the value of holding any grudge against ourselves is almost pure illusion. The reason lies again in the mechanism by which the bait and switch are performed.

The mechanism is *hindsight* bias or a tendency to retrospectively overestimate our ability to predict events, since as the saying goes, "hindsight is 20/20."[25] Thus, when I tell myself that I "should've, could've, and would've" done something that I did not do, I am essentially saying that I 'should've, could've, and would've" known better. But the catch is that I am saying these things in the *present* about events in the *past*. And when this happens, any necessary sadness and grief are prevented in at least two ways.

First, I hold myself to an unreasonable, if not impossible, standard of omniscience. I believe that, somehow, I 'could've, should've, and would've' predicted the future, but I most likely forget that I am basing this conclusion on information that I now have, which means it is information that I could not have had in the past. This sort of logic is very *unfair*, as well as *unreal*.

Further, such "should" statements can be especially heavy-handed, since they imply an absolutistic kind of moral evaluation and an emphasis on failure. It is not the absolute or "should" per se that is the problem, but rather the way in which criticism of a past decision takes the place of acknowledging what is now

25  Inman, M, (n. d.) "Hindsight bias." In brittanica.com. Retrieved September 16, 2018, from https://www.brittanica.com/topic/hindsight-bias

missed or lost. In these ways, regret undermines sadness and grief via unnecessary harshness.

Second, because I am identifying something that I should or should not have done (or should or should not have left undone), I am essentially trying to reverse the past in retrospect.[26] By doing this, I do not get to *accept* those aspects of my past that I wish had been different. This is a significant, albeit subtle, way I interfere with my own grief. I essentially prevent myself from being able to affirm whatever has been lost or missed out on. And often, probably unwittingly, I give myself cause for even more grief, because in addition to missing out on a past alternative way of doing something, I am now losing the time to seize the moment and address my interest in living more productively overall. What is necessary, then, is to return to certain principles, see the crafty nature of regret, and realize that the only thing that could have possibly spared me would have been something akin to a crystal ball.

As a case in point, my game show answer is essentially evidence for how I *did not realize* that the letter "T" had already been used. The fact is that my answer, albeit incorrect, represented my best attempt with the information that I knew at the time. Although it may sound redundant, it still needs to be affirmed that if I had *known* the letter "T" had already been used, I would only probably not have guessed, "Fast," and, more than likely, I would have answered differently. However, the clock was ticking and more importantly, at the time, I really thought that my answer was correct.

Also, it is interesting to note that even if I had seen that the letter "T" had been used and even if I had answered differently, this still would not have guaranteed a "better" outcome. For example, I might have made a different error altogether by miscounting the number of spaces in the first word and said something like, "Fresh Food for Thought." While this may seem far-fetched, the point is that regret also often operates on (mistaken) assumptions that "if only" things had been different, problems would have been avoided. However, what's to say that if things had been different, the outcome might not have been even worse?

---

26   I am, again, indebted to Patricia Resick's Cognitive Processing Therapy for this insight.

These dynamics of regret can be seen across contexts, whether a gameshow or a relationship. And either way, while the oversight *seems* obvious looking back, it is still counterproductive for me to heap harshness upon myself by saying I "should" have done this or that. After all, an oversight is precisely an experience of *unintentionally* overlooking or not seeing something. And so, it would be neither accurate nor fair for me to say that I "could" or "should" have seen differently. I saw what I saw, and I acted accordingly.

Regretting my decision is understandable, and at the same time, the more adaptive response is to accept the loss, minimizing extreme thinking as much as possible. If I had been a gameshow contestant, this might have taken a form such as "I wish I had looked more closely before answering" or "I feel sad to think of how I missed out on the win, the prize money, a chance to advance to the next level of the game show, etc." Moreover, true grief would probably also entail acknowledging aspects of the experience that were not lost—the fun of being able to play and get as far as I did, the thrill of getting to be on television, or even the opportunity to learn from an honest mistake.

---

### "...guilt is content to accompany anything that "should" have been..."

---

Regardless of the situation, the bottom line is that I will move on to the extent that sadness rather than regret is felt. Sadness reflects acceptance of the actual losses, and regret places attention on what could be considered a "non-event." And, ultimately, there is no need to accept something that has not taken place—in oceanspeak, energy invested in accepting "non-events" could itself be considered a form of harshness that interferes with our Atlantic passage.

*Guilt*

Guilt is the third form of misdirected sadness that can interfere with grief. For our purposes, guilt can be defined as that emotion we feel when we think we have done something bad, inappropriate, or wrong. In this way, guilt is closely related to regret, and regret could be considered a specific type of guilt. Regret is concerned with the past, and its focus is on an imagined different outcome. Guilt, on the other hand, is broader in its emphasis on how things ought to be done, at any given point in time. Thus, guilt can be about past, present, or future events, and it can pertain to either imagined or actual circumstances. Whereas regret is preoccupied with what "could" have been different, guilt is content to accompany anything that "should" have been or that "should be" different.

Let's say a woman is feeling guilty because she let a friend down. The guilt is associated with the belief that she has made certain mistakes and therefore failed at her goal of being a reliable friend. The emotions may include experiences with regret (e.g., if she keeps thinking about how she could (and would now) do things differently if given a second chance). Guilt is particularly on the table since she is aware of creating a rift while continuing to dwell on how this rift should not have been created in the first place.

As soon as someone determines that certain behavior should have been done or should not have been done, guilt can be expected. Again, guilt can be thought of as one word that describes the complex assortment of feelings and sensations that accompany any behavioral prescriptions or proscriptions, e.g., I think I should have done this or I think I should not have done that, respectively. And because guilt requires such an evaluation of behaviors, it, along with anger, is an emotion that has a "moral" feel to it. In a way we might say that guilt is a blend of sadness and anger (and possibly, as we will see later, fear). Since the primary determinant is a belief about how one should or should not act, anger is most likely more dominant than sadness. To the extent that this anger overshadows a situation where sadness might also be called for, we can also regard guilt as another form of misdirected sadness.

Consider our example of the woman who offended her friend. Embedded in this example is an experience of *loss*, perhaps of closeness in the friendship or the hope of the relationship going differently. As such, sadness seems appropriate, and healthy grief is important for moving forward from one's mistakes and even for minimizing or eliminating such mistakes as soon as possible. Further, healthy grief will involve an assessment of the losses that are as accurate as possible.

Since "should" statements about behavior operate as the bricks and mortar of guilt, the foundation guilt rests upon is often shaky to begin with. Unlike regret, guilt can be very necessary and very rational. If I have done something harmful to another person, guilt is warranted, since I should not have harmed a fellow person. Many times, however, guilt can also be just as damaging as regret, and this makes it a trickier form of misdirected sadness. As important and indispensable as guilt is, it is quite unreliable as a guide for at least two reasons.

The first reason is that guilt relies on should-statements, and "shoulds" very often do not correspond to reality.[27] For example, there are many things that we "should" do (such as take a certain medication, be on time for a meeting, go to bed in a disciplined manner) that we often simply do not do. Therefore, as soon as I start telling myself what should or should not be done, I put myself at risk for a less than accurate assessment of the loss. When I tell myself that I should not be doing something that I am actually doing, I am essentially not being honest about my actual experience, my reality. I might give myself a fine scolding, but a "good" scolding does not usually stop the behavior that is assumed to be inappropriate. In fact, if I continue the inappropriate behavior, my criticisms will likely be counterproductive. The more I scold, the more guilt I am prone to feel, and the more my mistakes will become self-fulfilling. Guilt, then, is more likely to create a vicious cycle that distracts me from what is most real, namely the loss of things important to me. In a way, the should-statements that promote guilt can be in competition with the loss-statements that promote sadness, and the more I focus on the former, the more the latter will get short shrift.

The second reason can be found in the connections between guilt and obligation. Again, this is not to discount the utility of "shoulds" altogether. Rather, it underscores the way in which pointing out moral shortcomings does little, by itself, to motivate me to make better behavioral choices. If anything,

27  This concept was first introduced to me through a Professional Education Systems, Inc (PESI) seminar on Cognitive-therapy taught by Jeff Riggenbach, PhD.

decisions based on guilt are less likely to be sustainable since, at the end of the day, the motivation is primarily one of compliance (because the person should, is required, has to, ought to, must, etc.). Moreover, compliance, as a form of obligation, is one way in which we operate when "survival mode" is at work. Guilt therefore has an added potential to undermine sadness because it is fundamentally rooted in a survival mindset, and it is often very difficult to allow ourselves to feel anything unpleasant when survival mode (necessary or not) is at work.

*Shame*

Shame is the fourth way in which anger can detract from situations where sadness is predominantly warranted. Whereas guilt is harshness toward specific behaviors, shame is harshness toward one's very sense of self. Where guilt says, "I should *do* something else" or "I should *not have done* what I did," shame would have me believe, "I should *be* someone else" or "I should *not be* who I am."[28] Shame cuts more deeply and leaves more lasting scars. Because it is about one's sense of self, its impact can be far-reaching and at the same time subtle and hardly noticeable. It is likewise often deeply rooted and resistant to change, growing up like a thick vine around a person, presuming to protect and preserve but ultimately constricting and strangling. In this way, shame "harms to protect," making it by far the most insidious form of misdirected sadness.

Shame is essentially alien to our original design. At the same time, because of its deep impact on our core understanding of ourselves, it lends itself to deeper discussion.

The Genesis account of humanity's creation culminates with these words: "And the man and his wife were both naked and were not ashamed."[29] This is profound. According to this account, there was a time when relationships were free of the debilitating effects of shame. It was possible to be naked, physically bare before another, and not conscious of this being any problem whatsoever. Without clothes and without concern. Comfortable with sexuality in its purest state. Completely natural and completely safe. No risk of being taken advantage of, manipulated, or degraded. And there was no risk of supplanting

---

28  Tangney, J. P., & Dearing, R. L. (2002). Shame and guilt. New York, NY: Guilford Press.

29  Genesis 2:25

sadness because there was no need for sadness—no sense of loss, even though protective coverings were entirely lacking.

Nevertheless, as Genesis unfolds, it is only a matter of time before shame rears its ugly head. The man and the woman partake of the only fruit that God forbade, and suddenly, their nakedness is the center of their attention. "Then the eyes of both of them were opened, and they knew that they were naked. And they sewed fig leaves together and made themselves loincloths."[30] And immediately following this, the man and woman hide from God. In an ironic twist, their nakedness is now visible, and as a result, they try to make themselves invisible. This begins the epic story of our race's downfall and our ongoing struggle to face all that was lost.

Perhaps this story can serve as a blueprint for our understanding of shame and the way in which it can corrupt, among many things, a healthy grieving process. Upon eating the prohibited fruit, Adam and Eve have every reason to be sad. They have lost so much—their innocence, harmony with God, the bliss of natural intimacy with one another. They have lost their nakedness in the best and purest sense of the word. But in transgressing God's instruction, this good nakedness and naked goodness suddenly become an awful awareness—of no longer having what they used to have. And for the first time ever, they experience themselves as deficient and endangered.

But, interestingly and tragically, instead of acknowledging the loss, they hide. Behind fig leaves. Among the trees. Trying to evade the God who made them and the truth of what has happened.

And, in this hiding, they take on harshness. They take on the harshness of guilt, for they have eaten what they should not have eaten. They take on the harshness of blame, for they each try to attribute their actions to the other, Adam to Eve and Eve to the serpent. They take on the harshness of regret, for in their blame they are implying that if another had acted differently, they too would have acted differently. And ultimately, these all amount to the harshness of shame, for their defensive self-justifications are just that, attempts to explain away the truth

---

30  Genesis 3:7

about *themselves*. Neither can own their own agency in the matter. Neither can face this new awareness of nakedness.

And further, the hiding is harsh because it prevents them from the only fair approach to the situation—to acknowledge that they have eaten what was forbidden and to respond honestly to God. This in turn interferes with their opportunity to face themselves. And perhaps most severe, the hiding is harsh because it deprives them, albeit only as an attempt, from allowing themselves to be seen by God.

On one hand, their hiding is completely understandable because as the story reveals, there are painful and far-reaching consequences for their actions. And, on another, hiding from God is unnecessary, not only because of its impossibility but also because the new vulnerability of their nakedness is about to become the next focus of God's ultimate intention to bless them. And so, as the story continues, in a striking and tender gesture of compassion, "...the Lord God made for Adam and for his wife garments of skins and clothed them."[31]

Harshness is bound up in this story, for the man was told that the eating of the forbidden fruit would bring death. Death is introduced the moment the fruit is eaten, and their *unawareness of evil* is lost. Death continues with every loss that follows—of innocence, of unity with each other, of right relationship with God, and of the opportunity to stay in Paradise.

## Sadness and Freedom

*Sadness over Shame*

Death is also presumably required of animals for God to cover and clothe Adam and Eve. Similarly, to this day, we continue to be faced with two competing realities. On one hand, death continues to wreak its havoc on our race, and so survival mode serves as a natural default and a rather trusted companion. On another, God continues to find ways to bless us, amid the death and havoc, transforming, often outside of our awareness, our losses into gains. So, while our survival instincts constantly press in on us, often with the force of shame, we have

---

31  Genesis 3:21

compelling reasons to also transcend our very history and live and even thrive. And, in keeping with the focus of this chapter, the more we learn to feel sadness instead of shame, the closer we will come to the psychological strategies that will help to make such thriving possible.

For example, suppose a woman carries the all but intolerable burden of a past riddled with tragedy and trauma: abandonment at an early age, emotional and sexual abuse, divorce and the sudden deaths of former husbands, and resultant compulsions related to diet, exercise, and cleaning. Nonetheless, she works courageously to reconnect with peers, face her fears, and recover her life. She comes one day to therapy, sharing how, despite her best efforts to make recommended changes, she finds herself caught up in the frustrations of old patterns. Among other things, she notes that she is making certain decisions that she still does not understand. She feels she must clean her home and bathe to rid herself of the disappointment she feels towards herself, even though it will mean less sleep for her that particular night and fatigue that will leave her vulnerable to repeating the patterns in some form the next day. And at the end of her sharing, she concludes with the question, which is more of a slam on herself than a question per se, "What's wrong with me?"

And, in this question, there is shame. A fundamental sense of wrongness about oneself. Not only what one has done, for this alone would be guilt. Not wrongness in general, for this would be blame. Not wrongness with missed opportunities, for this would be regret. Rather, wrongness with *who* one is. A sense of deficit and deficiency that goes to the core. So deep that for temporary relief this woman resorts to almost ritualistic ways of simultaneously punishing and cleansing herself. These exercises, however compelling and understandable, offer only temporary consolation.

If we are honest, we all know the desire to wash ourselves of our past demons and we can relate to how the stains can be so deep that villainizing ourselves becomes second nature. And so, we scour and scrub and scrape and gouge at ourselves but to no avail. These efforts are empty because they are all the ways of shame, and shame, like all forms of punishment, has little power to take us to true, lasting, sustainable transformation.

Harshness with ourselves is ultimately not the answer. If we, like the brave woman described above, have been robbed, stripped, deprived, imposed upon, abandoned, coerced, or in any other way mistreated, then deep down, what we really need, perhaps more than anything, is to grieve. We have already been exposed to enough harshness, and we need not trouble ourselves with an ounce or iota more.

So, sadness, marked by an accurate assessment of our losses, is our first hope. This involves acknowledging the awful truths about what we have lost or what we long for, what we've missed out on, and what we wish were different. It involves facing the holes and gaps and empty spaces that various wounds have left in our hearts. And it involves acknowledging the heaviness that ironically accompanies these wounds—the heaviness that leaves us feeling so vulnerable.

When we carry gaping wounds, the heaviness of confronting whatever is absent can seem so daunting, even dangerous. Often, consciously or not, we block our own awareness of these wounds. It seems easy enough to try and bury our past and just move on, but of course, our wounds have a way of rising to the surface since the past is always "buried alive."

If we do venture to unearth our pain, the memory of what has been inflicted upon us can combine with our awareness of what is missing within us and leave us feeling undone. The effect might seem much like the psychological equivalent of the hypothesized explosion that results when matter and antimatter collide to annihilate each other. We shield our own eyes thinking the blast will be too blinding and brace for the resulting black hole that will inevitably be generated. We turn, run, hide, take cover, cover up, deny, distort, fabricate, lie, pretend; anything to get away from it all. But, of course, the expected catastrophe is essentially a science-*fiction* and therefore so much more benign than dangerous.

More importantly, no amount of maneuvering will work because the crisis is embedded. In us. In our very hearts and minds, and skin and blood and bone. This is the overwhelmingly personal and insidious nature of shame. It turns us against our own selves and creates a vicious cycle. We punish ourselves to cleanse ourselves, but in the end, this only deepens our wounds. Harshness alone never heals.

## Gentleness

Healing presupposes loss. Just as physical lacerations require new tissues to form and grow, emotional damages call for dressing and addressing the wounds of loss. And, if we are honest, wherever losses are involved, sadness is the salve we so desperately need because sadness signifies realistic acknowledgment of such losses. This acknowledgment means sadness is, in contrast to blame and regret or guilt and shame, surprisingly gentle. Gentleness is the better response to our longing and pain because losses are almost always harsh.

And so, when it comes to these forms of misdirected anger, we will benefit as we find gentle approaches to appraising those things that are not the way that we would like for them to be. More specifically, it is vital to interpret *ourselves* with such gentleness. This will include: finding strategies of acceptance that do not slip into resignation; ways of more accurately assessing both what is not and what still is; and methods of remaining emotionally "fit" via awareness of how our thinking can transcend most situations.

Perhaps when it comes to decisions that could easily lead to blame, regret, guilt, or shame, a gentler response could be summed up in the sage words of poet and Nobel Laureate, Maya Angelou, in an early conversation with her friend and admirer, Oprah Winfrey. At one point, after Oprah had confided in Maya about some of the things that she wished she had not done in her 20s, Maya quite matter-of-factly but gently suggested, "you did in your 20s what you knew how to do and when you knew better...you did better."[32]

This may seem an odd quotation to end a chapter on sadness. After all, we might not think of Angelou's words as sad at all. She is simply stating the facts, and what's more, she is incorporating a positive twist. When we know better, we do better. But, if we think about it, this matter-of-factness and positive focus are

32  Winfrey, O. (2011, October 19). The powerful lesson Maya Angelou taught Oprah [Video file], 01:50. Retrieved December 10, 2017 from http://www.oprah.com/oprahs-lifeclass/the-powerful-lesson-maya-angelou-taught-oprah-video

indicative of true, healthy grief. Angelou's words encourage ownership but there's no hint of blame, regret, guilt, or shame. Once we fully accept our actual, objective losses, we live more closely in line with reality, with truth. And as we align ourselves more and more with truth, we experience less encumbrances and more freedoms.

Sadness, with its serious and heavy tones will be a part of this wherever we miss, wish, or long for what used to be. But if we are open to feeling sad, we won't be unnecessarily weighed down by its misdirected forms. And, somewhat paradoxically, as we accurately acknowledge what no longer is, we'll be more able to fully embrace what *is*, what life still has to offer. Often, being more present to what we still have, we'll turn a corner.

Amid sadness, we'll discover deeper appreciations. Through grief, we'll arrive at stronger gratitude. Our losses will also mean our letting go.

This is the goal, so to speak, of sadness. Through pain and often excruciating encounters with our own limits, we'll get glimpses of a grace that's deeper still. The following song, written by Tim and Laurie Thornton upon the occasion of an agonizing decision to relinquish a dream, captures this:

*All that I know, is Love has come around*
*Like the grass beneath the golden sun pushes through*
*the ground*
*All I know, is Love has come around*

*All that I know is Peace has come around*
*Like the rain beneath the silver moon glistens to the*
*ground*
*All I know, is Peace has come around*

*And I will kiss the days behind me now*
*And thank You for the beauty that I never saw*
*And I will say goodbye to what is gone*
*And welcome what I know has been here all along*[33]

33  Thornton, T., & Thornton, L. (2009, July 23). All that I know [Video file]. Retrieved December 10, 2017 from https://www.youtube.com/watch?v=oFTyxqFbYVo

# Chapter 10: Pacific

*Most people are about as happy as they make up their minds to be.*
*Abraham Lincoln*

*I have said these things to you, that in Me you may have peace.*
*In the world you will have tribulation.*
*But take heart; I have overcome the world.*[1]
*Jesus of Nazareth*

"...It was a mighty ocean, resting uneasily to the east of the largest continent, a restless ever-changing, gigantic body of water that would later be described as pacific..."[2] So begins James Michener's sweeping novel, *Hawai`i*, and as we continue to discuss the principles of oceanspeak, Michener's words provide an interesting platform for us to transition to our discussion of the third major category of emotion: happiness.

On the vast ocean of relationships, happiness is that experience which most closely approaches our overarching goals of freedom and joy. And just as the Pacific dominates the global ocean, so we long for happiness to characterize most of our interpersonal experiences.

## A Universal Pursuit

*An Elusive Target*
As I begin this chapter, I am rounding out a family vacation on Maui. Looking out from our balcony, I can see the beautiful waters off Ka `anapali, where just yesterday my daughters and

---

1   John 16:33
2   Michener, J. (1959). Hawaii. New York, NY: Random House, p. 1.

I snorkeled among a rainbow of fish, made mermaids in the sand, and then marveled at the sight of two humpback whales frolicking offshore. Even as I write, there is a wedding about to take place on the lawn below our villa, and the party is all smiles as they pose for photos with shimmering waters in the background. Happiness seems alive and well on all sides, and the atmosphere holds a sense of peace and well-being. Tranquility. Calm. The Pacific.

> **"...while positive implies good, good is often quite different from *better* or *best*."**

But many times, happiness can seem so much more elusive than an easy, idyllic vacation. In fact, if we are honest, vacations abound where conflict seems to be easier to achieve than happiness. On a more general level, things that would surely seem to procure happiness—money, fortune, fame, material goods, even relationships themselves—so often seem unable to deliver. How do we account for these discrepancies, and how do we, as a society, best arrive at experiences where happiness, like the Pacific, presides over our ocean of relationships? The answers begin to emerge as we begin to understand the focus of happiness, happiness relative to time, the dual nature of happiness, and how happiness functions in emotional fitness overall.

*The Focus of Happiness*
It may seem obvious, but the driving strategy for managing happiness is to understand what makes us happy. For this, let us return to our acronyms where happiness is represented by the G for *Glad* in MSGS and corresponds to the G for *Gain* in FLGT. The implication is that we feel good when we get good things. Happiness then is about obtaining, acquiring, earning, accomplishing, having, receiving, or any other experience where we add something positive to the picture of our lives.

Nevertheless, while positive implies good, good is often quite different from *better* or *best*. This principle is crucial to understand in our quest for happiness, and we will return to it throughout this chapter. The central distinction here is how to experience the good without settling for something less than better or best.

*Happiness and Time*
   A first step is to consider where the "gain" that brings happiness is located, relative to the past, present, or future. In this way, happiness is like all emotions in that it implicitly involves the relationship between our experiences and various points in time.

   Another dimension common to all emotions is the relationship between what is actual and what might be considered imagined or hypothetical. Take as examples anger and sadness. We might say that anger and sadness as negative emotions pertain to discrepancies between how things are and how they "should be," between the actual and the hypothetical. In the case of anger, the focus is on the difference between what is (actual present) and what should be (hypothetical present) or what should have been (hypothetical past). Sadness focuses on the difference between what used to be (actual past) and what no longer is experienced (actual present).

   In both cases, something is lacking, and tension is created between actual and hypothetical experience. This focus on what is lacking or absent is precisely why we can regard anger and sadness as negative emotions (in addition, we might also say that the inherently difficult nature of anger and sadness contribute to the negative "charge" of these emotions).

   By contrast, happiness is pleasant because it is fundamentally about positive things that *are* experienced. At the same time, it too has the potential for tension. Again, because "good" does not necessarily ensure "better" or "best," happiness always contains the potential for a tension between what is (actual present) and what *still could be* (hypothetical future).[3] And depending upon where we place the emphasis, e.g., on what is or what still could be, happiness can, at any given point, still be experienced as

---

3  The term "hypothetical future" is admittedly redundant. We do not experience "actual future" since the future, by definition, refers to something that is yet to happen and once it happens, it is regarded as present or past.

not quite satisfying or fulfilling. Happiness, then, can certainly be felt as having an "unsettled" dimension or even a "dark side." Like Michener's mighty Pacific, happiness can indeed be found "resting uneasily" amid the other waters of the ocean of relationships.

---

**"...happiness always contains the potential for a tension between what is (actual present) and what *still could be* (hypothetical future)."**

---

*The Dual Nature of Happiness*

Like anger or sadness, happiness has the potential to be both constructive and destructive. This may sound counterintuitive since happiness is again experienced as a positive emotion. However, we need only reverse our strategies with anger and sadness to see how happiness can also be both an asset and liability. Anger, for example, is negative in that it pertains to injustice and carries a harsh tone, but rightly understood, it can be used to energize and advance justice. Sadness also is negative in that it pertains to loss and an ironic sort of heaviness, but when accurately applied, it can promote healthy grief and gratitude for what remains. In both cases, these emotions can still be harnessed to accomplish much good.

Happiness can similarly be positive (in that gladness is connected to a sense of gain) and at the same time far from optimal, even detrimental. This is especially the case when other negative emotions are neglected or avoided and when happiness must be experienced at any cost.

Consider the simple example of a child who does not want to do her schoolwork and plays with friends instead. Or consider the adult who does not want to face the hurts or frustrations of a relationship and instead seeks relief in some sort of escape—work, television, alcohol—any activity that might distract him from the interpersonal conflict. In both examples, the child and adult are finding something to do instead of the "sadness" of school or relationship, respectively. And the distractions themselves are very much gains, in that during the time the child or adult are distracted, they "feel" good (pleasant, enjoyable, entertained, etc.). Both the child and the adult are probably very "happy" at the moment. However, we do not have to look very far to see the unhealthy trajectory that these happy activities will create. Given just a little time, such happiness will give way to unhappiness, and the sadness that was initially avoided will resurface. This time, however, the sadness will be much less necessary and so therefore more unfortunate. Again, *most* of life does not *have to be difficult.*

The dual nature of emotions in general and of happiness specifically is rooted in the difference between the "charge" of the emotion (determined largely by a focus on either what is absent or present) and the value of the emotion (determined by whether the emotion yields good or bad results). Just as positive does not necessarily mean good and negative does not necessarily mean bad (consider, for example, in medicine, the "good news" of a "negative biopsy"), good is not equal to "better" or "best" and bad is not equal to "worse" or "worst."

This is all distinguished from what we might think of as a morality of emotions, since the primary emotions that we are considering, i.e., anger, sadness, happiness, and fear, are usually not right or wrong in and of themselves. While emotions are always valid, in that they reflect personal experience, emotions are not always accurate to the situation at hand. Morality thus enters the picture when the situation at hand involves relationships and when categories of right/wrong and good/bad become the focus.

Relationally, morality enters the equation if an emotion works against reason or against what we might call the "reasonableness of the emotion." As such, emotions are moral, right, and good to the extent that the behaviors they inspire are accurate to the reason and reasonableness of the emotion. Conversely, we might say that emotions are immoral, bad, or wrong to the extent that they inspire behaviors that are a distortion of reason and reasonableness. For example, since anger is about justice and fairness, using anger to impose injustice or unfairness is a moral problem. Similarly, if sadness is about loss, then using sadness to deprive becomes inappropriate. Since happiness is about gain, happiness that works against progress and productivity risks being inappropriate as well. Of course, it is important to consider how we identify what makes for progress and productivity.

Likewise, happiness can be paradoxical. It may again seem counterintuitive or contradictory to say this since happiness is about feeling glad when we experience gains. We feel good when we get good things. At first glance, there is nothing tricky or complex about this. A second look, though, reveals happiness is not always this simple. Again, good does not necessarily translate into better or best. As a result, relationships or other experiences that lead to happiness are always subject to comparisons. And comparing, as necessary as it may be, insistently, and sometimes even detrimentally, reminds us that there is "always room for improvement."

In addition, most gains can, at some point, become losses. At any given time, happiness carries the potential for its emotional counterpart: sadness. As soon as we acquire, achieve, earn, obtain, receive, or win anything, we are reminded that the prize bears no guarantees. With the thrill of any possession comes the reminder that nothing will remain forever. Indeed, if we stop and reflect, we "possess" very little, and so the specter of impermanence seems always to loom. Again, to quote Robert Frost: "Nothing gold can stay."[4]

These ways in which happiness can, at any moment, give way to comparisons, losses, or sadness, are great mysteries. Like the deep canyons beneath the Pacific, they challenge the most seasoned mariners, especially those who aspire to plumb their depths. Fundamental questions arise: Are happiness and sadness compatible? How, if at all, can loss become gain? What makes a gain meaningful and can such meanings last? What is the cost of happiness? What are its risks?

As is often the case with paradox and mystery, attempts at simple answers will likely generate even more questions. At the same time, we are on a mission to simplify our understanding of emotions to better navigate and enjoy relationships. So, let us venture another principle, maybe two: True, lasting happiness

---

4 Frost, R. (October, 1923). "Nothing Gold Can Stay." Yale Review.

(joy), requires courage, and courage requires humility.

Courage can be defined as the ability to face fear by taking strategic steps towards whatever it is that we find threatening. We will return to this theme in our next chapter, but for now, let us focus on the deeper role of the prerequisite for both courage and happiness: humility.

## Happiness through Humility

### Accurate Self-Appraisal

Of all the character traits and personality variables we might consider, why humility? I propose humility because, again, the heart of the matter is the matter of the heart and because better relationships are the goal of this exploration. I also believe we can focus on humility because love of neighbor is optimized as we learn to love ourselves. Of course, loving ourselves is a tricky endeavor that calls for a healthy balance between awareness of ourselves and of others.

And so, humility is the "tie" that binds these tasks together, the skill that strikes the balance so critical to healthy interactions. Quite literally, humility is the "happy medium" we seek in our quest for happiness. On the ocean of relationships, it is a particularly useful compass for navigating the elusive waters of the Pacific.

For the purposes of our discussion, I will define humility simply as accurate self-appraisal. It is a way of rightly and fairly viewing oneself, strengths and weaknesses, weaknesses and strengths. In the words of English preacher Charles Haddon Spurgeon, to practice humility is to "make a right estimate of oneself."[5]

I contrast humility with pride, which I consider a preoccupation with oneself that is based on inaccurate self-appraisal. Such preoccupation manifests as an inordinate amount of self-focus that especially occurs to the exclusion of

5   Spurgeon, C. H. (1856, August 17). Pride and humility. Sermon given at New Park Street Chapel, Southwark. In Aaron Armstrong's Bloggingtheologically.com, retrieved December 10, 2017, from : https://www.bloggingtheologically.com/2010/02/20/charles-haddon-spurgeon-what-is-humility/

others. This excessive self-awareness can take the shape of either an *inflated or deflated* understanding of one's importance.

Many tend to focus on self-inflation as the primary expression of pride to avoid, and many aspire to be humble by seeking a rather low view of themselves. This is understandable for a couple of reasons. First, we live in a rather narcissistic culture, where self-absorption and self-obsession are rampant. Therefore, less self-emphasis is a useful corrective to the overarching philosophy of "looking out for 'number one.'" Second, it is easy to associate humility with humiliation. Both come from the root *"humus,"* which refers to the ground. However, as we have seen, what is understandable can also be very unnecessary. Equating humility with humiliation risks equating humility with low self-esteem, and this is more likely to lead to misery than happiness per se.

In *The Purpose-Driven Life*, pastor and author, Rick Warren, captures the essence of C. S. Lewis' insights, saying "Humility is not thinking less of oneself; it is thinking of oneself less."[6] Lewis' original words follow:

> Do not imagine that if you meet a really humble man he will be what most people call 'humble' nowadays; he will not be a sort of greasy, smarmy person, who is always telling you that, of course, he is nobody. Probably all you will think about him is that he seemed a cheerful, intelligent chap who took a real interest in what you said to him. If you do dislike him it will be because you feel a little envious of anyone who seems to enjoy life so easily. He will not be thinking about humility; he will not be thinking of himself at all.[7]

Lewis goes on to talk about the insistent, ubiquitous nature of pride and his belief that the critical first step toward becoming humble is "to realise that one is proud."[8] If this is the case, and if pride can exist as either self-inflation or self-deflation, then

6   Warren, R. (2002). The purpose-driven life®: What on earth am I here for? Grand Rapids, MI: Zondervan, p. 148.

7   Lewis, C. S. (1952, 2009). Mere Christianity. [HarperCollins e-books], p. 260. Retrieved from iBooks.

8   Lewis, C. S. (1952, 2009). p. 261.

happiness calls for first assessing our own tendencies toward either extreme. Overall, what is our tendency? Do we over or under-value ourselves?

Again, many will argue that we do far more to overestimate our value than to underestimate it. Indeed, Lewis himself points out the competitive nature of pride which seeks "the pleasure of being *above* the rest (italics added)."[9] It would seem then that people think too much of themselves. I suggest that an equal, albeit much subtler, danger can be found in the mirror image of what Lewis is describing. To borrow from Lewis' words, perhaps there is also a form of pride that competes to be "*beneath* the rest."

There is a paradoxical common ground here in that both expressions of pride trace back to excessive concern with oneself that simultaneously misunderstands one's actual value. Interestingly, overvaluing oneself has the same effect as devaluing oneself because the person misses out and comes up short relative to how things could be and how they could be so much better in particular. In these ways, both overvaluing and devaluing result in missing out on happiness.

Humility is the better pathway to happiness and ultimately, to freedom and joy. We experience these qualities as we live in line with reality, and the ground of humility is reality itself.

Some words on spiritual matters are important here. That is, if humility is the mystery behind the art of happiness, then recognizing our position in the cosmos is vital to happiness.

Spiritually, the secret to humility is being able to rightly assess ourselves in light of our relationship to God. Again, as theologian Paul Tillich so eloquently puts it, God is the "ground of being."[10] Furthermore, by definition, God is supreme, or, to borrow again from Lewis, "above the rest." God is therefore Alpha and Omega, Beginning and End, Floor and Ceiling to all of existence. An accurate self-assessment will include accounting for God's supremacy on at least two levels.

9   Lewis, C. S. (1952, 2009), p. 250.

10   Tillich, P. (1951). Systematic Theology, volume 1: Reason and revelation, being and God. Chicago, IL: University of Chicago Press, p. 21.

172 | MAYBE THE WHOLE OCEAN

## Worthy: Supremacy and Sovereignty

First, we will do well to take seriously how we are *unlike* God— we are dependent upon Him, He is different from us, and indeed, we are *not* Him. This includes taking to heart the ways in which He alone is perfect and the attendant ways in which we fall short of His splendor.

This is probably the more difficult aspect of accounting for God's supremacy. It involves that aspect of humility which we usually associate with "swallowing our pride," and "humbling ourselves." It very appropriately can be seen in certain postures of worship such as bowing, kneeling, even prostrating ourselves before one who is "wholly other" and completely deserving of reverence and awe. It involves the crucial move of acknowledging our own deep-seated desires to control things in ways only He can, inclinations that we all have to essentially be our own god, so to speak. This is crucial because so many of the ways we pursue happiness can be attempts to control areas that are not ours to control. So, this side of humility offers an important corrective to the extreme of self-inflation. It essentially reminds us that God alone is *worthy* of all honor, since He alone is supremely and exclusively good.

## Worth: Embodied and Embossed

Second, and just as important, I believe we do well to take seriously where we are profoundly *similar* to God. According to the Judeo-Christian tradition, we are "made in God's image."[11] As God's image bearers, we still reflect Him to others, and so, "similar" is very different from "identical." Nevertheless, as His image bearers, we are unique in all of creation in ways that almost defy description. Whether we like it or not, we carry the essence of the divine in our very persons.

The concept of image-bearing pertains to a couple of ancient contexts. The first was the process of creating a statue or even an idol and the second was the process of minting coins. In the first, the artisan sought to sculpt an object that would be a fitting embodiment of a deity. In the second, the coin was given value once it was stamped with the impression of a ruler such as a king or emperor.[12]

11  Genesis 1:26-27

12  Hoekema, A. A. (1994). Created in God's image. Carlisle, U.K: Paternoster Press.

In both cases, the image bearing was integral to the value and the purpose of the object. And the object (statue/idol or coin) pointed to an original source of honor and glory—the deity, the emperor, etc. In the same way, the notion that we are made in the image of God, that we bear the *imago Dei*, points to the immeasurable *worth* we have as human beings, precisely because of God's splendor as both architect and blueprint. This then is another equally important dimension of humility. If we are to understand ourselves rightly and accurately, it is imperative that we also acknowledge and even affirm the preciousness and pricelessness we each bring to the world. And, when we are open to valuing ourselves accurately, we will increase the chances of experiencing true happiness and even joy. Simply put, we treat well that which we value well.

### Humility and Happiness in Relationships

*Limits and Abilities*

Seeing humility from a spiritual perspective can lead to at least two practical approaches to happiness in relationships with others. The first is especially difficult and yet critical. It is this: humility leads to happiness because it frees us to *embrace our limits*. This is counterintuitive for sure. Personally, I do not gravitate towards my limits, and in fact, I dislike them very much. I do not enjoy the various encounters I have with experiences outside of my ability or beyond my control. And, of course, the situations that seem outside of our control nearly always are impacted by...other people—family, friends, acquaintances, employers, employees, patients, clients, customers, colleagues, peers, neighbors, or even complete strangers. I want them to cooperate with me, listen to my suggestions, follow my instructions, meet my expectations, and essentially do things that will make my life run more smoothly. But alas, other people often have their own ideas! And herein lies the rub, since true relationships require the freewill of all parties. And so, other people and their ideas amount to more limits to be embraced.

I believe that it is neither inappropriate nor wrong to *want* things to go my way. This is normal and probably healthy overall (of more concern would be the person who does not want things to go their way). However, when I am honest with

174 MAYBE THE WHOLE OCEAN

myself, wanting things to go my way is essentially, or at least often, my way of saying that I want others in my life to treat me as if I were *most* important. In fact, sometimes I may even be wanting to be treated as supreme—honored, esteemed, and dare I say it, worshiped, in the same way one might glorify a deity. Perhaps this an extreme way of putting it. Still, even if I do not consciously want people like my children or wife to bow down to me, I do desire their attention, affection, and even adoration. So, what really is the difference?

Again, these desires are not bad per se—but *requiring* them to be granted would be problematic for a couple of reasons. First, it would give me too much power or importance. Second, it would give other people in my life (such as my wife and children) too little power or importance. To reiterate, only one being in the universe is *worthy* of total praise—God. In addition, if others in my life are required to love me, they are not free to feel or choose for themselves. Thus, the experience is most likely something other than true love.

This is where humility enters as a beautiful and paradoxical corrective. By acknowledging first the supremacy of God, I allow myself to live in sync with His ways which are naturally higher than my own and always superior overall (I get to experience God as God). Furthermore, when I accurately understand this, I am more likely to also see others in my life as *equally* important to me and to treat them accordingly. Relationships can then be cultivated and built on things other than control and reactivity. In the words of the apostle Paul, there is room to be "rooted and grounded in love..."[13] And when this happens, it is as if happiness and joy are invited into relationships, for a deep sense of gain becomes almost inevitable when love is the foundation.

Second, and perhaps equally surprising, a spiritual understanding of humility will mean we also *embrace our abilities*. When we take the *imago Dei* seriously, we cannot help but pursue the potential we have for good things as we value God, ourselves, and those around us. We value God because He is the source of all that we experience as good and beautiful and

---

13  Ephesians 3:17. This may be particularly powerful to think about, considering what it means to have humility before God who is again, to borrow Paul Tillich's description, "the ground of all being" (italics added).

true. We value ourselves because we are aware that something within us is glorious and wondrous. Indeed, with the psalmist, we can celebrate how we are "fearfully and wonderfully made."[14] And finally, but certainly not least, we value others because we recognize that they too are treasures and masterpieces. And just as a connoisseur or curator takes special care to respect and honor a work of art, so we will approach relationships with a sense of sacred appreciation. This too will be humility, to the extent that human *worth* is distinguished from divine *worthiness*. And this too will be fertile ground in which happiness and joy can grow.

*Content and Process*

Let us now focus on tying these concepts in with our FIT model. We have begun with the notion that happiness can be paradoxical in that it can be found in even difficult situations or in situations where there is a potential for loss. Paradoxical happiness then is an example of thought-focused rather than incident-focused feeling. The situation is transcended by a certain way of thinking. This is especially important to consider in the context of relationships, and it ultimately can be traced back to humility and courage.

Interestingly, however, it seems society's dominant model of happiness, even in relationships, is more incident-focused. Consider the opening lines of the song, "Happiness," from the Broadway musical, *You're a Good Man, Charlie Brown*.[15] Charlie and friends recount all the simple experiences in life that contribute to their happiness and sing,

> *Happiness is finding a pencil, pizza with sausage,*
> *telling the time*
> *Happiness is learning to whistle,*
> *tying your shoe for the very first time*
> *Happiness is playing the drum in your own school band*
> *And happiness is walking hand in hand . . .*

As much as I enjoy the musical and the song, I reluctantly tend

14   Psalm 139:14

15   The song, Happiness, was composed by Clark Gesner for the 1967 musical, "You're a Good Man, Charlie Brown" and originally performed by Orson Bean (Charlie Brown), Bill Hinnant (Snoopy), Clark Gesner (Linus), and Barbara Minkus (Lucy) Retrieved January 18, 2020, from https://peanuts.fandom.com/wiki/Happiness

to think it illustrates what we have been referring to as happiness in "survival mode." These lyrics suggest that happiness is *outside* of a person. In this way, happiness is essentially an experience that requires certain conditions. Pencils, pizza, or even the skill of learning to whistle are all external—and therefore they can all be taken away. What happens if I lose the pencil? Or what if the pizza is missing the sausage? Or what if I have no one to walk with me?

Quite understandably and appropriately, the song does not explore these possibilities. Still, when we locate our happiness, or any emotion for that matter, outside of ourselves, the incidents in our lives must be changed for our feelings to change. As silly as it may sound, this is a reactive approach to emotions. To borrow from earlier metaphors, this understanding of happiness corresponds to "prairie chicken and *mahi mahi*" decision making. The result is that we stay tethered to the situation at hand, and ultimately we don't get to experience the "wireless" freedom that flows from a different approach.

For the most part, if we are on good terms with others, we feel good about these terms and enjoy the resulting happiness. This is all fine until things change and we are no longer on such good terms. When this happens, it seems inevitable that happiness too will diminish and change.

But if we think about it, in relationships, it is almost impossible for changes to not happen. Bringing two or more lives together in any way usually involves an adjustment and, often, some type of clash.

> **"...it seems society's dominant model of happiness, even in relationships, is more incident-focused."**

*State and Trait*

Suppose two people are "happily married." We can say this is a *state* of happiness. The connotation is obviously positive, and this is overall good and pleasant, to be celebrated and enjoyed. Still, there is an implied condition—some sort of satisfaction with the *marriage*. But, what if the marriage itself becomes unhappy? Can a couple be happily married if the marriage is less than ideal? If happiness is dependent upon a certain state, it seems a change to that state will inevitably result in a change in happiness.

The state of being happily married often pertains to an earlier season of relationship, the proverbial "honeymoon period." In this phase of a relationship, *differences* are generally celebrated. Interestingly, part of the initial bliss is discovery of the person as somebody *else*. But almost always, after a certain point, the differences become *difficult*. One person I know puts it this way: "Opposites attract and then opposites *attack*." And after the supposed attack, unfortunately, many relationships have difficulty staying *intact*.

Ironically, the "attacks" are usually not intended. They are most often differences of opinion, preference, or even style. Suppose one person is more of an extrovert while the other is more of an introvert. Or when it comes to time, suppose one person is more event-focused and the other more guided by the clock. One spends, the other saves. One is an early riser, the other more productive at night, and on and on.

Over time, frustrations can set in and differences can present as personality or character issues. Once this happens, it is not long before such "personality" differences are either resignedly expected or emphatically protested. Familiarity, as they say, begins to breed contempt. Ways of life that used to be fresh and new now become "same old, same old." Matters of opinion and preference become somehow non-negotiable. And before too long, even small, inconsequential details can become suddenly very consequential deal-breakers. In the catchy words of George and Ira Gershwin, "You like poh-tay-toh, I like poh-tah-toh, you like toh-may-toh, I like toh-mah-toh" until one day we may cite the song's tragic title and say..."Let's call the whole thing off."[16] When this happens, it is not uncommon for the couple to call

16   The song, Let's Call the Whole Thing Off, was composed by George Gershwin and Ira Gershwin for the 1937 musical, "Shall We Dance" and originally performed by Fred Astaire and Ginger Rogers. Retrieved January 18, 2020,, from https://digitalcommons.library.umaine.edu/mmb-vp-copyright/1543/

the differences "irreconcilable" or the marriage "irretrievably broken" and disband.

## "Opposites attract and then opposites *attack*."

This is admittedly a caricature, since each couple is unique and there are undoubtedly extenuating circumstances for many couples that contribute to legitimate moves to separation and divorce. The *content* of each relationship is important to consider. At the same time, what we are concerned with is a *process* that might be common to most relationship obstacles and how this process relates to, of all things, happiness.

I suggest that the process behind most relationship fall-out is the same survival-oriented, incident-focused, default approach to emotions we have been describing throughout this book. The problem then is precisely that emotions are treated as external—either as problems to be fixed or as necessities to be attained, at virtually any cost. And when people see each other as the cause of what they feel (i.e., one person becomes another's incident), then they inevitably react to each other via some combination of "fight, flight, or freeze" strategy. This is all unnecessary, however, because relationships are fundamentally not survival contexts. Again, *most* of life does not *have* to be difficult.

When it comes to emotions, and happiness specifically, the alternative is to shift to a non-survival, thought-focused approach. This allows us to attribute our feelings to matters within our control rather than outside of it. Perhaps, in this case, we could say that happiness is more of a *trait* than a state in that it is primarily internal and intrapersonal. Nonetheless, it is also a trait that is cultivated and developed, since living from a non-survival stance takes considerable effort in a world which is largely in survival mode.

*Theme Parks and Tiger Sharks*
It might still seem rather extreme to say that the world is largely living in survival mode. Again, however, what we are

referring to as survival mode is essentially the way we approach our emotions, including happiness, where what we feel is believed to be caused by something external or outside of our control. In this light, consider the following rather widespread references, and identify the apparent "sources" of happiness:

1) "The Happiest Place on Earth"
2) "Happy Meal" ®
3) "Happy Hour"

It seems clear that in each of these instances, happiness is *outside* of the person, and for our purposes, this is what is meant by a survival approach to emotions. There is a parallel between each of these references and actual survival situations where emotions (usually negative) are generated by external circumstances.

For example, suppose a person encounters a shark while swimming in the ocean. And suppose it is a kind of shark that occasionally attacks humans, such as a tiger shark. It seems fair to say that if this person were to feel afraid when encountering the shark, the fear would primarily be due to the shark (rather than their fear being due to ideas about the shark). This is so because it's practical—meeting up with a tiger shark is dangerous and so it makes sense to do something *about the shark*. The standard reactions here are again to fight, flee, or freeze, and behaving in any of these ways could lead to escape from a very real danger.

It may seem silly to compare tiger sharks to the references above, but if we will allow the parallels, we will be on our way to better understanding, managing, and experiencing true happiness. The main difference is that, in the references above, the emotion is not caused by an oceanic predator, but rather by a theme park, a lunch, or a beverage service, respectively.

This is important to relationships, because if emotions in general are treated as external to the people involved in the relationship, these emotions will be "outsourced" and subject to circumstances. When this happens, if a person initially feels some sort of discomfort, the primary strategy for feeling better (happy) will be to react rather than to respond. Reacting, however, leads to increased chances of unnecessary problems occurring (primarily because relationships are not actual survival-oriented contexts). Ironically, this makes the desired happiness more difficult to sustain. Further, when relationship successes hinge on environmental cues, the people in the relationships are likely treated more as a means to an end rather than an end in themselves.

Conversely, when happiness is thought-focused and therefore internal to each person, the relationship can be enjoyed as an end in itself. This also allows for the relationship to be more manageable, more streamlined, and more flexible. If I am focused on understanding how my perceptions contribute to corresponding feelings, I can allow for certain inevitable changes in a relationship to occur.

## Sex, Money, and Happiness

*Causation and Correlation*
At the top of the list of inevitable changes in a relationship, sex and money are repeatedly identified as two areas where difficulties most frequently happen. These are obviously very personal topics and there will undoubtedly be intricacies outside the scope of this discussion. However, let us consider two ways in which both areas can lead to conflict.

First, it seems these two areas are quite easily associated with happiness, provided they support the expectations of the relationship. It seems safe to say that when sex and money are available in satisfactory amounts, people are generally happy. Conversely, when sexual and financial satisfaction are less than expected, happiness decreases as well.

This strong correlation points to the second way that these areas can be challenging to relationships in that they both are easily and naturally associated with survival. Sex is associated with survival because it has physical implications and is ultimately necessary for procreation. Money is associated with survival because it is necessary for us to obtain resources (food, drink, shelter) that are themselves necessary for our physical existence as well. Because both areas overlap so closely with a survival paradigm, it is easy for the *correlation* they share with happiness to be mistaken as *causation*. This is understandable but unfortunate because happiness that is *caused* by sexual or financial success is dependent on circumstances, generally outside of the individual.

For example, suppose a man wants to be sexually intimate with his wife. He happens to see her getting ready for her shower, finds her stunning, and this slightest sight of her transports him to blissful memories of passionate times together. On this day though, she is undressing for a shower and apparently nothing more. And so that is what happens. A shower. By herself. Without him. He stays quiet, trying not to overanalyze the situation. He goes about his business (say, writing a chapter on happiness for a book on relationships!). He strives to think that she does not mean to create any frustration, and that indeed, she cannot make him frustrated. In fact, it seems she is well-intentioned, because after she showers and dresses, she pours him a cup of coffee and pecks him on the cheek. He expresses his appreciation, sips his coffee, and strives to not think of her kiss as an example of being "so close, yet so far." And, in that moment, for him, it seems happiness in the relationship depends on one thing—one elusive, evasive, extraordinary thing . . .

Suppose a couple jointly operate a business, and the stress of working together is impacting financial decisions and affecting their personal relationship. He is working overtime to make service calls, and she is operating the office but frustrated with him for not giving her the information she needs to keep up with the scheduling and accounting. Stakes are high because this business is their livelihood. They need to keep up with the mortgage, the tuitions, and basic grocery shopping. It feels very much like a matter of survival to them—almost as if receivables and payables and revenue in general are the equivalent of food and water and air. And so, when business is strong, the couple can relax, and the world is comfortable, safe, and right-side up. And, when business suffers, the stress takes a toll and all that matters is getting back to where matters used to be. It is as if the couple's commitment and obvious work ethic enter a feedback loop with their feelings, making it seem irresponsible for them to be happy when the finances are not in order. Happiness fluctuates like the stock market, and their "stock" only goes up when business is running smoothly. For them and countless other couples striving to make ends meet, the "bottom line" is that one thing that would seem necessary for a happy life together—that one elusive, evasive, extraordinary thing . . .

## Means and Ends

These two scenarios illustrate a general trend. At any given point, we seem to be just "one thing" away from happiness. Sex, money, food, drink, sleep, commitment, marriage, job, success, baby, car, boat, house, grade, promotion, respect, health . . . we scramble for these things and go to great lengths to attain them. But are they ever enough?

In relationships, scrambling often means we invest inordinate amounts of time and energy into wishing, hoping, expecting, even demanding that *others* make a change. And, when this happens, the relationship carries the primary responsibility for the happiness of the individual rather than the other way around.

This reversal can have far-reaching effects. In our examples, financial hardships can be trying and tiring. And, of course, if bills are not paid or food is scarce, actual survival is literally jeopardized. Financial stress, especially conditions that approach poverty, are very real causes of both unhappiness and physical threat. Likewise, the sexually frustrated person is understandably struggling and easily unhappy. Still, the question remains as to where people locate the primary responsibility for their feelings.

Again, in relationships, money and sex are two areas where people's feelings are often at the mercy of their circumstances. Sex is especially experienced as an ostensible cause of emotion. When sex is desired, many people experience pleasure and happiness if it occurs or frustration and disappointment if it does not. These strong correlations are bound up in the close connections between money, sex, and survival, since, among other things, these areas indirectly and directly impact both brain and body. Experiences like food, drink, and sleep are also significant to survival because of their physical implications.

However, the brain and body are only partly responsible for happiness. The mind is essential as well. After all, we are *homo sapiens,* and our capacity for thinking and wisdom are what distinguish us from the rest of the animal kingdom. In fact, if we did use our instincts alone to guide us into happiness, we would be at risk for the very opposite of happiness. Taken to an extreme, the results would literally be "brutal," since we would be no different from wild beasts, if not worse.[17]

In fact, when people take extreme survival approaches to other people, e.g., treating others as direct, physical vehicles of gratification, there is great potential for relationships to be profoundly violated. A moral line is crossed when people are treated as objects and "used" to somehow make others feel better, and when this crossing ventures further into actions such as theft or abuse, we rightly call the violations criminal. And, tragically, in extreme cases, when people become means to ends, indulgences of brain and body can figuratively, and at times even literally, degenerate into skull and bones.

## Happiness, Surviving, and Thriving

*Situations and Interpretations*
The alternative is to use our *minds* to regulate our happiness and other emotions. So, for example, if physical survival is not in question, the financially stressed person can seek to view the financial situation in a larger context, possibly exploring how hardship can be a chance to reevaluate and identify creative solutions. Similarly, the sexually frustrated person can consider the value of waiting for intimacy with their partner and, in so doing, embrace limits consistent with relationship.[18] In both of these situations, focusing on more than one interpretation involves true humility because this affirms the dignity of people over the difficulties of the circumstances. Further, looking for new interpretations is also an expression of courage, since delayed gratification is hardly for the faint of heart.

This will primarily happen as two things are considered. First, a mixture of desire and frustration can be acknowledged

---

17 Dallas Willard suggests that "brutal" refers to a kind of cruelty that is beyond even what brutes or beasts would express.

18 The challenge of such waiting can range from being inconvenient to extraordinarily difficult (especially when the person is still searching or waiting for a suitable partner!), and so one important option for support is to seek the assistance of a skilled individual and/or couples/family counseling or spiritual direction.

and respected because the relationship is not an actual matter of life and death. The context is not an emergency, even if financial status or physical romance can seem like urgent matters. True, these people may not experience what they want, but they will live to tell about it.

By contrast, we can imagine a person who is prevented from experiencing what they want and who might not, for lack of a better phrase, live to tell about it. Take, as examples, a diver whose gear catches on a piece of coral and so is prevented from swimming to the surface; or a person whose foot gets trapped on a railroad track with a locomotive barreling towards him; or a hiker lost in the mountains with no way of calling for help and no remaining food or water. These are extreme and far-fetched situations, but they illustrate something important. Frustration for these people is a matter of life and death, so the frustration is itself dangerous. To cite our FIT model, the incident (rather than any specific thought about it) determines the feeling and the nature of the incident means the feeling is itself a threat.

This kind of survival-oriented frustration cannot be allowed to continue for long. Frustration in relationships is another matter, however, precisely because allowing relational frustration to continue can ultimately benefit the relationship. Allowing is a part of acceptance. And when people can truly accept (rather than merely resign themselves to) delays concerning money and sex and other pleasures in relationship, they will take the first step toward better chances of growing and flourishing.

The second step our model can facilitate is to provide us with the option of modifying our feelings if they are either undesired or too intense (or not intense enough). Therefore, the challenge of happiness is simply this—to shift to a focus on anything that can be considered a gain, meaning what a person does have at any given point in time. It is important that this shift be sincere since the person will experience happiness in proportion to the strength of her belief that she is gaining in some way.

This will be more difficult to do in certain situations such as those marked by actual losses, injustices, or threats. It is not helpful to minimize the gravity of these situations nor to recommend an unrealistic practice of naive optimism or overconfidence that goes nowhere. Minimizing and denying reality are potentially just different expressions of pride in which self-preoccupation obscures the view of what is real and true.

## Two Sides of a Coin

If overconfidence is not the goal of happiness, perhaps confidence is. In fact, let us consider that humility, or accurate self-awareness, is precisely the other side of confidence. The two work together like two sides of a coin, and I am inclined to say the coin itself is aligned with reality. When we truly understand ourselves, we experience a sense of certainty and security that goes to our core. Again, from a spiritual perspective, this is tempered by the recognition of how we as human beings are not God and yet, remarkably, we are made in His image.

The word confidence literally translates into a phrase akin to "with trust or faith." It means that something or someone can be counted upon, and it implies a sense of strength, goodness, and esteem. It is difficult to imagine confidence that is not "happy," assuming the confidence is itself healthy. In addition, when it comes to happiness, a logical follow-up is to identify the object of our confidence—what or who is the basis of the confidence that results in happiness?

It will be helpful to distinguish between confidence and *competence*. Whereas confidence generally involves a sense of certainty and positive expectation, competence can specifically be thought of as a good feeling associated with capability, qualification, or skill. Thus, confidence flows predominantly from *who* one is, while competence flows predominantly from *what* or *how* one does. Both are important, though it seems each is associated with a certain kind of happiness.

Returning to our FIT model, I propose that competence primarily relies on a "survival" paradigm of emotions and confidence primarily relies on a "non-survival" paradigm of emotions. Again, survival refers to the situation or to incident-focused emotion, with an emphasis on being "fit" for competition (survival of the *fittest*). Non-survival, on the other hand, refers to the influence of perception or to thought-focused emotion, with an emphasis on being "fit" for cooperation (emotional *fitness*). Further, since we are concerned with the ocean of

186 MAYBE THE WHOLE OCEAN

relationships, I believe a non-survival paradigm is particularly important for *thriving* in our interpersonal journeys, or what we might affectionately term a "thrival" paradigm of emotion.

## Doing and Being

*Feelings and Actions*

A closer look at the component parts of our FIT model will show additional differences between competence and confidence and their corresponding implications for happiness. Recall that FIT refers to an equation that depicts how feelings are essentially the product of incidents and thoughts:

### *Feelings = Incidents x Thoughts*

In this case, one inspiration for the FIT model is Albert Ellis' ABC model of emotional and behavioral dysfunction.[19] Here, A stands for adversity or activating situation (akin to incidents), B for belief (akin to thoughts), and C stands for consequences (feelings and behaviors that follow). So, we might write the equation like this:

### *Activating Event x Beliefs = Consequences (or resulting emotions and behaviors)*

The main point here is that consequences include both emotions and the behaviors or actions that follow. We will see the value of combining the two models if we consider (in parallel with our FIT model) how emphasizing activating events or beliefs have differential impacts on emotional and behavioral consequences, respectively. So, let us return to the notion that when activating events are the focus of why we feel what we feel (a survival paradigm), we tend to *react* (fight/flee/freeze or act first and then think afterward). In this case, feelings and actions (consequences) are *essentially one and the same*. We have no need to distinguish between feelings and actions because in survival mode, our feelings essentially inform interventions that are directed at our external environment. It is our environment (incidents, activating events, situations, etc.) that must change for us to feel differently.

---

19 For a very helpful synopsis of Albert Ellis' ABC model, please see http://albertellis. org/rebt-in-the-context-of-modern-psychological-research/, retrieved December 16, 2017.

By contrast, when beliefs are the focus of why we feel what we feel (a non-survival or thrival paradigm), we tend to *respond* ("face" our situations or think first and then act). And so, the feelings and actions we experience are *essentially distinct*. This is important because if survival is not at stake, it is basically unnecessary to equate feelings and actions. We can afford, so to speak, to have our feelings, and we do not have to feel differently right away. Feelings are not problems per se and can be approached instead as resources, which return us to our perceptions and interpretations. As mentioned earlier, perhaps we can think of feelings as simply *words* . . . words that ultimately point us back to our thoughts. On the ocean of relationships, this strategy allows us to most fully experience the range of our emotions without treating others in our lives as if they are responsible for what we feel. Moreover, if responsiveness rather than reactivity is a better "fit" for relationships, we will experience a better quality of life as we avoid the unnecessary difficulties that occur when we "act out our feelings."

In addition, if a person's happiness traces back to confidence more than competence, there are at least two additional ways relationships have a better chance of thriving. First, when happiness derives from confidence, individuals can invest in their relationships even if or even when circumstances are difficult. When the issue is not "what" is going on but rather the "meaning" of what is going on, external circumstances can often be transcended. Further, since meanings can change, confident people can adjust their perceptions and essentially create options that best fit their aspirations and goals. As such, I find it useful to say, "confidence sees opportunity."

Second, happiness that springs from confidence more than from competence is more conducive to relationships, because each person in the relationship is more focused on *being* themself rather than on *doing* things that "make" others or themselves feel good per se. The overarching question is whether happiness is based more upon *identity* or *performance*.

Overall, increased freedom is an interesting and important feature of the kind of happiness that comes from humility. A primary reason for this is found again in the concept of acceptance. This happens when a balanced understanding of ourselves, our abilities, and our limitations forms the basis for happiness. Spiritually, this means that I can locate happiness in an abiding sense of worth and belonging rather than having to convince myself or others that I am worthy. Since worthiness belongs to God alone, happiness rests on a foundation of identity rather than performance, and this again is necessary for freedom that is independent of circumstances.

*Reactive and Responsive Happiness*
There is a potential relationship between our character and our ability to distinguish between our perceptions and beliefs and our circumstances per se. Most of us are probably acquainted with expressions like, "It's not what you do; it's who you are" or, "We are human beings, not human doings." Nevertheless, so often it seems our focus is on *how* we are doing rather than *who* we are being. In fact, I am persuaded that most interpersonal concerns that people discuss in counseling reflect this latter pattern. My goal here is to contribute to the discussion by connecting the doing/being distinction with survival/non-survival paradigms of emotion, respectively. I am also interested in the ongoing process of learning the relationship benefits of emotional responsiveness over emotional reactivity.

If we rely on certain conditions to be happy, our happiness is fundamentally reactive. If we shift our focus inward to what our conditions *mean* to us, our happiness will become more responsive. In a nutshell, or perhaps a seashell, this is what navigating the ocean of relationships is all about.

The goal here is not actually to just be happy all the time. Hopefully we have seen this in our previous chapters. There are legitimate reasons to not be happy and to experience other, more negative emotions, such as anger or sadness. By extension, avoiding legitimate negative emotions is essentially reactive, since such avoidance of emotion is usually, by definition, unnecessary.

Rather, let us consider how we can experience happiness as more accessible and less elusive—to increase the chances of successfully navigating and enjoying the waters of the Pacific—while also recognizing the tricky ways these waters can be found to be "resting uneasily . . ."[20]

Of course, the context of Michener's reference to the "uneasy rest" of the Pacific, is precisely one where something very significant is going on beneath the ocean's surface—namely, the gradual, relentless, volcanic creation of the Hawaiian Islands. Similarly, we can say that the waters of happiness are challenging precisely because there are potentially deeper purposes to being happy—specifically, profound opportunities to improve, enhance, and optimize relationships.

For these purposes to happen, people must be accepted and pursued for who they are, rather than as means to ends. Situations, also, must be experienced with an awareness of what they mean to each person, so that some sense of gain is retained, even amid more difficult details. And finally, the ongoing task of shifting away from obligation to opportunity will particularly allow for more openness to experience and pathways to living life as fully as possible.

---

**"Perhaps because we are so intricately wired for survival, we tend to focus on how things can be better..."**

---

These are, of course, general descriptions of how happiness can relate to our overall purposes of deepening and strengthening relationships. An even closer look at our new paradigm of emotions will point to three strategies whereby these purposes can be accomplished. Broadly speaking, these purposes can be called the Location, Challenge, and Direction of happiness.

### Happiness and Purposefulness in Relationships

*The Location of Happiness*

This entire chapter revolves around the notion that the focus of happiness is always some sort of gain. For us to be happy, it is important to have some way of calling our experience positive, enjoyable, or even good. We have seen that this gain

20  Michener, J. (1959). Hawaii. New York: Random House, p. 1.

can be objective, subjective, or some combination of the two. Overall, we have considered how emphasizing the subjective (thought-focused) dimension of happiness is most conducive to sustaining and enhancing relationships.

At the beginning of this chapter, we also briefly touched on how happiness relates to time, and more specifically, to the ways in which potential tensions exist between past, present, and future experiences. Accordingly, our non-survival paradigm of emotions points to a single principle for resolving these tensions: *Happiness in relationships will be optimized as we learn to locate our happiness in our present, here-and-now experience.*

Perhaps because we are so intricately wired for survival, we tend to focus on how things can be better than they currently are. This is fundamentally good in that it motivates us to constantly seek new and improved ways of living. Still, if we are not careful, this focus on what we do not yet have can work against us. Always looking ahead, we can fail to miss out on life-in-the-moment. The result is that we are left in suspense and waiting for something more to happen, all while life slowly passes us by. Ironically, this skill, so vital to our existence, can prevent us from truly living; this very "good" quality can become the very enemy of experiencing something better.

This is cleverly captured in the words of a song by Colin Hay and Thom Mooney, aptly titled, "Waiting for My Real Life to Begin."

*Any minute now, my ship is coming in*
*I'll keep checking the horizon*
*I'll stand on the bow*
*And feel the waves come crashing*
*Crashing down, down, down, on me*

*And you say, "Be still my Love*
*Open up your heart, let the Light shine in"*
*But don't you understand, I already have a plan*
*I'm waiting for my real life to begin.*[21]

---

21  Hay, C., & Mooney, T. (1994). Waiting for my real life to begin. [Recorded by C. Hay]. On Topanga [CD]. Los Angeles, CA: Lazy Eye Records.

This tendency to "check the horizon," to cast our "real life" and ultimately our happiness into the future, is understandable. We likely have people, "loves," in our lives who encourage us to be still and "open up" our hearts to the light that is already shining. Or maybe, the song could even be taken as a prayer, and God is telling us to just be still and open ourselves to His light. Whatever the circumstances and whoever is speaking to us, it can seem so hard to be "still" and "open" when the waves are ever crashing down upon us. So, we wait for our ship, our reason for happiness, to appear on the horizon.

*Something More*

The problem, however, is that there is no guarantee that our ship will come in. The waiting can seem endless, and, depending on what we expect to bring happiness, the wait might continue indefinitely. But what if, on the ocean of relationships, we are essentially already on the ship?

It's interesting that in Hay and Mooney's song, the singer too, is standing "on the bow"—apparently, he, too, is already on a vessel. The emphasis, however, is not on the ship he is waiting *on* but rather on the ship he is waiting *for*. And so, his "real life" is on hold; he is in a "holding pattern" until something *more* occurs.

Waiting is a vital skill for our lives, but interminable waiting can drain us of "real life" and keep us from really living. The horizon is an exciting but elusive (indeed impossible!) target, and so it functions best as a marker for where we are at rather than where we are heading. Moreover, if the horizon is our objective, we will be living for the destination rather than the journey. And when it comes to the ocean of relationships, the journey is the destination. We might expand our metaphor here to that of a cruise ship, where the adventure and enjoyment take place *on* the ocean, as opposed to a commercial airline, whose primary purpose is to transport passengers from one location to another *above* the ocean. In this regard, it seems worth noting that "holding patterns" apply more to navigating the skies than the seas.

The point, again, is that locating our happiness in the future is understandable and yet unnecessary. This is not to say that happiness is guaranteed or that waiting is not a part of relating to others. Rather, it is in waiting that we can discover our opportunities to experience more sustainable happiness. This is because it is precisely the absence of guarantees and the presence of delays that point to how we experience the ocean of *relationships*. People, perhaps by definition, cannot be forced into "boxes" to be controlled or automated, and this is a good thing. In fact, true happiness would likely not be possible if people were so programmable and predictable.

So, it is better to locate happiness in present-day experience rather than the future per se. Of course, there is a subtle yet vast difference between saying the locus of happiness is found in present-day *circumstances* and the locus of happiness is found in the *meaning* of present-day *circumstances*. This, again, is what this book is all about. Once we identify the meaning of our circumstances as the opportunity for happiness, we can experience more of what life has to offer. And as we experience more of what life has to offer, we will really live, and our relationships will thrive.

A phrase that I hear quite often is that "winning the lottery" will bring happiness. Ironically, I have heard this expressed by a range of people, from unemployed to very wealthy, and the implication is that no matter where people are in life, what they have is not quite enough—financially, just a little more will make all the difference. In fact, I just heard it today from a family member! We were talking about how it would be a great idea to install a hot tub next to the pool, and my family member quipped, "an even better idea would be winning the lottery." And, of course, this is not new. When asked how much money would be "enough," the billionaire oil tycoon, John D. Rockefeller, is believed to have said, "just a little more."[22] Even King Solomon, who "became great and surpassed all who were before [him] in Jerusalem," lamented the "vanity" of all things and the essential futility of accomplishments and possessions.[23] As our *Declaration of Independence* affirms, we are all endowed with certain inalienable rights which include the "pursuit of

22   John D. Rockefeller. (n.d.). In Newworldencyclopedia.org. Retrieved December 16, 2017, from http://www.newworldencyclopedia.org/entry/John_D._Rockefeller

23   Ecclesiastes 2:9-11

happiness."[24] And, we are all equally capable of complicating our own pursuit of happiness by locating it outside of ourselves, in external circumstances, and in the future.

*Sayings and Say*

The "lottery" represents our tendency to hold out for something more, something bigger, some *thing* that will bring happiness. But if happiness is found in a *thing*, whether an object, a place, a time, or even another person—we are back to emotional survival mode and our happiness is ultimately not up to us. When emotions are driven by a survival paradigm, we essentially find ourselves living between two sayings: "It is what it is" and "The grass is always greener on the other side."

Thus, if "it" is not "just right," we find ourselves resigned to the factual details of our circumstances, placing our attention on how we just "have to" deal with what we've been dealt. This can sound like a worthwhile approach, but it risks us giving in to matters outside of our control and giving up on finding happiness in the here and the now. At the other end, we can lament whatever "it" is we are experiencing, while seeming to console ourselves that somewhere down the line "it" will get better or that getting to the "other side" will result in greener pastures. When circumstances dictate our happiness, we risk the "hamster wheel" of emotional survival mode, caught in a cycle of continually casting happiness into the future while putting real life on an indefinite hold.

But what if we define "it" as the *meaning* of our circumstances? If we can find a way to really believe that our *opinions* about our circumstances are equally important to, if not more important than, the *facts*, we might have more emotional space to work with. When we shift to, for example, "it is what it means," then we have a sense of say and therefore increased influence over our own happiness.

Or, what if we start saying something like, "the grass is always greener where we water it"?[25] If we can get past the temptation

24   U. S. Declaration of Independence. Paragraph 2 (1776)

25   Benson, K. (2017, August 17). "The grass is greener where you water it." In Gottman.com. Retrieved December 19, 2017, from https://www.gottman.com/blog/the-grass-is-greener-where-you-water-it/

(and it is a strong temptation indeed) to see this as a gimmick, then perhaps we will redirect our attention from the color and condition of the "grass" to the resources at our disposal that may yet revitalize the very ground beneath our feet.

The goal is to transition out of the life-sapping suspension "between the sayings" to the creation of a new wisdom and sense of "say" altogether. And the idea is that this is especially possible when relationships are the context. The first step is focusing on how the here-and-now, whatever it may be, can be our ever-present opportunity.

*Reframing "Unhappy"*

To illustrate, I have Keri's permission to speak generally about how she and I seek to keep these things in mind when there is a tension in our marriage (though, humorously, she asked if I would change her name!). As a couple, when we are not happy, the fundamental reasons trace back to our departure (and mine in particular) from the very principles I am trying to set forth in this book. At such times, we are in survival mode emotionally and still very much in the process of working through our differences. In the middle of our conflict, either Keri or I can remind ourselves that what we each have  (an "unhappy marriage") is our very opportunity to experience a more sustainable happiness overall. To do this, several steps are important. First, we can realize that the meaning of marriage, rather than the state of it per se, is the priority. That is, we can either focus on how "We have an **unhappy marriage**" or focus on how "We **have a**n unhappy **marriage**."

Admittedly this looks, and can even feel, forced. Nevertheless, when we italicize and put in bold only the "a" in the word "an," we take one sentence and change it to something quite different. We go from "we have an unhappy marriage" to "we have a marriage." This is the first step and perhaps the most important. If we can believe that this shift is meaningful, we will be prepared for further steps, such as tracing our unhappiness to specific thoughts (we *think* we have fundamental incompatibilities). Or we can modify these thoughts (we may have incompatibilities, yet this does not have to mean we are incompatible; apparent incompatibilities can be opportunities for growth; our areas of incompatibility might be part of a bigger picture of how we complement each other overall). These last modifications are the more difficult steps, though they are perhaps not as difficult as the misery associated with our initial tendency to categorize the entire marriage as unhappy. Who knows what kind of happiness might be found as we give these shifts our every consideration and believe that whatever is going on *right now* could represent something good, something gained, and maybe even *better* than initially expected. Alternatively, Keri, who is generally much more efficient at these reframes than I am, simply navigates similar circumstances by sincerely telling herself, "It could be worse!"[26]

## Reframing "Unsuccessful"

Several years ago, my brothers and I decided to try our hands and paddles at deep-sea, kayak fishing. Many hours were spent gathering information online and materials at various stores, and on a designated day, we woke ridiculously early, drove to the west side of the island, and embarked on our journey from the boat harbor to the deep blue water approximately a mile and a half offshore. The water was perfect, with hardly a cloud in the sky, and at times the ocean's surface seemed surreal, glossy, and opaque, like molten silver. We could taste the anticipation like the salt in the air, and it seemed we were going to make family history by catching our biggest fish ever. But alas, we fished all morning without a single bite. Visions of reeling in good-sized "pelagics" —*mahi mahi*, wahoo, or tuna—filled our heads, but during the entire trip, our bait remained completely untouched.

At that time, being in the middle of writing this chapter, I found myself trying to learn the value of being happy in the moment. I felt an ongoing discrepancy between the dream of hearing our reels scream with a strike and the unavoidable awareness of no such sound, no such strike, and, ultimately, no such fish. We had a great time, but it was difficult to escape the notion that the time would have been *greater* had we hooked and landed a fish.

This seemed obvious even several days after the fishing trip.

---

26  I want to affirm Keri's extraordinary patience as my wife as a major reason she and I can continue to indulge these interventions. I further appreciate her openness to me sharing about our relationship experiences and her forgiveness for the times I can be downright difficult (the former hinging, to use her word, on me "knowing" the latter!).

Nonetheless, this suggested a survival paradigm of emotions at work. In some ways, survival mode was inevitable because fishing is particularly about being skilled at a certain situation, namely catching fish. Still, even when situations are central and the objective facts inescapable (no fish were caught that day), there was still the potential for us to put *subjective layers* of opinion and meaning on the facts. So, it was interesting and worthwhile for me to look for reasons to be happy *before* any fish took our bait, which happened to characterize the duration of our kayaking trip!

This meant putting my attention on those things that might still be considered *gains* . . . on all that I *did* have at any given moment of the trip. Time with my brothers. A pristine morning with peaceful waters. Sunshine. The opportunity to exercise. Occasions to chase seabirds apparently tracking smaller fish. The anticipation of the *possibility* of catching a whopper. Even the thrill of seeing several whales.

Ironically, for me, because we never actually hooked up with any fish, none of these "simpler pleasures" were overshadowed. In fact, at the risk of sounding ridiculous, not catching fish somehow preserved the opportunity to find a certain happiness that was within personal reach rather than having to wait for certain circumstances to occur. When viewed this way, not catching fish took on a sense of very subtle gain, and so a new, albeit similarly subtle sense of happiness was felt. Perhaps this is one reason anglers are fond of saying, "That's why we call it *fishing* instead of catching!"[27]

### The Challenge and Contradiction of Happiness

The second application of our thrival paradigm for emotions is yet another paradox: *On the ocean of relationships, the challenge and contradiction of happiness is this—if we want to please people, it is important to first let them be "upset."*

---

27   It seems important to note that while I was probably the least disappointed of all my brothers that day, they are also all much better fishermen than I am. And, there is likely a strong correlation between them directly associating happiness with catching fish (rather than just the meaning of fishing) and their commitment to developing their skills. Since that day, they have gone on to become quite successful ocean kayak fishermen, hooking and landing a variety of "whoppers," and I will readily agree that the result has clearly been more "fun" than just "fishing instead of catching!"

As surprising as this may sound, this principle traces back to rather ancient writings. For example, consider the parables attributed to Aesop, a Greek fable writer who is thought to have lived around the sixth century before Christ. In one particular fable, Aesop details the efforts of a man and his son who, while walking their donkey to the market, try to accommodate the criticisms of various people. While the journey begins with the man and his son walking beside their donkey, it soon involves the man and his son taking turns riding the donkey, depending on the feedback they hear from the different people they encounter. When these efforts are still criticized, the man and his boy both sit on the donkey at the same time, only to be scolded again. This leads to them both carrying the donkey, only to drop their animal into a river when trying to cross a bridge, thus losing the donkey altogether. According to Aesop, the moral of this fable is sobering—*Please all, and you will please none.*[28]

*Pizza, Puzzle Pieces, and Epiphany*

I first heard this fable as a child, and I continue to grow in my understanding of it. In fact, allowing others to be upset is a concept I am still very much in the process of learning. From an early age, I also learned the value of being a "people-pleaser." Indeed, one of my earliest memories, from first grade, is of "saving" a class pizza party by confessing that I was responsible for throwing away some perfectly good food. As a class, we were all excited about the party until our teacher found half an apple, wrapped in aluminum foil, in the wastebasket. She informed us that the party would be canceled if nobody accepted responsibility for the apple, presumably because she did not want good food like apples and pizza to be wasted. So, I stepped forward and ate the apple, we had the party, and everyone was happy. It is a pleasant memory for me overall, with one small caveat: I had not thrown the apple away in the first place.

I had taken responsibility for something that was not mine, and I, along with the rest of the class, had benefited. It was a formative experience for me in "keeping the peace," and I remember it helping me to find favor with my teacher even though I had, in fact, lied to her by saying it was my apple. I never found out if she knew the truth, though I think it was

---

28  Aesop (6th Century B.C.). The man, the boy, and the donkey. In Bartleby.com. Retrieved June 6, 2020 from https://www.bartleby.com/17/1/62.html

reported to my parents as an example of something good I had done for the class. Either way, I learned that there were rewards for putting myself out for the sake of others' happiness, and I continued along the path of striving to please others.

Fast-forward to my second year of graduate school and my first experience working as a clinical intern for a community counseling center. One memorable day, a supervisor I will call Mary made a comment that caught me by surprise.

"Brian, you're a nice guy," she said.

"Thank you, Mary," I replied, feeling good about what now had become the very familiar pleasure of hearing others' approval.

"I didn't mean it as a compliment," she smiled, as she watched the appreciation on my face turn to what must have looked like a pile of assorted puzzle pieces.

"Oh, then how did you mean it?" I timidly ventured.

In that moment of disorientation, I do not recall Mary's explanation, but I do remember her giving me something. It was a copy of an article from a periodical with a title that caught my attention—something like, "How Being Nice Can Be a Form of Controlling Others." Skeptical, I took the article home and read and reread it. And, after wrestling with the content, I came to the troubling conclusion that much of my life may have in fact been characterized by controlling others or at least inadvertently trying to. This was troubling because I had sought to live for the promotion of others' happiness, precisely because I did not want to be inconsiderate, mean, or of course, controlling. Nonetheless, I now see that even though I do not think I was being inconsiderate or mean, I was, unwittingly, being rather controlling. How? According to the article, I was being controlling because by doing whatever I could to make and keep others happy, I was not allowing them to be upset.

This experience as an intern was an epiphany but not yet a full paradigm shift for me. I continued my formal study of psychology for another seven years, but all the while continued to feel unevenly matched with my own people-pleasing tendencies. Other supervisors and professors would give me comments that reminded me of Mary's initial comment. I would even experience tensions in relationships related to my own desire to keep the peace that inevitably led me to overcommit and overextend myself. In addition, I engaged in ongoing confrontations with what I have come to call the two "cousins" of people pleasing: perfectionism and procrastination.[29] And then, one day, I experienced my own "drop in the bucket." One drop. Maybe two. And the drops continued to fall, until at some point, they began spilling over the container. My own ocean of relationships would never be the same again.

*Splashes of Insight*
Like simple water droplets, the initial change was subtle, without any fanfare or any differences that would have been observable to others. And like the first lesson, this change occurred in the context of my work as a counselor. By this time, I had begun my own private practice as a psychologist, and I was working with a specific client to address challenges related to her experiences with anxiety and people-pleasing. Together, we were discussing a book she was reading about these topics, and as I thumbed through the book, I thought to myself *What really is the problem with being compelled to please others? How could something so good make life so difficult?*

Answers eluded me for a while, until a simple logic provided me with an explanation that, at the time, seemed almost too basic and yet for me, it continues to be profound. I am sure that others have written about this, but in all of twelve years of my undergraduate and graduate training in psychology, I do not recall ever seeing or hearing it articulated in the way that struck me that day. The trajectory of the logic went like this:

*1) If feelings are determined largely by our thinking (one way to explain emotions as a personal responsibility), then each person essentially has control over what they*

---

29  In my experience, these are "cousins" of people-pleasing tendencies because both can also be traced back to reactive understandings of happiness involving certain external requirements. Perfectionism binds happiness to an absence of mistakes, and procrastination binds happiness to immediate gratification. As such, more emotionally responsive strategies can also help both, including rethinking our conditions for happiness and the ways happiness may not always be as necessary as we think.

*feel.*
*2) If this relates to negative emotions, then it must also relate to positive ones, such as happiness.*
*3) Further, if I am responsible for my own happiness, it must follow that others are responsible for theirs.*
*4) Therefore, if these premises are true, pleasing others, i.e making others happy, is not only difficult, it is impossible!*

This droplet splashed into my bucket like the first sign of a coming rainstorm. It occurred to me that I had essentially been basing my whole approach to relationships on an illusion. I was investing my energy in something that could never be.

Shortly after this first droplet fell, the second one followed, with similar force and eye-opening potential. I had repeatedly been told, "You can't please everybody." But, if it was true that it was literally impossible to please others, then not only could I not please *everybody* . . . I could also not please *anybody*!

*Snowboards and Smiles*
There is strange liberation in being able to see something for the first time, or at least with new eyes. I am reminded of the first time I tried snowboarding. I had been struggling to understand how to stand up, keep my balance, shift my weight, and of course, fall. And falling was certainly an integral part of the package. But there was a distinct point in that first day of snowboarding when I realized I was falling much more than necessary, maybe more than most beginners. My brother, Jeremy, pointed out to me that I needed to position my board differently. For some reason I had been pointing the wrong side of the board down the mountain. Once I made a simple adjustment and faced the other side of the board downhill, the whole experience changed for me. To be sure, I still fell and felt like the mountain gave me a beating, but the falls were more predictable and the rides much more enjoyable. It was, quite literally, a pivotal moment for me.

---

**"...the principle of allowing others to be upset also extends to our own feelings towards ourselves."**

In the same way, my new awareness of the *impossibility* of being the source of others' happiness was also a turning point, a pivotal moment, for me. I now had a way of making sense of seemingly untenable situations, a way out of apparent dilemmas, and a way into deeper relationships.

Admittedly, it is not an easy way, but, ironically, I believe it is a way that minimizes the difficulties that could quite easily occur. This is not to say that my people-pleasing tendencies are not still with me. In fact, they are very strong and still very much a default—in part because the number of years I have relied on them far exceeds the number of years I have not. In addition, there is something very decent about wanting others to be happy. Still, there is a significant difference between wanting something and making sure that it happens. Nevertheless, a new logic is taking root. And as with my snowboarding experience, not only are my falls more predictable, but the rides are also much more enjoyable—and both are happening as I am decreasingly inclined to "believe" that the pressure to *make* others happy is practical.

Of course, the principle of allowing others to be upset also extends to our own feelings towards ourselves. When survival is not at stake, it is important and valuable to also allow ourselves to be upset. It may sound strange, but as we do this, we will find freedom, because when we are honest about our disappointments and frustrations, we align ourselves with reality, which is a position vital for personal emotional health. Also, we make it possible for others to see who we really are, which is a position vital for interpersonal closeness. On the ocean of relationships, both are necessary because caring for both ourselves and for others is essential.

Allowing ourselves to be upset may not seem a good strategy for deepening a relationship. Many of us are familiar with the words of another classic song that recommends, "Smile, when your heart is aching..." The idea is that a cheerful outlook on life, even when life is hard, is the way to retain a sense of hope and optimism that will eventually lead to seeing "the sun come shining through."[30] Or, as another tune suggests, "when you're smiling, the whole world smiles with you."[31]

These are certainly inspiring words which imply we can choose both how we feel and influence our situations—I like to sing them myself and experience their uplifting qualities. At the same time, they assume happiness is good and other emotions are bad, and this assumption is ultimately not conducive to deepening our relationships. Instead, emotional connection hinges upon our ability to value the entire range of our emotions.

*The Freedom to Feel*

Many of us are so accustomed to paying attention to others' happiness, that we do not realize the energy we spend masking our own negative feelings. Slipping in and out of smiles and affected tones occurs with such ease that we hardly notice what we are doing. A moment's reflection, however, reminds us that those who see us when we are not happy are those who know us best. This is, of course, part of the challenging and contradictory nature of happiness. When we can allow ourselves to be upset with others (and vice versa) in healthy ways, we can connect more deeply with them. The challenge is to experience negative emotions with one another in respectful, measured ways.

Such respect begins with tracing our feelings back to our thoughts. Whether we are unhappy with others, they are unhappy with us, or we are unhappy with ourselves, linking feelings to thoughts gives us options for being able to find our own happiness through modifying our own approaches to processing difficult information.

And, here, of course, the operative word is "difficult." At some level, challenges and contradictions *are* difficult—they are difficult to understand, difficult to work with, difficult to accept. Still, as we have seen, true acceptance of what is difficult is integral to interpersonal health, especially insofar as it is

---

30   The song, Smile, was originally composed by Charlie Chaplin in 1936 and lyrics were added in 1954 by John Turner and Geoffrey Parsons. The song with lyrics was first recorded by Nat King Cole in 1954. Retrieved January 18, 2020 from http://www.ednapurviance. org/chaplininfo/smile.html

31   The song, When You're Smiling, was originally written by Larry Shay, Mark Fisher, and Joe Goodwin and made popular by Louis Armstrong who first recorded it in 1929. Retrieved January 18, 2020 from http://musichealth.net/songs1/when-youre-smiling/

part of aligning ourselves with reality. We can allow ourselves and others to be upset precisely because every individual is responsible for their own emotions.

The freedom to have uncomfortable, negative, or unwanted feelings, is just as important as the freedom to have feelings that are comfortable, positive, and desirable. In a society enamored with "feeling good," this might seem counterproductive. However, another brief pause suggests otherwise. In fact, we might consider how openness to less-desirable emotions is actually a necessary condition for our cherished, "self-evident" claim, that all are "created equal and are endowed by their Creator with certain inalienable rights, among them . . . the pursuit of happiness."[32]

The pursuit of happiness *includes* the range of forlornness and fatigue and frustration and fury that we inevitably feel along the way. In fact, any effort to escape or avoid these and other difficult feelings risks thwarting happiness. Conversely, when troubling emotions are processed well, more happiness becomes available. This dual process, like blood-flow in and out of the human heart, forms a rhythm that is central to emotional vitality. And, in fact, as we will see, our ability to both experience and process negative or difficult emotions, lays the groundwork not only for happiness but for joy as well.

## The Direction of Happiness

The 2011 documentary film *Happy* begins with the story of a young rickshaw driver from India named Manoj Singh who cheerfully appreciates his life despite the challenges he faces. He shares:

> *In the summer, my feet and head burn in the heat of the sun. It is painful. But winter and the monsoons do not bother me. Even if my clothes get soaked with rain, I know they will dry when I run with a passenger. My home is good. One side is open, and air flows into the room nicely. A plastic tarp covers the exterior, but one side has a window. During the monsoon, we have some*

32  U. S. Declaration of Independence. Paragraph 2 (1776).

*trouble with rain blowing inside. Except for this we live well. When I return home in the afternoon, my son is sitting at that tea shop and waiting for my return, and when he calls out to me 'Baba!' I am full of joy. When I see my child's face, I feel very happy. I feel that I am not poor, but I am the richest person. Sometimes we eat only rice with salt, but still we are happy. My neighbors are good. We stay together and that makes us happy. We are all friends!*[33]

Even though Manoj doesn't specifically say this, it seems to me that his words point to how he is a very "thankful" person. Similarly, we might say that the final principle for happiness, suggested by a thrival paradigm of emotions, is this: *On the ocean of relationships, gratitude is the ultimate direction of happiness.*

*Direction and Essence*

When we consider some of the other principles already discussed, gratitude captures the essence of interpersonal happiness. First, happiness is about gain, and when we experience good gains, the natural, or at least healthy response, is to be thankful. Second, if the location of happiness is in our interpretation(s) of what is happening here and now, then the focus becomes what *is* currently experienced rather than what is not experienced. And when we put our mind on something that is in existence that is also good, we again have room for gratitude. Further, if relationships are more about the journey than the destination, our focus can shift to the ways in which others are fellow travelers rather than just means to an end. Thus, we embrace any interpersonal event as an opportunity and shift away from the unintended tendencies we can have to see "different" people as obligations or burdens.

To say that gratitude is the ultimate direction of happiness is to say that happiness is felt to whatever extent a person can identify some object of appreciation. In oceanspeak, this ability to appreciate is our doorway to the Pacific, and it can apply at any given time. And once we are in these warm waters, our explorations of this area of the ocean only widen, lengthen, and

---

33   From Happy (2011), written and directed by Roko Belic and produced by Emotional Content, Iris Films, and Wadi Rumi Films.

deepen as our appreciations grow. Gratitude, as the principal direction of happiness, is also deeply multidimensional.

And, on the ocean of relationships, the many-dimensioned recipients of our appreciation are . . . *people.* Fellow human beings. With hopes and dreams and sorrows and pains every bit as real as our own. A primary problem, however, is our inclination to attribute our own dissatisfactions to people directly.

When we do this, when we treat people as the "reasons" for our dissatisfactions, we essentially attach our emotions to people and detach our emotions from reason. Separated from reason, emotions ironically become occasions for a sort of over-and-under-thinking. People overthink, or think too much *for others* and underthink, or think too little *for themselves.* These dynamics, among other things, are sure routes to *unhappiness,* since there is likely no sense of gain accomplished when people are treated like problems to be solved or when people are prevented from thinking for themselves. Ultimately, when one person determines another person's emotions, it leads to forgetting our common ground as fellow persons and our unique personhood as individuals.

*Unearned and Given*
Gratitude, like a gentle reminder, whispers a different way. There is a saying, made popular by the animated film, *Kung Fu Panda,* which is helpful for pointing out the nature of this way:

*Yesterday's history.*
*Tomorrow's a mystery.*
*Today is a gift—that's why we call it the present.*[34]

Embedded in this simple, familiar statement, is a gem of limitless value—the reminder that today, and, in fact, this very moment, is a gift. Something to be received. Unwrapped. Opened. Experienced and possibly, enjoyed. A present. *The* present.

---

34  From Kung Fu Panda (2008), written by Jonathan Aibel, Glenn Berger, Ethan Reiff, and Cyrus Voris, directed by Mark Osborne and John Stevenson and produced by Dream-Works Animation and Pacific Data Images (PDI).

If we will allow it, this approach to whatever is going on right now can become for us a sort of compass that points toward happiness. A beacon on the ocean of relationships. A reliable North Star for finding our way back to the Pacific, most any time. There are two characteristics of gifts that can help us make this connection. The first is that a gift is *unearned*. Nothing is done to merit it.

This returns us to the concept of grace which plays such an important role in doing away with a need for striving and in shifting from surviving to thriving. The pressure is off.[35]

Seeing life and relationships through the prism of grace therefore allows people to be themselves with each other. And room to breathe means more life can flow back and forth.

Of course, mistakes and hurts will still occur, and personal efforts will still be vital to the growth and maturity of the relationship. However, seeing the whole situation as a gift provides a larger context for whatever may be occurring at the time.

Another description for this larger context is the "bigger picture." And here, the bigger picture that emerges is the sense that something more is available if only we will have the eyes to see. Not surprisingly, the way we "zoom out" to see this larger perspective is to consider the possibility that the meaning of a situation is even more important than the situation itself. Once we take this view, we are afforded a remarkable new vista. *Feelings themselves*, positive or negative, become gifts, and relationships become opportunities to bless and be blessed.

In addition to being unearned, gifts are also *given*. This presupposes a *giver* of the gift in the first place, and this at once makes the situation much more personal. There is an intention when one person gives something to another. Gifts are not accidental. A gift is different from an experience that comes about by luck or chance or even coincidence. And while there can certainly be a sense of appreciation for lucky or fortuitous

---

35   I want to acknowledge psychologist and author Larry Crabb for the connection between grace and the idea that "the pressure is off" (this specifically occurs in his discussions with Dallas Willard and John Ortberg in the video curriculum for Dallas' Willard's Renovation of the Heart (2002, LifeSprings Resources).

circumstances, it seems there is a line between such appreciation and what we are calling gratitude. After all, what or who is there to thank if good things are encountered as a matter of mere happenstance? And if there is no one or nothing to thank, then how can one be thankful? To fully recognize the present moment or person before us, requires some acknowledgement of the goodness and generosity behind the gift itself.

In relationships, the "givenness" of whatever is going on can become for us a moment-by-moment opportunity to experience gratitude. There are two implications of this. First, relationship dynamics themselves might be considered gifts to us from whomever we are interacting with at the time. Whatever the other person does can become a catalyst for new growth and maturity. This will especially be the case to the extent that our feelings point us toward a healthy examination of ourselves instead of a controlling sort of scrutiny of others.

Second, as we grow in gratefulness for various positive and negative facets of our relationships, we experience the potential for a new baseline and ultimately a new sense of what we might consider "normal." When interpersonal circumstances are viewed as opportunities and our emotions are seen as gifts, new assumptions can be made about the very things that once led to conflict or frustration. And when this happens, we can, both literally and figuratively, regard the details of our relationships as "givens," only with more acceptance and less resignation.

Even as I move forward with implementing this principle in my own life, I find that it is again a tough sell. It is very challenging to think of relationship difficulties in the same categories as gifts and generosity. In fact, some might call this kind of thinking delusional (I continue to find myself wondering if my ideas qualify for this at times). I would like to suggest, however, that these reservations, while valid, simultaneously point to survival or situation-focused ways of thinking. Inevitably, if we trace relationship "problems" back to their source, we will find certain assumptions at work: that feelings are determined by incidents rather than thoughts; that negative feelings are problems rather than resources; and that agreement is prioritized over understanding. Moreover, while seeing relationship problems as gifts is difficult, it is quite another thing to say that this means such thinking is delusional. Indeed, we might say that the very idea that something is "difficult" means it is not impossible.

## Grace and Choice

At some point, gratitude has the advantage of returning our relationships to themes of grace and choice. It returns us to grace because we realize that everything we have has been given to us. And it returns us to our choices because gifts are experienced if, and only if, they are received. And when we choose to receive a relationship itself as a gift, the relationship becomes that much more personal. We begin to see ourselves and others through a new lens and one that better captures the remarkable complexity of everyone. The relationship then becomes a primary vehicle for helping us to feel we are truly living rather than just existing. Slowly but surely, relationship dynamics themselves become an integral aspect of an all-encompassing generosity.

Again, as a Christian, the story of Jesus seems to me the epitome of such generosity. And, since it points to principles that undergird the thesis of this book, one passage from the Bible is important to note. The apostle Paul, in his letter to the church at Rome, explains the ultimate accomplishment of grace:

*"For the wages of sin is death, but the free gift of God is eternal life in Christ Jesus our Lord."*[36]

While a full explanation of this teaching could become a separate book, suffice it to say that in these words we have the potential for an entirely different quality of life. Another paradigm shift. A subtle yet radical move from one way of thinking to another—and one that might transform our understanding of happiness and relationships altogether.

One droplet, maybe two. From wages to gift. Earning to grace. Death to life. Why is this important, indeed vital, to our discussion? Because relationships are central to life, and more specifically, to having meaningful lives. Because relationships are an apparent priority for even God, and nowhere is this more evident than in God's own trinitarian nature and the provision of Jesus who, in this passage, is here declared to be the source of undying, eternal life and meaningful living.

36  Romans 6:23 (ESV, NIV)

And because, in this passage, we have the epitome of the very transformations this book seeks to explore for relationships in general—transformations from fear to hope; from obligation to opportunity,[37] and from basic survival to true thriving.

And the catalyst for such transformation is none other than a gift.

Again, when we look at relationships as a gift, we go deeper. To return to previous chapters, we not only plunge into the waters of the Pacific, we have the potential to experience the mysteries of the ocean's deepest depths. We gain access to emotional equivalents of the Marianas Trench and Challenger Deep, only more unfathomable in the best sense of the word.

*Becoming and Belonging*

In fact, I would like to suggest that when we consider relationships and all their dynamics, positive or negative, as part and parcel of the larger gift of life, we go beyond even happiness. For when we can be persuaded, and indeed convinced, that all of life is given, then we move from happiness to...joy. The difference between these two might be regarded as the difference between a gain and a gift, between having and receiving, and between getting and giving. And if we think about it, in relationships, joy comes when people become, for one another, the very personification of acceptance and grace.

This kind of becoming is both non-possessive and empowering. In the language of the hymn writers, joy can be found in a sense of *belonging* to another "just as I am,"[38] and most especially, in the welcome of the Creator God, who Himself is "our eternal Home."[39] It is also important to acknowledge that this joy is not independent of trouble, though this need not surprise us since we are seeking the kind of emotional "fitness"

---

37  Interestingly, earlier in his letter, the apostle Paul directly associates wages with obligations, saying, "Now to the one who works, wages are not credited as a gift but as an obligation . . ." (Romans 4:4 (NIV)).

38  The specific hymn, "Just as I am" was originally written by Charlotte Elliot in 1835 and was first published and put to William B. Bradbury's tune "Woodworth" in 1849. Retrieved January 18, 2020 from http://www.hymntime.com/tch/htm/j/u/s/justasam.htm

39  From the hymn, "Our God, Our Help in Ages Past," written by Isaac Watts in 1719 to the tune composed by William Croft in 1708. Retrieved on January 18, 2020, from https://hymnary.org/hymn/PsH/170

that traces back to interpretations (thoughts) rather than situations (incidents) per se. Again, the waters of the Pacific can often be experienced as a twofold reality, "resting uneasily," on the ocean of relationships. And, ultimately, joy intertwines with freedom—to form the double-stranded DNA of our very humanity and the twofold goal of deeper relationships.

This concludes our exploration of the emotion of happiness and three strategies that can make it less elusive in our lives. Perhaps we can think of these as the three "least common denominators" (hence, Location, Challenge, and Direction) that, certainly, have their difficulties and so will no doubt be "easier said than done." Nonetheless, I am here proposing the most modest and simple of strategies for overcoming these odds: to examine some of the smallest units of meaning available to us, namely, our very words. If our words can be embraced as having this much importance, then we can begin our own deeper exploration of what we are telling ourselves and what we truly believe. And in so doing, we may possibly find happiness to be not only less elusive but also more accessible.

To review, we can do this first by asking ourselves if it is really the situation or our interpretation that is primarily determining our feelings. Second, we can consider that, in relationships, because emotions are not a matter of survival, it is our interpretation that has the most impact. Third, we can sincerely look for interpretations that point to ways of identifying different gains that any situation might present. And fourth, we can open ourselves to the possibility that such gains might even be . . . *presents*—gifts, opportunities—sometimes blessings in disguise, with the potential for longer-term benefits, including deeper, closer relationships. Of course, these claims will have their critics, and it is important to take them seriously. After all, to the extent that this discussion points to something true, it could also lead to significant changes in the ways we approach our relationships and our lives. And any discussion of change eventually can raise awareness of our fourth and final category of emotion—fear.

CHAPTER 11: INDIAN | 211

# Chapter 11: Indian

*The cave you fear to enter holds the treasure you seek.*
*Joseph Campbell*

We turn now to the final emotional frontier of our exploration, fear. In this case, we also arrive at the Indian Ocean as the last remaining metaphor for this part of our discussion. The pairing of fear and the Indian Ocean is entirely coincidental, though it is important to note that this is the only ocean named for a country, and it is a country that has rich connections to the ocean historically, spiritually, economically, and emotionally. Interestingly, one ancient Sanskrit word for the Indian Ocean is *Ratnākara*, meaning "the treasure-house of jewels."[1]

Treasure house of jewels and fear. We are not likely to think of these together. Still, I would like to suggest that, when we apply our current model of emotions to relationships, fear can become a catalyst that releases additional gems, which are indispensable to our journey. Let us take some time to consider these treasures.

## Befriending Fear

*Venomous and Benign*
Again, we are probably not inclined to think of fear as an experience that yields riches or wealth. In fact, our first approach will likely be characterized by some type of avoidance. We may think of monsters or heights, spiders and closed spaces, or other types of phobias. Perhaps we will recall President Franklin D.

---

1  Devaraja, N. D. (1967). The mind and spirit of India. Delhi, India: Motilal Banarsidass, p. 108.

Roosevelt's timeless assertion that "the only thing we have to fear is fear itself." Some may even be drawn to the motivational acronym that suggests that fear stands for "False Evidence Appearing Real."[2] In each instance, fear is painted as a *problem* that itself must be addressed. Very often, fear is viewed as a foe or an adversary to be shunned, defeated, or overcome.

This tendency is both reasonable and ironic. On one hand, fear does not feel good, and it can mean that a legitimate problem exists. We naturally want to eliminate fear, and there is something very important and good about this, because we do well to steer clear of harmful situations. On another hand, from a behavioral perspective, avoidance can often be a form of "negative reinforcement" which means that the act of staying away from the feared object will likely lead to relief. This, in turn, will lead to the fear continuing, even if what is feared is not bad per se. This is how anxieties, aversions, and phobias are helped along, since fear has the last word every time avoidance takes place.

Let us look further into how these things can happen. Take, for instance, a fear of snakes, which results in an avoidance of snakes. We can call this kind of fear of snakes a reactive understanding of emotion in that the apparent cause of the fear (i.e., the snake) is external to the person. It is the incident. This can further be a survival approach to emotion since 1) fear as a negative emotion is treated as a problem and 2) the strategies for solving the problem involve directly addressing the feared object by either fighting the snake, fleeing from it, or freezing in its presence. The outcome of all of this is that the fear results in a competitive solution, where an individual strives to be more "fit" than the incident by somehow acting upon the circumstances rather than by thinking differently.

In the case of snakes, the competitive approach would be vital if one were confronting, say, a cobra, and much less necessary if faced with, say, a garter snake. And, in the case of relationships, it is remarkable how often it can seem like the threats we are dealing with are more like vipers rather than like

---

2   This is one of many acronyms for "FEAR" that is used in Alcoholics Anonymous recovery groups. For a more comprehensive list of these and other acronyms, see http://www.barefootsworld.net/aaacronyms.html, retrieved January 19, 2018.

the more harmless "garden varieties."

I can think of several situations in my own life that are ongoing, where I feel an anxious discomfort with certain people. These people are, I believe, very well-intentioned and do not want me to be uncomfortable. Interestingly, the ways that they "scare" me are equally part of their good intentions—gestures such as advice, innuendo, or even humor, all seem to simultaneously get in under my radar and activate my defenses. Of course, it is not just advice, innuendo, or humor that evoke my guardedness. For me, the red flags are raised when it seems another person is criticizing, scolding, or somehow disappointed with me. The operative word here is "somehow." I think I can take it when a person tells me that they are disappointed with me, because when people own our own emotions, relationships have room to breathe. It is the guesswork that feels unsafe. Perhaps because I have become so passionate about the themes in this book or perhaps because of a deeper sort of intuition, I feel unsettled when I think another person is attributing *their* feelings to *me*. It amounts to the proverbial "guilt trip," and I am increasingly interested in opting out of *that* ride.

However, if I leave it there, I will potentially miss out on my own opportunity to respond rather than react. Again, survival mode is a rather tenacious tendency! In the words of Wordsworth, the "world" is still very much "with" me.[3] And, in the words of the apostle Paul, I am seeking to "not be conformed to the pattern of this world" but rather to "be transformed by the renewing of (my) mind."[4] So, as we embark on this particular region of the ocean, I am challenging myself, as much as anyone, to rethink my own assumptions about "fear itself" with the intention of experiencing even more freedom and joy in relationships.

*Anticipation and Assumption*
Let us return to the final letters in our MSGS and FLGT acronyms. When it comes to fear, the final letters in each acronym, S and T, suggest a correspondence between the feeling

---

3  Wordsworth, W. (1807). Poems in Two Volumes (1st ed.). London: Longman, Hurst, Rees, and Ormes, Paternoster Row. Retrieved January 18, 2020, from http://www.potw.org/archive/potw44.html

4  Romans 12:2

of being *scared* and an experience with anything that might constitute a *threat*. For the sake of discussion, let us regard threat as the possibility of something bad happening. Two important implications of fear emerge: first, fear is *anticipated* in that it is primarily concerned with the future and second, fear operates on the *assumption* that things will not go well. In ways that might not be immediately obvious, these two characteristics provide key information about fear that will help us to both navigate it and utilize it to our advantage.

---

## "As future-focused as it is, fear can come to fill our hearts and deprive us of the present."

---

The anticipatory nature of fear means our imagination is inevitably involved. In our "mind's eye," we prepare for some scenario that is either expected or projected to be, in varying degrees, less than ideal. Sometimes we are not conscious of this, and our preparation manifests in our bodies before reaching our awareness. So-called "lumps" in our throats, "pits" in our stomachs, and "butterflies" can be relatively subtle signals that something is amiss. At other times, the prospect of something bad happening is more obvious and vivid. With extraordinary amounts of detail and flair we can convince ourselves that disastrous outcomes will occur, even to the point of outright paranoia. As future-focused as it is, fear can come to fill our hearts and deprive us of the present. When this happens, it makes sense to say that fear has become "self-fulfilling." In these ways, fear's anticipatory nature can certainly work against us.

Fear can feel very much like a trap. The built-in sense of threat means that whatever lies ahead is coiled and ready to snap. A suspended sense of tension hangs in the air, and, in one way or another, freedom is at stake. This already-but-not-yet, drawn-and-ready-to-close-in quality of fear leads me to associate it with a sense of *pressure*. Whereas sadness feels *heavy* and anger parallels being *against* something, fear exerts a type of force upon us that simultaneously pushes down and pulls us in. Whether tugging and gnawing like the jaws of a pesky animal or looming ominously like some vortex ready to envelop our entire being, fear presses in upon us and vies, sometimes relentlessly, for our attention.

But even as the anticipatory nature of fear points to conditions that contain some amount of threat, deeper understandings of this dynamic can point to ways fear can also be harnessed, utilized, and even befriended to become an ally instead of a foe. Let us consider these details, especially as they pertain to both the importance of living in line with reality and the potentially protective nature of fear.

*Make-Believe Alligators and Misleading Assumptions*
As we have already discussed, anticipation refers to the future. This points to the undetermined and essentially unknown nature of fear, and even more importantly, to the risk of focusing on an as yet *un-real* outcome, since, at any given moment, the future is still a non-event. Thus, fear risks living apart from what is real, and, as we have already seen, this sets the stage for understandable but unnecessary problems. In relationships, this is especially the case since the ostensible threat is another person. When people are experienced as the reason for our feelings, it is important to consider the role of our interpretations. Let us remember though that in relationships, fear often pertains to "nonvenomous snakes."

In addition, self-protection is the whole reason we are inclined to anticipate threat in the first place. Thus, we want to ensure that whatever we fear is appropriately addressed. In relationships, fear exists to protect us rather than to harm us. And so, if relationships are about more rather than less depth with others, fear, among other emotions, will be utilized to the extent that it promotes more, rather than less, understanding. Ironically, in relationships, fear will be effective to the extent that it protects us from overprotection.[5]

This returns us to the second facet of fear, namely that it operates on the *assumption* that things will not go well. This assumptive quality of fear can serve to remind us of another

5   While this book focuses on minimizing unnecessary difficulties in relationships, actual dangers are always important to consider and discern. For an invaluable resource on how listening to fear can protect against actual life-threatening circumstances, please see: De Becker, G. (1997). The gift of fear: Survival signals that protect us from violence. New York, NY: Dell Publishing.

simple yet vital principle:

*In relationships, threat does not necessarily mean danger.*

Another brief story from our family comes to mind. Some years ago, we were spending some time at a relative's house and getting ready for the drive home, and the following conversation between my child and me ensued:

*"Please use the restroom and brush your teeth, so that you can fall asleep in the car and we can just tuck you into your bed when we get home, without having to wake you."*
*"Oh Daddy, I don't want to use the restroom."*
*"Why not, honey?"*
*"Because I'm scared."*
*"That sounds uncomfortable. Why are you scared, darling?"*
*"Because there are alligators in the bathroom!"*
*"Oh, that sounds frightening! How do you know that there are alligators in the bathroom?"*
*"Because I'm scared..."*

This type of logic, technically called "emotional reasoning,"[6] illustrates how fear can operate on the assumption that threat means danger. However, in relationships, we can say that such an assumption is almost always misleading. Unless the person we are relating to is physically about to harm us or physically about to be harmed, fear can point us to our interpretation of them rather than to them per se. So, as with other feelings, once we shift to focusing on our interpretation rather than our situation, we are positioned for fear to work for rather than against us.

*Crossing an Apparent Impasse*
Let us consider a very general example of how this principle might work in a relationship. Suppose both person A and person B are at a crossroad in their relationship, and A is afraid

6  Burns, D. D. (1981). Feeling good: The new mood therapy. New York, NY: Penguin Books. For two excellent applications of Burns' work to Christianity and mental health, see McMinn, M. R. (2008) Cognitive therapy techniques in Christian counseling. Eugene, OR: Wipf and Stock Publishers and Tan, S.-Y. and Ortberg, J. (2005). Coping with depression. Grand Rapids, MI: Baker Books.

of repeating the past while B is afraid of missing out on the future. This can happen in various ways. For example, imagine A feels hurt by B's lack of commitment or fidelity, and B believes time will heal and now wants to move on. In such situations, both parties often feel stuck or unable to move beyond an apparent impasse. A will likely be hindered by their desire to protect against something familiar, and B will be blocked by concerns about losing out on opportunities to come. How then to move forward? How to make progress without slipping into either unhealthy regression or unhelpful digression from the relationship?

As technical as it seems, what if we first consider what it means to say the *relationship* is the context for the fear? If we can allow this to have meaning, it might create other options. At this point in the book, reiterating these steps might seem unnecessary. If so, let us further consider that repetition is key to practice and practice is key to training our minds to think and ultimately believe differently about our circumstances. And if we are correct in our theory that relationships are essentially *not* a survival context for emotions (there is no imminent physical danger to either party), seemingly tedious repetition might be a part of aligning ourselves with reality that leads to even deeper relationship.

So, suppose both A and B begin to entertain the notion that they are afraid not of a specific outcome per se but of what they think about what that outcome might mean. Suppose they start to explore their ideas about either repeating the past or missing out on the future. Suppose they allow themselves to make interpretations as important, if not more important, than situations.

Our thesis suggests that beginning to entertain this way of thinking would be the beginning of something new. And if allowed to continue, the new trajectory could lead to new discoveries altogether. In relationships, such a shift could then move the whole paradigm.

Because relationships need space to thrive, opening ourselves to the power of ideas can create that space. In relationships, moving from facts to opinions, allows for others to have their opinions, and further, it puts the focus on a cooperative rather than competitive arrangement. Even more, this move can allow the emotion to stand as the emotion is being processed. When it comes to fear, this can particularly take some of the pressure off, while simultaneously revealing the ways in which certain pressure can also be valuable.

So, as an example, A starts to think about what repeating the past might mean, and B starts to think about what missing the future might mean. And as both experience the connections between their thinking and feeling, we can imagine the following conversation:

**A:** *I'm afraid of making this decision because I think that if we try to move forward from here we will only go backward.*

**B:** *Going backward would be unacceptable to you.*

**A:** *Well, I think so.*

**B:** *You're not sure. It might be different but you're afraid that it will be bad.*

**A:** *Yeah, what happened earlier was just so painful.*

**B:** *You think it would be more painful than what we're experiencing right now.*

**A:** *Well, yeah, otherwise I wouldn't be hesitating with this decision. What do you think?*

**B:** *Thanks for asking. I'm concerned too—for me, it's just I don't want to miss what's possible. I think that would be terrible.*

**A:** *That sounds pretty bad. What do you mean by terrible?*

**B:** *I think it would just be a shame to miss an opportunity.*

**A:** *So, you want me to speed up my part in this decision.*

**B:** *Well, maybe. I only want you to speed up when I think that you taking your time will make us miss something. But if the past was so painful, then, of course, you wouldn't want to rush anything and maybe you're not really "taking your time."*

**A:** *So, does that help you to think of my hesitation differently?*

**B:** *Yes. I know you're trying to work with me. Do you think I'm rushing you?*

**A:** *Not anymore. I think you're working with me, too, and I appreciate your patience to allow us to have this talk before we do anything else.*

**B:** *I'm glad to hear that. You're more important to me than the decision itself.*

**A:** *Thank you. I hope you know that I value you more too.*

This is another contrived and possibly excessively positive conversation. Still, it illustrates a few things about how we can learn to respond rather than react to fear. First, we can see how being aware of the role of thinking can influence communication. In this case, the word "think" (intentionally) occurs ten times, with five uses per person. In addition, both parties reference feeling "afraid." This is noteworthy because very often conversations occur in which there is no direct identification of what feelings are involved. And the failure to identify specific emotions suggests that the person, consciously or not, may feel their emotions are problematic, not their own, or both. Treating emotions as problems to be fixed is one way of living in survival mode, and if fear is involved, this will risk becoming overprotective to the detriment of the relationship.

### From Surviving to Thriving

*Snakes and Ropes*

At this point, it is important to recognize one more aspect of fear that can particularly influence inclinations towards survival mode. Specifically, fear may exist because current threats may resemble actual dangers from the past. If so, even more understanding and patience will be necessary.

We have been using the fear of snakes as an ancillary metaphor for understanding fear in relationships, and so let us take this a bit further. There is an expression, I believe Chinese in origin, which suggests: "once bitten by a snake, one is terrified at the sight of a mere rope."[7] If this is true (and I believe this expression captures the reverberating impact of traumatic situations quite well), how can it be applied to our task of making fear into an asset in relationships?

---

7  Cohen, J. (2007, June 26). Rightist wrongs. Time.com. Retrieved December 21, 2017, from http://world.time.com/2007/06/26/once_youve_been_bitten_by_a_sn/

For example, suppose a person was in a previous relationship where they were assaulted and now their current partner's behaviors remind them of the abuse. Or suppose a child was bullied by an older child and now has difficulty making new friends. Or what if a military service member returning from combat situations in another country now has difficulty trusting loved ones at home? How do these people make their current fear into an ally and mitigate the possible recurrence of all-too-familiar, self-fulfilling prophecies?

Such situations can be quite complex, and an intentional process of healing and overcoming (perhaps through a professional counseling relationship) may be indicated. In addition (and very likely part of the counseling process itself), I would consider the following as ways of moving out of survival mode and into a place of more thriving.

First, as pedantic as it may sound, it cannot be stated too strongly that if there has been an actual "snakebite" in the past and if there are concerns about "ropes" in the present, the person is a "survivor." Therefore, their fear has, to some extent, been valuable and worked for them. This concept is critical to embrace.

### Vital Signs

In situations involving natural disasters such as floods or earthquakes, a distinction is made between "rescuing" survivors and "recovering" victims who did not live through the disasters. We are assuming that, if people are experiencing fear in the context of a relationship, they are not victims in any ultimate way. They have lived to tell of their experience, and their awareness of apparent similarities to other situations testifies to their resourcefulness.

There is a world of difference between "rescue" and "recovery," and the first step to rescuing a person is to identify all signs of life. In this case, fear itself could be considered such a sign. The person is concerned for their safety, and if what or whom they are afraid of is in fact a dangerous "snake," then some type of avoidance or escape is both necessary and healthy. On the other hand, if what or whom they are afraid of is in fact a "rope," then the fear can signal opportunities to respond rather than react which is also critical for diminishing the likelihood of fear becoming self-fulfilling.

So, broadly speaking, all emotions, including fear, can function as "psychological vital signs," and we can say that the "life" that these emotions signal is a desire for a situation to improve (or in the case of happiness, perhaps a desire for the situation to remain the same). More simply, emotions point us to how we care about our circumstances. And our MSGS and FLGT acronyms can again direct us to the general "causes" that we care about at any given time (feeling anger/mad suggests we care about fairness, sadness suggests that we care about loss, etc.). The central issue, then, is how we best help such causes, especially when significant aspects of the circumstances are not within our control.

*Naming*
Second, if there is no danger (the "rope" rather than "snake" scenario is indicated) once fear is observed and accepted as an important cue, the next step in responding versus reacting to fear is to identify or name it. Naming is an act of authority. Again, to reference the Judeo-Christian tradition, we can recall the biblical account of Adam naming the animals.[8] In this case, let us define naming as actively and purposefully standing outside of another person or thing and saying something about who or what it is. Essentially, we give an entity an identity that in one way or another distinguishes it from other entities, including ourselves. We, as the "namers," then remind ourselves that, in some way, we are more mature than our "namees." And so, naming our fears allows us to assert that we are greater than the fear we have named that might threaten us.

More specifically, naming means we stand outside the threat and realize that we are separate from it. We define it rather than allow it to define us. Thus, we can use it instead of allowing it to use us. And when this happens, fear becomes another emotion that moves from being a problem to becoming a resource that can be used for personal and interpersonal gain. Thus, naming a fear reduces the likelihood of that fear *interfering* with our relationships.

---

8   Genesis 2:19-20

How then do we name our fears? We name them by tracing them primarily back to certain thinking patterns that undermine our sense of safety. More importantly, it is valuable for us to be convinced that the power of our thinking is greater than the power of our situations themselves. As this conviction grows, we can again return to our practice of explaining our fears using language that reminds us to consider our thoughts about threats or our thoughts about bad things happening.

> **"The opportunity we have with fear is to challenge the status quo and align ourselves with something that is even more real to relationships... thriving."**

So, the person who has been bullied in the past might say something like: "I am feeling afraid because I think that I am going to be hurt by this person."[9] Though this is quite simple, we can allow it to be profound. Again, linking our awareness of fear with specific thoughts allows us to both have our fear (which is the first step in being able to use our fear, namely via better understanding of ourselves) and to identify how it is generated by our thinking even more than by situations per se. As such, we have the option of decreasing or even not experiencing fear—if we can find a way to honestly and sincerely think differently about the situation.

It is important to be both honest and sincere in our efforts to rethink situations. If we start to give more weight to our thoughts, we may start to wonder if we are being naïve or even deluding ourselves. Indeed, this is normal and expected as we begin the process of shifting our paradigms.

So, rather than fight our reservations, we can allow for the discomfort of thinking that we are fooling ourselves. Allowing for this discomfort means that we do not try to make the situation more comfortable than it is. To be more precise, it means that

---

9   It is critical to note here that this approach is only practical if there is no risk of physical harm.

we embrace the difficulty and discomfort of the work, namely the work of adopting a different belief system. We may tell ourselves that the difficulty exists because our former belief system has worked quite well and has become a very comfortable default. Again, this default will become even more compelling to the extent that we have experienced actual dangers in the past and relied more on reactivity than responsivity in order to survive. Even so, if actual dangers are in the past, then staying in survival mode is akin to living by an illusion. The opportunity we have with fear is to challenge the status quo and align ourselves with something that is even more real to relationships . . . thriving.

## Threat and Danger

### Dying and Living

Considering these things, we might ask ourselves, which do we fear more: death or life? Is death more threatening or is life more threatening? Put another way, does death contain the most potential for something bad to happen or does life? And lastly, how do we discern whether the threat is dangerous?

These are general questions, but they can be applied to almost any experience. The assumption behind this book is that in relationships, emotions, including fear, are usually not matters of physical survival, and so when fear is experienced the threat is usually less dangerous than supposed. This view is reinforced when we consider a spiritual perspective that also speaks to those things in life that *actually* threaten physical survival.

An event that I am still processing comes to mind. As I recall, it happened during a particularly challenging year for me and one in which I remember feeling some distinct anger and fear about various things. On one specific Sunday of that summer, I happened to be raking some leaves. That day I was feeling frustrated and worried, as I thought about important preparations for my son Jacob's one-year-old birthday party, and yard work was a part of the preparation. Among other things, I was grumbling about raking the leaves when there seemed to me other more important tasks in the yard, and my time was limited.

A prayer that has become especially vital to my own emotional life is, "Lord, soften my heart, and help me to not react." On this particular day, while raking the leaves, I finally allowed myself to breathe this prayer, and almost immediately after doing so, I looked down and noticed that in just the spot where I was going to rake, in the middle of a pile of leaves, was a tiny, trembling, baby bird.

I was caught off guard. To be honest, my heart was still very much in a state of anger and anxiety, but it seemed to me that this fragile life was part of how God was responding to my prayer. I put the bird in a safe place, finished my yard work, then shared my find with Keri and our girls, who went about filling a shoebox with shredded paper and making a fruit puree for the bird to eat. Over the course of that evening and into Monday morning, we had good success with getting the bird to eat from a syringe. That afternoon, I put the bird in a secure place, indoors, away from possible outdoor predators, looking forward to feeding it upon my return from work.

Monday evening, just as I was leaving work to go home, I received a voicemail from my daughter, Ella, telling me in a shaky voice, "Baby Bird died." Still taking in this whole experience, I wondered if there was any purpose to this turn of events, and if so, how it might relate to my initial, simple-but-difficult-to-utter prayer. When I arrived home, Keri told me that when she had returned that day from running some errands, she had found the bird dead and the house very warm. I recalled with some guilt how earlier that day I had stuck to my usual routine of locking up the house, including all the windows and the one window which would have given some ventilation to the room the bird had been left in. A Bible passage that had initially come to mind when I found the bird, returned, this time with more clarity:

> "Are not two sparrows sold for a penny? And not one of them will fall to the ground apart from your Father. But even the hairs of your head are all numbered. Fear not, therefore; you are of more value than many sparrows."[10]

The interesting thing about this passage is that it is found in

10   Matthew 10:29-31

a larger teaching Jesus gives on the topic of fear. Immediately, before He talks about the "sparrows," Jesus gives this ominous admonishment, "And do not fear those who kill the body but cannot kill the soul. Rather, fear him who can destroy both soul and body in hell."[11] His audience is a specific group, twelve newly appointed disciples, and the larger context of the passage revolves around His words to them about the cost of following Him.

Curiously, Jesus seems to be preparing His disciples for *actual dangers* they will be facing and still telling them *not to fear*. Remarkably, the actual danger that He specifically says they do not need to fear is death.

He does clarify that fear is called for if the threat continues after death, and yet, the ultimate point of His counsel seems to be that those who follow Him will be secure both during and after death. And then, for some reason, He talks about . . . birds.

At this point, I would understand if the reader is thinking that I am spending too much time on this story. Indeed, I wonder if I am reading too much into it. Is there any parallel between Jesus' words to his first-century followers and my own inability to keep a baby bird alive? I consider, "birds die all the time, this bird was nothing special, so why make such a big deal about it?" And then a little voice within whispers, "that is why it is such a big deal—precisely because it is nothing special." That is, the death of a bird is so commonplace that it quite possibly happens *at any given moment*. Jesus' point seems to be that His Father knows when every bird "falls to the ground." And, if God is this aware of the plight of *all* birds, and if people are "of more value than many birds," then perhaps we are much, much better off than we realize.[12]

According to this passage, God both knows and values people. It is this combination that ostensibly motivates Jesus to tell his followers to *not fear*. By contrast, it seems that if only one of these qualities is represented, then there is reason to be afraid.

---

11   Matthew 10:28

12   I am particularly grateful for Dallas Willard's point of view on this. For example, in perhaps his best known work, The Divine Conspiracy, while reflecting on the enormity of the concept of God being love, Willard writes, "With this magnificent God positioned among us, Jesus brings the assurance that our universe is a perfectly safe place to be." (p. 66).

If God only knows everything about people but does not value them, then who can withstand that kind of scrutiny? Or if God only values people without knowing them, then what happens to concepts like justice or truth? Neither a graceless nor a truthless world is tenable, at least not without debilitating fear. Jesus seems to be saying that it is not the nature of the world, per se, but the nature of God who makes it possible for us to live without fear. What will it take for us to begin comprehending the implications of being "of more value than many birds"? Moreover, if we are so known and so valued, what better way to respond than to truly live?

### Allowing the Unwanted

All this to say that if it is possible to not be afraid in the face of actual danger (death), then how much more possible will it be to not be afraid if a situation is non-dangerous (as in the case of relationships)? The answer to this question will be experienced to the extent that we believe that threat in a relationship does not necessarily mean danger. So, if I am concerned with what someone will think or say about me when I share difficult information, their unwanted opinions or words may be quite threatening. And if so, then fear will exist.

But what if I allow the other person to have their thoughts, even though I would rather they not think them? What if I trace the threat back to not what the person is thinking but to what I think about what they are thinking? It seems that if I do these things, I will likely be treating my fear as an opportunity rather than an obstacle, separating threat from danger, and essentially giving myself more space to move within the relationship. Fear may still exist because of a perceived threat, but this fear will not have to be regarded or experienced as a problem per se.

All of these shifts will be signs that I am moving out of survival mode and into a non-survival or even thrival stance. In survival mode, treating fear as a problem will be followed by some sort of avoidance. The avoidance involves doing something, such as refraining from initially sharing an opinion or emotion with another person, perhaps to prevent the other person from having their thoughts and feelings. However, non-survival and thriving are made possible as I consider how both my feelings and the other person's feelings are important, relevant, and valid.

If what I say influences another person to be hurt or angry, and if I do not prevent them or myself from having such feelings, then their hurt or anger have been "allowed." In addition, if I am open to their hurt or anger influencing my fear, then my fear is also "allowed." By allowed, I mean the feeling is more than permitted—it is considered and acknowledged as appropriate and deserved (as in the case of a financial allowance).

Put another way, both allowing and validating feelings shift us into non-survival/thrival mode because the unwanted nature of the feeling is treated precisely as a matter of *want* rather than *need*. Thus, fear, hurt, or anger are given space to be felt, because as undesirable or unpreferred as they may be, I am not required to be free of them. They are unwanted rather than unneeded feelings. And, ironically, when I refrain from having to have what I want, I open myself to true freedom, namely, the freedom that comes from knowing and experiencing "truth"—in this case, the idea that in relationships, my feelings, including fear, are not dangerous per se.

When all parties are "allowed" to have their feelings, each person can be experienced for who they are and who they might become. Possibly more than anything, this potential for people to both be and become most fully themselves is the purpose and power behind relationships. To borrow from the words of an African philosophy known as *ubuntu*, "A person is a person through other people."[13]

*Negative Outcomes*
This discussion raises an interesting consideration: in the context of relationship, if fear can be more of a resource than a problem, what might we say about fear of relationships? Or how do we take a fear of relationships and make it strategic for enhancing the very relationships that we fear?

One follow-up question to this inquiry is what exactly is threatening about relationships? Of course, there are any number of outcomes that might be indicated—being rejected, judged, smothered, offended, embarrassed, found lacking, and

---

13  Flippin, W. E. Jr. (2012, April 6). Ubuntu: Applying African philosophy in building community. Retrieved January 18, 2020, from https://www.huffpost.com/entry/ubuntu-applying-african-p_b_1243904

so forth. These are legitimate concerns and can represent very real problems in relationships. For example, there is perhaps no greater pain than that of rejection from another person. At the same time, the avoidance of relationships carries its own risks.

Take for instance, the experience of loneliness. Elsewhere this has been referred to as "social pain"[14] or a "fear of love."[15] Rather ironically, it might be argued that loneliness is the underlying reason for the threatening nature of relationships in the first place. We fear relationships, because we fear certain outcomes, and we fear these outcomes because we do not want to be lonely.

Opting out of relationships to avoid pain simultaneously makes no sense and perfect sense, because relationships are at once a test of two dimensions of our will—control and surrender. This is vital because the full realization of both of these dimensions represents the full potential of relationships. To draw again from another facet of *ubuntu*, "I am because we are, and we are because I am." Fear, however, can lead us to various forms of imbalance in both control and surrender, such as attack and withdrawal or passivity and aggression. So again, how do we proceed?

Not surprisingly, our strategy will be both simple and difficult—respond to the fear. Or even better, use the fear to respond to the situation. That is, we can remind ourselves that the situation (rejection, loneliness, or other potentially painful relationship outcome) is not a matter of survival. It does not have to be experienced as damaging to our personal well-being. The well-being of the relationship may be damaged (the relationship may even end), but the end of a relationship does not have to mean the end of each individual person. Of course, the paradoxical effect of this is that, to the extent that each person in a relationship is healthy on their own, the relationship has a greater chance of surviving and indeed thriving.

When fear is present, there is a threat, but in relationships, the threat is not lethal. In keeping with our theme, it is neither

14   Cacioppo, J. T., & Patrick, W. (2008). Loneliness: Human nature and the need for social connection. New York, NY: W. W. Norton & Co.

15   Tanner, I. J. (1973). Loneliness: The fear of love. New York, NY: Harper & Row.

rejection nor loneliness that are the reasons for our fear but rather what we think about these experiences. The question is can we honestly and sincerely think of rejection and loneliness differently? Can we legitimately consider these and other negative outcomes as non-threatening? To the extent that we can make this shift, we will be sailing, as it were, this final part of the ocean of relationships in a new way and minimizing the likelihood of fear interfering with our journey.

## Gems for the Journey

*Treasures*

Just as the *Ratnākara* literally refers to a mine of precious gems, so fear can yield its own wealth, as we learn its dynamics. And, if fear involves a sense of pressure, then just as carbon can be transformed into diamond, fear can be converted into a valuable resource as well.

Indian leader and peacemaker, Mohandas (Mahatma) Ghandi taught, "fear has its use, but cowardice has none."[16] So what then is fear's "use"?

I believe that fear affords us certain opportunities to cultivate certain virtues that will help us to become better people. And as we learn to recognize these opportunities, I believe fear can also be a catalyst for deeper, stronger relationships.

The Chinese philosopher Confucius noted that "wisdom, compassion, and courage are the three most universally recognized qualities of men."[17] To be sure, fear is not the only emotion that lends itself to these three qualities and there are even more virtues we might consider, but there does seem to be a rather compelling link present between this particular triad and fear specifically. As such, let us take the remainder of this chapter to explore the possible ways in which the *Ratnākara* might be mined for each of these precious treasures.

---

16  Mahatma Gandhi quotes. (n. d.). In Brainyquote.com. Retrieved December 22, 2017, from https://www.brainyquote.com/quotes/quotes/m/mahatmagan122431.html

17  Confucius quotes. (n. d.). In Brainyquote.com. Retrieved December 22, 2017, from https://www.brainyquote.com/quotes/quotes/c/confucius386106.html

## Wisdom

Fear can first become the pathway to wisdom. King Solomon, who is described in the Bible as one who received from God "wisdom and understanding beyond measure, and breadth of mind like the sand on the seashore,"[18] makes the following claim: "the fear of the Lord is the beginning of wisdom and the knowledge of the Holy One is insight."[19] This is worth noting. In this one statement, we are afforded a specific description and definition, of wisdom and insight—from a person widely regarded as one of the wisest persons who ever lived.

For Solomon, wisdom originated with a certain quality of fear, namely fear that is concerned with God. In fact, in the account of how Solomon initially asks God for wisdom, God himself is recorded as saying to Solomon, "I will do what you have asked. I will give you a wise and discerning heart, so that there will never have been anyone like you, nor will there ever be."[20]

So how do Solomon's words about wisdom and fearing God pertain to our daily interactions with others? To address this question, it is important to first define and nuance our terms. For example, I believe fearing God is fundamentally about recognizing and even embracing God's supremacy. And, because fear implies some type of threat is present, fearing God can also mean recognizing the disastrous nature of missing out on acknowledging this supremacy. "Fearing" God in this sense certainly points to respecting and revering but in a qualitatively different way from how we would treat any other entity or experience. It connotes awareness of God as formidable, with an ultimate trajectory of worship and awe. Furthermore, if God is ultimately good, then fear is also ironically related to trust.

Wisdom and insight are essentially about skillful living, based on an awareness of reality and how life "works." They imply application of knowledge. When God is involved, fear and wisdom go hand in hand precisely because life is put in perspective. For example, if God is the one "uncaused cause" then God's nature is not determined by anything and God

---

18  I Kings 4:29

19  Proverbs 9:10

20  I Kings 3:12 (NIV)

determines the nature of everything. If God is the source of all of life, then recognizing Him as such will position us for accurate living.

Another prayer comes to mind. When I was in graduate school, my roommate and good friend Steve would occasionally repeat a certain request to God. Aware of the amount of information he was expected to know, he would pray, "Lord, free me from the burden of omniscience." As a fellow student, I came to appreciate Steve's prayer and I now find myself benefiting from praying it on my own. In fact, though we graduated years ago, Steve and I still refer to this prayer in our conversations today. Whereas the context back then was school, it has now broadened to all of life. That is, anytime I have a "need to know" information that is not mine to know (which can range from questions about why people (including myself) do what they do to questions about how certain circumstances are going to turn out), I now believe that I am taking on the "burden of omniscience." I have come to think that such knowledge is burdensome precisely because it is akin to expecting myself to know what God alone can know. And, now as a relationship counselor, I find it particularly useful for navigating interpersonal fears in a constructive manner.

For instance, suppose a couple is trying to rebuild after each person has done something to offend the other. Both want to heal, and neither wants to be hurt again. The possible scenarios for such difficulties are endless, ranging from inadvertent words to intentional violations. Still, the fear is essentially the same—the concern that extending oneself will not pay off, that vulnerability will lead to more pain. So how might understanding this fear be useful? And how specifically does the fear of the Lord help us with this?

We hesitate to become vulnerable (apologize, forgive, understand another's perspective, share our own feelings) because we do not know if vulnerability will be worthwhile. And so, if fear is about threat, then one threat relationships face is the threat of the "unknown." Up against the possibility of a situation worsening, familiarity can be strangely comfortable and seem safer by comparison. And so, we often opt for the safety of not sharing over the potential growth of risking sharing certain information.

But what if we can be freed of the "burden of omniscience"? What if we consider that it is God's role, and God's alone, to know the future? Might we be able to address the prospect of the unknown with more confidence and more openness to deeper relationship?

For that matter, what if we can also be freed of the burdens of omnipresence or omnipotence? What would it look like to really believe that it is not our responsibility to be all places at all times or to make everything work?

These are certainly all part of embracing our limits and recognizing where we fit in the larger context. And, though rather obvious, a major aspect of recognizing our position is recognizing that we are not God—a necessary prerequisite for relinquishing omniscience and other "powers" reserved only for God. In the end, as we embrace our limits, we are helped to approach relationships with a more realistic sense of control, namely self-control which can be effective for better influencing the relationship. Again, confidence and humility go hand in hand. Once these are in place, we are that much more prepared to live accurately and wisely. The fear of the Lord is indeed the beginning of these things.

## Courage

If wisdom is the first gem, courage is the second. Courage, in this case, is the opposite of avoidance. It is the strength to face what is feared. It is the ability to will oneself out of certain comfort zones and "into the fray." It is the capacity to engage situations that are threatening and often actually dangerous. So if, as Ghandi affirmed, fear has its "uses," then perhaps courage is fear's most challenging use. Courage implies sacrifice and putting oneself at risk for what is good, right, or true. Its purest forms are always humanitarian, promoting the well-being of others and the aims of love.

Courage thus points to internal strength. It derives from the Latin word for heart (*cor*), and so it concerns a person's deepest convictions. As such, it is interesting to consider how it relates to fear. If fear connotes a sense of threat and pressure, courage is the ability to deliberately choose an openness to these possibilities.

Therefore, courage is intentional despite the intensity of a situation. It is purposeful—when others would shy away, courage steps up. It is persistent—where others leave off, courage moves forward. It is bold—while others stay safe, courage takes risk.

But courage is not just concerned with risk-taking for its own sake. As mentioned at the beginning of this book, risks are a given. Courage discerns which risks promote justice, peace, and love, and it recognizes how these can be attained in ways consistent with the truth.

---

## "...courage is intentional despite the intensity of a situation."

---

And, we are exploring the possibility that, when it comes to relationships, the truth is that emotions are opportunities for enhancing our interpersonal experiences.

However, all too often, rather than inspiring courage, fear can take on its more familiar reactive "survival" forms. For example, when threat is unnecessarily equated with danger, fear can shift into misguided forms of sadness such as blame, regret, guilt, or shame. Or if the danger is taken to be unfair, defensive or aggressive forms of anger can develop. Ultimately, when left in these states, fear can become stuck or decline into unnecessary and unhealthy expressions of anxiety or depression. So, given enough reactivity, fear can morph into actual danger. The challenge  again is to minimize problems that do not have to happen.

Our theory can point us toward strategies for utilizing our fear. As a beginning point, it is important to acknowledge the usefulness of wanting to stay safe. Because hurt is already likely involved in the relationship, it makes sense to not want to repeat or intensify pain. Of course, certain forms of "staying safe" also risk missing out on the possibilities of growth or improvement, and so it is equally important to "count the costs" of both sides.

These dynamics can be particularly relevant to relationship decisions, especially when at least two different perspectives are involved. For example, imagine another scenario involving persons A and B, and in this case, A has somehow not treated B well and each is struggling to move forward. So, suppose A is reluctant to apologize because this requires admitting fault and it could just lead to B blaming A more. Or perhaps A is not so concerned with being blamed but just does not want to feel vulnerable (it is a curious thing to feel vulnerable with another person, especially when there is no clear danger other than that of stepping outside of our own comfort zone). And, on the other side, B does not know what to say and may be tired of hearing apologies since it can seem like A does not change and inevitably repeats hurtful mistakes from the past.

If left here, fear will lead to reaction. A and B will find themselves in the survival dynamics of fighting, fleeing, or freezing. Apology, for example, may be thwarted because it is perceived as a form of either manipulation or defeat. Walls may go up around comfort zones. Each person might begin to feel paralyzed and unable to step toward the other, especially if the pain of doing so means something detrimental could occur (for example, sometimes moving toward a person who just *seems* to be an enemy can be more arduous than even extreme physical discomfort).

So, how can fear be the catalyst for the courage to forge closer relationships? And how can wisdom continue to inform our steps?

As already mentioned, there are many times I am afraid, even deeply afraid. I am afraid of certain evaluations others might make of me. Or I am afraid that I will not have enough of one thing or another—of time, of money, of favor with people. I am afraid of being weak and of not being self-sufficient. I am afraid of being uncomfortable. I am afraid of not being liked by others and of not being like others. I am afraid others will win and I will lose. I am afraid of wasting and maybe deep down, of being scolded for doing so. I am afraid of falling and of failing. There are many times I am also afraid of God, because I can repeatedly act or think in ways that, in my mind, certainly disqualify me from His divine favor. In the end, as much as I endeavor to help others to face their own lives and fears, I too can be driven by fear, intimidated by so many of my own demons, finding myself knee or even chest-deep in survival mode. So again, how to move forward?

Courage will come as I move in the direction of my fear, recognizing that whatever is not a matter of literal survival may very well be *worth facing*. In relationships, fighting, fleeing, or freezing are all, at some level, unnecessary.

Again, let us consider that *most* of life *does not have* to be difficult. And the premise of this book is that relationships constitute most of life, much the way the ocean covers most of the earth.

So, all of my fears—whether of others' opinions, of failure, or even of disappointing God—can be construed as opportunities if I will allow them to be so. In fact, this reveals another way we can conceive of courage—namely, *the consent we give ourselves to view and treat non-dangerous threats as opportunities*. In this way, courage is also a willingness to live as closely in line with reality as possible, regardless of the consequences.

Fear exists because of perceived consequences, but it also paves the way for wisdom to discern what is really at stake and the ability to press on despite the cost.

American poet, Mrs. Karle Wilson Baker, concludes her insightful poem, "Courage," with the line, "courage is fear that has said its prayers."[21] Prayer, of course, implies addressing God, and this can itself be an exercise in shifting our perspective. Moreover, if I consider the supremacy of God over all things—including even matters of life and death, a sort of "downsizing" can happen. Next to God's greatness, does not everything scale down?

Interestingly, it seems we are free to answer this question as we see fit. So here again, our consent is involved. And when it comes to how we relate to God, the freedom that we are afforded to be consenting participants is especially remarkable on at least two levels.

21  Popik, B. (2014, November 20). In Barrypopik.com. Retrieved December 22, 2017, from http://www.barrypopik.com/index.php/new_york_city/entry/courage_is_fear_that_has_said_its_prayers

First, our freedom to consent is remarkable because of a contrast. That is, many would say that God, by definition, is completely sovereign, in total control. God answers to no one, and many people (including me) believe that all will one day answer to God. God alone is entirely self-dependent, self-sustaining, and self-sufficient. And this raises the contrast. Because against this backdrop of God's complete prerogative to ordain that things be however God sees fit, we can still talk about our own consent! Somehow God's total authority does not cancel out our ability to express our preferences and sense of say over our lives. In fact, this thought is so remarkable that some traditions would not and do not consider the coexistence of God's complete sovereignty and human will to be a viable option. With all respect to these traditions, I do not see any other way for the notion of a "personal relationship with God" to be itself an option apart from the coexistence of both divine sovereignty and human choice. For now, let us just consider that there is a deep irony in the fact that God and the reference to our consent can even be used in the same sentence.

Second, our freedom to consent is remarkable because it implies a boldness. This is the boldness it would take to consider allowing ourselves to *not* have everything scale down when God enters the equation. And, truth be told, we can all be so bold. I know for myself that life can bring many problems—including the fears listed earlier, which can seem insurmountable. They can loom before me, larger than life and, it would seem, larger than even God. Of course, most often we do not consciously think that a trial is greater than God. Perhaps if we were more aware of God's presence, the "downsizing" would happen more automatically. It seems that very frequently we have the audacity to forget that God is in the picture. I do not mean to be critical. Indeed, it seems God graciously chooses to have us experience this freedom—permitting and even empowering us to do so. Still, it begs the question: Might we be able to more boldly face our fears and be equipped to experience more courage if we were more mindful of God as an even greater reality in our lives?

I believe the answer to this question is a resounding yes. Specifically, the more mindful we are of God and God's greatness, the more wisdom and courage will inform our steps. We might put it this way: wisdom begins the process and courage continues it.

---

## "Wisdom begins by recognizing and revering God's greatness."

---

Wisdom begins by recognizing and revering God's greatness.[22] And, in a very real way, reverence is a way of fearing God, since God's greatness means God is potentially the greatest threat imaginable. Being all-powerful, God is entirely capable of overwhelming or even destroying whomever God chooses. In the face of this threat, however, courage leads us to persevere with seeking God because courage counts on this pursuit being worthwhile. In fact, we can forge ahead because as threatening as God may be, courage considers that God is ultimately not dangerous. Again, if "courage is fear that has said its prayers," then perhaps courage has also heard God say that He is ultimately the One who initiates and continues the pursuit and the persevering. Maybe the most marvelous thing of all is that, as awful and awesome as God is, He is *committed to relationship* with us far more than we could hope to imagine. Put another way, what if, in addition to being *supreme*, God is *supremely good*?

Ultimately, where God is concerned, it is love that guarantees our safety. For example, at the end of a harrowing description of severe circumstances that seem to be attributed to God, the author of the book of Lamentations declares,

> *"I remember my affliction and my wandering, the bitterness and the gall. I well remember them, and my soul is downcast within me. Yet this I call to mind and therefore I have hope: Because of the Lord's great love we are not consumed, for his compassions never fail."*[23]

So, if love—great, supernatural, committed, and protective love—prevents us from being consumed, then we can truly say there is no danger. And if there is no danger, then survival is not at stake. And if survival is not at stake, we are free to respond

---

22  Proverbs 9:10

23  Lamentations 3:21-22 (NIV)

rather than react.

In this case, we can even respond to our fear. This is the logic of thriving, even and especially amid various feelings that seem to threaten relationships. We have considered briefly the ways thriving can result as we allow fear to create the treasures of wisdom and courage. Let us conclude this chapter with an exploration of one more gem, already referenced in the Lamentations passage above: compassion.

### Compassion

"Compassion" literally means "to suffer with" another. So how does this relate to fear? Specifically, how do we use fear as a springboard for living more compassionate lives?

As mentioned, it is worth noting that God's compassion obviates fear. If God's compassions never fail, we will be spared, and more than that, we will truly thrive. Our survival is not at stake and our flourishing is ultimately ensured.

Nevertheless, though this is our reality, we still experience fear to the extent that we experience threat, and ironically, relationships are no exception. So, a couple hesitates to practice more transparency with one another. A parent loses control upon hearing of their child's misbehavior. A friendship grows distant because of jealousy. And on and on.

If not addressed, fear will erode relationships even if survival is not initially at stake. This, as we have already seen, is the stubborn, curious momentum of emotional reactivity—when it seems another can scare or hurt us, we use various strategies to protect ourselves. Our intentions are good and may yield short-term benefits, but the longer-term result is almost always the same—the relationship suffers. And very likely, much of the suffering is unnecessary.

It is an unnecessary suffering because the interpersonal nature of the conflict means the emotions are more within our power than we may realize. In this way, emotions, including fear, can be considered more optional than the situation may lead us to believe, precisely because we recognize the importance of our interpretations.

Compassion, almost by definition, is responsive rather than reactive. To "suffer with" another requires an ability to enter into various levels of their pain. Although this can increasingly become a character trait and therefore more and more automatic, sharing in another's suffering is more voluntary than accidental. One way or another, we choose to feel some version of what the other person is feeling. And choosing is the quintessential type of response.

Choice implies accessibility, and this is particularly the case in emotional responsiveness. For our purposes, we might say the chosen emotion is accessible both in how the emotion is not harmful and how it is within personal control, again via the content of our thinking.

It is one thing to feel compassion for a person who is suffering unnecessarily or because of the actions of some third party (be it another person or other specific events). It is quite another if the suffering involves us personally, especially if it appears we are the innocents or that the other person is responsible for why we are suffering. And this is what makes it so difficult to convert fear into compassion. If the other person is the reason for why we are suffering, they may essentially be feared because they are perceived as a threat. Since we naturally move away from threat and since compassion involves a movement toward pain, compassion seems counterintuitive. In a curious twist, we almost automatically assume that a person who threatens us is not also hurting in their own way.

And this is because a natural, survival-preserving approach to emotion is disconnected from logic. Persuaded that "negative" emotions (anger, sadness, and fear) are "bad," we view these feelings as impositions and do what is necessary to avoid such feelings altogether. When we reconnect emotion to logic (via openness to the idea that most of our feelings are determined more by thoughts than incidents per se), we can engage without being overly attached. And as we consider that emotions and fear specifically are "more thought than caught," compassion makes more sense. We see how threat can still be motivated by its own pain. Though we previously took issue with the statement, we can still appreciate the spirit behind it: "hurt people hurt people." And once we translate threat into hurt or pain, we are more inclined to address the person as a person rather than as a situation. We see that another's feelings derive primarily from their own thinking and not from us as their situation, and we can respond even if they react.

So, the lover can share difficult secrets, maybe even past indiscretions or sins, with their partner, because the possibility of being truly accepted is prized above even the pain of being rejected. Or the parent can face the discomfort of their child's "failure," because they can see the even greater benefit of modeling self-control in a difficult circumstance. And a friend can draw near to another who seems somehow superior because they take to heart the notion that friendship is fundamentally more cooperative than competitive. And on and on.

These are all compassionate moves because the people we are inclined to avoid are approached and valued. And again, this is certainly not easy. For example, rejection and abandonment are extremely painful. At the same time, when it comes to emotions, pain is heavily impacted by the meanings we give to events.

For example, suppose the confessing partner views their lover's anger or hurt as their lover's prerogative and a necessary risk for arriving at deeper intimacy. Or suppose the threats posed by certain risks (rejection, disrespect, defeat, etc.) are not treated as final because they are important for identifying how the relationship can be strengthened rather than weakened. If fear comes by thinking a threat exists, it is possible to change such fear by changing the thought process. And if threat can be converted to some type of underlying vulnerability that we can identify with, then new understanding, understanding that might itself better address the situation, is possible.

With new understanding comes new potential for relationship, and where relationship is promoted, so the welfare of the individual is as well. This too can be considered compassionate because it is uncomfortable, sometimes painfully so, to consider what another is feeling, especially if that other seems to not have our best interest in mind. Still, this process of entering the discomfort of the other has the potential to accomplish our best interest precisely by addressing the best interest of the person we are seeking to understand. One person's gain means the other person wins—this is the aim of relationship and the very reason fear can contribute to thriving rather than mere survival overall.

Compassion is always a noble endeavor. When we feel for a person in need, we show kindness and our true humanity. And when we feel for a person who seems to be or even is somehow against us, we practice a particular kind of kindness, one that may even approach the unconditional acceptance of the God whose compassions never fail. It is this form of compassion that is curiously compatible with fear because once we see that we have a say in what we find threatening, we can opt to view the threats differently. In much the same way that wisdom involves affirming our limits and courage involves converting threats into opportunities, compassion involves embracing the power of being vulnerable.

## Engagement

*Masks and Mirrors*
Like everyday treasures, these gems are hidden in plain sight, until we believe enough to look for them and look enough to believe. But believing and looking are two of the most difficult endeavors, especially in relationships with others. When it comes to our fears, we tend to avoid what threatens us, and so it is so much easier, both literally and figuratively, to avert our gaze. And this is the ironic fork in the road that relational fears present us with. On one hand, loaded with self-fulfilling potential, fear can easily and routinely grow as threats morph into dangers and dangers produce more threats. On the other, if the fear truly involves relationship concerns, then averting our gaze and equating threats with dangers will likely be unfortunate since relationships increasingly involve two or more people facing each other.

If fear results in protecting ourselves from one another rather than turning toward each other, then fear functions as a mask that prevents us from being able to see beyond ourselves. In this chapter, we have sought to remove the mask by suggesting that, in relationships, fear is more influenced by threatening interpretations than by dangerous situations.

But, if a mask, fear is also simultaneously a part of the face the mask conceals. For a fear that can be attributed to interpretations can also be a pathway, a window, into the interpreter. In a way, another name for a window into oneself is a mirror, and the primary function of a mirror is self-examination. So too, fear can reveal to us those things we hold dear, even if it is through an initial awareness of the potential jeopardization of such things.

When this perspective is lived out, the things in relationships that daunt us can likewise be overcome, to the extent that our interpretations can be reconsidered. By contrast, externalizing our fears risks unnecessary and convoluted dynamics where initial hiding leads to even more hiding. These dynamics are unnecessary because turning against and away from one another is antithetical to relationship. They are convoluted because if fear is from without, our natural reaction is to avoid other people, but if our own interpretations are not recognized, we simultaneously avoid ourselves. And so, ironically, we move to a place of again becoming "overprotective," undermining the very resources that might lead to more growth and trust.

This is especially challenging to our experience since fear, with its host of different expressions, can so often overpower our scary circumstances themselves. As we conclude this chapter, one more illustration, fairly related to oceanlore, seems pertinent. In his classic book, *The Life and Adventures of Robinson Crusoe*, author Daniel Defoe relates the experiences of Robinson, a lone shipwreck survivor who learns to fend for himself for twenty-eight years on a remote island off South America. At one point, after Robinson has lived fifteen years on the island without seeing a single person, he describes an encounter with a somewhat ambiguous sight, a single footprint on the beach. Obsessed with the possible ways in which there may be other islanders who are hostile nearby, Robinson recounts his battle with fear itself, saying,

*"O what ridiculous resolutions men take when possessed with fear! It deprives them of the use of those means which reason offers for their relief...Thus, fear of danger is ten thousand times more terrifying than danger itself when apparent to the eyes, and we find the burden of anxiety greater by much, than the evil which we were*

*anxious about.*"[24]

Though relationships and the adventures of a castaway are two different things, both involve emotions related to dangers that are not "apparent to the eyes." And interestingly, when danger is more perceived than actual, we tend to take even more precautions, donning masks and maybe layers of masks to prevent us from clearly seeing or from being clearly seen. As we have noted, in relationships, masks are unnecessary protections, since they keep us from truly connecting with one another. Mask removal, then, calls for some assurance that our faces are not dangerous, even if they are sometimes threatening. Just as we can learn to look at ourselves, it is important to trust that beholding one another will not prove harmful or fatal.

This trust begins with the belief that emotions in relationships are not matters of personal survival. This is the theme of this chapter and, indeed, this book. So, in a word, when survival is not at stake, fear can operate as an invitation to *engage* rather than as an impulse to protect.

It seems counterintuitive to engage the very thing that seems to threaten. It seems more logical to resist rather than give in to pressure. Still, threat and press are only problems if they derive from an external danger. When fear operates instead as an internal source of information, it can be used to engage and enhance relationships.

*Buried Treasure*
To this end, the fourth ocean, the *Ratnākara*, can be mined for its interpersonal treasures—by a process of redefining and rethinking:

1) those things that would usually intimidate and trouble us
2) those things that characterize the anxieties which so quickly flow within and between us
3) those experiences that would separate and divide us

This process further calls for redefining and rethinking:

---

24  Defoe, D. (1867). The life and adventures of Robinson Crusoe. Boston, MA: Crosby and Ainsworth, p. 185.

1) Limits to help obtain wisdom
2) Opportunity to help obtain courage
3) Vulnerability to help obtain compassion
4) Engagement to facilitate action

And as we experience the combined effect of these facets, we will increasingly witness the transformation of fear.

Intentionally, these concepts form a symbolic acronym: LOVE. And as we will soon see, love, being the epitome of any relationship is also the antithesis of fear. As the apostle John so beautifully claims, "There is no fear in love, but perfect love casts out fear."[25] Of course, the love John speaks of is simultaneously none other than God himself and the same love that John exhorts us, as God's children, to practice with one another.

The hope of this chapter is that implementing the principles just discussed will be one approach to practically and strategically embodying such love. When we begin with the notion that fear in relationships is not a problem, we are equipped to treat one another as people rather than as problems. And it is precisely when we treat fear as a resource that we are free to embrace the people who initially seem to scare us. Perhaps this then is one way to understand the apostle John's insights into the mystery of the incompatibility between fear and love. For just as fear implies threat, love implies safety. And if safety is in place, threat holds no ultimate terror.

On this important note, we turn to the final three topics of our exploration. Beginning with communication, we will consider several principles for how we can utilize emotions to enhance interpersonal connections. Following this, we will consider forgiveness as an indispensable and powerful strategy when connections inevitably break down. And finally, we will look again at love, along with faith and hope, and the ways each can help guide our continued navigation of the ocean of relationships.

# Chapter 12: Surf

*We're all equal before a wave.*
*Laird Hamilton*

*Being creative on the waves is challenging,*
*but we each create art in our own way.*
*Bethany Hamilton*

Now that we have "visited" each ocean, we can turn to a more in-depth look at what we might call the very waters of relationship: communication. More specifically, by communication, let us consider the overarching goal of connecting with one another. Let us define connecting as the experience of encountering and experiencing another person through a process of sending and receiving messages. Put another way, connecting is a process of mutual communication. And, on the ocean of relationships, connecting is ultimately about arriving at a sense of belonging and an increasingly settled feeling of being at home with one another.

Of course, navigating our various emotions and growing in personal control can be challenging. Getting to places of increasing comfort and ease with one another can seem like solving an elaborate puzzle. Looking at the significant number of scattered pieces can be overwhelming and sometimes even discouraging. But once a few strategies are in place, even the most daunting puzzle can yield to a step-by-step process that becomes progressively less difficult and even more enjoyable.

I remember an occasion when my family and I experienced this together. One of my daughters had put together a simple jigsaw puzzle on her own, and shortly thereafter, she began telling people she had "found her hobby." It was a joy to see her expand from this simple puzzle to a more complex one. And it was especially rewarding to talk with her about strategy.

Since she had been working with rectangular puzzles, a first step was to find all the pieces that comprised the edges of the puzzle and construct the frame. And, of course, as she did this, she kept an eye out for the four pieces that have two edges, otherwise known as the cornerpieces.

## Connecting

*Cornerpieces*
In relationships, it seems to me that there are four principles that form the corners to the puzzle of connecting. And so, in keeping with both our water theme and the theme of repeatedly returning to a sense of being at home with one another (returning to "shore"), let us consider another acronym: SURF.

Although I was born and raised in Hawai`i, I do not consider myself a surfer. I feel a little left out when I see the t-shirts developed by the Billabong surfwear company that say, "Only a surfer knows the feeling." The feeling, of course, that I imagine is being referred to, is the feeling of riding a wave, especially being in the tube or barrel of a wave, being propelled forward, perhaps almost fully enveloped by water. And, to be sure, this seems a feeling that must be experienced physically; no amount of describing it will do it justice.

In a much less glamorous way, perhaps we can say the same of connecting with another person. Only those who know how to meet people "where they are at" know this feeling, and I suspect that these people are in a minority, with most people knowing how to communicate but not necessarily connect. In fact, leadership expert John Maxwell has written a book on this topic entitled, *Everyone Communicates, Few Connect.*[1] The goal of this chapter is to explain some of the basic principles (again following the acronym SURF) that I believe will allow for more connection on the ocean of relationships, namely: Safety, Understanding, Reaching out, and Fun.

---

1   Maxwell, J. C. (2010). Everyone communicates, few connect: What the most effective people do differently. Nashville, TN: Thomas Nelson.

## Safety

*Physical Safety*

For relationships to thrive, people need to be free to be themselves, and so the priority is Safety. In this case, there are three levels of safety to consider. Imagine three concentric circles, working inward from the outside (see Figure 2).

At the outer level, we have physical safety. This is self-explanatory but essential to our goals. Anything that is physically dangerous is not conducive to relationship. So, as a minimal requirement for good relationship and connection, there should be no physical aggression or violence towards anyone or anything (people, animals, physical property, etc.). In my estimation, this includes both actually and potentially damaging behaviors. For example, just as striking a person would be physically unsafe, so would slamming a door or exceeding the speed limit while driving in a vehicle. When it comes to physical safety, it is very important to be as careful and thorough as possible.

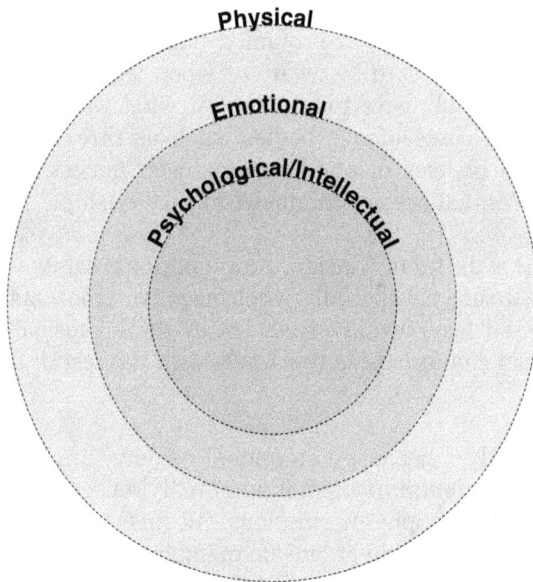

Figure 2:
Levels of Safety in Communication

*Emotional Safety*

The second circle, working inward (middle circle) represents emotional safety, which pertains to how we communicate and especially to how we communicate our emotions. This involves aspects of communication such as language, tone, volume, and gestures. Behaviors encompassed by this circle are also self-explanatory but more difficult to attain as far as ensuring safety is concerned.

---

**"All instances of emotions being communicated in an unsafe manner will involve what we have been referring to as emotional reactivity or survival mode."**

---

Since we often limit our sense of "safety" to the physical, we can become much less aware of how certain ways of communicating can feel unsafe. This area reminds us to beware of using language such as profanity, put-downs, and sarcasm. It is also important to be aware of when we raise our voices or use critical, abrasive tones. Finally, what we might regard as "symbolic" uses of our bodies, such as threatening facial expressions or uses of our hands or even fingers can create atmospheres that are not conducive to relationship.

Here it is useful to consider how emotional safety is related to physical safety, especially when negative emotions (anger, sadness, and fear) are involved. Let us think especially about how we can connect these two levels with the rest of this book in mind.

Specifically, because emotional safety involves *how emotions are communicated*, it potentially reflects the person's underlying philosophy of emotions. All instances of emotions being communicated in an unsafe manner will involve what we have been referring to as emotional reactivity or survival mode. And so, whether it is the use of profanity or an intimidating tone, the effect is the same: the message is sent to something or someone *external to oneself.*

Such externalizing is akin to a wild animal snarling or baring its teeth. By exhibiting such behaviors, the animal is not causing physical harm per se, but it is reacting, essentially saying, "Stay away." Similarly, when we scowl, glower, glare, or swear at one another, no physical harm is inflicted but the message is the same: back off; stay away.

In this way, emotional reactivity essentially deviates from the priority of treating emotions as a personal responsibility. So, the source of emotions is assumed to be outside of oneself (and often this means another person). Moreover, it operates on a second assumption that negative emotions (anger, sadness, and fear) are not just negative but also "bad." Neither assumption is conducive to relationship, because if another person is "making" me feel something that is "bad," that other person becomes the focus of my attention, and I need something about them to change in order for me to feel better. This is problematic because in this type of situation, not only are my emotions treated as problems, but those who seem to be causing these emotions will also be treated as veritable targets. And since people do not like changes to be imposed upon them, much less to be treated as targets, externalizing emotions this way will likely work against relationships.

*Intellectual Safety*

Finally, to return to our concentric circles of safety, the innermost circle of intellectual safety is probably the most difficult and the most strategic to achieve. The simplest way to describe this aspect of safety is to consider whether a person would feel safe if they could "read my mind" (thoughts) about them. For example, suppose my observations of another person lead me to think, "this person is lazy" (or stupid, ridiculous, boring, or any other similarly negative adjective). Would the person I am evaluating feel safe? How will such an evaluation lend itself to deeper connections?

These last two queries are intended to be "leading questions." That is, I am assuming that if the other person could read my mind, they would not feel safe and that labeling people generally does not lead to deeper connections. They also raise a third question: What alternatives are available if I truly do see a person as lazy (or stupid, ridiculous, boring, etc.)?

Can I not think of a person as I please without threatening the relationship? Of course, I can! The problem is not so much what one person thinks about another. *The problem is that so often the "thought" is not acknowledged in the first place.* Having opinions is not problematic if I identify them as such.

This is admittedly a very technical point; at the same time, it is very relevant to the themes of this book. There is a subtle but significant difference between saying "Bob is lazy" and "I *think* Bob is lazy." In the first case, laziness is stated, and therefore treated, as fact, and if this assertion is the reason for another person's emotion, such as frustration, then we are firmly planted in the realm of survival. That is, when the "facts" are the reasons for why we feel what we feel, then we are likely not managing our own emotions. Instead, circumstances or incidents are doing the managing, which unnecessarily complicates the relationship.

Conversely, if I say, "I *think* Bob is lazy and therefore, I feel frustrated," now my opinion is the primary reason for why I feel what I feel, and this gives room for the relationship to work. My frustration is not tied to Bob's actions but rather it is tied to my thoughts about Bob's actions. Likewise, if my frustration is not tied directly to Bob, Bob is not tied directly to my frustration. Since Bob is not tied to my frustration, he and I are both free to allow me to be frustrated. This both increases the chances of me taking responsibility for this frustration and allows Bob to make changes that are more sustainable if he so chooses. The chances of Bob changing (for example, Bob becoming less lazy and more diligent) are much better if it makes sense for him to be more diligent rather than if he makes changes just to make sure I am not frustrated with him.

---

## "Intellectual safety is one of the most difficult and yet pivotal aspects of safety."

---

*Safe Self-Talk*

Here, an interesting concept related to all levels of safety, especially the topic of intellectual safety is how we think about ourselves. Am I, for example, critical or accepting of myself?

Do I call myself lazy (or some other self-denigrating adjective), and if so, what might the implications be for my relationships with others? In general, it seems that the more negative my own self-perceptions, the more likely others will pick up on these perceptions and possibly see me similarly. Relationships are two-way streets, and so there is bound to be a reciprocal impact. So, to the extent that my self-opinions are not in line with the facts, the relationship could also suffer unnecessarily.

Intellectual safety is one of the most difficult and yet pivotal aspects of safety, because we are so acquainted with equating thoughts with situations. This, in turn, can make it difficult to know where our feelings are coming from. In my experience, most arguments between couples stem from this tendency. Suppose two people, John and Jane, have been talking about an upcoming event and, in the process, one says something that unintentionally leads to hurt:

| | |
|---|---|
| **Jane:** | *You don't respect me. You wouldn't say that if you respected me.* |
| **John:** | *That's not true, Jane. You always accuse me of not respecting you, but it's not true.* |
| **Jane:** | *There you go again telling me I'm wrong. If you respected me, you wouldn't be so critical.* |
| **John:** | *You're not listening to me, Jane.* |

This interaction illustrates the compelling way in which emotions can quickly become more complex than necessary. As the dialogue develops, we might ask, does Jane feel more respected or less respected when John replies? Or conversely, does John feel Jane is being more truthful or less truthful when Jane replies? It is likely that the answer to both of these questions is no, especially since this brief conversation apparently ends with a mutual sense of disconnection: Jane calling John critical and John saying Jane is not listening to him. What is happening here and what can be done to address it?

Sometimes an obvious observation can be a strategic place to start. What is happening between John and Jane? What seems most obvious is that they are both arguing about how they want to be treated better by one another, and they are likely disappointed that this is not happening. I would venture to say that what is slightly less obvious is that their disappointments are good and healthy. That is, it is good to not want to be mistreated, and it is healthy to want to be treated well. At the risk of sounding sarcastic, it is far less healthy to want to be mistreated or to not want to be treated well.

Why are these observations important? When coupled with the concept of intellectual safety, they can provide either John or Jane (or both) some recourse for being able to have the conversation go in a different, more positive direction. In our snippet of dialogue, since Jane is the first one to speak let's begin with what John can do. By keeping in mind that disappointment reflects something good and healthy—the desire to be treated well—John can allow Jane to protest what he is doing.

This, in turn, is consistent with the goal of intellectual safety. One way of illustrating this is to imagine what it might be like for us to "read" John's mind as the conversation is unfolding (indicated by statements in parentheses):

> **Jane:** You don't respect me. You wouldn't say that if you respected me.
>
> **John:** That's not true, Jane. You always accuse me of not respecting you, but that's not true. (I can't believe you are saying that. That is ridiculous and so unfair of you.)
>
> **Jane:** There you go again telling me I'm wrong. If you respected me, you wouldn't be so critical.
>
> **John:** You're not listening to me, Jane. (I don't know why I try. It's like talking to a wall.)

If this is in fact what John is thinking while he is talking to Jane, is it any wonder why Jane perceives him to not respect her or to feel he is being critical? The same could be considered if we could read Jane's mind:

> **Jane:** You don't respect me. You wouldn't say that if you respected me (You won't ever respect me).
>
> **John:** That's not true, Jane. You always accuse

| | |
|---|---|
| | *me of not respecting you, but it's not true.* |
| **Jane:** | *There you go again telling me I'm wrong. If you respected me, you wouldn't be so critical (You never change, John. This feels so pointless).* |
| **John:** | *You're not listening to me, Jane.* |

Again, if this is what Jane is thinking, then can we blame John for feeling that Jane does not listen to him?

An intellectually safe conversation means that if actual mind-reading could happen, then the mind-reader would not feel threatened. At a minimum then, intellectual safety means that what is said is an accurate reflection of what is thought. More than this, an intellectually safe conversation means *the way I think about another person is respectful of the way that the other person thinks.* Therefore, I am open to whatever the other person says because I am open to them having their opinions. Of course, this is complicated by how often we express our opinions as if they are facts (for example, John telling Jane, "you always accuse me of not respecting you" or Jane telling John, "there you go again telling me I'm wrong").

*Overt Operations*

Related to this, an important strategy for clarifying communication and increasing connection with others is what we have previously called *translation* or converting apparent statements of "fact" into opinions. The first step occurs when one person's thoughts about the other are acknowledged as such. Second, intellectual safety can increase when covert thoughts shift from a second-person format to a third-person format, for example: "I think that is ridiculous and so unfair of *her*" rather than "I think that is ridiculous and so unfair of *you*". This, like so many points in this book, is a small detail, but it might particularly lend to one person feeling safer if they could read the other's mind. By shifting to this format, we are, both literally and figuratively, working with "*self*-talk."

So, it would be better if both John and Jane would at least be more explicit about their opinions, respectively. Thus, John's self-talk could be modified to, "I think that is ridiculous and so unfair of Jane" and similarly, Jane's self-talk could be "I think

254 | MAYBE THE WHOLE OCEAN

John will never change."

To many, these changes will undoubtedly seem superficial or possibly even petty. What difference can such minute issues really make? To see how this critique is understandable, we need only think of situations where the "facts" seem to speak for themselves, times when there seems to be a consensus that a situation is bothersome. What if, for example, after I am given a traffic ticket I say, "I feel frustrated because I *think* I got a ticket" as opposed to "I feel frustrated because I got a ticket"? This likely sounds absurd because I already "know" I was given a ticket. Still, I ask the question this way to demonstrate how certain situations can be particularly emotionally compelling. In fact, when I say "I feel frustrated because I think I got a ticket," I am really saying, "I feel frustrated because of *what I think about getting a ticket.*"

Once, when I tried to explain this approach to my brother, he very cleverly picked up a large exercise ball and knocked me off balance with it, saying with a smile, "I didn't hit you, the ball did." Touché! On one hand, traffic tickets and physical altercations are in a different category from relationships, especially when it comes to the role thinking plays in emotions. We are so accustomed to believing that our emotions are situational, as in the case of traffic tickets and others' physical actions "making" us feel certain ways, that it is silly and tedious to even consider that these events might be more interpreted than we realize.

On the other hand, and at the risk of seeming too literal (again, I affectionately think of these strategies as "Literal Therapy"), I am trying to train myself to consider the value of saying that frustration, even with a traffic ticket, is due to thinking certain things about how or why I got a traffic ticket. For example, my focus may be on the unexpected nature of the ticket, the regret I have about speeding, or the problem it may represent for my budget. With some chagrin, I agree with my brother that yes, the exercise ball hit me directly, so he hit me only indirectly. Still, if my thoughts, like the exercise ball, have a more direct impact upon my feelings than my situations do, I have more say over what I feel. And this say extends to how my feelings can lead to being more responsive than reactive, especially in my relationships. So, while I dislike conceding to my brother, it is a small price for me to pay to have the option of retaining such say!

Either person in a dialogue can initiate this kind of responsiveness. In our working conversation, since the conversation picks up with what Jane says, let us consider what John can do differently to respond. If John can simply start by acknowledging the role of thinking on both sides, this could make a difference. First, as soon as he hears Jane speaking, he can consider translating what she is saying into a reminder to himself that it is important for Jane to have her perspectives and opinions. Moreover, if John can covertly acknowledge that he thinks that Jane is being ridiculous or unfair, he will likely be on his way to being able to also say, more overtly, that he thinks she is not saying something that is accurate. Awareness of his thinking will precede his actual response, which, of course, will be the first step in John being more responsive. Prioritizing his thinking will then make the conversation more intellectually safe. The goal will be for John to better distinguish his thinking from what Jane is saying (which likely would feel safer to Jane if she could read John's mind). Hopefully, this will also empower John to be more emotionally attuned to Jane, thereby addressing her expressed concerns in the first place. By focusing on increased intellectual safety, the transaction might shift to something like this (with parentheses indicating each person's *self-talk):*

**Jane:**     *You don't respect me. You wouldn't say that if you respected me.*

**John:**     *(I think that Jane saying this is extreme. I think that it is ridiculous and unfair of her. To be balanced and fair though it will be good for me to be open to how she sees this and attentive to how important this is to her, so...) I don't think that is true, Jane. I think you always accuse me of not respecting you, but I don't think that what you are saying is accurate.*

What might Jane say at this point? To see how John might still influence this situation, apart from Jane's help, let's consider what John might be able to continue to do differently:

**Jane:** *There you go again telling me I'm wrong. If you respected me, you wouldn't be so critical.*

**John:** *(Jane already feels I am being unfair. I think I am being fairer than she realizes, but telling her this is likely to leave her feeling I am still being unfair. What can I tell her that will help her to see 1) I'm not saying she's wrong and 2) I do respect her even if I don't see it her way?). Jane, you want me to respect you.*

**Jane:** *Well, yes...*

Is this too ideal of an outcome? Perhaps. Alternatively, some might say it's hardly a change, too small to be considered an improvement. Again, just a drop in the bucket. The goal here is to demonstrate how prioritizing safety (in this case, intellectual, but at all levels overall) can lead to better communication and in fact new places of connection. Small as it may seem, Jane's use of the word "yes" can indicate such connection. And, once a connection has been established, a *precedent* has been set. Something new can now occur, and the hope is that the new direction will lead to even more connections down the line. Just a drop. Maybe one. Maybe two and then three, and then maybe we'll increasingly experience more connections in our conversations.

### Presence of Positives

Finally, it may seem obvious, but safety is not just a matter of avoiding danger. Safety is also about promoting an atmosphere of security and protection. So, consistent with the various levels discussed, refraining from physical aggression, threatening gestures, or disrespectful thoughts are all necessary but not sufficient. The other half of safety involves focusing on behaviors that build up the relationship. For example, in addition to the nonnegotiable of not striking or cursing another, it is vital to be gentle and encouraging. Similarly, as we minimize our unspoken criticisms, we can also speak sincere and affirming words.

To summarize, safety is the first step towards endeavoring to SURF, towards riding the waves of freedom and joy in relationship. When safety is in place—when a sense of mutual respect and trust imbues all physical, emotional, and intellectual arenas—people can be themselves with one another. In these ways, the threat of being somehow hurt by another person is mitigated because each party involved is acting, feeling, and thinking in accord with an awareness that both interpersonal similarities and differences have value.

> **"Safety is also about promoting an atmosphere of security and protection."**

### Understanding

*Peaks and Troughs*

One of my closest friends, Aaron, is a surfer. On occasion, he reminds me that, as a surfer, he knows that for waves to exist, there also must be both peaks and troughs. The two are inseparable. Sooner or later, one will give way to the other. Keeping this in mind, he knows that good riding conditions will be followed by bad riding conditions and so forth. This allows him to embrace both the active and inactive phases of the surfing experience. Applying his knowledge of waves to his life in general, he is seldom thrown off by circumstances, positive or negative, easy or difficult, comfortable or painful. Aaron likewise seems to take this openness into his approach to relationships, and as a result, there is an ease about him with just about anyone—he is free to be himself continually.

Aaron's approach to surfing, relationships, and life can help introduce the second principle of connection—understanding. To the extent that understanding is practiced, freedom is also experienced. To the extent that freedom is experienced, relationships can thrive.

What is understanding? Perhaps the best way to address this is to begin by clarifying what understanding is not. And, in a word, understanding is not agreement. This may come as a surprise, since the two are often used interchangeably, and in fact, understanding does have a connotation of "mutual agreement." However, when we consider just what it means to practice emotional responsiveness rather than reactivity, I hope it will be clear that distinguishing between the two can be strategic for relationships overall. To illustrate this, it will help to explore two other concepts: reflection and empathy.

## The Breakfast Club

*Pancakes*

When I think of these two concepts, several experiences with my daughters come to mind, all involving, of all things, breakfasts together. The first was with my oldest, Jessie, when she was six years old. On this day, I was rather excited because I had the opportunity to start the day with Jessie and a meal of homemade blueberry pancakes and boysenberry syrup. In my enthusiasm, I announced to Jessie what we were about to eat:

> *"Hey Jessie, it's so great to be having breakfast with you this morning! We're gonna have blueberry pancakes and boysenberry syrup!"*

As I said this, I was expecting her to join me in celebrating the prospect of sharing the delicious food that was before us. Imagine my surprise then, even shock, when she looked me in the eye and with a flat expression on her face said, *"Disgusting."* In fact, as soon as I heard this, my shock turned to disappointment, and I wondered just what was going to be necessary to correct her apparent rudeness.

At the same time, however, I was in the beginning of developing my own private counseling practice and talking with various folks about listening strategies. So, in an effort to "walk the talk," I paused, literally bit my tongue, and tried to clarify with Jessie what had just occurred.

> *"What do mean by disgusting, sweetheart?"* I asked, trying my best to not take offense at the word even as I repeated it.

*"Well, Daddy, you said **poisonberry**!"*

I did a double take, caught off guard by her simple and unabashed innocence. And then it occurred to me, she really was innocent. *"You mean you thought I was going to serve you poisonberry syrup?"*

*"Uh-huh"* came the reply, signaling the first point in the entire conversation that felt like a connection.

Almost as instantly as it had shifted from excitement to disappointment, my attitude changed again, this time from disappointment to gratitude. I was glad to realize that my daughter was disgusted at the thought of eating poison!

*"Oh no, sweetheart, I would never give you poison! I said **boysenberry** syrup, see the picture on the label here?"*

*"Ohhh, I see..."* And with that, we proceeded to enjoy a lovely meal together.

*Bagels*

A second story takes place around the same time in our family's life, when my middle daughter Ella was around two or three. I recall a certain day when I was getting ready to go to work, saying goodbye to Ella for the day. In her hand was about an eighth of a bagel. Not wanting it to go to waste, I encouraged her, *"Ella, please eat your bagel."* Barely a toddler, Ella quite predictably answered, *"I don't want to."*

Now this posed a curious situation for me. On one hand, it was just an eighth of a bagel and hardly worth a struggle. On the other, as her dad, I think it is important for me to have a certain amount of authority and follow-through. If I give my children an instruction, even if it is to finish a small amount of food, I want them to give it their every consideration and quite frankly, follow the instruction. So, before continuing, I encourage you, as the reader, to pause and consider, given these circumstances, what course of action would you find most effective?

\*\*\*

My inclination was to try and accomplish a sensitivity to Ella's toddler mentality while also respecting my own prerogative to give instruction as her dad. And, in fact, at the time, I was aware of wanting to understand the concept of reflection. So, I said to Ella, *"You don't want to eat your bagel because you're not hungry. Is that right, Ella?"*

She nodded.

*"Anything else you want to tell me?"*

She shook her head.

So, I told her, with some hopefulness, *"Ok, well then, please eat your bagel."*

My hope sank though when Ella insisted, *"But I don't want to."* Of course, she's a toddler, I thought. Again, hardly a big deal but I also did not want her to leave with the notion that she could just call the shots, so I stood my ground.

*"I know you don't want to, Ella. You just told me that. Please eat your bagel; you'll have a great day."*

By this time, it was important for me to be in the car. And as I was backing out of the driveway, I could hear Ella, saying, somewhat playfully, *"I don't want to have a great day!"*

I went to work that day around 8 a.m. and returned shortly before 8 p.m. As was our custom, when I walked in the door, Jessie and Ella jumped out from behind a wall, and I did my best to pretend to be scared. Then, a few minutes later, Ella looked at me with a smile and said, *"Daddy, guess what?"*

*"What, honey?"*

*"I ate my bagel!"*

I don't remember exactly what happened at that point, but I am pretty sure an outside observer would never have guessed that the cheering and dancing I broke into was because we were celebrating news about what had earlier been an eighth of a bagel! And wanting to preserve the memory, from that day over 10 years ago to the present, I occasionally will remind Ella of her success, saying, *"Do you remember the waffle?"*

She's quick to nod and equally quick to remind me, *"Dad, it wasn't a waffle, it was a bagel."*

In similar fashion, I recall an experience when my youngest daughter Zoe was about four, she was eating cheese chips for breakfast. In addition, Keri had just, I believe, spoken to Zoe about putting on her stockings since we were going to church. I said, *"Zoe, I know you want to eat those cheese chips for breakfast, and at the same time, I think it will be better for you to eat something healthier. So please eat just one more and then close the bag and put a clip on it."*

She said okay, and I left the room. I returned a few minutes later to find the bag clipped and Zoe smiling, *"Daddy, I chose to put the clip on the bag, **and** I put on my stockings!"*[2]

On one hand, these are just family stories about very specific situations that happened to, thankfully, work out well. On another, I am compelled to think that however simple and elementary, these stories illustrate the potential for a world of connection to take place. One drop. Maybe two, in this case three, and then maybe years later we will still be telling these stories.

*Reflection*

Through these separate occasions and many other follow-up experiences, I have become convinced of two principles. First, the "pancake" incident illustrates the principle of reflection. Jessie and I learned, in a rather humorous way, the power of a certain kind of reflective listening. In the words of relationship guru, John Gottman, and colleagues, "Good communication means having the impact you intended to have, that is Intent

---

2   Although it is not a "breakfast" story, I want to also recognize our son, Jacob for his debut demonstration of "choosing" something difficult and mature. He wanted Keri to buy him a certain toy truck, yet still agreed to wait and forgo the purchase when she asked him to, despite previously carrying the toy around the store for nearly the entirety of the shopping trip!

equals Impact."[3] Jessie had said something that did not sit well with me ("disgusting"), and it was important for me to first see if what I had heard lined up with what she had meant to say. Upon hearing Jessie's reasoning, I realized that we had much more in common than had initially seemed to be the case. If I were to express the principle in a statement I would say: *Reflection makes hidden connections visible.*

During the pancake breakfast, I came very close to reacting. For a brief amount of time, I took issue with Jessie's words, to the point where I was persuaded that she was essentially "making" me feel disappointed. However, if I had corrected her it would have been premature and most likely have led to extra misunderstanding. It was better for me to delay my reply until after I had given full attention to what she had shared. I cannot recall if at the time I was thinking about emotions, but in retrospect, one explanation is that I was able to better hear Jessie by connecting my feeling (disappointment) with what I thought Jessie was meaning (rudeness) rather than just what she had said (disgusting). By making this connection, I was thus better able to respond rather than react.

## "Reflection makes hidden connections visible."

The reflection process in communication can also be compared to how light interacts with glass surfaces. The words we use in any exchange can be likened to either a transparent or reflective surface such as a window or a mirror.

It seems our default is to interact with one another as if we are talking through windows. This is intuitive since we often aspire to a type of interchange that involves a natural verbal back and forth rhythm, with question and answer, call and response, e.g., How are you? I am fine, thank you, how are you?

However, when feelings enter the picture, the "window" approach can often, and ironically, be reactive. In the "pancake"

3  Gottman, J. M., Notarius, C., Gonso, J., & Markman, H. (1976). A couple's guide to communication. Champaign, IL: Research Press, p.1.

example, this might have looked like me telling Jessie she was being rude or inconsiderate as soon as I heard her say the word, "disgusting." Upon hearing this, assuming she would have felt that she was right and I was wrong (and that no clarification took place), Jessie might have told me that I was being unfair, mean, or judgmental. I, in turn, might have been further reinforced in my belief that she was out of line and sent her to her room. Though this is a caricature, the point is our words would have been like clear glass, and each of us would have been talking about our own perspective or position, likely without hearing the other's. This approach may be accompanied by the assumption that emotions were generated from without, that each of us was "making" the other feel frustrated, irritated, hurt, or criticized. Often, and again, ironically, a "window" approach to communication can leave each person feeling like they are "talking to a wall."

In the end, an accurate awareness of oneself is necessary for being able to practice reflective listening with others. Following our working model, a vital part of self-understanding is recognizing the primacy of interpretations in our emotional experience. This is likely a significant reason for why many self-help and counseling approaches emphasize the use of "I-statements" (e.g., "I feel angry because I think what just happened was unfair") for acknowledging individual ownership and responsibility for feelings. And I believe that, when this happens, difficult dialogues can be circumvented as each person shares their own experience with the other rather than saying things that could sound blaming. So, instead of saying "What you did just ticked me off," person A might say, "I feel angry because I think what happened was unfair."

Now, suppose A expresses this kind of ownership, and person B still appears to react:

*A:* I feel angry because I think what happened was unfair.
*B:* Well, that's your problem.

This can be a cue to A that B was not ready for what was just shared. In such situations, it is quite likely that the apparent "defensive" reactions of the other person are ways in which that person is processing their own personal material. In this regard, additional strategies might be stated thus: *"The answer to projection is reflection,"* and this can be accomplished by taking a *"suspend (me) to attend and extend (you)"* approach.

In this scenario, if B has just told A that A's anger is A's "problem," A might consider ways of focusing on B's interests and concerns. For example, A might say something like, "You would like to see me take more responsibility for myself" or "You wish I wouldn't blame you for my feelings."

Of course, this "suspend to attend" approach is neither easy nor comfortable, and it again relies on genuine sincerity. Nevertheless, it can be relationally strategic in at least two ways: 1) it prioritizes the other person's readiness, focusing on what they seem most inclined to discuss and 2) it is consistent with personal ownership of feelings via awareness of thoughts, thereby continuing the emphasis on self-understanding and responsiveness.

*Empathy*

In the bagel incident, I witnessed a small, though powerful example of empathy. I think of this as an illustration of empathy because, by trying to reflect what Ella had shared, I was able to allow her to "have" her feelings.

In this regard, I have found that an especially useful definition of empathy is, "putting yourself in someone else's shoes while retaining your own feet."[4] Putting myself in Ella's shoes involved doing my best to see how it made sense to her to not want to eat her bagel. It was not my job to change what she wanted or did not want, rather I was concerned with showing her that I took seriously what was important to her. At the same time, it was important to maintain optimal influence as her father, so it was also strategic to "retain my own feet." While my kids' desires and wants are important to me as a father, it is also important for me to teach them the value of often refraining from doing what they want in the short-run to experience something else they may want even more in the long-run.

---

4   I am grateful to Professor Jeffrey Bjorck at Fuller Theological Seminary for introducing me to this very practical definition of empathy.

The alternative to empathy is sympathy—putting myself in another's shoes and essentially taking on their feet. Or, put another way, inspirational author and speaker, Brené Brown defines sympathy as "feeling for" while empathy is more akin to "feeling with."[5] For example, I might have so identified with Ella that I took pity on her to the point of just letting her have her way. Incidentally, I find it telling to consider the literal overlap in sympathy and the part of our nervous system identified as "sympathetic" which is involved in the fight-flight-freeze reactions that are so key to survival. This is not to disparage sympathy, only to say that it reflects a certain approach to negative emotions that can easily lend to "rescuing" a person from their feelings or trying to "cheer them up." As well-intended as these efforts are, they can create unnecessary problems later.

By contrast, empathy empowers people to own their own emotions and thereby freely entertain options that are more sustainable in the long-run. I believe that even though I left for work that day without enforcing my instruction to Ella, because I took time to try and follow her viewpoint, she was subsequently more able to volitionally go against the grain of her own desires. If I were to express the principle in a statement it would be: *empathy facilitates choice.*

I realize that these are only a few examples, again fairly silly, with benign consequences. How do we generalize to other, more "significant" communication problems? For example, as a counselor, I will talk with people about various interpersonal conflicts, ranging from infidelity to financial worries to health concerns to academic challenges to grief and traumatic experiences. Can stories about my kids' morning meals really pertain to these larger situations? With full respect for how severe life's challenges can be, I suggest that, yes, these stories carry powerful implications, albeit very subtle, for addressing the interpersonal dynamics of even the most trying circumstances.

**"Understanding requires more than one viewpoint and often involves a process of learning something new."**

5    Brown, B. (August 15, 2013 RSA Talk). The power of vulnerability . 06:40. Retrieved on August 8, 2020, from https://www.youtube.com/watch?v=sXSjc-pbXk4

One way of thinking about this is to consider that understanding is only one type of communication strategy. There are other strategies such as information exchange or problem-solving, both of which are more conducive to the "window" or "sympathy" approaches. For example, when trying to adjudicate matters of right and wrong, a problem-solving approach to communication may be indicated, e.g., "Did you take Johnny's toy? Yes or no?" However, at conversational impasses, such as, "I did not!" "Yes, you did!" "No, I didn't," understanding can be a pathway through and to new, interesting, and clearer places.

Understanding requires more than one viewpoint and often involves a process of learning something new. It is about embracing and honoring our differences and seeing them as vital to relationship. Again, it involves reflection and empathy. If I simply agree with another person, I risk losing or missing the importance of differences that might otherwise enhance the relationship. In addition, if I agree, I essentially am at risk for putting on another's shoes *and taking on their feet*. This is like cloning the other person, but clones have little to no reason to relate to one another. If they do relate to one another, it is, as others have suggested, redundant. In the words of American businessman, William Wrigley, Jr., "when two men always agree, one of them is unnecessary."[6]

True intimacy requires the kind of difference that often accompanies disagreement. The challenge is getting to the place where this compels us to see *both our position and another's position* as equally important, even equally valid. This is indispensable to the kind of connection that we are after as we seek to experience the full ocean of emotional and interpersonal experience.

## Reaching Out

*Small Waves, Big Waves*
Although I am not a surfer, it is my understanding that one of the most challenging aspects of surfing is standing up on the board and catching the wave. This involves the ability to read the

---

6   Clark, N. M. (1931, March). Spunk never cost a man a job worth having. The American Magazine 111(3), p. 63. Retrieved January 23, 2018, from https://quoteinvestigator.com/2015/04/04/agree/#return-note-10916-1

wave, time the situation, and move into a relatively vulnerable position.

Reaching out is the third aspect of connecting and involves similar steps. Much like the surfer who paddles into position and then ventures to stand, the person who reaches out in relationship takes a risk. It is a unique sort of risk, and the challenge it represents can be quite remarkable. On the ocean of relationships, when we risk reaching out to another, we are primarily dealing with emotional stakes.

For our purposes, let us consider reaching out to be any move towards another person that is an attempt to strengthen a relationship. Thus, attempts to initiate conversation, repair past hurts, apologize, coordinate meetings, share personal feelings, or hear about others' experiences are all forms of reaching out. Naturally, when this happens, and the relationship is already strong, it is easier to continue reaching out. If I am feeling good about a friendship, then call my friend to further develop the bond, this kind of reaching out is marked by mutually positive and beneficial emotions. Perhaps it is akin to surfing small waves, where the act of standing up is less of a risk. Staying connected in such situations requires less effort overall.

However, the waves get bigger and the standing gets riskier, when there is tension or strain in a relationship and emotions are less positive. Again, it is striking how daunting reaching out can be in a negative atmosphere. We will go to remarkable lengths to avoid hurting others or our own egos. Whether we are trying to not offend or whether we have been offended, we often refrain from doing the things in relationship that will make for more depth, more closeness, or more connection. At the center of why we so often refrain from reaching out is one overarching reason: avoidance. And, of course, what is so interesting is that we avoid certain emotions.

Again, we can allow our $f\,i\,\boldsymbol{T}$ model to address this and help us to increase our chances of connecting. Take for instance person A, who is hesitant to ask a favor of person B. A may not want to impose on B. Or A may be concerned that B will say no. Either way, A might refrain from asking B for help, because the request could lead to unpleasant emotions.

A deeper look at the situation reflects an approach to emotions that is characterized by the $fIt$ model. If A does not ask B because A does not want to introduce unpleasant emotions, it would seem either A's question or B's answer are the assumed causes of such unpleasant emotions. If so, an incident is the main determinant of the feelings. Moreover, trying to prevent unpleasant emotions from occurring is an avoidance of the emotions themselves. This points back to survival mode which is often accompanied by the possibility of unnecessary problems, such as not being able to experience the help of a friend. This is again akin to missing out on riding a "smaller wave."

Now, consider a situation that is more tenuous, where the stakes are much higher. Suppose there has been some sort of rupture in a relationship and A wants to apologize to B. There is uncertainty about whether B will be receptive to the apology. In addition, A is aware of guilt or shame regarding their part in the damage that was caused. In both ways, A feels vulnerable, though not necessarily because of anything B has done. Rather, the vulnerability is due to how sharing one's feelings, and specifically feelings about a mistake, can be very uncomfortable. Such vulnerability can be so uncomfortable that many times the risks are not taken; so often the waves never get ridden.

In such situations, the stakes seem higher because the feelings are more pronounced, and the well-being of the relationship can seem much less certain. Nevertheless, the same principles apply. If our primary concern is that feelings will somehow be damaged, we have an opportunity to remind ourselves that strong assumptions about feelings are at work. Many times, however, instead of focusing on the priority of beliefs, we would rather avoid potential conflicts, especially if there is already a strain in the relationship. Our intentions are usually good, but the benefits of conflict avoidance are often short-lived.

Attempts to connect that include acknowledging feelings will likely seem silly, gimmicky, canned, inauthentic, or awkward. The more we embrace and affirm the role our thinking and beliefs play in our emotions, the more the awkwardness will give way to increased closeness and appreciation.

*Epic Surfing*

One of the most difficult yet significant ways we can reach out in relationships is through the process of acknowledging past hurts and experiencing forgiveness. We will explore this further in the next chapter, but it seems worth mentioning here as a particular kind of connecting, a particular kind of "surfing."

Since emotional stress is painful, there are many potential barriers to forgiveness. And while forgiveness is integral to thriving in relationships, our survival instincts are strong. So, forgiveness is always a very intentional act, often against tendencies to fight, flee, or freeze emotionally.

Depending on the severity of the emotional wound, achieving forgiveness can be compared to surfing waves that seem to dwarf the surfer. It is important to remember that deeper, more intimate connecting is a process that again takes time. Moreover, there may be many times it feels like reaching out will lead to "wiping out." If we keep our *f i T* principles in mind, however, we can be assured that as far as emotions go, "wiping out" is not a matter of individual survival per se. Of course, there are times when the support of others will be necessary, such as the help of other friends or counselors for facilitating the connection/forgiveness process. In such cases we might consider the waves massive enough to require "tow-in" assistance. Regardless of the size of the wave, anytime forgiveness is experienced or trust is restored, we will have experienced an epic ride.

Just as a surfer does not directly manipulate the waves, the use of our emotions to enhance relationships is ultimately about influencing rather than controlling others. When I asked a friend, John, who is quite an accomplished surfer, what the hardest part of surfing is, I was pleasantly surprised when he replied, "Knowing how to get in the wave." He followed up by saying that this involves "ocean knowledge." In relationships, this is also true of reaching out. We need to understand both the dynamics of connecting (how to get in the wave) and the ways in which emotions can work (ocean knowledge).

As these are learned, we get progressively better at finding the mysterious balance between going with the flow of the relationship and going in the directions that we desire. We will learn to discover the thrills of new skills and "carving up" the waves of our relationships. And as we gain more and more mastery, we will see how part of the joy of surfing is the wild, unpredictable, and even precarious reality that the ocean of relationships, like the sea, is never completely ours to control.

## Fun

*Creative Connecting*

Finally, our comparison of interpersonal connecting to surfing would not be complete without acknowledging the importance of having a little fun. In fact, this is vital to interpersonal thriving. Just as the primary motivation for catching waves is often the sheer pleasure of the ride, so the goal of relationships might very well be the enjoyment of being with other people and experiencing the synergy of "doing life" together.

Another way of putting this is to consider the role that *creativity* can play in our relationships. Indeed, since relationships, by definition, require at least one person to interact with another, including interacting with oneself, there may very well be no limit to how we can creatively connect. By now, I hope that this book is an example, with all the quirkiness of what I term oceanspeak, of how far our ideas can take us in our interpersonal journeys—especially as we emphasize the notion that ideas, even more than situations and circumstances, are that powerful.

It is difficult, and indeed I would say impossible, to overstate the importance of creativity in our approaches to interpersonal connecting. Again, this traces back to our original blueprint as people made in the image of God. In fact, the very notion that we are "made" indicates the involvement of a creator. And to say we are designed in the very image of this creator is to say that each of us possesses a built-in tendency to create in some way or another. Whether one is a person with an artistic talent or simply a child who pretends a stick is a sword or magic wand, we all have within us an inextinguishable drive to imagine new possibilities.

All too often however we do not access the full potential

of our creativity when it comes to relationships. In fact, we can tend to "turn off" our creativity, even with those who are closest to us. This is part of survival mode. When situations take precedence over thinking, we have less reason and less motivation to emphasize interpretations. As a result, we operate more automatically and instinctively.

*"Outside the Box" Thoughtfulness*
Creativity in connecting with others, however, calls for both thoughtfulness and "thinking outside the box" of natural problem-solving strategies. Thoughtfulness involves observing and learning what is important or special to other people. For example, in my own life, my sister, JoAnna, continues to be an inspiration and model of this kind of *gracious awareness of others*. Whether she is blessing someone with a personalized gift, reaching out to address a practical need, or simply recalling details of memories that show her extraordinary care and concern, JoAnna always seems ready to meet people where they are, on their terms. In addition, she usually manages to inject some laughter or humor into these thoughtful ways, resulting in memorable and enjoyable experiences, especially since she is a genuinely "fun" person by nature.

---

## "When situations take precedence over thinking...we operate more automatically and instinctively."

---

We have discussed how connecting focuses on understanding rather than agreement. Thus, at an emotional level, connecting affirms and utilizes various emotions instead of treating them as problems to be solved per se. This can seem very unnatural and even impractical, at least in the beginning. Nevertheless, this is because what we call "natural" is largely shaped by assumptions related to years of living by more reactive solutions that derive from the $fI\,t$ (rather than $f\,i\,T$) paradigm.

As we close out this chapter, I'll share several methods that reflect my own attempts to creatively apply more responsive solutions inspired by the $f\,i\,T$ paradigm. Admittedly, these often

272 | MAYBE THE WHOLE OCEAN

involve subtle nuances in language because emotional "fitness" is precisely about prioritizing what we think and, ultimately, believe about our feelings. Indeed, this is part of the creativity and fun of the process. And while these may seem mere drops in the bucket, I find they are increasingly making an ocean of difference.

*Syntax*

In an earlier chapter, we considered the potential power of changing one letter (from "o" to "e") in our way of framing a situation—specifically, noting the difference between saying that I "get to" do something rather than I (have) "got to" do something. While this is easily dismissible as a silly gimmick, it can also be useful, as well as fun, if we want it to be so. It can be a step towards making the shift from obligation to opportunity, which often forms the main difference between reacting and responding, surviving and thriving. The implication here is that freedom (which is the aim of opportunity) is vital to truly connecting with others.

Here are two other ways in which our approach to language can influence the extent to which we feel something is either obligatory or optional. Next to actual letters and words, another basic building block to communication and connecting may be the order—the syntax—of our words. Changing the syntax of certain words is an interesting, albeit subtle, way of shifting our perspective. A helpful example of this in popular culture is Yoda, the Jedi wizard from the *Star Wars* films. Specifically, he is known for such memorable phrases as "help you I can" or "a powerful ally it is."[7] The effect of this is a sort of "out of the box" way of thinking that has helped to endear "Master Yoda" to millions of viewers worldwide and set him apart as one of the most well-known science fiction characters of all time.

Being fond of *Star Wars*, I have been inspired to practice a similar "Jedi mind-trick" of my own. It again derives directly from my own passion to employ words as carefully as possible and applies to the all-important (in my mind) task of shifting from obligation to opportunity. For both reasons, it seems to

---

7   From Star Wars: Episode VI—Return of the Jedi (1983), screenplay written by Lawrence Kasdan and George Lucas, directed by Richard Marquand, and produced by Lucasfilm.

be quite versatile to me, as long as I can believe that it will be worthwhile.

In this case, the "trick" is to, like Yoda, rearrange syntax to shift perspective. And the reason it seems to work is the way in which certain words can have multiple meanings. For example, consider this simple phrase: "I have to take an examination." The word that particularly applies here is a curious one: "have." According to the *Random House Dictionary*, "have" can be used as a verb to mean "to possess or own" (I have a pet dog) or as an auxiliary verb to mean "to be required, compelled, or under obligation" (I have to go to the store).[8] At this point, I will consider it a particular success if the reader can predict the syntactic change I am about to propose. In fact, I would encourage you, the reader, to pause here to evaluate your own application of this before reading further.

***

The main change that will reflect a shift from obligation to opportunity is this: "I have an examination to take." Or the actual Jedi way might be: "An examination to take I have," which accomplishes the same purpose but with slightly more "force" (pun intended!). In my home, I enjoy implementing this in my conversations with my children—for example, shifting from "I have to take a shower" to "I have a shower to take" or "I have to go to work" to "I have work to go to," in the hope that even in our everyday interactions, we will learn to live more consciously where we might otherwise feel obligated. Grammatically speaking, we are making the indirect object into the direct object, but emotionally, we are incrementally setting ourselves free.

*Insert the Opportunity*
The second way to achieve a similar shift is even more simple. If the first instance relies on words having multiple meanings, this next move relies on how certain phrases can have multiple meanings as well. I have come to call this "inserting the opportunity" because this is precisely what is accomplished, both literally and figuratively.

---

8  have. (n.d.). Dictionary.com Unabridged. Retrieved December 22, 2017, from http://www.dictionary.com/browse/have

Consider again the statement, "I have to take an examination." On its own, there is a very rigid feel to this phrase, especially because the concept of an exam is easily associated with pressure and obligation. However, we can move fairly quickly from a sense of pressure to openness by quite easily adding the phrase "the opportunity" before talking about what apparently "has" to be done. So, the statement becomes, "I have (the opportunity) to take an examination." For those interested in optimizing a sense of freedom, I hope and trust that this will come as very good news! Of course, this, again, will only work to the extent that we really believe that it will be valuable for us to make this extra reminder to ourselves, and it may take some time before we experience the full benefits. Indeed, taking the time to do this for ourselves can seem downright tedious and it might appear more convenient to just say we "have to" do this or that at just about any turn and just live with the sense of pressure this subtly, yet inevitably, engenders. And it is my observation that this is very much what we, as a society, so often do. We can be so acquainted with obligation that we resist the steps that lead to more freedom. Nevertheless, as understandable as this is, it is frequently unnecessary.

It is intriguing to consider the extra stress we put on ourselves via the unnecessary ways we talk about what we "need to" or "have to" do. This is ironic because in most cases we can usually get away with *not doing* what it is we *have* to do (for example, we may say we have to wake up early and yet sleep in late). Of course, there are often consequences to not doing what seems mandatory, but the consequences are usually not dire enough to prevent us from violating the apparent mandate. It is stressful to have something required of us and even more stressful to fail to meet this requirement. More interesting to me though is the effective way in which we can use the double meanings of words and phrases to minimize this stress. If I move from "having to take a test" to "having an opportunity to take a test," I symbolically move from a passive to an active role. We might say I am positioned to be more "open" to taking the test even if I am not "okay" with doing so. Like an incessant visitor, opportunity may be continuously knocking, and we may just not realize it because we mistake the visit for an intrusion.[9]

*Gold Mines and Gold Lines*

When I was in middle school, one of my favorite teachers had a policy of giving tests that contained what he called "gold mines"—where answers to certain questions at the beginning of the test were embedded in specific questions later in the test. So, for example if question #5 was "What is the name of the tomb in India that was built for Shah Jahan?" question number #20 might be something like, "What city is the Taj Mahal located in?" The teacher was making the test easier and giving us "free points," because if we were even remotely familiar with the material, we would at least get certain questions correct (in this case, we would see that the answer to question #5 is the "the Taj Mahal"). Our teacher called these kinds of questions "gold mines" because they contained little nuggets of treasure if we just knew where to look.

> **"We convey to others that they, as the originators of the ideas, are more important to us than the outcomes of our interactions with them."**

Our conversations can contain similar "inside information" that can help us to better connect. Such information can be useful when we find ourselves feeling like the person we are talking to is not understanding what we are trying to say. Consider the following interchange from a previous example in Chapter 7, with numerical indicators added:

*A1:* *I feel like you don't care about me anymore.*
*B1:* *I can't believe you said that. Of course, I care about you.*

---

9  Sometimes going from obligation to opportunity can feel dishonest or forced, especially if the initial circumstances feel particularly negative. At such times, an interesting and effective strategy is to stay "neutral." In this case, one way of doing this is to reframe an apparent obligation as an "option" (e.g., "I have the option of taking the test"). This has the dual benefit of shifting from a survival to nonsurvival (though perhaps not yet "thrival") mode and of feeling more honest about simply stating a fact. For an excellent resource on neutral thinking, see Trevor Moawad and Andy Staples' (2019) very practical book, It Takes What It Takes: How to Think Neutrally and Gain Control of Your Life (HarperOne: New York, NY).

> **A2:** *Well, if you cared about me, you would take me more seriously.*
> **B2:** *You're too sensitive. I am taking you seriously; you just don't see it.*

In this case, a "gold mine" can be found in what each person says the second time. So, line A2 reveals that person A would feel more cared for if they were taken more seriously, and line B2 reveals that person B does not think A sees how seriously B does take A. Here is one way the conversation might turn, beginning with B making a change:

> **A1:** *I feel like you don't care about me anymore.*
> **B1:** *I can't believe you said that. Of course, I care about you.*
> **A2:** *Well, if you cared about me, you would take me more seriously.*
> **B2:** *So, I could show you I care about you if I could take you more seriously.*
> **A3:** *Yes!*

Or A might change the conversation this way:

> **A1:** *I feel like you don't care about me anymore.*
> **B1:** *I can't believe you said that. Of course, I care about you.*
> **A2:** *Well, if you cared about me, you would take me more seriously.*
> **B2:** *You're too sensitive. I am taking you seriously; you just don't see it.*
> **A3:** *So, if I could see how seriously you take me, I would feel how much you do care for me.*
> **B3:** *Yes!*

In the language of gold mining, the "veins" of gold that lead to improved connections are discoverable whenever someone shares from the heart. Thus, when it comes to communication, the gold mines are also "gold lines" that can be drawn between various ideas that are shared back and forth. Hopefully these examples, as contrived as they might sound, demonstrate new ways we can follow what others may be trying to say. And since we generally do not work with transcripts of our conversations (though these might be useful for more creativity), tracing these unseen lines that run throughout our interactions could be yet another way to both listen better and to truly hear what is being said.

### Convergence and Divergence

Another way that we can utilize creativity in our efforts to connect is to work with what we might call convergent and divergent topics or "inside-and-outside-the-box thinking." The idea here is to follow the gist of what the other person is sharing so well that we develop their main topic as much as possible, in ways that are more or less expected. So, again using our sample conversation, here are some possible examples of convergence:

*A1:* *I feel like you don't care about me anymore.*
*B1:* *You used to feel that you were important to me, but now it seems like something has changed and you miss what it used to be.*

or

*B1:* *I can't believe you said that. Of course, I care about you.*
*A1:* *It should be obvious to me how much you care about me.*

Divergence, on the other hand, is still a way of developing ideas but by using less conventional means such as extrapolation or metaphor. Returning to our examples above,

*A1:* *I feel like you don't care about me anymore.*
*B1:* *Maybe it feels like someone else is more important to me than you or maybe you feel like you've been replaced.*

or

*B1:* *I can't believe you said that. Of course, I care about you.*
*A1:* *You weren't expecting me to say what I just said. It's like I just threw a curveball at you, and maybe you're hurt by my words.*

It is difficult to say when convergence ends and divergence begins (or vice versa), and there really is no right or single way of using either. Instead, we experience the benefits of these strategies as we employ them to consciously elaborate upon other people's ideas. Moreover, while the ideas are important, the real impact of these strategies occurs when we convey to others that they, as the originators of the ideas, are more important to us than the outcomes of our interactions with them.

*Curiosity*

Related to divergence and thinking outside-the-box is the simple and yet surprisingly difficult task of being curious about one another. In relationships, the opposite of curiosity is a disinterest that results from feeling like people are boring or predictable. I suggest that such disinterest is yet another risk of a reactive approach to emotions. This might help to explain the popular expression, "familiarity breeds contempt." When we attribute emotions, especially negative ones, to others' behavior, we can quickly begin to experience such emotions as problematic and grow irritated with the people who seem to "make us feel" the irritation we are feeling. One sign that this is occurring is if we find ourselves, in one way or another, resorting to any form of labeling others or their behaviors. As examples, this could be occurring if we find ourselves asking of another "Are you kidding me?"; if we think of others' words or actions as "ridiculous,"; if we seem caught in patterns of relating that are "same old, same old,"; or if if we find that people "always" do this or "never" do that.

> **"...attributing emotions to beliefs rather than situations can be the first step toward addressing this 'paucity of curiosity'."**

As we have seen, one of the problems with operating as if others can "make" us feel whatever we feel is that this results in disproportionate power (us having too little and others having too much or vice versa) over emotions. Ironically, when this happens, both sides lose the ability to be themselves. If I start to make claims about why someone does what they do or about what they should or should not do *without acknowledging that these claims are a matter of my perspective*, I essentially set myself up as an expert over that person. Once I make such claims, I also make it very difficult to truly hear others' perspectives, much less discover new things about them. This is a very subtle yet prevalent way in which we prevent ourselves from the kind of curiosity that fosters true connection and intimacy in relationship.

Alternatively, attributing emotions to beliefs rather than situations can be the first step toward addressing this "paucity of curiosity." For example, when I am frustrated with another person and link my frustration to my *perspective* on what they are doing rather than to what they are doing per se, I am free to experience my frustration, *while still taking a genuine interest in them, on their terms*. This process of *differentiating*, of keeping parties sufficiently separate, ironically affords those parties a better, fighting chance of eventually growing closer over time.

*Savoring*

As a final way of creatively increasing connection, I suggest that we embrace the concept of "savoring" our approach to emotions in general and to our relationship experiences. Recently, I saw a chocolate commercial that contained a reference to the value of "savoring" each morsel, closing with the tagline "Life is delicious."[10] For most people, chocolate is an easy sell, but what about life itself?

There is much in life that is sweet, but there are other experiences that are quite different—salty, sour, spicy, bitter. For life to be delicious, the whole range of flavors is necessary, and the true art is in the proportions. Whereas basic taste is fairly objective—sucrose is sweet, sodium chloride is salty, citric acid is sour, capsaicin is spicy—our experiences with emotions in relationships can be less clear. A woman coming to me for counseling recently confided that a difficult relationship was a source of stress but was also the catalyst for our meeting and the opportunity to learn new, positive characteristics about herself.

10   Staffen, J. [John Staffen]. (n. d.). Hershey's 'life is delicious anthem' [Video file]. Retrieved December 22, 2017, from https://vimeo.com/159503435

The option we have to see the glass as half full or half empty and the notion that "beauty is in the eye of the beholder" both bear witness to the ways in which we play a role in what is deemed to have value.

Still, savoring is different from enjoying. I can purchase a tasty meal, then voraciously devour it in such a way that I enjoy it without savoring it (for example, I might be in a hurry and only have a limited amount of time to eat). If I can enjoy without savoring, what if I can also savor without enjoying? If so, then it seems possible to savor something even when it is difficult to do so. For our purposes, this is vital to consider because in relationships, it can be difficult to connect with those we disagree with and even more difficult to connect with those whom we find to be disagreeable. If I can learn, however, to be "open" to these people whom I am not necessarily "okay" with, I might be able to experience levels of depth and substance I might not have thought possible otherwise.

This will take a certain amount of trusting that the relationship is worth it, and trust involves counting on something ultimately being beneficial or good. In the Bible, the psalmist makes an interesting statement that seems relevant here, tying in the act of tasting with the ultimate goodness of God: "Oh, taste and see that the Lord is good!"[11]

If we can learn, then, to take in all of life the way our taste buds take in flavors or the way our eyes take in sights, what might this mean for relationships? Might even experiences with frustration or disappointment be evidence of the good gift of any relationship and if so, the goodness of the author of all relationships as well? I believe that we can be open to these experiences, especially to the extent that we can allow unpleasant emotions to be a function of our interpretations. And, as we open ourselves to all aspects of our lives, we will ensure that we do not miss out on living life more fully.

---

11  Psalm 34:8

# Chapter 13: Trades

*Life is an adventure in forgiveness.*
*Norman Cousins*

*It's one of the greatest gifts you can give yourself,*
*to forgive. Forgive everybody.*
*Maya Angelou*

As we prepare to conclude this exploration, it is important to remind ourselves that, on the ocean of relationships, we will inevitably and repeatedly encounter conflict. Whether it comes in the form of a storm, ranging from choppy waters to gale-force winds and monster waves, or an equally difficult, doldrums-like season of interpersonal avoidance and lifelessness, conflict can threaten even the strongest of relationships. And when this happens, there is one primary alternative for continuing in the face of the hurt and the pain: forgiveness.

In oceanspeak, we can compare forgiveness to the trade winds that fill a mariner's sails in certain tropical regions. Whether the conditions have been violently active or overwhelmingly, dangerously passive, the balmy trade winds, or trades as they are sometimes called, are a welcome, healing experience for even the saltiest of sailors. Even if we like conflict and find ourselves gravitating to it, there is always room for the freedom that can come from letting go of past injuries and moving forward with new possibilities.

In this chapter, we will specifically consider just how forgiveness can pertain to our understanding of emotions and how this can benefit our relationships overall. We will consider one approach to forgiveness and the ways in which it can inform not only how we relate to one another but also how we live.

## Uncommon Sense

*A Tale of Two Candlesticks*
   When I think of forgiveness, two scenes from two different stories come to mind. The first is a comical one, from *Far Side* cartoonist Gary Larson. It features a rather bizarre interaction between a piano store employee and an aspiring thief. The thief is making his way out of the store with a suspicious look on his face, wearing sunglasses and a huge overcoat that is hiding, of all things, the ridiculous and unmistakable shape of a grand piano! The reader gets the impression that the thief is completely out of his mind until seeing the rest of the picture, which involves the store employee running after the thief, holding a candelabra, saying, "Excuse me sir, but did you drop this on the way out?" The caption reads, "Stupid clerks."[1]

   The second, much more serious and timeless scene is from the beginning of Victor Hugo's monumental novel, *Les Misérables*. A kind bishop, Monseigneur Bienvenu, has just given refuge to a paroled convict, Jean Valjean, after many other people have rejected Valjean's requests for help. Nevertheless, in the middle of the night, overcome by an impulse from the past, Valjean steals Bienvenu's silver plates. Valjean is arrested the next day and deceptively tells the armed police that Bienvenu has given him the silver as a gift. Brought before Bienvenu, Valjean fully expects this to be the end of his freedom, so he is utterly shocked, "with an expression which no human tongue could describe," when Bienvenu lavishes him with additional kindness.[2] Not only does Bienvenu tell the police that he did indeed give Valjean the silver, he insists that he had also intended for Valjean to take his two silver candlesticks as well! And then, in a gesture of incisive wisdom and generous faith, he solemnly whispers to Valjean,

1   Retrieved April 28, 2018, from https://www.bing.com/images/search?view=detailV2&ccid=VDBKgcNp&id=64BDF1BC3CB83483C51603AF48C24E5CB00F93C5&thid=OIP.VDBKgcNp9Ql89AAZskChBAHaJz&mediaurl=https%3a%2f%2fi.pinimg.com%2f736x-%2f24%2fb6%2f85%2f24b685e2399df4615d1ebad364c7df7b—cartoon-jokes-funny-cartoons.jpg&exph=975&expw=736&q=stupid+clerks+gary+larson+far+side&simid=608007310853081466&selectedIndex=12&qpvt=stupid+clerks+gary+larson+far+side&ajaxhist=0

2   Hugo, V. (1862, 1992). Les misérables (C. E. Wilbour, Trans.). New York, NY: Modern library, p 91.

"Forget not, never forget that you have promised me to use this silver to become an honest man...Jean Valjean, my brother: you belong no longer to evil, but to good. It is your soul that I am buying for you. I withdraw it from dark thoughts and from the spirit of perdition, and I give it to God!"[3]

Two stories. In one, a clerk who does not necessarily have a big heart, just a huge deficit in common sense. In the other, a bishop who has both a magnanimous heart and an overflow of uncommonly good sense. Both involving candleholders, robberies, and favorable outcomes for the would-be thieves.

*Into the Wind*

Forgiveness breaks the mold. It's in a class of its own and takes uncommon sense. And it is both powered by and directed towards grace. On the ocean of relationships, it is none other than the breeze, the boon, and even the breath of life for the disappointed, discouraged, disrespected, and disillusioned. But all too often, it can seem elusive and scarce. Why is this and how can we do more to catch the trade winds in our sails?

In keeping with our theme, it is my humble contention that a fundamentally reactive understanding of emotions is a significant reason for why forgiveness is so hard to experience. This is so because of the two "legs" that reaction stands on— namely, the idea that emotions can be caused by something or someone external to us and the idea that negative emotions are also "bad" or "problematic" in and of themselves. When we see and behave as though someone else can somehow "make us feel" upset in some way (angry, sad, afraid) and when we say it is bad to feel upset, we inevitably see the other person as a problem as well.

---

**"...when competition is involved, we are again inclined toward a "survival of the fittest" mentality."**

---

3  Hugo, V. (1992), p 92.

Suppose the other person has hurt us. Most likely, we will be inclined to either protect against this hurt or hurt them back. The alternatives (for example, neither protecting nor avenging ourselves) will seem like we are simply allowing the hurt to continue. However, as we have seen before, whether the posture is one of protection or aggression, of fleeing, freezing, or fighting, it is reactive. In essence then, reactive ways of thinking about emotions promote reactive ways of acting out or acting upon such emotions. Once this happens, we are fundamentally at odds with the other person, and competition (whether subtle or obvious) marks the overall dynamic of our relationship. And, when competition is involved, we are again inclined toward a "survival of the fittest" mentality.

*Supply and Demand*

The potential for reaction to develop into competition plays a key role in our difficulties with forgiveness. As we have seen, when emotions take place in a competitive context, others are (unintentionally or intentionally) treated as problems or obstacles that must be fixed or removed for us to be happy (rather than sad, angry, afraid, or some combination of these feelings). Once people are perceived as *obstacles*, it is only a matter of time before they are treated as *objects*.

Certainly, people are not objects. We take issue with occasions where we feel treated, for lack of a better term, as "things." Certain language, for example, grates against us, especially when it comes to how we are "made" to feel. Consider the following words as examples of what we do not want to feel in our relationships with others: Used. Played. Taken. Stepped on. Manipulated. Abused. We are neither tools nor toys, utensils nor trophies, doormats nor instruments. As Fyodor Dostoevsky so perceptively proposes in chapter VIII of his *Notes from Underground*, "the whole work of man really seems to consist in nothing but proving to himself every minute that he is a man and not a piano-key!"[4]

Human dignity's demand that people never be treated nor

4  Dostoyevsky, F. (1918). Notes from underground (C. Garnett, Trans.). [eBooks@Adelaide]. Retrieved December 23, 2017, from https://ebooks.adelaide.edu.au/d/dostoyevsky/d72n/chapter9.html. I am again grateful for the work of Dallas Willard who first brought this quotation to my attention through his Divine Conspiracy lectures.

treat others as a "means to an end" is central to the topic of forgiveness. This is the case both for why we need forgiveness and why it is so difficult to come by. Regarding the first, there is no way to reverse pain. We cannot take back hurtful actions or words. We cannot "go back in time." So, if we are to heal, there must be another alternative. As political philosopher Hannah Arendt notes in her work *The Human Condition*, "the possible redemption from the predicament of irreversibility—of being unable to undo what has already been done—is the faculty of forgiving."[5]

And yet the demand for forgiveness seems to significantly outstrip the supply. Even as we need forgiveness, we so often would rather not offer it and, many times, we even resist receiving it. Why is this? We can again find our answer in our universal tendency to react and to compete with one another, which in turn can be traced to survival understandings of emotion.

*Uneasy Patterns*

Competition can lead us to a type of ledger or scoreboard mentality, where the good and bad things we do increase or decrease our overall standing or score. This pattern has a way of coloring our relationships, such that one-upmanship becomes a type of hidden agenda.

We are usually not aware of this agenda and probably do not mean for this to happen, but therein lies the rub; this is what happens when we treat external circumstances, other people specifically, as the primary "causes" of our feelings. We default to taking a survival approach, seeing emotions as both externalized and problematic, to a non-survival context (relationships). And when this happens, *we simultaneously lose our sense of agency and community*. Allowing other (most likely well-intentioned) people to come between our head and heart fundamentally puts us at odds with both self and neighbor. This internal and external disconnect leads us to experience discrepancies between what we intend and what we experience.

Since relationships are usually not matters of actual survival,

5  Arendt, H. (1958). The human condition. Chicago, IL: University of Chicago Press, p. 257. Retrieved December 23, 2017, from http://sduk.us/afterwork/arendt_the_human_condition.pdf

treating them as though they are creates additional problems. For too many people, the subtle, but vicious, cycle continues, captured again by the haunting reminder that "the road to hell is paved with good intentions."

And, just as most of life has one thing or another to do with relationships, most of the hurt and pain we experience in our relationships is probably a spinoff of something that was originally "well-intended." Indeed, as we've seen, significant portions of the private hells we experience in this life can be easily attributed to the phenomenon of how "hurt people hurt people."

And so, this uneasy pattern is what poses such a challenge to forgiveness. In our inadvertent tendencies to compete, we continually try to balance the ledger, even the score, and generally outdo one another. If a person hurts me, it is as if they score a point against me. Again, most of the time, I do not register this in any conscious sort of way. Nevertheless, I know (and I think we all do) that too often I am guided by a tit-for-tat, quid pro quo, stance, where I essentially rewrite the Golden Rule and "do unto others the way they do unto me."

This tendency applies in reverse as well. When someone does something positive, like a favor, there is something in me that wants to return the kindness. True, there is a genuine interest in expressing my gratitude and promoting the other person's well-being. Still, if I am honest, there is often also a subtle desire within me to reciprocate simply because I don't want to do less than them, and I don't want them to do more than me. This is uncomfortable to admit, if not embarrassing, but the bottom line is when it comes to how others "treat" me, I neither want to "lose" nor allow them to "win."

Similarly, when it comes to how I treat others, I also want to win and do not want to lose. Thus, it is very difficult to feel there is any fairness in doing good to those who hurt me, unless of course, doing good is somehow a way of "getting back" at them. Why would I purposely put myself in a one-down position? In sports, this would be the equivalent of forfeiting or "throwing the game." In business, this would be professional suicide. In battle, this would be risking defeat.

Many times, we assume these same rules apply to relationships, especially when it comes to emotional pain. When somebody hurts me, it seems, either consciously or unconsciously, quite legitimate to "return the favor." Interestingly, because of the competitive streaks that underlie all of our survival instincts, it seems that every time we score our own points or prevent others from scoring theirs, we are doing *ourselves* a favor.

But, like boats in a race, this leads to constantly vying for the top position, going back and forth between leading and trailing. Even if this is more than basic survival, it might be characterized, at best, as a kind of striving. As we've discussed earlier and as the author of Ecclesiastes notes, all our striving in life and certainly in relationships is vanity, "a chasing after the wind."

*Thriving*, however, is an entirely different matter. And understanding these challenges can be the first step to shifting from grasping at the wind, to catching it in our sails.

## Defining Forgiveness

*Reaction, Response, and Replacement*
So, just what is forgiveness? What happens when one person forgives another? For example, some time ago, my daughter took my son's toy without asking, and my son, in turn, pinched my daughter. In my effort to intervene, I found myself coaching them to each say they were "sorry" to the other, followed by instructing each to tell the other, "I forgive you." Though they were still likely much too young to understand (at the time one was 5 years-old and the other not quite 3 years-old), I believe those were vitally important expressions to teach them. But again, what exactly was I trying to teach?

So far, the focus of this chapter has been on *emotional reaction* and how it is both the reason forgiveness is so important as well as the basis for how it can be so challenging. Let us turn now to the alternative, namely *emotional response*, and how it both addresses the concerns raised by reactivity and is itself epitomized by the forgiveness process.

If reaction is characterized by viewing negative emotions as predominantly external and problematic, then response will focus on these same emotions being internal and useful. This is important for understanding what the forgiveness process entails. And while there are multiple ways of understanding forgiveness, I would like to focus on one model that particularly fits our present discussion. In this case, I will draw primarily from the work of psychologist and forgiveness researcher, Dr. Everett Worthington, Jr.

Both professionally and personally, I am choosing to focus on Worthington's approach, because it has had the most influence upon my own forgiveness experiences for more than two decades. In addition to knowing how it has informed and enhanced my own life, I have found that it dovetails quite well with the predominantly cognitive model that forms the basis of this book. If this is not compelling enough, it is my understanding that it is a model that Dr. Worthington has successfully applied to his own life, including to profoundly difficult situations where awful tragedies such as murder and suicide took the lives of some of those closest to him.

According to Worthington, forgiveness can essentially be defined as "emotional replacement."[6] If the reader will indulge me, I think it is worth pausing to reflect on this idea.

In these two words, anyone interested in this topic is potentially afforded an extraordinary opportunity. In fact, these two words are precisely on my mind when, as a father, I seek to explain forgiveness to my kids. Likewise, they are in the background when I talk with clients entrusted to my professional care. And, of course, they certainly helped Worthington in his own efforts to forgive what anyone might easily think of as "unforgivable."

*Replacement.* Emotional replacement. Two words. Two drops. And then, maybe . . . a sea change.

6  Worthington, E. L. Jr., (2003). Forgiving and reconciling: Bridges to wholeness and hope. Downers Grove, IL: InterVarsity Press. It is important to note that Worthington distinguishes between emotions and feelings. For example, he notes that emotions are "whole-body experiences" whereas feelings primarily pertain to the words that our conscious minds use to label such experiences (p. 35). Worthington particularly acknowledges the research of Antonio Damasio in this regard (see Damasio, A. R. (1994). Descartes' error: Emotion, Reason, and the human brain. New York, NY: Avon Books).

*Investment Opportunity*

The opportunity we are afforded in Worthington's definition is just that—an opportunity *to see forgiveness as an opportunity.* This further affords us a way of placing forgiveness in the same category as concepts like freedom and flourishing and thriving; a way to see forgiveness as part of what it means to really live.

Forgiveness, we will see, is a gift that, at a minimum, benefits the forgiver. To understand this potential, let us further unpack what Worthington is proposing.

My intention here is not to give an analysis or summary of Worthington's model, but to explore just what might be possible if we take to heart some of the details embedded in the definition that guides his thinking. Specifically, Worthington's expanded, operational definition of emotional forgiveness or emotional replacement suggests this sequence:

*"Forgiveness is defined as the emotional juxtaposition of positive emotions (such as empathy, sympathy, compassion, agape love or even romantic love) against (1) the hot emotions of anger or fear that follow a perceived hurt or offense or (2) the unforgiveness that follows ruminating about the transgression, which also changes our emotions from negative to neutral or even positive."*[7]

If we allow it to, this approach to forgiveness can be particularly rich and valuable in at least two ways: it is chosen, and it is unconditional.

*Chosen*

First, forgiveness is a choice. By suggesting that emotional replacement characterizes forgiveness, Worthington is essentially saying that forgiveness is always up to the individual. In fact, emotional replacement is, for Worthington, a way of emphasizing that forgiveness is an *intrapersonal* experience in that it takes place *within* an individual. By using language related to temperature to describe the sequence, he further gives us a helpful metaphor for understanding what might otherwise be an abstract process. To better grasp the full implications of

7   Worthington, E. L. Jr., (2003). p. 41-42.

the chosen or volitional nature of forgiveness, let us consider this sequence a bit further.

The logic goes something like this: When a person is initially hurt by another, a typical result is that the injured person experiences what may be considered "hot emotions"—anger, fear, and hurt. Given enough time, if this person ruminates on the hurt long enough, these "hot emotions" can morph into "cold emotions"[8]—a harder, icier complex of "delayed negative emotions, involving resentment, bitterness, hostility, hatred, residual anger and residual fear, which motivate people to reduce the negative emotions." Collectively, Worthington refers to these cold emotions as "unforgiveness."

For Worthington, there is a difference between forgiveness and merely "getting rid of unforgiveness." This is because forgiveness not only involves letting go of the "cold emotions" but also taking on what might be considered the "warm emotions" listed above: "empathy, sympathy, compassion, agape love or even romantic love." These are what Worthington terms "pro-transgressor" emotions. It is one thing to take measures to eliminate feelings of unforgiveness. For example, pardoning or condoning an offense or even getting revenge might be ways of discharging unforgiveness. It is quite a different matter, however, to take feelings of unforgiveness and replace them with feelings that are in favor of the transgressor.

All of this points to how forgiveness is optional for a person who has been hurt. If a person is interested in learning a way of addressing an offense that is qualitatively different from either harboring resentment or different from just avoiding unforgiveness, Worthington offers a model that sheds important light on the process: the process of finding a way to move from either hot or cold feelings to warmer pro-transgressor feelings. Furthermore, if one is interested in a simple mnemonic, Worthington has proposed five steps which follow the acrostic: REACH: (recall) the hurt; (empathize); (altruistically) give the gift of forgiveness; (commit) to forgive; and (hold) onto forgiveness.[9]

8  Worthington, E. L. Jr., (2003). p. 33.
9  Worthington, E. L. Jr., (2003). pp. 73-74.

At this point, however, it would be completely understandable to ask *why, in the first place, would we be interested in having feelings that favor the person who hurt us?* Why, some might ask, would anyone in their right mind choose to think or feel well towards a person who did them ill?

There are several answers to these questions that are worth noting. Worthington mentions that even though unforgiveness can be valuable (in motivating people to work for more justice), it also has potential health risks such as cardiovascular problems, endocrine or immune concerns, or even extreme anxiety related to anticipating being hurt again. In addition, here is where we can revisit the implications for what have become two very important themes, namely the intrinsic value of choice, and the connection between thinking and feeling.

Choices are the heartbeat of relationship; without them, people interact as robots and have difficulty getting beyond interpersonal dynamics that are characterized by a "survival of the fittest" approach to life. This is, in part, because without a sense of choice or will, people are hardly free to experience the full range of their emotions with one another. As we have seen, when one person is truly "allowed" to be upset with another, each person's individuality is respected, and future potential problems are paradoxically minimized.

Moreover, the relationship between thinking and feeling (specifically, the notion that, in interpersonal contexts, thinking is the primary determinant of feeling) is key to understanding the role choices play in our emotional experience. If others "make" us feel certain ways, we are essentially at the mercy of their actions. However, if we, by our particular interpretations, are better able to "own" our own feelings, we will feel more free to be ourselves and this will likely be true of those we interact with as well. When this happens, we can affirm the other person's emotions, even if we would rather they not have those emotions. Furthermore, we might say that this underscores a certain kind of *maturity* in the relationship, where we can choose to experience what we might not necessarily want at the time, in order to experience what we do want to experience later on.

Earlier we likened this awareness of our choice, this

Motivational Shift, to the air that we breathe. As we learn both how priceless and readily available this air really is, we begin to see how the breeze of forgiveness is likewise a gift. Indeed, every choice we freely make is a gift to ourselves, but forgiveness as a way of *freely choosing to think and feel differently and more compassionately towards a past offender* is essentially an investment.

Whereas the general ownership of our choices can be compared to using personal funds for personal enjoyment, the choice to forgive is like taking those funds and purchasing properties or stocks that have the potential to appreciate in value in the future. In this case, the investments are in one's own health and character, which have the additional likelihood of enhancing relationships in the future. There are, of course, costs and risks associated with choosing the path of forgiveness, but this is true of any investment. And, for the most part, these costs and risks trace back to a survival understanding of emotions.

If another person can directly hurt my feelings, holding that person's actions against them makes good sense. There is some gratification in harboring a grudge. It gives us a sense of power in situations where we otherwise might feel vulnerable and scared. It keeps us from the chance of being similarly hurt again. It seems like justice to repay harm with another sort of harm. We might even conclude that we are superior, since our retaliation is more "controlled" or "dignified," or at least less blatant or less rude.

Nevertheless, this still assumes that our emotional pain is directly caused by the other person. This, in turn, assumes that such a direct impact is somehow possible in the first place. It is almost as if we expect that, by holding a grudge, we can even the scales by using the same magic that our offender used against us.

When we do this, we are, of course, using reactive, survival-mode logic and a peculiar form of it at that. Rather than free us, grudges only weigh us down. It is as though we seek to build our offenders a prison cell but end up locking ourselves inside. And as comedian Buddy Hackett notes, "While (we're) carrying a grudge, they're out dancing."[10] Or more seriously, when we prefer grudges over forgiving, we risk not only our freedom but our very health and lives as well. And the cumulative effect can be lethal, if not to our bodies, to our souls. As writer Anne Lamott so poignantly notes, "not forgiving is like drinking rat poison and then waiting for the rat to die."[11] Again, if it were possible to kill rats this way, it would be hard to explain other than to regard the killing mechanism as a sort of magic or at least acknowledge that it would require a very peculiar sort of logic.

But Worthington's model points to how forgiveness can be even more compelling. For, if at any given time, we can choose to exchange the pain and discomfort of hot/cold feelings for the healing of warmer ones, we have a whole new dimension to consider. We are afforded a way of applying the logic of *thriving* rather than just being limited to what would mainly seem to ensure survival. In this way, we can see that, at best, grudges rely on the power of illusion rather than any form of true magic or special logic. And the idea that one person can ordinarily manage another person's feelings is itself the illusion.

*Unconditional*
Worthington's model points to forgiveness as unconditional. Again, we may balk at this idea and find ourselves doubting its practicality. *Should not an offender be required to somehow make amends for their offense before being forgiven?* This is a reasonable question, if indeed the offender directly caused the offense. But is this not a residual effect of believing that emotions are primarily externally determined? Indeed, this again points to the illusion we have just mentioned. What if we continue to shift away from the idea that others have the power to hurt our feelings?

In an indirect way, Worthington's model gives us one more

10   Buddy Hackett quotes. (n.d.). In Thinkexist.com. Retrieved December 23, 2017, from http://thinkexist.com/quotation/i-ve_had_a_few_arguments_with_people-but_i_never/323986.html

11   Lamott, A. (1999). Traveling mercies: Some thoughts on faith. New York, NY: Pantheon Books. Retrieved December 23, 2017, from https://books.google.com/books?id=Myp2lp3S-LZMC&printsec=frontcover&dq=like+drinking+rat+poison+anne+lamott&hl=en&sa=X&ved=0ahUKEwjylNnD_KDYAhVmlmMKHUg8CZoQ6AEIQDAE#v=onepage&q=not%20forgiving&f=false

way of applying this shift by considering the larger nature of forgiveness. Specifically, he notes that in addition to being characterized by emotional replacement, forgiveness can motivate people to seek reconciliation which he defines as "reestablishing trust in a relationship after trust has been violated."[12] In one sense, this is another way of developing the idea that forgiveness occurs within the individual, that it is intrapersonal. In another, it points to an even deeper implication, namely the difference between forgiving and reconciling.

By positing this difference, Worthington makes forgiveness an option even if reconciliation is not viable. He is also emphasizing the *conditional nature of reconciliation*, indicating that it should only be pursued *if* it is "safe, prudent, and possible." Forgiveness, by contrast, is always possible since it is an emotional shift that hinges on changes taking place within the forgiver rather than within the forgiven.

Whereas forgiveness involves a transformation within one person, reconciliation involves at least two people making changes. Forgiveness, as emotional replacement, involves changes that can occur even if one never sees the offending party again. Reconciliation, however, is characterized by both parties coming back together. Still, both imply injury, hurt, offense, or some other sort of wrongdoing have taken place. As such, if changes are to take place for reconciliation to occur, these changes must include an acknowledgement that something wrong occurred and a sincere commitment to make things right.

In a word, reconciliation requires *repentance*, or a turning away from what is acknowledged to be harmful and turning toward what would be truly good—a change of direction that begins with a change in how we think. Repentance, then, is a critical and necessary condition for reconciliation to take place. Moreover, repentance is certainly helpful if a wrong has occurred and the wronged person is interested in forgiving their transgressor.

But, according to Worthington's model, while repentance can help to facilitate forgiveness, it is not required for forgiveness to occur. And here we find the second way Worthington's

---

12  Worthington, E. L. Jr., (2003). p. 42.

definition affords us a gift. Since nothing is required, the forgiver can choose to feel differently towards an offender regardless of whether the offender makes changes or not.

If we place this idea alongside the idea that forgiveness is a choice, we have the potential for very good news. That is, the benefits of forgiveness are available on an ongoing basis, anytime, anywhere, for anyone. And if there is any question about what the benefits of forgiveness are, we need only consider just how good it will be, for our bodies, our souls, and our relationships when our lives are marked by all that can come from "empathy, sympathy, compassion, agape love or even romantic love."[13] If forgiveness is an investment, it is one that not only comes to us on our terms but also one that is, so to speak, *always affordable.*

> **"...the forgiver can choose to feel differently towards an offender regardless of whether the offender makes changes or not."**

Of course, there is a difference between what is affordable and what we are willing to pay. The question is why would we not be willing to pay for forgiveness? Perhaps we want something that is free rather than just always affordable. As we've seen, however, true freedom is never free per se, never without its costs. The bigger question still might be whether what is bought is worth the price. After all, we are not aiming to eliminate difficulty, just minimize its occurrence, especially when it does not have to happen.

More than likely, when we opt out of forgiveness, we do not yet realize its value. Moreover, when we choose to hold onto unforgiveness we are very likely reflecting our old, default, survival logic, which again can be so simultaneously self-appealing and self-defeating. For, if forgiveness has its benefits, why would we forfeit them? Does it make sense for us to cope with the pain of offense by further depriving ourselves of something good? In any other context, this might seem like adding insult

---

13   Worthington, E. L. Jr., (2003). p. 41-42.

to injury. Ironically, we can be so used to our conditions and obligations, that freedom can seem foreign, even threatening. The chosen, unconditional nature of forgiveness is an excellent place to take risks then, especially if we would experience more thriving in our relationships.

## Control

One more comment is in order regarding why we can stay unnecessarily in survival mode and how this can have an impact on forgiveness. The issue can be summarized in one word: "control."

A brief story comes to mind, again from my experiences as a father. When we first moved into our neighborhood, my youngest daughter Zoe was not yet a toddler and therefore not yet able to say much that could be understood. This caused some of the neighborhood kids to find her particularly adorable and fun to play with.

One day, Zoe was playing with two of her older friends, who were being quite affectionate with her in a very well-meaning but, for Zoe, somewhat overwhelming, way. And Zoe, being particularly independent even from a young age, protested the attention by expressing her displeasure with what might be termed rather high-pitched "squawks." Her friends found this amusing and so proceeded to hug Zoe even more, smiling and giggling as they did so. Very predictably, Zoe protested again, this time by adding some foot-stomping to her even higher-pitched squawks. Like clockwork, her friends, still very well-intentioned, hugged Zoe even more tightly, adding some kisses as well.

I had been watching this all take place from a distance, and I could simultaneously see that Zoe was getting frustrated even as her protests were becoming increasingly cute. So, what happened next was curiously not surprising and yet not what I would have expected. After the third show of affection, Zoe, apparently tired of squawking, gritted her teeth and made a more muffled, angry sound while *pinching her own cheek*. Seeing that her frustration had now escalated to a point of *harming herself*, I quickly stepped in (though, in retrospect, not quickly enough) and gently asked her friends to give Zoe her space.

Why is this story important? In my estimation, having a sense of control was so vital to Zoe that, when her efforts to gain control seemed ineffective, she found a way to recover this control *even when it meant taking control by harming herself.*

While some people may not quite resonate with the earlier argument that we are deeply competitive, I believe everyone wants a general sense of control. I believe we can affirm this *desire* for control as vital to our health and to our very dignity as human beings. As we have seen, it traces back to our original design as image bearers of a sovereign God.

However, this is where a curious irony emerges. On one hand, this same God, whom we are patterned after, has full control, yet He so often refrains from wielding it. On the other hand, He is completely free even as He routinely seems to limit Himself. *He is in control but not **into control**.*

We, on the other hand, are hardly inclined to be self-limiting. Paradoxically, we are all too familiar with bondage. We can so easily and regularly get stuck in well-intended but extraneous stress as *we move from wanting to be in control to having to have what we want.*

Whereas desiring something is consistent with thriving, converting that desire into a need is more consistent with surviving. Made in God's image, we are built with a very legitimate longing to have a say over what does and does not happen in our lives. And, at the same time, since we are not God, our limitations require that we selectively discern which desires to pursue. Unlike God, we cannot will everything we desire and expect this to always lead to thriving, because unlike God, we are imperfect and our desires do not necessarily align with what is good.[14] Moreover, when we are honest, we are faced with the deep ways we actively desire to go *against* what God has expressly deemed to be not only good but best. This becomes particularly poignant when God's instruction, as it were, is not only in conflict with what we want but also seems to directly call for a relinquishing of control.

---

14  I am very grateful for Dallas Willard and the influence of his speaking, writing, and example on this and many other topics that pertain to relationships and faith.

There is probably no more profound intersection of all these challenges than the topic of forgiveness. When we are hurt, we so often want to hold onto the offense and the unforgiveness that naturally results. Holding onto offense gives us a sense of control, of power, possible reassurance, or even "insurance" against future hurt. Since we are, by nature, patterned after God, we want justice and feel that our offender should somehow answer for their wrong actions. Thus, any talk of *unconditionally choosing* to release them from the offense can seem categorically naive.

And yet, this is the path of forgiveness. The Greek word that is used in the Bible is "aphesis," which means to let go, release, dismiss, send away.[15] This makes sense since, as we've noted, forgiveness is ultimately about freedom. The complexity comes from how we often do not see who we are truly releasing when we've been offended, namely *ourselves*. In the words of forgiveness exemplar, Nelson Mandela, upon his release from years of incarceration for opposing the racist policies of apartheid in South Africa, "As I walked out the door toward the gate that would lead to my freedom, I knew that if I did not leave my bitterness and hatred behind, I would still be in prison."[16]

Mandela's wisdom helped him to relinquish a certain kind of control in order to gain a certain, more sustainable, and more lasting kind of freedom. Years of adversity were not wasted on him. His life, character, and work on the Truth and Reconciliation Commission, together with Bishop Desmond Tutu and many dedicated people, serve as an inspiration to the world of what forgiveness can help make possible. In oceanspeak, this chapter is a modest comment on some of the details that might factor into us catching the same trade winds in our sails. To this end, let us consider a few more issues before moving on to our final chapter, specifically, the topics of betrayal, apology, intention, and, finally, a life characterized by forgiving.

---

15   Aphesis. (n.d.). In Biblehub.com. Retrieved December 23, 2017, from http://biblehub.com/greek/859.htm

16   Bourgeoise, T. (2013, December 19). The greatest gift—to: you and I, from: Nelson Mandela. In Huffingtonpost.com. Retrieved December 23, 2017, from https://www.huffingtonpost.com/trudy-bourgeois/the-greatest-gift_b_4469297.html

# Betrayal

## Cheaters and Traitors

When it comes to relationships, next to the crime of murder, there is probably no offense more severe than betrayal. And there is probably no more hurtful place to experience betrayal than infidelity (sexual or emotional) such as in a marriage or other lifetime commitment between two people. There are those who would say that death is more desirable than the pain inflicted by broken trust. In my clinical practice, I certainly find that the wounds inflicted by marital infidelity are among the most challenging and the most prevalent.

The especially heinous nature of betrayal is apparent in that, in the United States of America, "treason" or a betrayal related to an attempt to overthrow the government, is one of only several crimes where a guilty verdict could mean the death penalty for a person even if that person did not actually kill anyone.[17] If this is any indication of seriousness, any situation involving betrayal, where the offender might be considered a "cheater" or a "traitor," would be a particularly daunting match for forgiveness.

But, if so, what of all we have said about freedom? And what if we apply the principles of thriving rather than basic surviving? Might even infidelity be healed?

I believe so. While this again is not intended to be a handbook on either forgiveness or infidelity, I would like to briefly explore the former in the context of the latter as a way of considering how forgiveness can bring about sustainable new beginnings, using infidelity as a sort-of "worst-case scenario" that can also be generalized to other situations.

## Broken Trust

The painfulness of infidelity arises from the fact that a trust has been breached. I say "fact" because, where forgiveness is concerned, it is important to first acknowledge that something wrong has occurred. Forgiveness takes seriously the consequences of our offenses, even as it recognizes, with equal seriousness, the ways we may have more participation in our

---

17  I am grateful to my good friend Edwin Nam for this insight.

own "offendedness" than we may realize.

The acknowledgment that a violation has occurred is itself a process, and it is important to allow this as much time and attention as the wounded party believes necessary. This phase, which corresponds to Worthington's step of "recalling the hurt," is necessary before other steps in the forgiveness process can be taken. Although it may sound at odds with the general premise of this book, I also regard it as an important time for the forgiver to attribute the pain *directly* to the incident of the affair or even to the unfaithful person. While it is somewhat different from the message of this book, it seems to me often very practical to simply say, "infidelity hurts." In keeping with this, it is especially important for the unfaithful person to sincerely own their offense.

*Owning the Breach*
Owning an offense is a delicate task. If we are not careful, attempts at responsivity, responsibility, and response-ability will slip into blame, which ultimately will lead to forms of punishment that could perpetuate the reactive cycles that influenced the initial breach. Punishment is useful and effective for stopping bad behavior but often falters when it comes to initiating and sustaining good or better behavior. This is key for understanding how forgiveness can grow when a breach has occurred. To own something is to acknowledge a connection between the thing that is owned and oneself. In the case of an offense, owning includes having an accurate recognition of its seriousness and its impact.

Consider a husband who has stepped outside of a marriage and violated trust with his wife by becoming involved emotionally, sexually, or both, with another person. Owning this offense will mean that this husband acknowledges his wrongdoing and harm to his wife and to himself, along with being harmful to others in his community. He will not try to *excuse* his behavior either by dismissing, minimizing, or condoning it. This is different from explaining or identifying *reasons* for how or why he made his decisions. Explaining his reasons is an important part of the process but first there must be an unvarnished, courageous admission of wrongdoing and guilt.

When done carefully, this husband's admission of wrongdoing and guilt are acts of kindness toward both his wife *and toward himself*. The purpose and trajectory of forgiveness are both marked by the crescendo from mercy to grace. To say he was wrong is to acknowledge the illegitimacy of his unfaithfulness. To own his guilt is to say his actions were not only wrong and indiscriminate but to also say they were harmful and call for some kind of accounting. Here blame and punishment do make sense but as a means to an end rather than as ends in themselves. Correction will only be effective to the extent that one is able to value it and trust that it can bring about something better.

For the forgiver, owning offendedness also has the potential to be an act of kindness in both directions. Again, it is important to say that the blow was directly related to the extramarital involvement, though giving the offense this much "power" is primarily a means to an end. In our case, for the wife to say that she was hurt and even harmed by her husband does justice to the gravity of the situation. It is no mild thing to break a promise or betray a trust. In fact, recognizing the severity testifies to the value of the relationship, the sanctity of each spouse, and the perilous nature of unfaithfulness.

Allowing herself to feel the range of emotions will thus be essential to this process. Since infidelity is intrinsically unfair, detrimental, and threatening to both parties, it will be normal and indeed healthy for her to feel anger, sadness, and fear in varying degrees. It is not an exaggeration to say that the relationship will "never" be the same again. When trust is broken, a certain amount of innocence dies, and so there is a very real and legitimate place for survival mode. In the case of infidelity, the pain and scars are both real because the wounds can be so deep.

While the scars may never leave, they nevertheless point to the possibility of healing power. And while violation and violence are both inescapably and inextricably tied to any discussion of forgiveness, they can represent the darkness before the dawn. On the ocean of relationships, the squalls may be great but never have to be greater than the sea itself. If the storms can be weathered, eventually the craft will come into calmer waters.

Here is where we turn, so to speak, into the wind, and particularly into the trade winds that forgiveness can inspire. As we've noted, facing the sting and burn of broken trust are meant to be a means to a greater end. And in the case of forgiveness, that end is grace.

*Turning Point*

Continuing with Worthington's model, at some point forgiveness will mean that recalling the hurt develops into empathizing with the transgressor. The decision to make this shift, to attempt to see through another person's eyes, especially the eyes of someone who has done wrong, is gracious indeed. The transgressor does not deserve this kindness precisely because of the transgression. However, the more we understand forgiveness as a *gift*, the more we see that practicing kindness, especially towards those who do not deserve it, can be consistent with opposing the offense in the first place.

Once the forgiver has decided to consider the transgressor's perspective, the process of empathizing is rather straightforward. In the example above, the wife might imagine or listen long enough to her unfaithful husband's account of how an extramarital involvement made sense to him. She might consider how he could have felt desperate, sad, lonely, angry, or anxious. She might think of times when she has felt similar feelings and possibly acted upon them in ways that did not work or ways that she might have regretted. And, keeping with the principles in this book, she might further apply the idea that the marriage was violated to the extent that her husband perceived the marriage (rather than his perspective on the marriage) to be the source of his discontent.

At a glance this could seem ludicrous, and the condition stated earlier is a significant caveat in this way: Empathizing occurs *once the forgiver has decided to consider the transgressor's perspective.* Considering is difficult enough, but empathy hinges on one's ability to not only consider but also to value another person's vantage point. And when done well, it can breathe life into a relationship. After all, if empathy had been given more attention in the first place, there would likely have been less transgression overall.

Empathy facilitates choice, and empathy is the choice that facilitates the rest of the forgiveness process. Per Worthington's model, once this choice has been made, the forgiver is now positioned to altruistically give forgiveness as a gift, to both themself and to their transgressor.

In our example, the wife might, as a result of thinking about how her husband essentially betrayed himself, look at him with a heart of compassion. And, since compassion literally refers to suffering with another person, she might think about the pain he is in and allow her own suffering to include this awareness of his pain. This is different from pity, though pity would still be a step away from a judgmental stance. Pity might certainly be warranted, since any betrayal is ultimately a pathetic way of trying to solve a relationship problem. Still, it is difficult to think of pity as a gift since it is more forced than offered. Compassion, as companionship in suffering, is a more generous gesture. And again, the more we understand forgiveness, the more we will be compelled that both the receiver and the giver benefit from the generosity.

The remaining steps involve committing to forgiveness and holding onto it. In identifying these, Worthington again makes a valuable contribution to our understanding of the process. This is because of the curious relationship between painful experience and memory. "Forgive and forget" has become a popular expression. However, by suggesting that forgiveness involves both a commitment and a conscious decision to hold fast to such commitment, Worthington is noting that forgiving does not mean forgetting. Some wounds are too deep to ever forget entirely, and forgetting the past makes us vulnerable to repeating it. Instead, the goal is to remember whatever happened through a lens that potentially gives new meaning to the event.

In our example, this means that even the slightest detail can bring the offense back to mind, and this can happen on a repeated basis. When this happens, committing to and holding onto forgiveness will again mean engaging the first three steps. So, if a certain circumstance (a familiar situation or event) "triggers" a memory of the offense, each person can approach the trigger as a chance to move again from recall to empathy to altruism. And, when these steps are honestly taken, it is likely that the triggers will gradually decrease.[18]

## Apology

### Admission and Ownership

Let us turn now to the topic of apology and how it can relate to forgiveness. Some nuance will be useful here since the intrapersonal approach to forgiveness that we are considering means that nothing is required from the transgressor, including neither repentance nor apology. At the same time, if the transgressor does venture an apology this will certainly help to facilitate the forgiveness process.

What is an apology? I would like to suggest that it involves a person saying that they wronged another person, making no excuses or qualifications, and with a true sense of sorrow. In this sense, an apology is an admission of fault and an ownership of responsibility, particularly of one's own role in another's pain. Like forgiveness, an apology is a gift, to both the forgiver and the forgiven.

### Two Parties, One Team

At the outset, an apology will likely "go against the grain" of what we feel like doing. To the extent that we are competitive, it may feel like a self-defeating thing to call "foul" on ourselves. Perhaps some might feel it is like pulling the pin on a grenade that has been thrown at them or removing vital body armor in the middle of a fight. Again, giving our opponent a point or taking one away from ourselves feel like losses. However, here is where we can remind ourselves that relationships, by definition, are not intrinsically competitive arrangements, though they will often seem to be. If anything, the notion that an apology is a gift hinges on our ability to commit to the assumption that a relationship implies we are on the same team.

One question worth asking is if we are on the same team, who or what is our enemy? Let us consider that our enemy is *anything that makes us think our teammate is our enemy.*

---

18  This process will often benefit from the help of a trusted mentor or professional counselor since "recalling the hurt" can particularly create additional challenges for relationships.

And again, where relationships are concerned, the notion that people are enemies is itself a conflict of interest.

> ## "...an apology is an admission of fault and an ownership of responsibility, particularly of one's own role in another's pain."

A graphic, beautiful depiction of this can be seen in *Catching Fire*, the second film of the Hunger Games trilogy, based upon the novels by Suzanne Collins.[19] Briefly, the story further develops the saga of heroine, Katniss Everdeen (played by Jennifer Lawrence), a teenage girl who must fight for her life in an annual survival tournament (the Hunger Games) developed by a corrupt government (the Capitol), which pits her against other young participants or "tributes." In the first film, Katniss ends up being victorious (together with her friend Peeta Mellark (played by Josh Hutcherson) by finding a way to break the rules of the tournament. The sequel continues the story with Katniss and Peeta being accused of starting a rebellion by their rule-breaking, which results in them being re-selected for a second tournament called a Quarter Quell. Before the actual tournament, Katniss' mentor Haymitch Abernathy (played by Woody Harrelson) advises, *"Katniss, when you are in the arena, you just remember who the true enemy is."* In the end, this life-saving and strategic advice influences Katniss to realize that her fellow tributes are actually her allies in a larger struggle against the real enemy, the Capitol. In a decisive and symbolic move, she refrains from shooting a fellow tribute, cleverly using her arrow to electrocute the ceiling of the metal arena, providing a way for her rescue and destroying the Game altogether.

The literal "gamechanger" (and reason that the tributes can confidently treat each other as allies) is the fact that, unknown to Katniss, a coup, involving half of the tributes and the Gamemaker himself (played by Philip Seymour Hoffman), is underway. Precisely because of this plot twist, the apparent

---

19  From the movie Catching Fire (2013), screenplay by Simon Beaufoy and Michael Arndt, directed by Francis Lawrence, and produced by Color Force and Lionsgate, based upon Collins, S. (2003). Catching fire. London, United Kingdom: Scholastic.

or assumed enemy is not the "true enemy." Moreover, knowing about the coup casts a new light on the tournament overall. The viewer of the film can see how certain people are more good than evil, apparent threats are ultimately not true dangers, and certain subtle signs are foreshadowing hope all along.

Could this be analogous to relationship situations where a conflict might make it seem like fighting our significant others makes more sense than working with them? If so, what kind of plot twist might be unfolding, which could mean that our attacks against each other are exercises in "friendly fire"?

In my opinion, wherever relationships are concerned, the way emotions function is the plot twist that allows us to do things like apologize and forgive when feelings have been hurt. Both apologizing and forgiving can feel vulnerable, but we can have confidence that this is a kind of vulnerability that strengthens rather than weakens relationships.

It is important to trust that vulnerability is useful because vulnerability inevitably feels so uncomfortable. We are so acquainted with our "survival of the fittest" defaults that saying we are somehow not fit or less fit than we should be (which is essentially what we are saying when we say we are wrong on a matter) can really run counter to what we feel like doing. As such, apologies, like forgiveness, rely on uncommon sense. They are akin to redirecting our arrow toward the true enemy, which in this case might be the need to justify ourselves at the expense of the relationship. After all, in a relationship we are on the same team.

### Double Standard

Here, it is necessary to make a second nuance about apologies, namely how all of this pertains to our focus on emotions as a personal responsibility. Since apologies almost always imply hurt feelings, does apologizing mean that we must take responsibility *for* others' feelings?

My answer to this is both yes and no. With "apologies" for the ambiguity (pun intended!), what else would be expected from a book that repeatedly appeals to considering that there "may be two" (or more) ways of looking at any given situation?

One way of thinking of this is to say, *Nobody can hurt my feelings, but I can hurt theirs.* At the outset, this is admittedly a "double standard." At the same time, it seems to me the best strategy for addressing two goals overall: 1) minimizing my own tendency to take life too personally and 2) maximizing my ability to genuinely make a sincere apology without requiring that others do the same. Freedom for me to apologize is necessary lest I fall into the trap of self-reliance that is both impossible and at odds with vulnerability in relationships. At the same time, it is vital that I not "require" much of anything from another, lest I create a predicament where "allowing" another person to have inordinate power over my feelings just increases the likelihood of unnecessary problems overall.

I have found this principle of "double-standarding myself" to be as practical as it is quirky. And its application in my own life has been particularly influenced by two people. The first influence is my brother, Eric, through a conversation where he suggested to me that apologies do not go well when they begin with words like, *"I am sorry if..."* He pointed out that this approach is essentially, even if inadvertently, a way of making the other person responsible for the apology. That is, it implies that if the person's feelings were not hurt, an apology would not be necessary. Such a "conditional apology" hardly addresses the other's feelings, much less the likelihood that something wrong and hurtful was done.

This was initially a new way of thinking for me, but over time, I have found it to be very sensible. What I have also found helpful can trace back to how, in our initial conversation, Eric perceptively (in my opinion) added that the alternative to the conditional apology is to simply say *"I am sorry I"* rather than *"I am sorry if."* To do this, though, it is important to really consider that I do have a kind of power over another person's heart even as I do my best to not assume that they have that kind of power over me. If, for some reason, the conversation turns to how they can also influence their own feelings, then there is no good reason to rigidly insist that I exclusively caused their hurt, and we can consider the roles our interpretations played. Nevertheless, it seems important to say that it is very possible to be hurtful to another person, and their experience of me as such is enough evidence for this taking place.

The second influence was C. S. Lewis. Reflecting on the paradoxical nature of certain matters (in this case, the importance of both the concept of divine sovereignty and the concept of human free will), he writes,

> *"I think we must take a leaf out of the scientist's book. They are quite familiar with the fact that for example, Light has to be regarded* <u>both</u> *as a wave and as a stream of particles. No-one can make these two views consistent. Of course, reality must be self-consistent; but till (if ever) we can* <u>see</u> *the consistency it is better to hold two inconsistent views than to ignore one side of the evidence."* [20]

Lewis goes on to explain how this influences his own view of himself and others, saying,

> *"I find the best plan is to take the Calvinist (broadly speaking, divine sovereignty) view of my own virtues and other people's vices, and the other (human free will) view of my own vices and other peoples' virtues."* [21]

And so, I have found it very useful to apply a similar reasoning to my own understanding of "hurt feelings." Again, I am committed to believing (it is a lifelong process for me) that nobody can hurt my feelings, but I can hurt theirs. I do not expect others to take this view, though I enjoy discussing it with those who have interest, and I have found that when two parties do share this view it seems to open additional options for a relationship to thrive.

## Gift

If I can open myself to this kind of logic, this kind of uncommon sense, then an apology can function as a gift in several ways. First, and perhaps most importantly, an apology is a "gift" in the sense that it is a small but significant gesture of restitution, an attempt to restore something that was lost or stolen. The quotation marks above around the word gift are intended to show the figurative sense that an apology is a freely

---

20  Martindale, W. & Root, J. (Eds.). (1989). The quotable Lewis. Wheaton, IL: Tyndale House Publishers, p. 494. Bold and underline added.

21  Martindale, W & Root, J. (Eds.). p. 494. Parenthetical comments added.

given act of the will even if the wronged person "deserves" the apology. It is the transgressor's first way of saying that, when the other was hurt, something was essentially "taken" and needs to be accounted for. In some cases, the offense may not be very major and so the apology may be all that is necessary for the relationship to move forward. In other cases, an apology may be just the beginning of a long process of showing remorse and a desire to make things right. Regardless of the nature of the offense, an apology is a way of saying that one knows that certain damage has been done which, though unable to be taken back, can be acknowledged and hopefully understood in such a way that the offense will not be repeated in the future.

Second, an apology is a gift in that the person offering it has no expectations of anything in return. It is unqualified, with no hooks or strings attached. Whereas it may be beneficial for the apologizer to explain or give reasons for their actions, this is different from making excuses or trying to somehow say that what was done was not wrong. On a very technical level, I have found that I can make my apologies even more sincere if I consider offering my reasons before offering my apology and this seems to work even in situations where my apology may be more of a courtesy than a confession of wrongdoing. For example, if I unintentionally delay my response to someone trying to reach me, in my reply to them, I might say something like, *"I am only catching up on getting back to people now. I am sorry for the delay"* rather than the other way around.

Or, in cases where my actions were more hurtful, it would be important to first understand the damage done in order to apologize accurately. If it seems necessary to explain my own perspective, it seems I might either want to do this before offering the apology or perhaps after some time has passed. The point is that, when the apology is given, it can stand alone without any caveats or "fine print." We might consider this to be a way of offering an apology "unapologetically," with no pretense and no pressure, so that the person we have hurt is as free as possible to accept or reject it, according to their timeframe.

Since there is no guarantee that it will be received, an apology is a gesture of vulnerability. And, if it is not received or even if it is outright rejected, the person giving it accepts this as part of the package. For when we are truly sorry, we recognize that the person we have hurt does not owe us anything. Moreover, affirming their prerogative to deny may be just as important to the healing process as affirming the value of them accepting. Of course, in keeping with the themes of this book, it will be better if the wounded person sees that accepting an apology can ultimately promote their own growth (if the apology is sincere). Hopefully, the apologizer will "show" their reasonableness by being open to whatever replies (denials or acceptances) follow the apology itself.

Third, when freely given, an apology optimizes opportunities to learn more about oneself, including one's limits, shortcomings, and the ways these can negatively impact relationships. On a personal basis, if I can trust that relationships mean all parties are on the same team, then, my teammate's pain means I am somehow worse off. When the pain is related to my action or inaction, saying *"I am sorry I hurt you"* (again, as opposed to saying *"I am sorry if I hurt you"*) is not only an unconditional gesture of remorse but also an opportunity for me to heal as well (and if "hurt people hurt people," then I do probably need healing of my own to keep from wounding others). Strangely enough, it can take great courage to stand before another person and admit one's faults. Nobody is perfect, and yet we often have a very difficult time accepting this about ourselves. An apology is an opportunity to confront this challenge and to face our fear. When this is done skillfully and sincerely, we will find again that the vulnerability, though possibly very threatening, was not actually dangerous.

> **"Since there is no guarantee that it will be received, an apology is a gesture of vulnerability."**

*I am sorry I*. Rather than *I am sorry if*. Neither conditional, contingent, nor hypothetical. Just straight up and straightforward, with no props. Interestingly, the difference is again just one letter. One drop. Maybe t.w.o....and then perhaps, even more forgiveness.

## Intention

*Good or Bad Idea?*
Forgiveness is fairly simple when the transgressor sincerely apologizes and can honestly say that the harm was unintended. But what if there is no apology or the transgressor is not sorry? What if the person was outright malicious? In such situations, is forgiveness possible, and if so, is it even practical?

Two thoughts immediately occur to me as I write. Looking around my surroundings, I am first reminded of how, before writing this chapter, my home was burglarized. The carpet directly beneath me was smeared with mud from the burglar's shoes. I recall how seeing this mud left me feeling simultaneously violated and vulnerable. Some person(s) had come into this very room, tracked the mud in, gone through closets and drawers, and apparently helped themselves to whatever they pleased. It happened that Keri had cleaned her wedding ring that day, and so it was among the items taken. Likely just a way for the stranger(s) to make some quick money even as it represented nearly 17 years of memories for us.

We may never know who invaded our property, and we may never recover what was lost. Moreover, it would not be unrealistic to think that, to the intruder(s), we are essentially nonpersons. Quite possibly, we are just one of many "checkmarks" on their to-do list, feathers in their cap, or means for them to support some vice or bad habit. It appears their offense was clearly intended, maybe even planned and plotted out. Considering all of this, would forgiving them be a good idea?

Way more significantly, this morning Keri told me of a news alert she received on her phone. Yet another terrible shooting in a public area. More young lives cut short. More senselessness. I can hardly imagine what the victims' families and friends are feeling. My mind resists the idea almost entirely.

*Eye for Eye*
*Is the availability of forgiveness different for thieves and murderers?* This question vexes even as it vies for our attention. On one hand, this question goes beyond the scope of day-to-day relationship concerns. On the other, the way we answer it

can have major implications for how we address interpersonal offenses, even if they are somewhat routine and "ordinary." If forgiveness is neither available nor sufficient for very severe situations, what is to say that it will have power for the more mundane?

On a personal level, the question above is daunting. Both literally and figuratively, it is too big for me. Holding a grudge, for example, against our "family" burglar(s) seems much more manageable. And again, I cannot even begin to fathom the atrocity of losing a loved one to a person who, for all intents and purposes, is a "cold-blooded killer." Even mentioning forgiveness in this context seems naive and uncaring. It seems fairer and more natural to hold onto anger, or at least to simply not forgive.

Both retaining anger and withholding forgiveness often seem very fair and very natural. Nobody who knowingly and intentionally takes from another, whether property or life itself, deserves forgiveness. And, as we have seen earlier, anger is necessary wherever there is injustice.

Still, while fairness would mean my enemy is not granted forgiveness, it still begs the question what would really be fair to me? A larger question to ask myself, to ask ourselves, is *what kind of a world do we really want to live in?*

There is probably something in all of us that wants our world to be fair. We expect at a minimum that, when it comes to crimes and offenses, "the punishment will fit the crime." This derives from an ancient principle called "talion" or *lex talionis* (literally, "law of retaliation"), which essentially governed the extent to which retribution for a crime was carried out.[22] Commonly referred to as an "eye for an eye," it referred to the understanding that if person A took person B's eye, justice would mean B could take A's eye or the financial equivalent of what the eye might cost. This was to keep people from taking revenge or retaliation too far, such as in a case where a person might take the life of the person who took their eye. For practical reasons, this principle continues to be part of how punishments

---

22  Lex talionis. (n. d.). In Newworldencyclopedia.org. Retrieved January 18, 2020, from https://www.newworldencyclopedia.org/entry/Lex_talionis

are meted out today, but is a system of retribution ultimately the best strategy for how we approach relationships? In the words of Mahatma Ghandi, "an eye for an eye only ends up making the whole world go blind."[23]

*A Different Logic*
When it comes to resolving our differences and to ultimately healing from past wounds, forgiveness offers a different logic. As we have seen, this is a logic that is uncommon because it sees a connection *between one's well-being and the way one views or even feels towards a transgressor.*

To the extent that this connection is true, it would seem this logic would also find a way to forgive even if the transgressor intended or continues to intend to do harm. But how?

In response, I am repeatedly and inexorably drawn to the character and life of Jesus and to one particular point in time where he lived out His own teaching on forgiveness. It is likely a familiar passage since it occurs at a most critical time in Jesus' mission and includes, in my opinion, one of the most challenging and powerful lines in all of Christian scripture. Briefly, the occasion involves a moment during His execution, when He is crucified on a Roman cross even while innocent of all charges, literally in place of a guilty man (Barabbas), and in fulfillment of centuries of prophecy. And as He is dying, He cries out to God, whom He always called Father, *"Forgive them, for they know not what they do."*[24]

Who is He advocating for and how does He do this? At the very least, it seems the people He is concerned with are those who have just put nails through His hands in order to kill Him. How could they possibly not know what they are doing?

An argument can be made that Jesus is essentially saying that those responsible for His death do not know who they are killing. In other words, they do not realize that they are killing an innocent man whose death itself is unique from all other deaths they have overseen. This irony is initially present in

23  Mahatma Gandhi. (n. d.). In Bbc.co.uk. Retrieved December 23, 2017, from http://www.bbc.co.uk/worldservice/learningenglish/movingwords/shortlist/gandhi.shtml
24  Luke 23:34

Jesus' words in Luke 23:28-31 prior to his prayer from the cross when, apparently pointing to a future calamity (most likely the Roman destruction of Jerusalem in AD 70), Jesus likens His death to the unnecessary and untimely destruction of a tree when it is "green."[25] If we consider the meaning of Jesus' name, the people do not realize that they are killing the One who will "save them from their sins," the Messiah.[26]

This is profound in and of itself. In the middle of His agony and aware of how His killers are oblivious to His true identity, Jesus implores His Father to be merciful towards them. Just when it seems His mission is ending in utter shame and despair, He, the epitome of grace and truth (see John 1:14), remains steadfast in His compassion. As such, perhaps we too can confidently ask God to forgive those who are mistaken about us.

But is this all? Are Jesus' words primarily relevant to cases of "mistaken identity?" Actually, because of Jesus, I believe we are afforded much, much more. In fact, if we focus exclusively on how Jesus' killers did not know who they were killing, it seems less clear how His words can apply to us. It is not as if we will appeal to God asking Him to forgive because our transgressors do not realize we are the Messiah! So again, what does it mean that Jesus, hanging on a cross, seeks forgiveness for His apparently unrepentant torturers, claiming that they "know not what they do"?

I believe we can trust that when Jesus pleads for His killers' forgiveness, He is exemplifying a fiercely practical and strategic way of both reasoning and of life. This is therefore not an isolated moment for Him but rather a glimpse into the ongoing and intimate communion that He has had with his Father, on a continual basis. And so, when He intercedes to His Father on behalf of His killers, I believe the Father is already very familiar with this particular prayer and yes, is even the One who may have encouraged Jesus to pray this way in the first place. For example, throughout His ministry, Jesus constantly takes His

---

25 Jackson, W. (n. d.). What is the answer to the 'green tree' riddle? In Christiancourier. com. Retrieved December 23, 2017, from https://www.christiancourier.com/articles/640-what-is-the-answer-to-the-green-tree-riddle

26 See Matthew 1:21. The notion that the rulers at that time would not have crucified Jesus had they realized who He was is also indicated in the apostle Paul's words in I Corinthians 2:8.

cues from His Father, and He once taught that "out of the abundance of the heart, (a person's) mouth speaks."[27] Therefore, we can at least be certain that His prayer is a very deliberate and natural expression of a heart that consistently and continuously pulses with forgiveness for all who are in need of it.

---

### "By praying for forgiveness Jesus is acknowledging, in no uncertain terms, the sins of His killers."

---

And for Jesus, the reason His killers need forgiveness is... ignorance.. At a glance, this could be very troubling. In a more modern context, it could seem akin to an attorney claiming that a client is somehow not guilty of a crime by reason of insanity or mental incompetence. These kinds of defenses, of course, are aimed at diminishing personal responsibility, ultimately in the hope that the punishment will be mitigated. Is this what Jesus is doing?

I think not, and again, I am persuaded that Jesus is doing something much, much deeper. First, let us remember that forgiveness implies guilt. In the words of Miroslav Volf, author and theologian, "condemnation" is the "indispensable presupposition" of forgiveness.[28]

By praying for forgiveness Jesus is acknowledging, in no uncertain terms, the sins of His killers.

At the same time, as an act of pure kindness, His plea for forgiveness seeks to expose rather than diminish personal responsibility. In labored gasps, He is simultaneously declaring the depravity of his killers and the curious compulsion He has for them to receive compassion nonetheless. Far from trying to exonerate His enemies, Jesus is ultimately providing a way, through the gift of His very life, for them to correct their ways and experience lasting transformation.

---

27  John 5:19; Luke 6:45

28  Volf, M. (2005). Free of charge: Giving and forgiving in a culture stripped of grace. Grand Rapids, MI: Zondervan, p. 130.

And this is the backdrop against which He appeals to His Father, citing His transgressors' ignorance as His reason. While I recognize that it is risky to make arguments from what is not recorded, I still think it quite intriguing that Jesus does not say other things that would also seem reasonable such as forgive them for they are mistaken, misguided, selfish, wrong, cruel, wicked, abusive, or malicious. Instead, He points to His killers' lack of knowledge of what they are doing. And I am so glad He does this, for it seems to me that by doing so He reveals a secret to forgiving that cuts across all motivations.

*Ignorance is this . . .*

The darker motives, such as those above (such as cruelty or selfishness), seem incompatible with compassion. Compassion, as a response to an offense and a strategy for forgiveness, must be intentional and purposeful. In this case, Jesus' prayer for forgiveness is entirely consistent with His willingness, from the very beginning (again, especially because He trusted his Father), to die on a cross. His is a laser-focused mission to ransom and redeem any and all who acknowledge their need, and praying for forgiveness is one way of announcing that it is soon to be a "mission accomplished."

If His executioners are just mistaken or misguided, it would seem Jesus is minimizing the egregiousness of torturing and killing an innocent person. And, if they are purely and exclusively selfish, wrong, cruel, or worse, there is really nothing to redeem.

Bad is bad, and all bad is all bad. But ignorance is a particularly different kind of bad. In a word, it is blindness, and blindness without knowledge or awareness is especially dangerous.

There is an interesting relationship between lack of knowledge and the kind of blindness or "badness" that we might describe as "evil." For example, Dallas Willard points out that the philosopher René Descartes noted that all evil could be explained as "human will running beyond knowledge."[29] Scott Peck, a psychiatrist whose thinking has influenced much of this book, has elsewhere suggested that evil be defined as "militant

29  Willard, D. (. [Daniel dliver]. (2011, March 13). Dallas Willard—Divine conspiracy 01: Jesus & culture. [Video file]. Retrieved December 22, 2017, from https://www.youtube.com/ watch?v=ezbExj7pT1s. 37:30.

ignorance."[30] Peck sheds additional light on this summary of evil when he describes evil as fundamentally opposed to "life and liveliness" (he notes the way his then 8-year-old son observed that evil is "live" spelled backwards). Moreover, it involves ignorance because the "central defect" of evil is not sin itself but a self-deceiving refusal to acknowledge even the possibility of sin which ironically leads to the "subtlety and persistence and consistency" of the sin overall.[31]

As we have previously seen, evil as the opposite of life is a distorted, derived, and dependent phenomenon, devoid of any ultimate originality or intrinsic sustainability. In a way, the biblical narrative begins with both the world and humanity in a state of innocence that might very well be summed up as, "ignorance is bliss." Sin makes its debut when Adam and Eve partake of the forbidden fruit of the tree of *knowledge* of good and evil.[32] And ironically, a quantum reversal occurs as this "original" ignorance is lost and replaced with a terrible awareness of shame and increasing darkness. Left unchecked, this darkness will morph into a second kind of ignorance so narrow and consuming that it will blind both the mind and the heart.

Of course, no person aspires to be blind—that is, nobody tries to *not know* what they are doing. If anything, the fact that they are "doing something" suggests that in some way that action makes sense to them. They may be trying to be loving or they may be trying to be wicked, but either way, it is because they think that love or wickedness are somehow warranted. Overall, as human beings, we cannot escape the consequences of having a mind, and as long as we have the capacity for using our mind, we cannot stop thinking (even if we do try to stop thinking, we are really trying to just "think about nothing"). So, as long as this is the case, we will always do what, at some level, makes sense to us. Even trying to not make sense, to not know what we are doing, is done for a reason.

---

30  Peck, M. S. (1997). The road less traveled and beyond: Spiritual growth in an age of anxiety. New York, NY: Touchstone, p. 74.

31  Peck, M. S. (1983). People of the lie: The hope for healing human evil. New York, NY: Touchstone, pp 42, 69.

32  Genesis 2:17, italics added

And this is why Jesus' assertion that His killers are ignorant is both intriguing and profound—despite their purposeful violence, He finds a way to say they are acting without knowledge. They are apparently trying to torture and kill Him, either because they believe He deserves it or because they are just carrying out orders. Either way, killing Him makes some kind of sense to them. And even though they ultimately succeed, while He is still alive, he says that somehow, regardless of their own conscious decisions (and eventual "success"), they are ultimately not aware of "what they do." It is almost as if Jesus is saying that if they did know, they would not be doing what they are doing; they would not be trying to kill him.

If this is the case, from Jesus' perspective, what do his killers "know"?

I suggest that Jesus would say they "know" all the ways that go into a "survival" kind of life—the "pattern of this world"[33]—characterized by moves that are altogether reactive, quid pro quo, competitive, transactional, retaliatory, and obligatory. By contrast, Jesus, from a position of utter pain and surrender, exemplifies a completely free, responsive, and life-giving acceptance, not only of His suffering but also of His killers. When Jesus is first arrested, He makes several statements about how He is *not* leading a "rebellion"[34] and how the nature of His kingdom is so other-worldly that His servants do something other than "fight."[35] His is a way of peace and love, and He is elsewhere described as the Prince of Peace and God of Love.[36] Those who oppose these hallmarks of His kingdom and indeed those who oppose Him as the benevolent King, are truly blind; they "know not what they do."

*Bigger Picture*
To the extent that this is what Jesus knows about both Himself and His enemies, He is afforded a much, much bigger picture of what He is experiencing. And when a wider angle is used to view any situation, the details of the situation are inevitably scaled down. Moreover, when this happens, the situation is interpreted

33  Romans 12:2 (NIV)
34  Mark 14:48
35  John 18:36
36  Isaiah 9:6; 2 Corinthians 13:11

differently and, in this case, more compassionately. Remarkably and yet not surprisingly, Jesus can petition His Father for mercy and grace, regardless of the nature of the sins against Him because all of these sins are seen from a larger perspective. Always questioning the prevailing assumptions, He who taught His followers to "bless those who curse" and to "turn the other cheek,"[37] is now, from the cross, living out this new way.

Jesus' words call to mind other biblical scenes where "victims" of agonizing injustices are able to similarly speak love to hate. Of note is Joseph who is separated from his family and homeland for most of his life when his jealous brothers sell him into slavery after nearly killing him. Years later, following a remarkable rise to power which makes possible a very well-deserved revenge, he focuses instead on how their *intention to harm him* was part of God's larger plan. Even years after he has extended them kindness, when their father's death triggers new doubts, Joseph again reassures his brothers:

*"Do not fear, for am I in the place of God? As for you, you meant evil against me, but God meant it for good, to bring it about that many people should be kept alive, as they are today. So, do not fear."*[38]

Or consider Stephen, the young man who, though "full of grace and power," becomes the first martyr of the Christian church, ultimately because certain religious leaders "could not withstand the wisdom and the Spirit with which he was speaking."[39] Bloodied by stones being hurled at him, he is comforted by a vision of Jesus and makes his final words a prayer for his killers to receive mercy: "Lord, do not hold this sin against them."[40]

Timeless words, spoken at critical moments by people compelled by a peculiar logic. A logic as relevant today as it was for these people in the past. A way of reasoning that found and still finds a way of clinging to kindness *despite the clear desire of another to inflict severe harm*. A way of saying that somehow

37    Luke 6:28; Matthew 5:39
38    Genesis 50:19-21
39    Acts 6:8, 10
40    Acts 7:60

evil will not get the last word, and instead, it is possible to overcome it with good.[41]

## Sense and Sustainability

*Consent*

Of course, the real magic and true power of a larger perspective show forth when *new ways of reasoning become new ways of living and of life.* For example, Worthington notes that in addition to functioning as behaviors, both *forgiveness and unforgiveness* can become character traits, qualities he calls forgivingness and unforgivingness. In light of this, we can again ask: what kind of world do we want to live in?

I recently overheard my wife, Keri, talking with our girls about how their lives would be so much easier if they did not treat every conflict as though it was a crisis. Specifically, she encouraged them to allow various offenses to roll off themselves "like water off a duck's back." The expression is a helpful one for how we address hurt feelings in general. The less we allow people to insult us the greater will be our quality of life. As Eleanor Roosevelt so aptly put it, "No one can make you feel inferior without your consent."[42]

Forgiveness takes this idea a step further. Because forgiveness implies that something wrong actually occurred, it involves more than just not letting the wrongdoing affect us—it involves *finding a way to view the wrongdoer with compassion.* In addition to relying on ownership of personal feelings, forgiveness finds a way to see the offense in a larger context. Part of this larger context involves considering that a reactive approach to emotions was likely behind the offensive behavior in the first place. So, for example, if someone has expressly tried to insult me, I can imagine that this insult was further informed and motivated by the other person's beliefs that I deserved to be insulted (likely because somewhere in our past interactions, this other person felt insulted by me). Forgiveness is then a way of ending the "cycle of violence" by recognizing the place of pain

---

41  Romans 12:21

42  Templeton, J. M. (1994). Discovering the laws of life. New York, NY: Continuum, p. 158.

that the insult is coming from. Forgiveness, in three words, is responding to reaction.

In many instances, this means that if someone seeks to insult me, I can validate *the way in which it made sense* to the person to try to hurt me (which is entirely different from validating the insult outright), possibly to the point of apologizing for whatever was done to prompt the other person's insult in the first place. Whereas Eleanor Roosevelt reminds us that we don't need to be hurt if we don't want to be hurt (similar to encouraging us to *not be reactive* in our approach to emotions), forgiveness goes beyond this and sees empathy as a patently better *response*, especially since would-be injuries represent evidence of a different logic altogether.

The more compelled we are that our hurt (vs another's) is "in the eye of the beholder" or that resentment carries diminishing returns, the more equipped we will be to embrace the logic of forgiveness. In keeping with this, perhaps the most difficult aspect of forgiveness is trusting that it is actually better than other alternatives. Is it possible or even practical to really believe that, regardless of the circumstance, forgiveness is always the more sustainable, sensible, and beneficial option?

## "What if we start to see the feeling of "being devalued" as a misnomer or even a myth?"

The typical, even classic, objections to forgiveness are that it somehow opens an injured or wronged person to re-injury, or it means the perpetrator is pardoned. These arguments assume that forgiving somehow means the injury was allowable or justified in the first place. If this assumption were accurate, forgiveness would truly be an objectionable endeavor. Let us recall, however, that forgiveness is very different from condoning or excusing offenses. Indeed, forgiveness is first a way of acknowledging and lamenting that a wrong occurred. It is as if the forgiver says, "I was violated, and I refuse to further hurt myself by holding a grudge, so I will find a way to trade my hurt for compassion."

Nonetheless, for various reasons, we can still hesitate to forgive either because we feel certain hurts are insurmountable or because it seems our compassion reserves will run empty. Let us consider two metaphors that might help us respond to these concerns.

### Boats

The first metaphor pertains to motor vehicles, and for our purposes, let us use the example of a boat. In this case, let us say a boat is involved in an accident and there is an insurance company that determines that the vessel has been "totaled." This is another way of saying that the damaged boat is a "total loss" in that the costs of repairing the vessel exceed the value of the vessel itself. In other words, the insurance company would pay the owner the value of the vessel (minus any deductibles) rather than cover the higher expense of fixing it. Of course, since the damages are significant enough for repairs to be higher, often the vessel is hardly worth keeping.

When it comes to forgiveness, it is critical for us to begin by recognizing that people are different from vessels and vehicles. People, unlike inanimate objects, are of incalculable worth—priceless. Whereas a comprehensive insurance policy on a vehicle may pave the way for the owner to simply replace the lost boat or car with a brand-new model, no insurance policy is ever enough to cover the loss of a life. Because they are priceless, people do not "depreciate" in value. And since nothing can diminish a person's value, a person simply cannot be *"totaled."*

Why is this important, especially in the context of forgiveness? Simply put, *if people cannot be "totaled," hurt feelings are not a matter of permanent damage.* Therefore, no matter how hurt we are, our value cannot be taken away! It might be good for us to pause here and allow ourselves some time to process these concepts. We can begin by asking ourselves what it will mean if these concepts are true? What if, for example, even as we acknowledge that we are all physically fragile and finite, we also believe that we are emotionally indestructible? What if we start to see the feeling of "being devalued" as a misnomer or even a myth? What if there were a way to be emotionally bulletproof in such a way that relationships would be more strengthened rather than weakened? Would we take it?

If survival is not at stake, reacting, however understandable, is still unnecessary. More importantly, if survival is not at stake, responding is then always possible. Of course, the principal challenge to responding is *believing that what we believe about belief* can actually make more of a difference than situational changes, however relieving or helpful the situational changes might be. Like any process, this takes time, practice, and patience. The more convinced we are that people are never a "total loss," the more we are positioned to value the process *even more than or even regardless* of outcome. And the more appreciation we have for the process, the more natural forgiveness will become.

*Pipelines*

Let us turn to our second metaphor, in this case for addressing the concern that certain offenses might demand more compassion than we may have or than we may be ready to give. Several years ago, I enjoyed tending to a very basic saltwater aquarium in my home. When I began this hobby, I mixed my own saltwater using tap water and a salt compound that I purchased at our local pet store. It was simple enough to make sure I measured out the correct proportions of water to salt. I did not continue with this mixing process for very long, though, because living in Hawaiʻi, it seemed very unnecessary to essentially buy and make saltwater when I could collect natural water from the beach, just a short drive from home. However, collecting water at the beach proved to have its challenges, such as issues related to waves, sand, and filtration. So, it was "music to my ears," to learn about a particular public beach park, where there is actually a faucet that is connected to a direct pipeline to the ocean. This is a completely free, all-access, anytime-of-day faucet where all sorts of aquarists, fishermen, and pet store staff come to replenish their saltwater. Additionally, because the pipeline goes out to sea some distance from shore, the water is quite pristine in quality, all-natural and even much cleaner than water from the beach.

In the days when I used to mix my own saltwater, I recall a time I accidentally spilled the water while pouring it into the tank. I found myself frustrated with the waste and worried about whether I would have enough water, if it would be necessary to mix more, and further still, if I might need to buy another bag of salt compound sooner rather than later. Contrast this memory with a more recent memory of a particular drive to the park with the pipeline. On that occasion, I remember seeing that someone had apparently left the faucet on, resulting in water gushing from the spigot, flooding the ground. My initial thought was again that this was unfortunate and wasteful, immediately associating the scene with how I might feel if I had accidentally left the faucet or hose running at home. Of course, it did not take me very long to remember that this water was coming from *a direct pipeline to the sea*. The faucet could theoretically be left on indefinitely and except for the flooded ground nobody would know the difference. Indeed, I don't think it is an exaggeration to say that even if the faucet were left on for months or even years the water level of the ocean would not drop in the least. The Pacific Ocean is massive, and even if we could diminish it, we would still have to contend with the Atlantic, Indian, Arctic, and Antarctic seas!

*Unlimited Compassion*

The principles in this book show us how we can draw from a supply as vast as the ocean. In this case, the more responsive (rather than reactive) we are to emotional concerns, the more our experience with compassion will parallel a direct pipeline to the sea. Similarly, when it comes to the relationship between compassion and forgiveness, the issue is how to operate from a place of abundance rather than scarcity. And if another person's actions are the direct cause of our hurt, this would seem to indicate a starting point that is marked by scarcity.

As we have seen, another person essentially has leverage or power over us when they can "single-handedly" cause us emotional pain. It is as if they can somehow exceed our capacity for discomfort and push us over some undefined edge. And once this happens, we naturally brace and protect ourselves from further depletion. The very notion of others being able to "push our limits" suggests that we are concerned with limited supplies of energy, patience, or compassion. And once our own resources are threatened, survival becomes a priority. Not surprisingly, it is then much easier to push others back or away than it is to forgive.

Compassion takes a different shape, however, when emotional pain can be modulated from within. We see actions that would ordinarily be taken as offensive through a different lens altogether. We recognize that when we are hurt, the wound in question has at least two dimensions: first, it suggests an injury to someone or something we care about and second, the injury seems a personal concern, as if it was somehow intended to particularly harm us. In other words, there is a difference between caring and taking things personally; perhaps we might even say that there is a difference between having feelings that hurt and "having our feelings hurt."

---

**"Similarly, when it comes to the relationship between compassion and forgiveness, the issue is how to operate from a place of abundance rather than scarcity."**

---

Whereas feelings that hurt are up to us, "having our feelings hurt" is up to others. So, while it is always important to care, we do not have to experience the injury as personal or offensive. Admittedly, this position largely goes against the grain of many societal assumptions. Take again the ubiquitous use of language that implies people can "hurt our feelings." However, the ability to have the power to not be offended by others is potentially far greater—maybe even as measureless as the sea.

*Unoffended*

Before we can forgive, we must first judge and even condemn whatever it is that we are forgiving. Still, forgiveness recognizes that there is a fundamental difference between judging and carrying out a sentence or punishment. Moreover, forgiveness makes this distinction precisely because it is concerned with a bigger picture of justice.

The ability to be unoffended is particularly useful for keeping a bigger picture of justice before us. The two dimensions of an injury that we've just mentioned (care and personal concern) make it possible for a wrong to be acknowledged (something is judged or condemned) without the need for personal retribution to occur. Therefore, emotional punishments such as grudges can be released, even when actual consequences naturally take place.

There is, of course, one more lens that helps us to focus all these matters if we will allow the "eyes of our heart" to see through it. This is the lens of spiritual reality. Storms on the ocean look significantly different when we zoom out, so to speak, to a perspective that allows us to see our whole planet from a wider angle.

I will limit myself here to one verse from Christian scripture that seems integral to the discussion:

*"Put on then, as God's chosen ones, holy and beloved, compassionate hearts, kindness, humility, meekness, and patience, **bearing with one another and, if one has a complaint against another, forgiving each other; as the Lord has forgiven you, so you also must forgive.**"*[43]

Here the author is again the apostle Paul, and he appeals to his readers to clothe themselves with these virtues, precisely because of a specific kind of relationship to God. In the case of forgiveness, what does it mean to forgive "as the Lord has forgiven"? Let us consider that for Paul, this is a direct reference to an all-encompassing forgiveness of every sin ever committed, afforded by Jesus' own gift of His very life for all humanity in the mystery of Jesus' crucifixion and resurrection. For example, earlier in this letter, Paul reminds his readers that both he and they have been "made alive together with [Jesus], having forgiven us all our trespasses, by canceling the record of debt that stood against us with its legal demands. This he set aside, nailing it to the cross."[44]

This announcement that forgiveness of all violations is available because the "record of debt" has been "canceled" is elsewhere, in numerous places, referred to by Paul as the "gospel" or, literally, the "good news." This news is exquisitely good when we consider that what Paul is describing is Jesus' provision of having a *clean slate before God*.

---

43 Colossians 3:12-13, bold added

44 Colossians 2:13-14

What might it mean then if we apply this idea to Paul's appeal regarding our own forgiveness of one another? Does it make any sense at all for me to not forgive another person if God has forgiven me for sins against God? I encourage us to reflect on how this could be the most important question we ask ourselves regarding forgiveness. Moreover, if decisions to forgive flow, as Paul suggests, from the personal experience of being *forgiven by God*, the option is again available to draw compassion from a direct *pipeline to the sea*.

## True Nature

### Of Christ and Men

An additional tenet of Christian faith that seems a fitting (pun intended) way to round out this discussion is what many followers of Jesus affectionately cherish as the doctrine of the Incarnation. This belief has various dimensions to it, and for our sake, let us consider that it specifies that Jesus was, is, and always will be *completely divine and completely human* at the same time. It is the idea that, in Jesus, God became a mortal person in order to identify with and, ultimately, save people.

One implication of this doctrine is that Jesus lived, died, rose, ascended, and now lives forever as the perfect human being.[45] If this is the case, what does this mean for our understanding of forgiveness, regarding a spiritual, pipeline-to-the-sea power to forgive the way God has forgiven us?

In a now well-known line, Alexander Pope writes "to err is human; to forgive, divine."[46] This is a widely accepted view and perhaps a reason we so often say we're "only human" when we make a mistake or commit a sin.

However, what if we take the concept of the Incarnation so seriously that we allow it to transform our use of even these well-accepted lines from Alexander Pope? That is, if Jesus is the perfect human, then He is the epitome and exemplar of humanity.

---

45  This idea is especially implied in the Bible's depiction of Jesus as the "Word made flesh" (John 1:14) or as the High Priest who "always lives to make intercession" for people (Hebrews 7:25)

46  Pope, A. (1713). An essay on criticism. London: W. Lewis. Retrieved January 1, 2018, from http://www.eighteenthcenturypoetry.org/works/o3675-w0010.shtml

He shows us what is possible when, through Him, we recover our original design. I am persuaded that, instead of "human" being synonymous with fallible or sinful, "human" points to certain liabilities like weakness, frailty, or vulnerability. Jesus was morally perfect but still susceptible to bleeding and dying. Also, I believe that "human" captures the "so-close-yet-so-far" relationship we have to God in that we are uniquely made in His image and, therefore, very good, while being simultaneously, and most assuredly and thankfully, not Him.

What if forgiveness, precisely because it is divine, is also a most "human" thing to do because it is in the image of the divine? What if we found a way to believe and practice forgiveness in a way that it seems to us the *natural* thing to do? Indeed, based upon the principles we have discussed in this book, I would like to suggest that even as forgiveness requires uncommon sense, it also is possible to get to the place where we regard it as the quintessential form of "emotional common sense" as well.

*Swans*

Sometimes it takes significant time to recognize the true nature of a thing, especially, if certain defaults are quite firmly set in place. Hans Christian Anderson's 1843 classic tale of *The Ugly Duckling* is an interesting case in point. The story traces the painful adventures of a duckling who does not look like his "sibling" ducklings and culminates in him realizing that, much to his delight, he is not a duck but a swan. In 1993, British composer George Stiles and lyricist Anthony Drewe turned the story into a musical called, *Honk!*, which later won an Olivier Award in 2000 for best musical. In the musical, the lead character is naturally named "Ugly," and one of the features that makes him different is that he is unable to "quack." Instead, his voice comes out as a "honk," which continues to be a frustration for him until he finally discovers that he is a swan and that this was his native language all along.[47]

What if we apply this to forgiveness? What if we see forgiveness as our native, human language? Might the socially acceptable things we do to retaliate or to feed resentment sound more like "quacking"? Conversely, might the times we respond with gentleness, looking foolish or naive, be more like "honking"

47  Retrieved on January 18, 2020, from https://www.mtishows.com/honk

and what we were intended to do all along?

The truth is that when we bully and reject one another, we are living beneath our nature. Often these behaviors spring from reactive minds and reactive, even hardened, hearts. However, unlike the rest of the animals in the barnyard, we are baby swans, cygnets. Beauty, grace, harmony, and freedom are our birthrights, not bickering and vying for control. As such, when a relationship faces conflict, which is likely since reactivity is our persistent and compelling default, we might consider that there is another option besides reaction. Even amid the most painful emotions, we can do more than just limit ourselves to fighting, fleeing, or freezing. Instead of holding personal grudges, we have the option of facing our feelings, however negative they may be, practicing the truly human response of being open to forgiveness. As we do this, perhaps we might even think of the offense as rolling off of us, *"like water off a swan's back."* To the extent to which anger, bitterness, and hurt are routinely converted to compassion and the initial negative emotions decrease, we might also say that the forgiveness process is in place.

Emotional replacement. Two words. Words which could seem to be nothing but jargon, hardly even drops in a bucket. Or from a different perspective, two words that signify the option to make an exchange from pain and bitterness to healing and possibility. From obligation to opportunity. From surviving to thriving. And ultimately, from seas of hurt to oceans of grace.

If we can trust these things to be true, then forgiveness can keep its promises. To use earlier metaphors, it can become a gift or investment for all parties, like blue-chip stock, a profitable flip, or real estate that appreciates in value. In oceanspeak, it can become the balmy breeze that fills our sails and sends our craft slicing through the waters with a spirit of adventure and excitement. In other ways, it might be seen as a move from manufacturing saltwater to accessing it directly and free of charge from an infinite supply. Or a shift from thinking of ourselves in undermining, unhelpful ways to reclaiming our true and beautiful nature as people who forgive, having ourselves been forgiven. In each instance, movement. In each instance, change. And, in each instance, trades.

# Epilogue: The Navigator's Triangle

*And now these three remain...*[1]

We began this exploration sitting on a metaphorical beach, gazing at the distant horizon, and imagining the possibilities. We have particularly considered options for deepening, expanding, and strengthening relationships by delving into certain ideas about relationships, emotions, and motivations. And we have indulged the hypothesis that these ideas, appearing initially as mere "drops in the bucket," might be so significant that they ultimately apply and expand to the entire ocean of our relationships. Thus, we have sought to apply the inspiring exhortations of Mark Twain, one of the authors who helped us with the beginning of this voyage—to "throw off the bowlines" and "sail away from the safe harbor." And so now, if we have succeeded, we find ourselves on the open sea of additional possibilities, ready to continue with more exploring, more dreaming, and more discoveries. Let us entertain one final metaphor that might further guide us on our way.

The writing of this book overlapped with a fascinating journey. On June 17, 2017, a team of sailors and scientists from Hawai`i completed a three-year, 47,000 nautical mile voyage around the world! This journey, known in Hawaiian as *Malama Honua* or "Caring for Island Earth," involved two vessels, the *Hokule'a* and the *Hikianalia,* two double-hulled canoes that are patterned after the ancient canoes that first brought Polynesians to the Hawaiian Islands over a thousand years ago. Under the auspices of the Polynesian Voyaging Society, the crew of these vessels, led by master navigator Charles Nainoa Thompson, skillfully and successfully used the same traditional sailing methods that ancient sailors once employed. Remarkably, part of this tradition involved "non-instrument navigation" which was complicated by the fact that on the open ocean there are quite literally no "landmarks" to reference. Instead, the "wayfinding" of the captain and crew relied on other natural phenomena such as the sun and ocean swells by day and star patterns by night.

## Two Triangles

*Vertices and Virtues*

One such star pattern that continues to capture my attention is what the crew of the *Hokule'a* and *Hikianalia* refer to as Huinakolu or The Navigator's Triangle. And while this star pattern is itself less well-known and I admittedly have only a very limited understanding of astronomy, I still think it a useful final symbol, especially since the topic I will close with is a "triad" indispensable to navigating relationships, namely the "triangle" of faith, hope, and love.

Three stars, Altair, Deneb, and Vega form the three vertices of the celestial Navigator's Triangle.[2] The Triangle itself is technically not a constellation but each of its stars are the brightest stars in three separate constellations, respectively. Incidentally, the reader will recognize that two of these constellations happen to stand for creatures already familiar to our discussion, namely Aquila the Eagle (which contains Altair) and Cygnus the Swan (which contains Deneb). The third and brightest star of the three, Vega, is from the constellation Lyra the Harp.[3] The Navigator's Triangle is also known as the Summer Triangle since it is most visible, in the northern hemisphere, during the summer months. For the crew of the *Hokule'a* and *Hikianalia*, these stars are known in Hawaiian as Humu, Pira'etea, and Keoe, and are regarded as symbolizing the three points of what is also called the Polynesian Triangle consisting of Rapa Nui (Easter Island), Aotearoa (New Zealand),

---

2  Summer triangle. (2014, June 15). In Constellation-guide.com. Retrieved January 1, 2018, from http://www.constellation-guide.com/tag/navigators-triangle/

3  Interestingly, just outside of the Triangle, between Altair and Deneb, is a constellation that contains another animal we have previously discussed, namely Delphinus or Dolphin.

and Hawai`i.[4]

We have used the sea as our primary metaphor, but here and there, we have opted to look beyond the water, past the earthly bounds of our horizontal relationships, to ponder the heavens, so to speak, and acknowledge the spiritual. For me, this has meant repeated references to the Christian tradition and the use of certain stories and teachings from the Bible. I hope that I have done this with both conviction and humility, and I respect each reader's prerogative to say whether I have or have not done so. At the outset, there were risks to this whole mission that were important to acknowledge, and now as we conclude, I am convinced that they were risks worth taking. And so, it is in the spirit of continuing to "throw off the bowlines," that I now turn our attention to a very brief reflection on the place and power that these three virtues, faith, hope, and love, might have in and over the model we have been studying. Again, I will share my perspective as a Christian.

Specifically, to keep this conclusion focused, I have chosen three separate passages from the Bible as primary springboards for thought. These passages give important glimpses into the essential nature of each of these virtues and are thus packed with light for further illuminating our discussion.

And as we will see, one essential feature of each of these virtues is that they all pertain to the realm of the invisible. Of course, this is hardly new for us. Even as this book has focused on predominantly horizontal themes, our constant goal has been to develop an "invisible" principle: that where emotions are concerned, interpretations may often take precedence over situations. And all along, this principle has been propelled by an even deeper undercurrent, namely an interest in living a certain kind of life.

On one hand, this has been the question of how we move from just surviving life to thriving. Even more though, our journey to explore the what, how, and why of our feelings and relationships has been repeatedly connected to the question of who we are. Therefore, it concerns the matter of our character.

---

4 Hawaiian voyaging traditions. (n. d.). In archive.hokulea.com. Retrieved January 1, 2018, from http://archive.hokulea.com/ike/hookele/hawaiian_star_lines.html

As such, we have particularly delved into this in our discussions of morality, motivation, and forgiveness, and now we will finally immerse ourselves in these three virtues. Not that this will be an exhaustive discussion of these virtues; far from it. However, it is my hope that even the briefest bits of time spent pondering them will prove useful for taking us to even greater depths within ourselves, with one another, and with our Creator.

334 | MAYBE THE WHOLE OCEAN

# Faith

> *Now faith is the assurance of things hoped for,*
> *the conviction of things not seen . . .*[5]

Faith is the first star in our Triangle. Let us consider it to largely pertain to what we might think of as "confident belief." Its origins can be traced to the Latin term *fidere*, "to trust," which, in turn, is related to the word "confidence."[6] In the verse above, taken from the book of Hebrews, the word for faith is the Greek word *pistis*, which can also mean *belief*.[7] Another translation reads, "Now faith is being sure of what we hope for and certain of what we do not see."[8]

The larger context of this verse is a passage that is spiritual or theological in that God, or more precisely, Jesus, is the reason faith is exercised in the first place. In fact, the writer of this passage ultimately goes on to describe multiple people whose lives were characterized by faith in God and to point out that "without faith it is impossible to please [God]"[9] and that Jesus is the "founder and perfecter"[10] of such faith.

## Faith and Reason

*Favorable and Invisible*
Even as this passage on faith is fundamentally theological, I believe it can also speak to and inform our psychology. For

5   Hebrews 11:1

6   Faith. (n. d.). In dictionary.com. Retrieved on January 1, 2018, from http://www.dictionary.com/browse/faith

7   Pistis. (n. d.). In biblehub.com. Retrieved on January 1, 2018, from http://biblehub.com/greek/4102.htm

8   Hebrews 11:1 (NIV)

9   Hebrews 11:6

10   Hebrews 12:2

example, consider that this book has essentially focused on establishing the importance of *what we believe about belief*, with an emphasis on what this means for how feelings can be used to help us and our relationships. Both literally and figuratively, our focus has been on learning and practicing certain *habits of mind*. We might therefore say that, to the extent that we practice such habits, we are already practicing a certain kind of faith as we trust these habits to work.

In this way, faith involves trusting that certain beliefs will be beneficial or worthwhile.This may be redundant since trust implies that we are counting on experiencing something or someone as *good*. Nevertheless, it is important to emphasize that faith is interested in both the future and in what is good. At the risk of oversimplifying, the feelings we have previously considered appear to contain one of these elements but not both. For example, fear is a future-oriented anticipation of something bad happening. Happiness is focused on what is good, though, in a way, it is more about a gain that has already occurred or that is occurring. It is possible to be happy about the future, but such an emotion would seem to be crossing over into the category of faith or as we will see shortly, hope. Faith "looks" for those things that are future-oriented, favorable, and, by definition, not immediately apparent.

In fact, it might be more accurate to say that faith concerns itself with things that are both favorable and invisible. As the biblical author puts it, faith is "the assurance of things hoped for, the conviction of things *not seen*" (italics added). This "favorable and invisible" combination is common ground for all three of the virtues in our Triangle. Perhaps this combination is also what sets these virtues apart from the general emotions we have been discussing.

Focusing on good, invisible things is counterintuitive, and so it can seem highly impractical. We are much better acquainted with "things seen," especially when it comes to explaining our basic emotions and particularly if "things seen" include not just visible events but anything that can be detected with our physical senses. And so, we have examined the ways in which anger, sadness, happiness, and fear can be easily associated with literal or categorical injustices, losses, gains, and threats, respectively. Associating our emotions with such situational causes is an example of common sense. This is another way of seeing how happiness is about what has already been gained, since future gains are not yet "seen." What we see (hear, taste, smell, touch) is, as the saying goes, what we get.

This is important because life requires the physical, concrete, tangible, palpable dimensions, and these dimensions are a very good part of what it means to be alive. At the same time, this book is also about going beyond basic requirements to those things that will lead to flourishing and moving from good to better or even great. As such, we have also given serious attention to what might constitute a sort of uncommon sense—specifically, the proposition that our emotions may be equally if not more affected by the hypothetical realm of thoughts, perceptions, and interpretations. Our vessel was meant to go beyond the beach and the shallows to the open sea, and the stars help us to navigate the uncharted waters where life can really take off.

In the film *Religulous*, the narrator, Bill Maher, makes an interesting critique of faith saying it is the "virtue of not thinking."[11] On one hand this opinion is understandable. All too often, faith is used as an almost standard way of justifying decisions or actions that seem to have no basis in either reality or in logic. However, on another hand, this chapter and indeed this book are focused on the ways that faith can be compatible with reason. I am committed to showing that this compatibility becomes most evident precisely as we take seriously the role of reason in our emotional experiences. And so, we have spent the better part of this book focusing on strategies for interpersonal relationships (via a largely intrapersonal, cognitive approach to emotion management), arriving at a general process for reflecting on how to best respond rather than react.

Faith enters the picture when we turn our gaze towards the things we would rather experience that are not yet apparent and not yet experienced. Things hoped for that are still unseen. Take for instance, a relational disagreement, a disappointment, or even a disillusionment. Using our cognitive model, our first option is to define whatever "it" is that is disagreeable,

---

11  From Religulous (2008), starring Bill Maher, directed by Larry Charles, and produced by Thousand Words.

disappointing, or disillusioning in a way that brings the problem within our control. Therefore, if it is a problem for another person to disagree with us, what is it that we believe about disagreement that makes it problematic in the first place? Or if another person is disappointed with us, what is it that they think (concerning us or our behavior) that does not meet their expectations?

Let's consider this in a little more depth. If somebody in our lives is disillusioned with us, how can we use this cognitive model to move the relationship to a better place? As a start, we can remind ourselves that, because interpersonal emotions are largely created by our perspectives, another's disillusionment is reasonable whether or not we are at fault for something. So, if we can convey the reasonableness of their feelings, might our openness to them having such feelings begin to address their disillusionment (could such openness show rather than tell them we sincerely want what is best and fair for them)? It seems that when this is done effectively, actions will speak louder than words and the disillusionment will be much less necessary. Moreover, this kind of credibility is particularly useful because it addresses emotion through a respectful rather than rejecting process.

## Faith and Truth

*Trusting the Truth*

As we realize that we can engage others even when they are not pleased with us, faith can help our relationships to deepen. In fact, we will see that faith is an ongoing option anytime we genuinely care about the person and the relationship. First, faith is an option because God, as the author and source of all relationships, stands ready to help us. Indeed, He is likely already helping us more than we realize. Second, faith is an option because genuine care for a relationship can inspire and empower increasingly healthy interpersonal dynamics. In other words, in addition to faith being about confidence that what we hope for is possible, faith also means we can trust the truth to prevail.

Irony can be found in truth. One of the most ironic moments

in history occurs in the apostle John's account of the Roman governor Pontius Pilate asking Jesus of Nazareth, "What is truth?"[12] Curiously, John does not record any answer on Jesus' part, though earlier in his narrative, John does note that Jesus referred to Himself as "the way, and the truth, and the life."[13] In the same way, is it possible that even as we face something or someone who is true, we may not realize what or who is before us? And if this is possible, can we also learn to have eyes to see the very truth that was formerly hidden in plain sight? Faith would have us answer yes to both questions.

The goal here is to better understand what is really occurring, or even more importantly, what is possible as we take seriously certain assumptions we may have about truth. And, according to our scripture reference, faith suggests that the truth that we have "assurance" of is also apparently good, perhaps even in our best interest (that is, it is about "things hoped for").

This principle seems most salient to me in the specific relationship context of marriage. If I am honest, I have my own tendencies to be fairly matter-of-fact or slightly sarcastic when a couple first describes their marital difficulties. For example, it seems to me that the sentiment "I did not sign up for this" is such a common refrain that my first impression upon hearing it is often to think *it sounds like you're married!* To be even more transparent, perhaps this impression is also influenced by how Keri and I have both felt like this in our own marriage of more than 20 years. At the same time, I am learning to be more attentive to my own disillusionment and sarcasm and to *hear* what I would consider the truth behind my frustration.

Let's call whatever it was that was not signed up for "involuntary suffering." So, to the extent that it is sarcastic for me to associate involuntary suffering with marriage, whether another's or my own, I am saying that such suffering should not be happening. This is also another way of saying that marriage (or maybe my spouse) somehow should not be frustrating or frustrated. If I take our cognitive model seriously, I will remind myself that my disillusionment is primarily experienced because I am thinking marriage should not be frustrating. Therefore, by

---

12   John 18:38

13   John 14:6

extension, I will realize that others do not have the actual power to single-handedly frustrate me. My frustration is primarily my decision, and I can choose to be less frustrated, even if others do not make any changes to their ways of doing things. Also, important though, will be my awareness that because my frustration is largely up to me, it is more of a resource than a problem per se. As such, I can learn how my frustration can help me to "see" and "listen to" the deeper issues that are at work in my approach to marriage. These deeper issues, then, are what I would regard as the *truth behind my frustration.*

Frustration, therefore, is an opportunity for us to learn more about ourselves, regarding it as a kind of teacher or a window into our beliefs. But if so, it is commonly a window we would rather not use or a teacher we would prefer to avoid. This is because frustration pertains to interposing. Something comes between a person and their desire, and the result is the equivalent of a wall. The height and thickness of the wall can vary but regardless of its construction, the effect is the same—we are prevented from having a clear path to the object of our desire. Ironically, sometimes it is the thinner barriers that can leave us feeling the most helpless. Indeed, the "window" of frustration, can at times seem like a pane of glass *within the wall* so that we can essentially see ourselves apprehending our goal, even as the facts leave us admitting the imagined success is "so close and yet so far away."

### Factual and Actual

However, it is at such times that faith can work its own kind of interposing. This is because faith pertains to being certain of what we do not see. I like to differentiate here between what I consider the *factual and the actual.* The *factual* includes all of the empirically verifiable details of the situation—the physical, environmental, and circumstantial details. These are the things that are in one way or another experienced by the senses. But the *actual* issues involve all of these details *plus the impact of certain interpretations that can influence the facts to possibly be just part of a larger story.*

We have already seen some examples of this in our discussion of how communication, specifically *connecting,* can involve translating apparent facts, such as "you should take more responsibility," into opinions, like "I think you should take more responsibility." This strategy starts to move in the direction of certainty about the invisible. But if we are going to be operating out of faith, we will also be incorporating interpretations that are favorable. In our current example, perhaps faith will further translate an opinion such as "I think you should take more responsibility" into "I *believe* you *can* or even *will* take more responsibility." While this example is simple, it serves to illustrate a progression from essentially telling someone what to do to qualifying this as an opinion to affirming a belief in what is possible. In the last two steps, there is a subtle but powerful difference between thinking "what should be" to believing "what can or even will be." Interestingly, once this move is made and something possible is entertained, it seems the chances of the *actual* outcome changing (in this case, the other person taking more responsibility) will increase.

Before we move on, let us consider in even more detail how faith might make a difference in a relationship. Again, while I think that faith is relevant to all relationships, marriage seems to me the most compelling context, since it implies a unique commitment. Suppose there has been a conflict in a marriage, perhaps of a very serious nature such as an extramarital affair. Moreover, let us say that there is an interest from one spouse or even both in continuing the relationship despite the pain of sorting through the hurt. However, amid this difficult season, imagine that certain words are said that seem to do more harm than good. For example, let us say that the offending spouse, trying to be as forthright as possible, tells the offended spouse, "I am not in love with you anymore."

A statement like this could seem like more of a setback than anything else, especially if the comment was made as the couple was trying to recover from an infidelity. What is the faithful spouse to do upon hearing that their spouse is no longer in love with them, particularly if this is because an extramarital partner has had or even still has their loved one's heart?

At face value, it seems nothing can be said or done to address the kind of pain engendered by such a statement. Even if the unfaithful spouse were to apologize, recant, or promise to never again repeat the offense, the damage has already been done.

Certain things, once said, can never be "unheard," much less taken back. Indeed, some people might rather endure serious physical injury than be told by their loved one that their loved one is no longer "in love" with them.

We can call these the *facts*. Irreversible, irrevocable, and indisputable. And for so many, the facts painfully play themselves out day after day with almost mathematical regularity. These are repetitive, almost boringly dramatic cycles that can seem so predictable, because, if facts are anything, they are predictable. In the language of science, these are replicable patterns. In the language of the theater, they are "the same song and dance." Or to borrow from songwriter B. J. Thomas' witty line, "another somebody done somebody wrong song."[14] And while the words may vary, the theme remains the same. One person hurts another, and the hurt takes on a life of its own. Intentional or not, something is done to deepen or worsen the pain, insult is added to injury, and misery finds a way to keep miserable company. Again, at *face value*, any recovery can seem all but lost.

Still, at the risk of using more wordplay, what if we consider that there is also such a thing as taking facts at *faith value*? As we have discussed, faith will answer this question by "looking" for what is unseen. But how is this done?

We have considered looking for what we hope for—the invisible and the favorable. However, how do we start to do this if everything we "see" seems anything but favorable? I suggest that we begin with two things: First, it is important that we enter, as sincerely as possible, into the discomfort of acknowledging the facts of the situation. Second, it will be important for us to remain open to new options, regardless of how tedious, silly, or small they may seem. Let us briefly unpack each of these points and then see how they apply to our couple who is struggling to recover a mutual love.

---

14   The song, Another Somebody Done Somebody Wrong Song, was originally written by Larry Butler and Chips Moman and made popular by B. J. Thomas, who first recorded it in 1975.   Retrieved January 18, 2020, from https://www.songfacts.com/facts/bj-thomas/hey-wont-you-play-another-somebody-done-somebody-wrong-song

*Honesty and Perseverance*

First, honest appraisal is critical since any interest in seeing what faith sees will first take seriously the difficulties of the situation. Indeed, not taking difficulties seriously is probably a major reason for the perception that faith and rationality are incompatible (recall again Bill Maher's criticism that faith is the "virtue of not thinking"). However, rather than being illogical, faith employs a *different kind of logic* altogether. This "other" logic assumes that, most of the time, emotions do not have to be treated as matters of survival. Therefore, when survival is not at stake, ideas have the potential to be even more powerful than facts in determining the feelings we feel. And, the more these concepts make sense to us, the more we can honestly enter the emotional spaces we might rather avoid.

An indispensable part of honest faith is sincerity. For example, in both of his letters to his young protege, Timothy, the apostle Paul encourages and affirms "sincere faith" (see I Timothy 1:5 and 2 Timothy 1:5). The Greek word for sincerity in these passages is *anypokritou*, which literally means "without hypocrisy" or unfeigned.[15] It points to an ability to be genuine, without any need for acting or pretending.

This is especially intriguing when we consider the other kind of logic that faith employs—a logic that can clearly and confidently work with difficult situations and, in our case, even make such situations promote relationship. In my life, my brother Jon is a person who has particularly demonstrated this kind of sincere faith that also prioritizes relationship. Always up for a challenge, he seems to me to be constantly turning unlikely circumstances into occasions for more connection. So, whether he is negotiating a business deal, executing a creative practical joke, conspiring to bless his family or friends, or reaching out to a person less fortunate, Jon exemplifies for me a way of living authentically and intentionally that *naturally flows from a faith which wholeheartedly seeks to love God and people.* This kind of overflow begins with a willingness to engage situations honestly and sincerely as catalysts for deepening relationships.

Second, as we are equipped and empowered to move toward, rather than away from, difficult circumstances, we will benefit as

15  Retrieved August 11, 2018, from https://biblehub.com/greek/505.htm

we open ourselves to *anything in line with hope,* no matter how trivial it may seem. This is a most pivotal consideration since faith involves perseverance. And, when it comes to focusing on things that are invisible, perhaps there is no greater distraction that can undermine perseverance than feeling one's efforts are "ridiculous" or "insignificant." At the same time, attending to the trivial, the ridiculous, or the microscopically small is probably the best evidence we have that we are seeking to understand invisible things that align with hope.

> ## "...sincerity...points to an ability to be genuine, without any need for acting or pretending."

Maybe this is why Jesus spoke of the kingdom of heaven as "yeast" or why He taught that belief the size of a "mustard seed" meant a person could command a mountain to move.[16] At face value, these seem like ridiculous things to say. However, what if they are true? What if miniscule things really contain all the power necessary to radically alter reality as we know it? Yeast surely does this when it enters dough, essentially giving would-be crackers the possibility of becoming bread. And, given enough time, a single seed contains all the genetic information necessary to cover an entire mountainside with trees. So, what if faith has the potential to operate with the same strength? And what if it is so powerful that in even the tiniest amounts it can relocate entire mountainsides no matter how forested they may be with trees? Moreover, what if this could be true of the bleakest or steepest of relationship difficulties? Would not such transforming faith be worth just about any risk, even that of feeling or looking ridiculous?

*Risking the Ridiculous*
Let us explore this a bit further, using the situation previously mentioned. An affair has occurred, and the unfaithful spouse has told the faithful spouse that they are no longer "in love." Let us call the spouse who stepped outside the marriage person A and the spouse who stayed inside the marriage person B. B is

16   see Matthew 13:33; 17:20

particularly feeling re-injured upon hearing that A is no longer in love and now thinks *why try?* so discouragement is not far off. We can anticipate the following dialogue:

> **A:** *I'm not in love with you anymore.*
> **B:** *I can't tell you how much that hurts. But if I'm honest, I'm not sure I'm in love with you either.*
> **A:** *Then why are we even doing this? We're just wasting our time trying to find something that went away long ago.*
> **B:** *Well, what did you think would happen? What am I supposed to do with you telling me you're not in love with me anymore? Obviously, you love someone else. That's why we're here in the first place.*

Let us imagine what difference our strategies might make, beginning with new responses from the faithful spouse. Here is a brief sample dialogue, keeping in mind both the difficulties of the situation and an openness to the significance of small things:

> **A:** *I'm not in love with you anymore.*
> **B:** *It's hard to hear that, but I don't imagine it's easy to say it either.*
> **A:** *No, I hate admitting it, but it's true. Maybe we're just incompatible.*
> **B:** *Again, it must be frustrating to be at a place where you're telling me about things you hate. Do you think it's always been this way?*
> **A:** *I don't know. I just know I don't feel close to you anymore.*
> **B:** *I'm trying really hard to stay with you right now. And I definitely don't like hearing how hard it is for you to be with me. But if I'm in pain, I'm sure you feel it too, maybe even more. For what it's worth, thank you for sharing as much as you've shared right now. Is there anything I can do to make this easier for you?*
> **A:** *No. If anything, I wish I could do more to comfort you. I mean I'm the one who stepped out on you. I'm sorry I'm so confused and confusing, too.*
> **B:** *Thank you for acknowledging that. It's helpful.*

*Even though it's hard to know where this is all headed, it's just like you to always find something that is helpful for us. I'm grateful for your apology.*
**A:** *Well, it wasn't fair to you, and I feel horrible for it.*
**B:** *I feel horrible too. But do you think there's any chance that if we could feel less horrible about all this, we might feel more compatible too?*
**A:** *I hadn't thought about that. Maybe.*

Alternatively, let's consider now how it might go when we begin with new responses from the unfaithful spouse. We'll start the dialogue the same way and consider how it might shift after hearing the faithful spouse express pain.

**A:** *I'm not in love with you anymore.*
**B:** *I can't tell you how much that hurts. But if I'm honest, I'm not sure I'm in love with you either.*
**A:** *I don't blame you. I want to be in love with you again though.*
**B:** *Whatever. I thought you just said you weren't in love with me.*
**A:** *I did, but I don't think it came out the way I wanted it to.*
**B:** *What do you mean? You can't take back what you've already said.*
**A:** *You're right. What if I had said, "I miss being in love with you."*
**B:** *You miss being in love with me? Well, that would still have hurt but maybe not as much. You did cheat on me.*
**A:** *Yes, I did. And it's not fair to you for me to have hurt you even more just now. So, I wish I had said it differently.*
**B:** *Well, what's done is done, and I'm getting tired of feeling hurt.*
**A:** *This conversation isn't helping then.*
**B:** *Not really. But I suppose it's better than us not talking.*
**A:** *That's generous of you. Is there anything I can do differently right now to be more helpful?*
**B:** *I'm not sure. Thanks for trying.*
**A:** *I'm just glad you're being honest with me.*

> **B:** *Well, the reason we're even here is because of dishonesty.*

These clearly are idealized conversations, and many readers may find them far-fetched. In fact, "unrealistic" is the feedback I have received when I have shared these examples with various friends, family, and clients. At other times, I have been told I am on "planet Brian" or when I ask if my methods are frustrating, I often hear some version of yes, like "What else would you expect, Dr. Lim?"! Indeed, as I propose these scenarios, I am aware of mixed feelings within myself, including some embarrassment.

But what else did we have in mind? We are seeking to understand the role *faith* can play in even the direst of interpersonal circumstances. And a major way we are trying to gain this understanding is through an ongoing openness to the range of our emotions.

---

## "...unfaithfulness sets a stage that all but announces the merits of distancing rather than drawing close."

---

To the extent that people in our lives have done things that are *factually* detrimental or unfair, disappointment and frustration are par for the course. And, if we are honest, sincerely entering the discomfort of these emotions can feel embarrassing or even ridiculous. For example, in the scenario above when the faithful spouse (B) hears the unfaithful spouse (A) say that A is not in love with B anymore, B might feel silly at best, saying that it must not be easy for A to share this. Such selflessness can appear to undermine our sense of self-respect and seems like we are pointlessly lowering our standards.

In this regard, in a very eloquent and thought-provoking reflection on infidelity, relationship therapist Esther Perel suggests "If we used to divorce because we were unhappy, today we divorce because we could be happier. And if divorce carried all the shame, today, choosing to stay when you can leave is the new shame."[17] For so many reasons, and legitimate ones at that, unfaithfulness sets a stage that all but announces the merits of distancing rather than drawing close.

Nevertheless, we are looking for something favorable that is invisible. And this of course is a process that can leave us feeling quite foolish, maybe even ashamed. But what if the object of our search would somehow be worth all the subjective discomfort involved in finding it? And, what if even that discomfort could be addressed by leaning into it?

## Faith and Trust

*Faith and Influence*
These questions are more than just rhetorical, because faith opens very real and increasingly new possibilities. Faith pertains to belief, and belief is simultaneously about what makes sense to us and the driving force behind anything that we do. Thus, the apostle James teaches "faith apart from works is dead."[18]

Anytime I do anything—anytime I get in my car to drive somewhere, put on my shoes to walk someplace, call a friend, order a meal, check my inbox, write a note, pay a bill—I am acting thus because it makes sense to do so. I believe that my efforts will somehow be worth the time and energy. Also, anytime I scrutinize a person for hurting me, "see" another's disrespect, or feel weak when giving the benefit of the doubt to another—these experiences will flow from my assumptions about what is safe, respectful, and strong.

These assumptions are examples of belief. However, faith, being informed by hope, adds a positive expectation to how we make sense of things, going beyond simple belief to trust. As such, we *believe* that any number of things will happen, but faith looks forward to how the outcomes will be *good* overall.

In relationships, this means that faith has a wonderful ability to influence even if it cannot make guarantees. It is no

17  Perel, E. (May 21, 2015 TED Talk). Rethinking infidelity...a talk for anyone who has ever loved. 09:03. Retrieved on January 1, 2018, from https://www.youtube.com/watch?v=P2AUat93a8Q

18  James 2:26

exaggeration then to say that, in relationships, faith can stand on reasons almost imperceptible, to do what might seem almost insensible, and help make possible even the improbable. And, in relationships, even as unfaithfulness can give multiple, compelling reasons to give up, faith takes a different kind of inventory. It weighs the awfulness of the situation not just against the absence of that awfulness but against the potential goodness or even greatness that could lie beyond the awfulness once it is healed. In this regard, faith operates in ways that are similar to, and in conjunction with, grace. Per our previous discussion of the Coordinates of Grace, faith focuses on moving past a tolerable, if not lackluster or boring, baseline and into the upper, right-hand quadrant where thriving is possible.

Let us address an additional aspect of faith that, from a certain perspective, may seem opposed to faith and, from another viewpoint, might be one of faith's most compelling advocates: doubt.

How can doubt support faith? Is not doubt a lack of faith and, therefore, part of the problem rather than part of the solution? These are fair questions, though again they derive from a certain perspective. And they beg two more questions—what exactly is the problem, and what solution do we have in mind?

*Faith and Doubt*
Let us first distinguish between doubt and an *absence* of faith, which we might call a state of "faithlessness." Indeed, part of the reason for why we might think of doubt as incompatible with faith is that we equate it with being faithless. However, doubt is not the same thing as faithlessness or unbelief. Doubt is probably better thought of as a lack of *certainty*. Therefore, if I doubt something's existence, it is not so much that I do *not believe that* it exists but rather that I am *not sure if* it exists. If doubt is about not believing, then, yes, it is incompatible with faith, which is all about believing. However, if doubt is about not being certain of a thing then it may have more in common with faith than we realize (this last sentence may seem to contradict our working definition of faith, and I hope to address this shortly).

Recall that faith is about trusting or "being sure of what we hope for and certain of what we don't see."[19] Again, at the outset, this seems to preclude doubt because how can one be sure of something if there is a lack of certainty to begin with? But when it comes to doubt, we might also ask what exactly it is that we are not certain of. And, in response, it seems the uncertainty that characterizes doubt is about things that characterize the "seen" world.

I am reminded of an experience with fishing which involved doubt. My brothers and I were on our way home from a successful day of catching halibut in Kachemak Bay off Homer, Alaska. We had pulled up our anchor and left the productive "hole" our friends had taken us to where we had almost caught our limit for the day. We had some extra time, so we decided to try fishing while drifting, this time over an area that we had no prior knowledge of. When we first dropped our lines, it seemed like we were getting bites similar to when we were reeling in fish, but each time we pulled them up, we were disappointed to see our bait untouched. My brothers, Eric, Jon, and Jeremy, whom I regard as quite skilled fishermen, quickly deduced that what we thought were bites were really the sensations caused by our heavy weights bouncing along the ocean floor since we were drifting. As soon as this explanation was voiced, we all began to doubt that we would catch any more fish. The combined effects of knowing we were drifting over a fairly random part of the bay and the reasonable hypothesis that it was our weights rather than fish that were tugging at our lines led to great uncertainty, which led to increasing pessimism with each drop. Eventually, we pulled up our lines altogether and returned to the harbor.

In this case, our doubt was rooted in how we "saw" the *absence* of certain things—the anchor *not* being in the water, the coordinates of this second spot *not* being familiar, the bait *not* being touched, the halibut *not* weighing down the end of our line. And since, everything we "saw" was *unfavorable*, we only became more *uncertain* that the situation would improve. Or, put another way, we became more and more certain that everything we saw, the "facts," so to speak, of our situation, meant disappointment would get the last word. We became increasingly sure of our *disappointment* and certain of what we *did* see.

---

19  Hebrews 11:1 (NIV)

And, while it was unpleasant, this was an important and good position for us to take. Doubting that the situation would improve meant that we did not unnecessarily delay our return to the harbor, which meant other family members who were waiting could also have their turn at going out to fish the productive spot. While fishing, it especially makes sense to doubt when the doubt lines up with the facts. There are particular spots and particular techniques that are more conducive to catching fish, and learning when and how to doubt the unproductive ones is vital to experiencing better outcomes.

*Necessary and Unnecessary Doubt*

In relationships, it also makes sense to doubt when doubt lines up with the facts. The difference between fishing and relationships, however, is that in relationships, the "facts" are often not so simple, and indeed, they can be so much more complex and harder to define.

For example, if one person (A) says another (B) is "lying," this can be very difficult to prove. There may be any number of explanations for what might initially look like a lie. As examples, apparent lies may be explained by lack of clarity, forgetfulness, misinterpretation, accidental omission of information, or even purposeful withholding of information that may seem irrelevant at the time.

Interestingly, even using a traditional polygraph or "lie detector" is not a foolproof way of determining that someone is lying, since such a test, at best, only allows for "inferring deception."[20] The purpose of mentioning this here is not to condone inappropriate or false behavior but rather to consider a common relationship challenge and to point out that perhaps the main way an allegation of lying can be "proven" is by the alleged liar actually calling their statement a lie. In other words, when it comes to "knowing" a person is lying, confession is the best method of confirmation. And here is where we encounter another challenge, for useful, accurate confessions require certain kinds of conditions, namely coercion, deception, or the best alternative —trust.

--------

20  American Psychological Association. (n. d.). The truth about lie detectors (aka polygraph tests). Retrieved on January 1, 2018, from http://www.apa.org/research/action/polygraph.aspx

So, let us focus on lying as an example of a visible (factual) and unfavorable outcome in a relationship. By contrast truth-telling would be an example of a visible and favorable outcome.[21] So, if person A is lying, it makes sense for person B to doubt, and if A is telling the truth, it makes sense for B to trust or exercise faith. And since we are particularly interested in minimizing unnecessary difficulties, let us think about what might be most strategic if A is telling the truth but for whatever reason B is still inclined to doubt. To illustrate, let's return to our previous example of a couple recovering from infidelity, where the unfaithful spouse is A, and the faithful spouse is B. Suppose the following conversation takes place:

**B:** *Why are you late?*
**A:** *I'm sorry, I got caught in heavy traffic.*
**B:** *I expected you an hour ago. Why didn't you call?*
**A:** *I guess I didn't think it was going to be a problem. Again, I'm sorry.*
**B:** *Well, you not thinking something will be a problem is **the problem**.*

There are a few things to keep in mind in this simple exchange. First, though the context is a past infidelity, we are still assuming that A's tardiness is not due to any current infidelity. Second, because past infidelity is the context, it is going to be relatively easy for both parties to experience the situation unfavorably. B is legitimately concerned about A being late, and A will probably feel like the best option will be to offer an apology that B will find hard to believe. As a result, it is going to be very *easy for both parties to see the whole situation as a problem.*

It is also easy to imagine this situation turning into a kind of stalemate:

**A:** *I'll make sure it doesn't happen again.*
**B:** *We'll see about that.*

Or the situation could evolve into a more pronounced conflict:

---

21 Here, I find it interesting that, in the English language, we seem much more accustomed to talking about people "lying" than "truthing," though this latter expression is used by some, e.g., see https://www.urbandictionary.com/define.php?term=truthing

**A:** *You know, why would I want to call you if this is how I'll be treated? I can't catch a break!*

**B:** *Are you kidding me? You're going to complain about how I'm treating you when you're the one who **cheated** on me? Give **me** a break!*

When a relationship has been strained, it can seem like mistrust makes more sense than trust, even when all parties are telling the truth.[22]

*Even More and Working With*

We might say that faith is about *something else that makes even more sense.* It "sees" beyond the material world to realities that cannot be detected with our physical senses. It "looks" beyond obvious facts to the subtleties of emotions, opinions, and beliefs. And of course, when others limit their focus to the natural, it readily opens its awareness to the pervasive, abiding, possibility of the supernatural.

And so, faith *works with* whatever comes its way, precisely because it assumes that a bigger picture exists and that deeper truths are at work. In our present example, this might mean that when B points out A's lateness, A can respond to B, before apologizing, by saying something that better connects with B's concern:

**B:** *Why are you late?*

**A:** *You have every right to ask, though I imagine it's very frustrating. I got caught in heavy traffic. I'm sorry I didn't call.*

Or, alternatively, the dialogue could start the same way with B making the change:

**B:** *Why are you late?*

**A:** *I'm sorry, I got caught in heavy traffic.*

**B:** *I appreciate you letting me know. I would have liked it if you had let me know earlier, but I'm glad you're safe. Perhaps you can imagine that many things run through my mind when you're late. I am*

---

22 I am particularly grateful to my father, Dr. Francis T. O. Lim, for teaching me both this principle and the importance of valuing truth overall.

*struggling so much with trusting right now.*

These are again technical changes and probably difficult to think of as the conversation is unfolding. Still, the idea is to imagine how faith might inform even the most plain, basic kinds of conversations to increase the chances of different, more favorable outcomes. For example, in the latter dialogue, A noting that B has *"every right to ask,"* says that there is nothing wrong with B wanting to know and subtly affirms anything related to what B might regard as fair or unfair.

Moreover, since the context of this conversation is post-affair, B will be attuned to issues related to justice. Likewise, A can also acknowledge B's emotions that pertain to injustice, e.g., anger and frustration. As A "allows" B to feel angry or frustrated, A might *show* B that the lateness was an "honest mistake." We noted at the beginning that the tardiness was not due to an additional infidelity, so the situation may be difficult though still not a transgression or sin per se.

Similarly, faith can also be considered if we have B initiate the change. In this case, if B expresses appreciation to A for sharing about the traffic while simultaneously expressing a preference for an advanced notice, it is because B is counting on things hoped for that may yet be unseen. For example, B might look for reasons to trust A even when it seems doubt makes more sense.

Alternatively, if B is frustrated with A (which seems clear from the initial question), it is because B wants A to be more punctual. This interest in punctuality can be traced back to the pain B experienced from A's past infidelity. One way of explaining this might be that it would be easy for B to link the "surprise" of A's lateness with past "surprise" of learning about A's affair. The more aware B is of these emotions and associations, the more B can own them and use them to influence the situation in more positive directions.

This will understandably challenge B; simultaneously acknowledging frustration and affirming care for another takes effort. Maybe the most uncomfortable part of this effort is resisting the almost instinctive tendency to again feel silly. There is an inescapable irony whenever a wounded person shows compassion for their perpetrator.

## A Certain Kind of Kindness

We don't want to be naive, passive, or pushed over. Neither do we want to be short-sighted, self-defeating, or needlessly stressed out. This again is where faith reminds us of the reasonableness of a certain kind of kindness that can result in more lasting solutions. We might even say that this type of kindness is the *something else that makes even more sense.* Faith accomplishes this by "looking" for the favorable things that are often anything but obvious to the senses. And so, when interpersonal frustrations are involved, doubt can be the signal to continue investing in the search.

Perhaps this is another way of identifying or "giving" the "benefit of the doubt." Traditionally, this benefit is about acknowledging that there may be details that the would-be "doubter" is not aware of, which results in the other party being given a break. The person being doubted is thus the one who benefits.

The point of this discussion is to also consider that, when this happens, the "doubter" also has the chance to be helped. So even as the benefit of the doubt is "given," we might say that this same benefit is also "received." And our hypothesis is that to the extent that relationships are fundamentally more cooperative than competitive, whenever either person benefits, both can expect to gain.

Ultimately, when this happens, the *relationship* benefits because when one person is accurately trusted, a synergy between the parties takes place and a win/win is accomplished. I have come to think of this process as involving what I call "pro-relationship explanations." For example, if I greet a friend and that friend does not reciprocate, I can think something like *"they do not care about me"* (anti-relationship explanation) or *"they must have a lot on their mind"* (pro-relationship explanation).

Both explanations involve emotion and risk. The first explanation is likely to generate hurt or anger and risks unnecessarily assigning a negative motivation to another person.[23] The second explanation might generate compassion or concern and risks being unnecessarily kind and vulnerable to someone who may not care about me.

When negative things happen, one way of assessing the risks is to consider what actions each explanation might inspire and the costs of such actions if the explanation is less than accurate. So, in the example above, if I attribute my friend's lack of response to a lack of care for me, I will likely feel hurt and do something to protest my friend's behavior (ignore, withdraw, or criticize). Alternatively, if I believe they "have a lot on their mind" and so were too busy to notice me, I might *do something to show I still care*, like sincerely repeat the greeting or wish them the best.

Either way, both approaches use behavioral methods to address a motivational issue. Interestingly, if my friend truly does not care, how effective will it really be to do something that could also be experienced as unfriendly towards them? For example, will ignoring or criticizing them give them reason to change their mind so that they are suddenly friendlier toward me? If they really do not care about me then, as much as it makes sense to avoid them, it seems doing so with *the intention of rejecting them*, will only undermine any initial protest I may have had towards their unfriendliness in the first place. By contrast, faith can be a primary catalyst for interpretations that "believe the best" in others, since it counts on a certain kind of kindness being at work even if such kindness is not immediately detectable to the senses.

## Faith and Reality

*The Fuel of Faith*
One final question about this first star is in order before we explore the rest of the Triangle. Specifically, what makes faith work?

Let us entertain the following hypothesis: *Faith works*

---

23  This can be related to what social psychologists call the "fundamental attribution error" which refers to how we tend to over-emphasize internal factors in others' behaviors and over-emphasize external factors in our own personal behaviors. For additional information, see https://www.simplypsychology.org/fundamental-attribution.html

356 MAYBE THE WHOLE OCEAN

*because of the importance of human will.* And by will, we mean that aspect of a person that is essentially free.[24] This is not to deny that we can still be conditioned to behave in certain ways, nor does it mean that we escape someone who might still be "at large," so to speak, as a sovereign "Higher Power." Quite the opposite, to return to a word we have used throughout this book, our aim is to understand how human beings can *respond* in and to situations (especially those involving relationships) that they did not ultimately initiate.

Taken further, this hypothesis is concerned with situations that not only seem beyond personal control but that also seem unfavorable. And if we will dare, our aim is to particularly learn how these very situations can be viewed and valued as opportunities to count on something good happening. When all of these details are in place—when the human will is presented with a situation that looks like it is more bad than good and when something or someone inspires a belief that an impossibly good outcome is still possible—then the star of faith can burn brightly.

If we are honest, we have only further specified the conditions that make faith possible, and we have yet to identify just what about these conditions makes faith work. How is it reasonable to believe in an "invisible good," especially when all signs seem to indicate otherwise? To address this question, it is necessary to ask an even more fundamental question: what makes *good* work?

Again, I come to these questions as a Christian. Central to my understanding of Christianity is the notion that not only is a Higher Power indeed "at large" in the universe, but this Power is profoundly *personal*. Moreover, this Person is not only believed to be supremely good but also the source of love itself. And so, briefly, here are my proposed answers to the previous questions: Good makes faith work and God makes good work.

### Belief and Reward

If the above statements are true, then it also follows that faith is important to God. From a Judeo-Christian perspective, this theme seems to pervade the Bible. One verse in particular stands

---

24  When it comes to this topic, I am again grateful for the influence of Dallas Willard.

out, again from Hebrews 11, that has provided our definition of faith. The author states: "And without faith it is impossible to please (God), for whoever would draw near to God must believe that He exists and that He rewards those who seek Him."[25]

I am intrigued by this passage. If it is impossible to please God without faith, then it seems faith is what makes it possible to please God. Consistent with this, the British minister, Charles Spurgeon, says of this specific verse in Hebrews, "the negative is often the plainest way of suggesting the positive."[26] If we will allow it, this idea can be nothing short of astounding. The God of the universe not only values, but is *pleased* by, faith! Moreover, such faith seems to involve two conditions: belief in God's existence and belief that God will *reward* us as we seek Him.

> **"...when we give God the gift of genuine faith, we receive the greatest gift possible—relationship with God."**

Can we really please God? If so, can we do so just by believing that He exists and that He will reward such belief? Can such good, indeed greater than good, news be so amazingly simple? It certainly seems way too good to be true. However, if we pause to consider that this same God is the *source* of everything good, then can we not say it is way too good to *not* be true?

With all my heart, I want to say yes. There are a million reasons to say otherwise and easily billions of things wrong with this world. But, in the face of such countless counterarguments, I want, and maybe even have, to believe that good carries more weight, more originality, and more resilience, and that it will ultimately have the last word. Beyond just indulging desire or succumbing to some mysterious compulsion, I *choose* to believe this. I choose to believe that good is even more at large than evil and this good is deeply personal. As I believe this, I take heart in

---

25  Hebrews 11:6

26  See Spurgeon, C. H. (1889). Faith essential to pleasing God. A sermon given at the Metropolitan Tabernacle, Newington, United Kingdom. Retrieved January 2, 2018, from http://www.spurgeongems.org/vols34-36/chs2100.pdf

the thought that this all-good Person, God, is somehow *pleased with such belief!*

Why in the world, though, would the Sovereign of the universe put such a premium on belief, on faith? Maybe we can say that even as He is completely self-sufficient, God still seems to value the experience of *being believed.* Or maybe more accurately, if faith is what *pleases* God, then we can consider that God *enjoys being believed.* And if God is good then that which He finds pleasing is also good. So, if God would deem faith sufficient for pleasing Him, then by doing so God also declares that it is good when people freely exert their energies and incline their hearts and minds towards Him.

Another way of looking at this is that, from God's perspective, the "billions of things wrong with this world" are not people. On the contrary, people matter to God. Greatly. In fact, we might be so bold as to say that people matter so much to God that He is willing to take the risk of billions of things going wrong with the world if in the end it means people will experience what is good or even what is *best.* And, if God is good, perhaps the highest good that we as people can experience is for us to give God, so to speak, the *gift* of genuine faith. Moreover, perhaps this is the highest good because when we give God the gift of genuine faith, we receive the greatest gift possible—relationship with God.

*Supremacy, Goodness, and Willing Consent*
The first part of this may sound contradictory. If God is supreme and therefore needs nothing, how can anybody give Him anything?[27]

The best way that I know to answer this question is to return to a theme we have been developing throughout this book—the paradigmatic shift from obligation to opportunity, or in this case, the fundamental difference between a need and a gift.

If God's supremacy means that He needs nothing, then whatever we offer Him can be *nothing but a gift* (whatever we offer Him can neither add to nor take away from His self-sufficiency and goodness). At the same time, being supremely good, God is deeply committed to personal well-being—His

27   See Acts 17:24-25 and Corinthians 4:7

and ours. And ultimately, God's supremacy and utter goodness mean that He Himself is the highest good for any person.

Simultaneously, as the true, First Person of the universe, God ensures that genuine relationship is never forced. This flows from God's essential, interpersonal nature as the Trinity. So, wondrously, mysteriously, and often painfully, He preserves human freedom, practicing a kind of divine self-restraint that allows people to, by and large, take their own paths. This sets the stage for the option of living by faith—the exquisite opportunity to endlessly and *willingly* "see" the favorable amid the invisible, precisely because God is so good.

In the end, faith is important because human will is important to God. Quite simply, He delights in people trusting Him. Again, we will do well to remember that God's pleasure with human trust completely does away with any concern that He is needy or controlling. In addition to being at odds with His supremacy and goodness, neediness undermines confidence, and control obviates trust. On the contrary, even though it may involve significant hesitation or reluctance, trust always involves at least a modicum of voluntary risk and release.

It is this willing consent that actually blesses God, precisely because God cares about relationship. Moreover, this same consent, however small, is what preserves the possibility of continued relationship. It is no wonder, then, that this same kind of willingness is also what blesses God, especially when it is directed at blessing others.

*Faith and Freedom*
To conclude this section and repeat what has become something of a refrain, emotions experienced interpersonally are both a personal responsibility and personal opportunity. Thus, where feelings are concerned, the opinions we have about the facts are more important than the facts themselves. What does this mean for what we have been saying about how we can somehow please God by having faith in His existence and that He will reward us for seeking Him? Moreover, what can this leave us with as we consider how faith might inform our approach to relationships?

First, these questions underscore both the similarities and differences between people and God. If we return to the Judeo-Christian teaching that people are *imago Dei*, made in God's image, the principle of emotions as a personal responsibility is particularly related to the notion that people are like, yet far from identical to, God. Therefore, there are also similarities and differences between how people please people and how people please God.

Second, the similarities revolve around the notion that when emotions are a personal responsibility, feelings in one person are neither determined nor dictated by another person. Let us further say that "pleasing" God is something different from "making" God happy. Just as the point of this book is that people cannot ordinarily "make" other people happy, so too, people cannot make God feel emotions in any way that would make Him subject to people. At a minimum, this would be at odds with healthy relationships, since, as we've seen, the freedom to feel whatever emotions make sense is an important part of people truly being themselves. If a person is not truly free to be themself, then they are not able to relate to another person in any sort of true way. Moreover, it seems that this would be just as important to relationship with God since God cares about truth.[28]

Here, however, is where the plot thickens and where the thickening ultimately sheds light on the options for all relationships. On one hand, God, like people who are His image-bearers, has the autonomy to feel however He chooses and is not at the mercy of anyone. On the other hand, through no small twist, God, being deeply interested in relationship, has included a way for people to still please Him. Faith deftly accomplishes this plot twist by preserving freedom, so to speak, at both divine and human levels.

Faith reminds us that it is vital for relationships to be voluntarily experienced at any given time. This is all well and good and easy when things are going smoothly in a relationship, but it is another story altogether whenever one person or party feels that they "did not sign up" for the experience. We need to only consider any time a relationship involves a negative emotion

---

28  See Psalm 51:6 and John 4:23.

and, especially, any time such an emotion feels personal. In such circumstances, faith challenges us to consider, amid the uncomfortable emotions, how we can willingly move *toward* the other—precisely because we are counting on "things hoped for" to be true even when such things are hidden from view. If we can do this, ultimately counting on the situation to work out because God's goodness substantiates our hope, then it would seem such motivation would please God, and it is difficult to conceive of a greater outcome than this.

Interestingly, an integral piece of this strategy is the notion that, in relationships, negative emotions do not have to be taken personally precisely because we can trust, so to speak, that beliefs are the more direct reason for such emotions, rather than the facts themselves. Since facts, or apparent facts, most often seem responsible, this (trusting that beliefs have more power over most emotions than facts) takes faith. Particularly intriguing is what this means when we imagine God's perspective. See, if faith preserves human freedom (and thereby, human relationship) by attributing emotions to beliefs rather than facts, then this is also relevant to how God freely experiences relationship with His creation as well. The only difference is that, for God, *perception and belief are reality.* So, if God "thinks" something will be a certain way then His thoughts will supernaturally influence that thing's nature.[29]

So again, when it comes to faith, if "being sure of what we hope for and certain of what we do not see" is indeed pleasing to God, then we can rest assured that there is something about this way of living that is *actually* good and right before God. Further, it is difficult to think of anything greater than *actually pleasing* the Sovereign of the universe. It seems so utterly simple and yet, at times so difficult, to count on what we hope for, especially when this seems contradicted and contraindicated by the facts.

On one hand, it is profoundly simple—just believe, as the apostle Paul declares in his letter to the Romans, that "if God is for us, who can be against us?"[30] It seems this advocacy

29   If God's thoughts influence reality, perhaps the moment God's thoughts become reality is the moment God speaks, such as at the dawn of creation when God said, "Let there be light" and there was light ( Genesis 1:3).

30   Romans 8:31

from God applies regardless of circumstances, at any and every given time. On the other hand, perhaps because we are so accustomed to navigating our lives by sight rather than by faith, it also seems nothing could be more difficult than living by faith.[31] In the face of various local, global, physical, medical, financial, or interpersonal trials, worry, helplessness, and even despair appear to make more sense. In this regard, walking by faith, mindful of both the goodness and greatness of God, is not so much an event but rather a lifestyle that is cultivated over extended amounts of time.

Of course, faith is just the first star in our discussion, and so for us to more fully understand and benefit from its light, it is important for us to also ponder the other two vertices of our Navigator's Triangle. Let us now turn our attention to the second star and the virtue we now see as so integral to faith—that precious beacon we call hope.

---

31  Lest we lose heart, another facet of this topic that is so important it warrants a separate book is the notion that, in addition to living by faith in Christ, we also live "by the faith or faithfulness of Christ." See, for example, Galatians 2:15, 20 (New Revised Standard Version (1989)).

# Hope

> *But hope that is seen is no hope at all.*
> *Who hopes for what they already have?*
> *But if we hope for what we do not yet have,*
> *we wait for it patiently.*[32]

## Second Star

*A Real-Life Parable*

Since we began with a look at how faith involves assurance of "what is hoped for," we have, in many ways, already started to explore this second star of the Triangle. The Greek word for hope in Hebrews 11 and in the passage above from Romans 8 is *elpis*, which derives from *elpo*, meaning to "anticipate or welcome."[33] As with faith, we have a kind of looking forward or looking ahead to something, counting on that "something" to both happen and to be good. In this regard, if faith is confident belief, then let us consider hope to be "joyful anticipation."

Some years ago, Keri and I made the decision to transition my practice as a solo clinical psychologist into a group practice consisting of a team of counselors. I remember a host of mixed feelings when we were finally able, with the help of family and friends, to renovate a larger office space and officially change our business name from Brian R. Lim, PhD, Inc. to Paradigm Hawai`i Counseling, Inc. Instead of just a single office, we now had a small waiting room and two counseling rooms to work with. The only problem was that even though we had all this nice new space, I was essentially still the only employee of Paradigm.

For the next several weeks, we began the process of looking

---

32  Romans 8:24-25 (NIV)

33  Elpis. (n. d.). In bibleapps.com. Retrieved January 6, 2018, from http://bibleapps.com/greek/1680.htm

for counselors who shared our vision for the community, and I went about with "business as usual," meeting with clients who frequently told me that they were enjoying the "upgrade" and the increased space. I was making good use of the new waiting area and the first counseling room, but the second counseling room was used for storage. Whenever it was necessary, I would casually use the time between appointments to go in and out of this "storage room" to get supplies, without giving much thought to doing so.

And then, one day, going about my usual business at the office, as I pondered the relationship between faith and hope, as described in Hebrews 11, a new idea occurred to me. If we were going to be successful with our expansion and gradually add new counselors, it was important to continue preparing for this new reality. And so, I began to cultivate a new habit that felt rather silly for some time. *I began to knock on the door of the storage room.* Even though I "knew" that no one was inside (because I kept the office locked and I was the only one with the key, let alone the only one in the office), I began to train myself to softly knock before unlocking and opening the door. I believed that someday the dream would be a reality, the storage room would in fact become a second counseling office and I would work alongside a colleague without interrupting them. And so, I knocked. For weeks that grew into several months, I continued to knock on an empty office door, trusting that one day it would just be professional and no longer silly. In a subtle but very real way, I was "being sure of what I hoped for and certain of what I didn't see."

I'm grateful to say that since that time, Keri and I have continued to build our practice and now have five counseling rooms and a team of over ten colleagues, with whom it is my great privilege to work. Incidentally, we also have rather attractive color-coded door signs that slide from red to green to signify a counselor is occupied or available, respectively! Knocking before entering (even when the door signs are green) is now second nature for me. And though small and somewhat goofy, this gesture continues to point me to an ever-deepening paradigm shift: the process of repeatedly reminding myself of hope.

EPILOGUE: THE NAVIGATOR'S TRIANGLE: HOPE | 365

## Expectation and Anticipation

Just as we began by defining faith in terms of hope, our discussion of hope will build on what we have already said about faith. Still, while there is much overlap between these two virtues (both again involve the invisible and the favorable), it will also be helpful to consider what makes them distinct. As we have seen, if faith is about belief, hope is about anticipation. Further, if belief pertains to how we make sense of situations, anticipation pertains to how we plan for them. In my story above, I would say faith guided me to "see" the possibility of having colleagues joining me, and hope led me to look forward to and essentially prepare for their arrival by cultivating a specific habit, namely knocking on the door of an empty room.

We can think of faith and hope as "active ingredients" in each other. The Greek word describing faith in the Hebrews passage earlier is *hupostasis*, which literally translates as "standing under." Alternative words are foundation, substance, confirmation, assurance, and even a type of title deed to a property.[34] So we might say faith makes possible what is hoped for in the same way that a foundation allows for a house to be built or a title deed paves the way for property ownership to take place.

Similarly, just as faith makes hope possible, hope makes faith viable. Just as houses cannot stand without foundations and property ownerships cannot be proven without titles, so hope empowers what is believed. Whereas believing is certainly an action, it takes a special kind of energy to move from believing that something good will take place to anticipating and planning for the occurrence of that same good event.

## Numberless Stars

To illustrate this, let us briefly consider another story from the Bible, this time from the apostle Paul's letter that was written to encourage his readers in Rome. Specifically noting the necessary and vital role faith plays in being accepted by God, Paul recounts the way in which Abraham's faith in God simultaneously led to Abraham becoming both the biological father of the Hebrew nation and the spiritual father of the faith

34 Hupostasis. (n. d.). In bibleapps.com. Retrieved January 6, 2018, from http://bible-apps.com/greek/5287.htm

community. God had promised Abraham and his wife Sarah (then called Abram and Sarai) descendants as countless as the stars, and Abraham believed that this promise would be fulfilled even though he and Sarah were well beyond child-bearing age. Referencing this ancient story, Paul says of Abraham, "In hope he believed against hope, that he should become the father of many nations, as he had been told."[35]

*"In hope he believed . . ."* The context of Abraham's story is that God had apparently told him two other times that, among other things, he was going to have an inheritance of countless descendants.[36] In Romans 4, Paul seems to be referencing a third time in Genesis that God expressed His intention to bless Abraham. Interestingly, on this occasion, Abraham's response to God indicates that he imagines God will fulfill His promise through an heir who will not be blood-related to him. Thus, Abraham asks God, "O Lord God, what will you give me, for I continue childless . . . Behold, you have given me no offspring, and a member of my household will be my heir." This is the point at which God makes clear his intention to give Abraham a biological heir saying, "This man shall not be your heir; your very own son shall be your heir . . . Look toward heaven, and number the stars, if you are able to number them. So shall your offspring be." The next line in the Genesis account is later developed by Paul to illustrate the game-changing nature of faith: *"And he (Abraham) believed the Lord, and He (the Lord) counted it to him (Abraham) as righteousness."*[37]

I imagine Abraham was utterly beside himself with excitement when God confirmed that Abraham was going to have his "very own son." Of course, at the very least, Abraham must have felt a great curiosity about how this promise would be fulfilled since he and Sarah were well-past the age when they would expect to have a child (he was 75 years-old and Sarah was 66 years-old when God first made His promise). Nevertheless, the promise was coming from God, whom Abraham had previously called "Possessor of heaven and earth."[38] So, it seems his excitement and curiosity would have been laced with deep confidence. The

35  Romans 4:18
36  See Genesis 12:1-4 and Genesis 13:14-18
37  See Genesis 15:1-6, parenthetical names added
38  Genesis 14:22

cumulative effect of all this? Paul says, "in hope he believed."

Hope motivates belief, at least the kind of belief that characterizes faith. As we've previously discussed, faith is a way of seeing what is not visible. It might be analogous to a kind of thermal vision. If so, hope is the heat signature we seek. Hope motivates and demarcates the search. Wherever we find the risk of faith being taken, we encounter hope as the reason for the venture in the first place. And, like the promise of a long-awaited child, hope is characterized by an eager, even joyful anticipation.

Just as God used a sky full of numberless stars to validate His promise to Abraham, so too hope shines for us, like so many countless beacons, whenever we are afforded opportunities to practice faith.

Let us consider three additional principles (in this case, derived from the passage in Romans 8 above) that might help us to understand just how we can continue to find our way.

## Seeing and Seeking

*Looking at, Looking for*
Like faith, hope is concerned with unseen things. And, in a manner of speaking, hope "loses its job" once a matter is made visible. In this way, a first characteristic of hope is that it pertains more to the process of *seeking* something or someone rather than the outcome of *seeing* the results of the completed search. So, like faith, hope has a paradoxical relationship with our objectives. In a way, they are both integral parts of the journey and yet unnecessary once we arrive at the destination. As the apostle Paul states, "Hope that is seen is no hope at all."[39]

I once had the opportunity to talk very briefly with a world-class researcher who specialized in how expectations can influence behavior. Knowing my time was limited, I narrowed my many thoughts to one burning question: what is the difference, if any, between expectation and hope? As best as I can remember, I was very intrigued to hear the researcher tell

---

39   Romans 8:24 (NIV)

me that this question had not previously crossed their mind. Naturally, I felt rather sad when the researcher's response, plus the fact that many other people wanted to ask questions, meant that the discussion was essentially over. Now, nearly a decade later, this question continues to occupy my mind. And so, here is my latest thinking on how the difference between expectation and hope might parallel the subtle differences between expectation and anticipation.

The distinction between seeing and seeking seems particularly useful for understanding the way in which hope is more about anticipation than expectation. And again, I find it interesting to consider aspects of the words themselves. According to historian and etymologist, Douglas Harper (creator and author of etymonline.com), the word "expect" derives from *ex* (thoroughly) and *spectare* (to look),[40] while "anticipate" traces back to *ante* (before) and *capere* (to take). In his entry for the word "anticipate," Harper specifically notes "anticipate has an element of 'prepare for, forestall' that, etymologically, should prevent its being used as a synonym for expect."[41]

> **"...the absence of guarantees might also explain how life is anything but static or 'stacked'."**

Taking these together, I would like to propose that the distinction between seeing and seeking might be further illustrated if we associate expectation with "looking at" and anticipation with "looking for." And if, as Harper notes, anticipating involves a kind of preparation, then it also involves readying oneself for a future event. Further, I would say that in the case of hope, the future that is being prepared for involves something good or joyful. As a result, the search in question is undertaken with perseverance and even enthusiasm.

---

40   Harper notes that spectare (to look) is also related to specere (to look at). See Expect. (n. d.). In etymonline.com. Retrieved January 6, 2018, from https://www.etymonline.com/word/expect

41   Anticipate. (n. d.). In etymonline.com. Retrieved January 6, 2018, from https://www.etymonline.com/word/anticipate

Also, when it comes to anticipation, the focus of the search is specifically on what occurs *before* the future event happens. Thus, hope is always about what is yet to happen and, in this way, it may have a more limited scope than faith.[42] Hope is about seeking something good, and to paraphrase the apostle Paul, "a search for what is found is no search at all."

Expectation, on the other hand, is concerned with "looking at," which might be more akin to seeing (rather than seeking). When something can be looked at or seen, it is already in existence, already present.

Put another way, there is a difference between looking at something that is now in front of us and looking for or forward to something that is yet to occur. Once, when I shared the story about knocking on my storage-room door, a friend asked, "Weren't you disappointed every time you knocked and expected to find someone in the office?" I smiled and told them I was not disappointed "because I did not expect to find someone there at the time as much as I anticipated that they would be there later."

*Settling for the Seen, Seeking the Unseen*
My friend's question also sheds light on another matter—the relationship between disappointment and not finding what we expect to find, not experiencing something that we expected to experience. In fact, I tend to define disappointment as the emotion we feel when our expectations are not met.

Interestingly, one way that people attempt to balance hope and expectation is to live by the slogan, "hope for the best, expect the worst." Indeed, this phrase is skillfully developed in Mel Brooks' witty song of the same title. Consider the opening stanza:

*Hope for the best, expect the worst*
*Some drink champagne, some die of thirst*

---

42   Theologian John Piper points to Hebrews 11:3 saying, "For example, verse 3: 'By faith we understand that the world was created by the word of God.' Faith can look back (to creation) as well as forward. So, faith is the larger idea. It includes hope but is more than hope. You might put it this way: faith is our confidence in the Word of God, and whenever that Word has reference to the future, you can call our confidence in it hope. Hope is faith in the future tense." Piper, J. (1986, April 6). What is hope? In desiringgod.org. Retrieved January 6, 2018, from: https://www.desiringgod.org/messages/what-is-hope

*No way of knowing which way it's going*
*Hope for the best, expect the worst*[43]

In a very clever way, this accomplishes a theoretical win/win. If "the best" occurs, then hope is fulfilled. And, if "the worst" occurs, well, our expectations are met, and so ironically, we are, by definition, not disappointed.

Even more ironically, though, this slogan seems to encourage hopefulness that subtly implies we are helpless. Thus, outcomes are left to chance and hope is reduced to wishful thinking. Brooks' point that there's "no way of knowing which way it's going" is just the opening salvo to other witty ways of suggesting that life is fundamentally out of our control, and this is precisely the reason for us to live it with as much gusto as possible.

In so many ways, Brooks' lyrics are insightful, strategic, and even comforting. He seems to account for both sides of an equation and arrive at a kind of acceptance of life as both unpredictable and predetermined. And on the surface, it is difficult to argue otherwise. At a minimum, I think many subscribers of nihilism, hedonism, and existentialism would agree.

But is this really hope? On the contrary, this book intends to show how the second star of our Triangle shines with a qualitatively different light.

One detail that seems to make a big difference is the way life's fortunes and vicissitudes are interpreted. For those who espouse Brooks' approach, successes and failures seem to be matters of fate, and the optimal answer is to be aware of the possibility of either extreme, particularly since nothing can be done to change what has already been assigned. Again, this approach is about the things that are *seen*. As a case in point, consider the closing stanza of Brooks' song:

*Hope for the best, expect the worst*
*The rich are blessed, the poor are cursed*

---

43   Brooks, M. [Tobias Ryan]. (2015, February 4.). 'Hope for the best, expect the worst— Mel Brooks' [Video file]. Retrieved January 6, 2018, from https://www.youtube.com/ watch?v=W9FRqE7eMJQ

*That is a fact friends, the deck is stacked, friends*
*Hope for the best . . . expect the worst*

With uncanny candor, Brooks demonstrates the limitations of focusing on the visible "fact" that life is fixed. We see that, overall, everything is subject to chance, and any attempt to personally change one's lot is essentially futile. The "best" is confined to whatever luck life can provide now, and any kind of future improvements beyond this are hardly acknowledged.

This chapter aims to present another angle on hope that offers significantly different potential. And so, conversely and counter-intuitively, the absence of guarantees might also explain how life is anything but static or "stacked." Vital to this process is the continued focus on *seeking the unseen*.

This book prioritizes the psychological implications of this search by considering what we fundamentally believe about belief. I have also done my best to be clear that, as a Christian, I cannot escape certain theological markers that continue to inform the more personal side of this quest. And the notion that hope is a process of "seeking" more than "seeing" is no exception. With respect to Mel Brooks and others who affirm the "hope for the best, expect the worst," philosophy, I am looking for what I would like to think of as a "far-sighted" hope, one that counts on good and often invisible things happening, that extend beyond the limits of this life alone. The apostle Paul himself indicates quite strongly that, for Christians, hope that exclusively limits hope to this life is lamentable, saying, "If in Christ we have hope in this life only, we are of all people most to be pitied. But, in fact, Christ has been raised from the dead..."[44]

## Having and Holding

*Quantity and Quality*

A second characteristic of hope is that it is better described as something we *hold* rather than something we *have*. This difference is more than semantics. For example, traditional wedding vows often include the expression, "to have and to hold, from this day forward, as long as we both shall live." This

---

44  I Corinthians 15:19-20

phrase implies that having and holding are different, so what is the difference? I interpret "having" as a matter of belonging, or in some cases (other than marriage), owning. I interpret "holding" as a way of valuing or cherishing (as well as physically embracing). This difference might be seen in a situation involving the death of a spouse. The surviving spouse might still "hold" the deceased spouse in their memories even though they no longer "have" them in their life physically.

We might also say that having pertains to tangible, physical things whereas holding concerns intangible, nonphysical things. Because physical objects are quantifiable, they can be assigned a price. And so, anything we can experience with the senses (now including "virtual" goods and services) can be bought with currency of some kind. However, the experiences we classify as intangible, like accomplishments or relationships, are the ones we call priceless, precisely because they are not quantifiable.

Some friends of mine (husband and wife) told me of a trip they took to visit the Great Wall of China. The husband told of how good it felt to physically jog a certain section of the Wall with his daughter. His wife jokingly noted that she had run to the first rest point and then returned to the start, stopping at the gift shop, where she bought a little souvenir with an inscription that read, "I conquered the Great Wall." Ironically, the husband did not buy himself anything from the gift shop, and the wife had the inscriber put her name on the souvenir! This is a rather humorous example of how money can buy only so much. We might say that even though one "had" the souvenir, it was the other who "held" the experience. Another more serious example of this can be seen in the apostle Paul's own description of paradoxes that marked his ministry. For instance, in speaking of both the hardships and the joys he shared with his apprentice, Timothy, he describes himself and Timothy as "having nothing, yet possessing everything."[45]

## Holding Patterns
Hope is about holding to something we do not yet have while anticipating that we will eventually have it. Hope then is about the interval and the interim, between the time we first become aware of a desired change and the time that our desire is

45  2 Corinthians 6:10

fulfilled. Of course, the timing of this interval can vary, and this is where hope is tested.

Another helpful analogy that draws upon similar language, can be seen in the example of a "holding pattern" in aviation. In this case, a holding pattern is a flight maneuver that helps a pilot to keep an aircraft within a certain airspace while the pilot is waiting for a clearance to land. Interestingly, aircraft manufacturers will prescribe certain "holding speeds" that are slower than cruising speeds, to use less fuel when holding patterns are flown. And, of course, the longer the duration of the flight pattern, the more fuel is required by the aircraft and the more urgent it becomes for the pilot to land.[46]

> **"...the more comfortable our natural circumstances are, the more difficult it is to truly say we are *hoping* in the supernatural."**

For our purposes, we can liken hope to the fuel that makes flight possible for the pilot who is waiting to land. In life and especially in relationships, hope, like fuel, can be depleted. It waxes and wanes according to what seems most realistic and can exist in a range of degrees. There are risks at either end of the continuum. When hope is too high, we risk being impractical and delusional. When hope is too low, we may be vulnerable to hopelessness and despair.

So, hope implies a kind of suspense. We literally and figuratively find ourselves hanging in the balance, without resolution, "holding out" for closure. Since some sort of timeframe exists between wherever we are and our next destination, the potential for frustration is also always nearby. Depending again on how comfortable we are with staying airborne and postponing our landing, sooner or later we will feel increasingly emotionally depleted. It can seem as though, like a bird, we must flap our own wings, and the further we are from our destination, the more we grow tired and even exhausted. Is

---

46  Holding pattern. (n. d.). In Skybrary.aero. Retrieved January 18, 2020, from https://www.skybrary.aero/index.php/Holding_Pattern

there any recourse when the things we long and hope for seem so elusive?

One way through these challenges is to look at an additional thought-provoking reference to hope in the apostle Paul's account of Abraham's faith. We have given some attention to what Paul might mean when he says, "In hope he (Abraham) believed." Again, hope precedes and motivates faith. However, consider the full extent of Paul's sentence: "In hope he believed *against hope* that he should become the father of many nations as he'd been told..."[47]

"In hope . . . against hope. These are two seemingly contradictory approaches that Paul apparently treats as compatible. How might we explain this?

I think Paul's words point to two different kinds of hope, namely hope in the natural and hope in the supernatural. It seems the remainder of the passage bears this out when he writes, again of Abraham's pioneering faith:

> *He did not weaken in faith when he considered his own body, which was as good as dead (since he was about a hundred years old), or when he considered the barrenness of Sarah's womb. No unbelief made him waver concerning the promise of God, but he grew strong in his faith as he gave glory to God, fully convinced that God was able to do what he had promised.*[48]

Hope is not mentioned directly in this passage. Still, if hope does indeed motivate faith, it seems Abraham's faith meant that Abraham was hoping in God's promise of a biological son even as physical, bodily limitations for both him and Sarah were simultaneously against the odds, "against all hope." Rather than being contradictory, when it comes to hoping in God, some amount of "hoping against hope" is reasonable, especially to the extent that the hoped-for outcome is more supernatural or miraculous. We might even say that the more comfortable our natural circumstances are, the more difficult it is to truly say we are *hoping* in the supernatural. It is precisely when we *have* no

---

47  Romans 4:18, italics added

48  Romans 4:19-21

control that we *hold* to things both invisible and favorable.

## Wanting and Waiting

### *Immediate and Delayed Gratification*

Finally, hope pertains more to "waiting for" the fulfillment of a desire than to even the fulfillment of the desire itself. It is about the interval between the awareness of a new possibility and the realization of that possibility. In this way, hope returns us to themes like process rather than outcome, journey rather than destination, and future rather than completed action.

If we are honest, we often assume that if we want something, we pursue it. This points back to the $(f\textbf{\textit{I}}\ t)$ approach to emotions that relies on an external circumstance being a certain way for a person to feel a certain way. This approach is again incident-driven, reactive, and oriented toward survival. It assumes that there is no distinction between what we want and what we need. Therefore, if desire is the focus, immediate gratification is seen as ideal. While it is common and compelling, immediate gratification is the default we have been challenging throughout this book.

By contrast, hope is about waiting. This corresponds to the alternative approach to emotions which focuses on changing our interpretations to feel differently. This $(f\ i\ \textbf{\textit{T}})$ approach is thought-driven, responsive, and oriented towards non-survival, and thriving. As such, delayed rather than immediate gratification can be the focus. When it comes to hope, waiting is often preferred to having what we want, because desire is not equated with need, and there is the very real possibility that what is desired may not be best. In the first $(f\textbf{\textit{I}}\ t)$ case, to not have what we want is problematic; in the second $(f\ i\ \textbf{\textit{T}})$ case, to not (initially) have what we want is axiomatic.

### *Maybe t.w.o . . . kinds of hope*

This is not to say that hope is in any way opposed to desire. Rather, hope points to a difference between short-term and long-term desires. Skillfully applied, hope creates the potential for legitimate desires to be indulged, experienced, and enjoyed in lasting ways.

Of course, this is so much more easily said than done. Just over the course of the day that I am writing this section, I have been confronted with reminders of different difficulties, ranging from the almost insignificant to the deeply and painfully profound. Learning that a guitar repair will take longer than expected. A conversation with my daughter, who is in the throes of homesickness from 5,000 miles away. Hearing a friend lament a breakup with a romantic partner. Grieving with dear friends who have rather suddenly lost a beloved family member. In each of these situations, I would much rather not face the delays and pains associated with these difficulties. I would rather have what I want or see others have what they want. In the thick of a trial, waiting seems way less than ideal.

To be waiting for what we want implies varying degrees of interruption and discomfort. Delays are inconvenient at best and excruciating at worst. By contrast, immediate gratification can be intensely satisfying. So why would we willingly forgo such satisfaction?

If we stay with Paul's reasoning, the answer seems to be the value of hope itself. For example, a few verses after talking about Abraham's faith, Paul explains that hope begins with adversity. Sounding almost masochistic, he writes, *"we rejoice in our sufferings, knowing that suffering produces endurance, and endurance produces character, and character produces hope..."*[49]

Far from being masochistic, however, Paul is talking about maturity and the way it develops. Whereas masochism is about finding pleasure in pain, Paul is describing an appreciation for pain because of the growth and depth it affords. Moreover, the underlying reason for Paul's argument seems to focus on the supernatural when he goes on to say, *"and hope does not put us to shame because God's love has been poured into our hearts"*[50]

Contrast this with a passage in Proverbs which says, *"Hope deferred makes the heart sick but a desire fulfilled is a tree of life."*[51] Keeping with the idea that there are two different kinds

---

49  Romans 5:3-4

50  Romans 5:5

51  Proverbs 13:12

of hope, this verse from Proverbs seems to indicate that there is a kind of hope that *can* be deferred. And whenever such hope is deferred, then a person becomes disheartened. I take this verse to be descriptive rather than prescriptive in that I think the author (likely King Solomon) is saying that whenever hope gets postponed or put off, heartache is a frequent, though avoidable, occurrence. A corollary to this is that wherever we find people who are discouraged or disheartened, a deferred hope is probably nearby. Again, this is descriptive of a certain kind of hope, namely hope in natural outcomes since any natural hope or any hope structured around something other than God can be deferred.

*Hope, Patience, and Freedom*
    Although hope in general can be deferred, it is also potentially very resilient. So, even when we are experiencing suffering due to an interruption or disruption of hope (anything not going the way we would desire), this suffering does not have to have the last word.

    If suffering seems inevitable, hope can outlast it. If it seems inescapable, hope can outrun it. If it seems invincible, hope can outshine it. This is the nature of anything built from adversity. But while the possibility of hope is always present, real life reminds us that all too often this possibility remains dormant and many times slips away altogether.

    The difference between being hopeful and hopeless is not the suffering we endure but rather the nature of the endurance. Hopelessness results when endurance is so pointless and futile that effort is nothing more than sheer exertion and eventual exhaustion. Hopefulness, however, results when endurance, however exhausting, is marked by an effort that is peculiarly productive and meaningful. As Paul so succinctly notes, suffering leads to perseverance, perseverance to character, and character to hope.[52]

    A next step to take then will be to explore how perseverance transforms suffering into character. And here again, the apostle Paul sheds precious light on a certain aspect of the character that produces hope, namely patience. *"But if we hope for what*

---

52  Romans 5:3-4 (NIV)

*we do not yet have, we wait for it patiently."*[53]

Etymologically, patience is related to the word passion which, in turn, is related to, interestingly and now hopefully not surprisingly, suffering.[54] Similarly, in medicine a "patient" is "one who suffers." Moreover, an older English word for patience is "long-suffering." There is an important irony here for us to consider, particularly as we round out this reflection on hope. For, if we take anything away from this section at all, it is that the more patient we are the more short-term our suffering will be in the long run.

Hope relentlessly reminds us that something more is possible. In the words of Victor Hugo's narrator of *Les Misérables*, "Hope" is "the word which the finger of God has nevertheless written upon the brow of every man."[55]

If so, hope is part of God's design for our lives. Moreover, I would like to suggest that the goodness of God is such that we can trace the reason for this back to the two-fold purpose he has placed in every person, namely, to experience maximum freedom and optimal joy.

As we have also seen, the freedom we seek is both *freedom from* as well as *freedom to*. The first is perhaps more obvious, since none of us wants to be under anything that would confine, limit, or restrict us. The second is less understood, especially to the extent that we automatically treat our desires as though they are needs.

One of the virtues of patience is that it allows us to explore new assumptions about when to pursue what we want. The alternative is that we inadvertently enslave ourselves to our desires by an almost unconscious acceptance of the merits of immediate gratification. One strategy is to essentially not be put off balance (for example, "shocked") when a hope is delayed

---

53  Romans 8:25 (NIV)

54  Both patience and passion are related to the Latin word pati, which means "to endure, undergo, experience." See https://www.etymonline.com/word/patience and https://www.etymonline.com/word/passion. Retrieved January 6, 2018.

55  Hugo, V. (1862, 1992). Les misérables (C. E. Wilbour, Trans.). New York, NY: Modern Library, p 79.

or postponed, and we can begin to do this by being aware that hoping always implies a form of waiting and delay.

A similar approach might consider the following:
1) Since hope involves waiting, it contains a kind of built-in difficulty.
2) Acknowledging this difficulty prevents *extra difficulty* because we do not fight reality by saying that a naturally difficult situation "should" be easy.

In fact, patience might be thought of as a conscious awareness and practice of delayed gratification that aims exactly for the opposite experience of slavery, namely freedom.

Freedom from imprisonment coupled with the freedom to live can be called "sustainable freedom." Again, patience reminds us that sustainable freedom is directly related to what we think of as the *character* of a person.

Character here may be understood as an ability to live wisely and well. Such ability is also at the heart of this book since we are learning to be emotionally responsive in ways that promote relationships. Such responsivity forms a certain character in a person as it is cultivated over time. This responsivity is also particularly and directly related to knowledge about timing— namely when to wait and when to act. As we have also seen, this goes beyond morality to a person's volition, a person's will. It ultimately forms the basis for moving from an ability to do something that might be "right" (which could possibly be good) to an ability to choose something that might be better or even best.

A final way of understanding hope then is to think of it as a kind of optimism about the timing of things, precisely because as we learn when to refrain and when to move forward, we see opportunities regardless of or even because of the circumstances. Anecdotally, while writing this chapter, I have noticed how my scribbling of the word "optimism" has also looked to me like a new word—"optionism." Hope, as both an awareness of timing the value of waiting, perceives options wherever it looks. And again, where we find options, freedom is not far away.

In keeping with the rest of this book, these thoughts are simply my own way of packaging the much more eloquent words of philosophical giants who have gone before. For example, in his reflections on something quite different from hope, Henry David Thoreau notes that "the mass of men lead lives of quiet desperation," and ultimately he concludes that "it is a characteristic of wisdom not to do desperate things."[56] Or, in his gripping novel of revenge and redemption, *Count of Monte Cristo* novelist Alexandre Dumas concludes the entire tale with a type of thematic refrain, "has not the count just told us that all human wisdom is summed up in two words?—'Wait and hope.'"[57] And so, we see that hope is directly related to wisdom and wisdom to waiting, which in turn brings us full circle.

Wait. Hope. One word, maybe two . . . and then maybe wise seeking will reveal a tree of life.[58]

---

56   Thoreau, H. D. (1893, 2004). Walden. Boston: Houghton Mifflin, p. 6.

57   Dumas, A. (1844-1845). The count of Monte Cristo. In online-literature.com. Retrieved January 6, 2018, from http://www.online-literature.com/dumas/cristo/117/

58   See Proverbs 13:12

# Love

*There is no fear in love, but perfect love casts out fear.*
*For fear has to do with punishment,*
*and whoever fears has not been perfected in love.*
*We love because (God) first loved us.*[59]

## Greatest of Blessings

*Brightest Light*
We come now to our final virtue in this exploration—the brightest star in our Triangle. Indeed, the brightest light in our universe.

Love. It is referred to by the apostle Paul as "the greatest" [60]and "the most excellent way."[61] And yet interestingly but not surprisingly, in Paul's same description, it is neither proud nor boastful. Instead, it is patient and kind. Always protecting, always trusting, and always hoping, it perpetually encompasses and is illumined by its two other companions. Radiating both inclusiveness and uniqueness, love presides over all—preeminent, supreme.[62]

And, while books on love could certainly fill entire libraries and songs about it will never cease to be written, it remains a deep, deep mystery. So profound is love's mystery, that a full understanding of it would surely alleviate most relational suffering and possibly eliminate it altogether. However, if we are honest, we are probably more familiar with how our misunderstandings and misappropriations of it create more pain than peace, to say nothing of sorrow and heartache. Perhaps

---

59  1 John 4:18-19, parenthetical name added
60  1 Corinthians 13:13
61  1 Corinthians 12:31 (NIV)
62  1 Corinthians 13:4-13

singer Neil Young best captures this irony when he simply says,
"Only love can break your heart."[63]

Thus, love, or at least it's approximations, can either be
blamed for the proliferation of our relational woes or praised
for the healing of them. And so, in a book about the ocean of
relationships and the notion that most, if not all, of this ocean
is, traversable, we are left with one shining idea that can either
make or break our journey. How then shall we do justice,
especially in limited space, to this greatest of blessings?

*Returning to the Source*
The answer is embedded in this last question. For when we
call love a blessing, we remind ourselves that it is, above all, a
gift. Moreover, this gift transcends all gifts precisely because it
traces directly back to the transcendent.

> **"If faith is confident belief and
> hope is joyful anticipation, then let
> us consider love to be 'courageous
> generosity'."**

"We love because God first loved us."[64] Thus writes the
apostle John who, as a member of Jesus' inner circle, adopted
love, specifically the love of God, as his most cherished theme.
So personal is John's conviction about the centrality of this
love that he refers to himself repeatedly as "the disciple whom
Jesus loved."[65] So pervasive is his awareness of the intimacy he
felt with God in his friendship with Jesus, that John's claims
about God's love for all humanity naturally echo this very way
he approaches his own identity. We do well then to take note
when, in describing "perfect" love, John emphasizes that the
beginning of all loving is found in being loved and that by God
Himself.

63  Young, N. (1970). Only love can break your heart [Recorded by N. Young and 'Crazy
Horse']. After the gold rush [Record]. Hollywood, CA: Reprise.

64  1 John 4:19

65  See also John 13:23; 19:26; 20:2; 21:7

Can we bear to even attempt to entertain this claim? I will reluctantly acknowledge that I am shy and even skittish to approach the massiveness of this idea. I will also readily confess that, while I have tried to be clear about both secular and sacred dimensions of relationships (if such a distinction is even necessary), it will be useless for me to resist "taking the gloves off," so to speak, when it comes to the topic of love. If we are to do any justice to the topic at all it seems necessary to start at the source which appears to me to be patently spiritual. Concerning this source, when it comes to being loved by God, I imagine myself trying to fill a canteen from the thundering cascade of a formidable waterfall only to be stopped by the force of the wind that is generated by the spray alone.

I don't want to get too close; the awesomeness of the falls is intimidating enough. Even when I desire to approach, it seems the "winds" keep me at bay. These are the winds of guilt and regret or self-reliance and stubbornness. On one hand, there are haunting memories of things either done or left undone that would seem to automatically disqualify me. On the other hand, there is avoidance in all forms, taking the shapes of neediness, vulnerability, failure, pride, and everything in between. And behind all these, there is fear.

How then can we understand love that banishes fear? How can we expel not only the fear of an unsafe situation but also the fear that seems whipped up by the strength of love itself? How can we ultimately address the fear of both loving and of being loved?

I will address these questions by considering two aspects of love that, if not comprehensive, seem at least a good summary of just how this virtue can illuminate our journey. If faith is confident belief and hope is joyful anticipation, then let us consider love to be "courageous generosity." Moreover, as we do so, let us add one more image to the mosaic of metaphors we have been forming along the way. We have entertained various ways of traversing the ocean—sailing, paddling, surfing, even to some extent flying. As we wind down this discussion, one more way quietly calls: walking.

## Defying Gravity

*Stepping Out*
In his honest and unconventional ballad, "We Are Not as Strong as We Think We Are," singer and songwriter, Rich Mullins, poetically captures both the wonderful and fragile dynamics of love, saying:

> *When you love, you walk on water,*
> *careful you don't stumble on them waves*
> *We all wanna go there somethin' awful,*
> *but to stand there it takes some grace...*[66]

The words above, taken from the song's final verse, summarize, with Mullins' signature combination of child-like simplicity and uncanny clarity, the miracle that takes place each and every time one person loves another.

Of course, Mullins is alluding to the biblical occasion where Jesus supernaturally walked upon a stormy sea and then bid the disciple Peter to exit his boat and step out upon the waves as well. By faith, Peter did so and was temporarily able to defy gravity—as long as he was focused on Jesus. Interestingly, however, Peter began to sink when he "saw the wind."[67]

Whether from waterfalls or sea storms, the "winds" of life can distract and discourage us. When it comes to love, the winds of fear seem to constantly blow against us. Here again, the apostle John's diagnosis is at once intriguing and perceptive, for he says that the driving force behind all fear is—punishment. Keeping this in mind, let us look a bit deeper into two facets of love, courage, and generosity, to see how we can ultimately and intimately better know the grandeur of the waterfall and the miracle of walking on the ocean.

66   Mullins, R. W. (1996). We are not as strong as we think we are. [Recorded by R. Mullins and 'A Ragamuffin Band']. On Songs [CD] Brentwood, TN: Reunion. See also https://music.apple.com/us/album/we-are-not-as-strong-as-we-think-we-are/303182485?i=303182490 and https://www.youtube.com/watch?v=B9vogh4ll34 (retrieved January 6, 2018).

67   Matthew 14:30

# Courage

*Love does not envy or boast; it is not arrogant or rude.*
*It does not insist on its own way;*
*It is not irritable or resentful;*
*it does not rejoice at wrongdoing . . .[68]*

## Rejection

In many ways, this book, being about relationships, has been examining the topics of courage and generosity from the beginning. We specifically focused on courage in our chapter on fear that also ended with some thoughts on what courage might mean for love. We considered how courage can involve our consent to redefine as "opportunities" situations ordinarily regarded as "obligations" and how this can also mean emotions in relationships do not have to be treated as survival issues. Moreover, if fear pertains to threat and if survival is not at stake, then there is ultimately no danger. Finally, since there is no danger and since the apostle John points out that fear is fundamentally incompatible with love, then love or at least "perfect love" is about safety.

This is the big picture—where love exists there is safety and whenever we are safe, there is no reason for fear. As with many things in this book though, this is so much easier said than done. So, what accounts for the difficulty? Why does it seem fear so often jettisons love rather than the other way around? Let us consider two dimensions of courage: acceptance and affirmation.

Love, especially love that traces back to the God whose

---

68   1 Corinthians 13:4-6

character is defined by love, takes the risk of what theologian Paul Tillich might call, "the courage to accept acceptance."[69] And one of the clearest ways to explore this is to revisit what might be involved when the apostle John specifically attributes fear to a concern with punishment.

Interestingly, this is the only time, in any of his writings, that John uses the word "punishment" (see 1 John 4:18; the Greek word *kolasin* that John uses can also be translated "correction, chastisement, or torment").[70] To better understand John, we can consider that he clearly emphasizes that his purpose in this first letter is to optimize joy (1 John 1:4), and the underlying foundation for his joy is the forgiveness of sins made available through Jesus' sacrificial love in the gift of His life for all of humanity (1 John 2:2; 3:16; 4:10). This, in fact, is identified by John as the definition of love (1 John 4:10), and in this way, John's understanding of love is unequivocally theological. In fact, John not only traces love back to God (i.e., "this is love..." 1 John 4:10) but also traces God, so to speak, back to love, affirming as well that "God is love" (1 John 4:8, 16). So, if we are serious about understanding John's claim that perfect love casts out fear, we can, in the words of Isaac Watts' timeless hymn, "survey the wondrous cross,"[71] and see the undeniable love of God and the God of love in Jesus, giving His life for the sins of the whole world. Thus, if what John says is true, then we can take heart in knowing we are truly safe.

In addition, and consistent with his theology, John is quick to remind us that love is particularly "perfected" when people emulate God's love and when people specifically love one another (1 John 2:5; 4:12; 4:16-17). In this way, John's book is strategic for understanding both the "vertical" (theological) and the "horizontal" (social, psychological) dimensions of love. As such, let us return to our discussion of courage by looking at one way that people might especially experience fear getting the best

---

69  See Tillich, P. (1952, 2000). The courage to be. New Haven, CT: Yale University Press. Also, for a helpful review of this book, see http://people.bu.edu/wwildman/tillich/resources/ review_tillich-paul_couragetobe.htm (retrieved January 6, 2018).

70  Kolasis. (n. d.). In biblehub.com. Retrieved January 6, 2018, from http://biblehub.com/ greek/2851.htm

71  The song, "When I Survey the Wondrous Cross," was written by Isaac Watts and was published in Hymns and Spiritual Songs in 1707. See also https://hymnary.org/text/ when_i_survey_the_wondrous_cross_watts (retrieved January 18, 2020).

of love, namely through self-condemnation.

Ironically, John's reference to people condemning themselves is in a part of his letter that has the potential to be profoundly comforting and encouraging. Noting the importance of loving others with actions rather than words alone, John asserts,

> *"By this we shall know that we are of the truth and reassure our heart before (God); for **whenever our heart condemns us**, God is greater than our heart and he knows everything."*[72]

John goes on to also encourage those who do not experience self-condemnation by saying that they can have another kind of confidence. It is interesting, though, that John feels it is necessary to talk about self-condemnation in the first place, especially in a letter that is all about forgiveness and the love of God that casts out fear. Why?

### Acceptance

Self-condemnation is an especially treacherous form of fear. In our previous discussion on shame, we noted the distinction between guilt as wrong-doing versus shame as "wrong-being." Self-condemnation seems to take shame a step further to what we might think of as wrong-existing. So, where shame points to wrongness in "who" I am, self-condemnation points to wrongness in "that" I am, that I even exist.

Self-punishment, then, is even more of a given in self-condemnation; it is self-evident. Once we level a damning verdict upon ourselves, we can find any number of ways to carry out our own death sentence. In most cases, though, it is a painfully slow execution because the blows are frequently subtle and intertwined with critical survival instincts. However sincere this penance may be, it is never enough. Every self-inflicted punishment creates more misery, further reinforcing the belief that, for whatever reason, we not only deserve bad, but we are also undeserving of good.

Put another way, self-condemnation is truly a kind of fear, and one that is based on a two-fold threat: the threat of not

---

72  1 John 3:19-20, parenthetical name and bold added

receiving something bad and the threat of receiving anything good. And so, self-condemnation will tenaciously find ways to prevent us from anything good that might come from love overall.

Nevertheless, John joyfully tells people, specifically those of us who know the pain of being condemned by our own hearts, that, as we actively love, we can actually rest! And, astoundingly, of all places, we can rest *in God's presence!*

The apostle then gives two reasons that might directly address the two-pronged threats of self-condemnation: *"God is greater than our heart, and He knows everything."*[73]

In this case, any explanations for who we have been or what we have done will somehow be compatible with us finding rest in God. So, we might say first, if God is greater than our hearts, then God's judgments will ultimately prevail. Since the context points to how God does not condemn us, then simply put, punishment is no longer necessary—so, it is *not* a problem if we do not receive something bad. Second, if God knows everything, then God's knowledge is completely thorough and comprehensive. Since God again does not condemn, God's omniscience can be a comfort and, in this way, it is also *not* a problem for us to receive something good.

Can we possibly trust these things to be true? Self-condemnation and all other forms of rejection from ourselves or otherwise can be so diabolically compelling. But again, we need only return to the extravagant love of God, consider afresh John's words about this love, and ask: What if more real than the charges against us are both the mercy of not being punished and the grace of God's full knowledge and wisdom? Even when rejection is appropriate or deserved, what if acceptance makes *even more sense?*

If so, then there would be more risk in not believing than in believing. And we might say that not believing would flow from fear and that believing would flow from courage. In this case, courage would entail vulnerability since it would mean, at the very least, opening ourselves to trading the familiarity of what

---

73   1 John 3:20

is negative and condemning for the unfamiliarity of something so much better.

Where mercy and grace are true, there we can truly rest for we are again and indeed safe. Where there is safety, there is no fear, and according to the apostle John, the entire eviction is accomplished by... love.

### Affirmation
In his timeless hymn to love, following his announcement that love is patient and kind, the apostle Paul also gives five statements about what love is not and what love does not do. It neither envies nor boasts. It is neither proud nor rude. It is not irritable or resentful. It does not rejoice in evil. Situated in the middle of these statements is one that could very well sum up the other four and possibly capture the essence of courage altogether—love *"does not insist on its own way."*[74]

At a glance, this seems almost too obvious. Love is not "self-seeking,"[75] and love is not selfish. Why, we might ask, would Paul tell us what we already know? How does this even relate to courage?

From personal experience, a deeper look at this concept continues to take me way outside the bounds of my comfort zone with love. For me, the shift is accomplished by a perspective that focuses not on what love avoids but rather on what love affirms.

I must gratefully acknowledge theologian and author N. T. Wright, who, referencing an idea of philosopher Bernard Lonergan, simply states, "When I love, I affirm the differentness of the beloved."[76] Simpler still, love affirms another's way.

It seems another's way is all fine and good—if their way works for us. We can work with them—if we agree, identify, or align with whatever it is that they are saying or doing; as long as it is convenient or comfortable; as long as we do not have to make any changes.

---

74  1 Corinthians 13:5

75  1 Corinthians 13:5 (NIV)

76  Wright, N. T. (1999). The challenge of Jesus: Rediscovering who Jesus was and is. Downers Grove, IL: Intervarsity Press, p. 195.

However, what if changes are asked of us? What if such changes seem inconvenient, uncomfortable, or downright unreasonable? Even more, what if we regard what another is doing as inappropriate, immoral, or wrong?

If we are honest, certain differences can be very uncomfortable. We naturally gravitate toward the familiar and similar rather than the unfamiliar and dissimilar. Love, however, finds opportunities *amid the discomfort* to esteem. Again, it *affirms the differentness* of the ones we love.

Such love also finds a way to ascribe value to the very things we call irritations or frustrations or generally uncomfortable feelings. These feelings will signal differences that in turn will signal differentness. Awareness of differentness can be thought of as a fork in the road, leading to the option of taking one of two different paths. One path, which is often our default, is to have differentness move us away from each other, resulting in feeling less close.

The second path, the one that is much more rarely experienced, is the one that would have *differentness* lead to finding ways of feeling *closer* to each other. This begins with treating negative emotion as a reminder that the other person is doing something in a way that we would not do it. If we can believe that there is value in their different way, we can look well, even favorably, upon what might have been formerly "upsetting" behavior. We can look for the usefulness or logic of their ways—precisely because of *who* is behind the behavior.

Here is one way to look at this second option: Suppose that we would like someone to do something to help us. We can reason that if the other person shared our background, experiences, understanding, and perspective, there would be a high probability that they would do the very thing that we would find helpful. In fact, for the sake of argument, let us say that there would be a 99 percent likelihood that they would do what we want them to do. This would be a very comfortable arrangement for us. At the same time, there is still the very slim, 1 percent chance that the person might not "cooperate" with our preferences. When a person does not seem helpful to us, it is easy to feel "upset" and to feel distant from them.

## "Simpler still, love affirms another's way."

The principle of affirming differentness acknowledges that, whereas the 99 percent likelihood of another's help is a good prospect, we place a particular premium on the 1 percent chance that the person will *not do* what we want them to. We can enjoy the 99 percent likelihood of comfort and convenience, and at the same time, we protect against the 99 percent crossing over into 100 percent. In essence, we value and ensure the *absence* of the guarantee precisely because as soon as we have a guarantee that another will do things our way, we effectively have some control over that person, which also means that we no longer have *relationship*. As we recast "upsetting" things as evidence of relationship, we can also grow in experiencing relationship as a gift. Perhaps we can grow to where, even if we could ensure that another would do things our way, we would still opt out because the others' freedom is more important to us than getting "our way."

Three caveats apply here. First, I placed quotation marks around "upsetting," because when behaviors themselves create feelings, it is easier to emotionally react. The easier it is to react, the harder it is to be open to outcomes. When this happens, threats and fear are likely to increase.

Second, affirming differentness is not the same as accepting or approving behaviors. To reiterate an equally important aspect of Paul's description of love, "it does not rejoice at wrongdoing." [77]We may be strongly opposed to the behaviors of a person and yet embrace as good the freedom they have to be themselves. Depending on the differentness in question, this may take particular faith and hope.

Third, we will do well to remember Paul's initial description of love as "patient."[78] It is again one thing to bear with and tolerate those areas where another person is less like us. It is

---

77   1 Corinthians 13:6

78   1 Corinthians 13:4

quite another to acknowledge and to actually be open to *their* way of doing things.

The openness we speak of would again encompass all the variables that contribute to them being who they are and to them doing things in the ways that they do them. It would involve not just acknowledgment, but genuine affirmation.

The reality is that difference, and perhaps even more, differentness, can seem very threatening. We can talk about recognizing diversity, promoting tolerance, and championing the idea of forgiveness, but do we genuinely mean what we say? Are we really *affirming* how others are different? What if someone thinks our way of doing something is wrong? What if their way of protesting leads them to do something that we feel is wrong as well? What if they seem to criticize or just not show the support we yearn for? What if everything that is said seems to be defensive or contrarian? Or as we have already explored, what if trust is broken and betrayed?

The patient heart of love takes all of these questions seriously by taking seriously the other person's prerogatives to think, feel, and want whatever makes sense to them. At the same time, love's patient heart distinguishes between what is desired and what is done, and where appropriate, employs healthy boundaries to protect and preserve what is good.[79]

Still, amid all legitimate reservations and protests, love persists with additional questions: What do we really believe is possible? What kind of world do we really want to live in? *What if we can learn to sincerely value those who are both **unlike** us and those who initially appear even **unlikable**?"*

To these questions, love patiently replies by adhering, even clinging, to a possibility. It is the possibility that, as we do learn to value those who are unlike us or those who even seem unlikeable, our loving will actually and eventually give way to a kind of *liking* of such people. Moreover, this liking will focus on them, however different, *as people*, for who they are in their

---

79  For an excellent resource on this matter, see Cloud, H. & Townsend, J. S. (2004). Boundaries: How to say yes and no to take control of your life. Grand Rapids, MI: Zondervan.

own rights, with neither strings nor conditions of change. In so doing, love also whispers that as we truly see others for who they are, we will begin to resemble the kind of acceptance of and from God, who "knows everything" and who still encourages us to reassure our hearts and rest "in his presence."[80]

In summary, this continues our aim of setting a stage for genuine affirmation to take place by exploring strategies related to emotional responsivity. And since, on the ocean of relationships, responding lends to thriving more than just surviving, responding will also go hand in hand with facing fear. Fear is psychologically unnecessary because we are not in any danger (since relationships are rarely matters of individual survival), and courage is still called for since the default to feel threatened is so strong. It takes a certain kind of confidence and boldness to thrive when all signs seem to indicate survival is at stake. As this inner fortitude, this courage, is harnessed in such a way that the differentness of others is honored, we will experience a peculiar and double freedom—the freedom from others having to do things our way and the freedom to have them do things their way. As both occur, we will see love edging out fear.

80  1 John 3:19-20 (NIV)

# Generosity

*Love...rejoices with the truth.*
*Love bears all things, believes all things,*
*hopes all things, endures all things.*
*Love never ends.*[81]

*Benevolence*

In addition to courageously accepting and affirming others, love courageously gives. And so, let us briefly explore two ways in which this giving takes place: benevolence and sacrifice.

Philosopher and author Dallas Willard points out that a concept closely related to love is benevolence. He particularly explains how benevolence can be translated literally "good will" or "willing the good" of the beloved (from the Latin *bene* meaning "good" and *volent* meaning "will")."[82] He is also quick to distinguish what is good from what is desired and therefore, suggests that sometimes loving another person (or loving ourselves) means not automatically indulging what is desired. With this relatively simple teaching, Willard sheds additional light on how we can continue our walk upon the waves.

One aspect of benevolence may be seen in the apostle Matthew's account of Jesus' teaching what today is known as the Golden Rule: "So whatever you wish that others would do to you, do also to them, for this is the Law and the Prophets." [83]Jesus' identification of this principle with "the Law and the

---

81    1 Corinthians 13:6-8

82    Willard, D. (. [Daniel dliver]. (2011, March 19). Dallas Willard—Divine conspiracy 02: Human nature. [Video file]. Retrieved January 6, 2018, from https://www.youtube.com/watch?v=ArRHjUoatT8, 09:10.

83    Matthew 7:12

Prophets" is intriguing. Later, Matthew records Jesus telling a Pharisee "lawyer" that the two greatest commandments are to love God with one's whole being and to love one's neighbor as oneself, adding that "on these two commandments depend all the Law and the Prophets."[84] Moreover, in a parallel account, the apostle Mark records Jesus as saying,

> *"The most important is, 'Hear, O Israel: The Lord our God, the Lord is one. And you shall love the Lord your God with all your heart and with all your soul and with all your mind and with all your strength.' The second is this: 'You shall love your neighbor as yourself.' There is no other commandment greater than these."[85]*

The grammar is intriguing. By referring to "these" as a single "commandment," Jesus seems to be giving love for neighbor (which involves love for self) the same importance He gives to love for God. For Jesus, all the Hebrew scriptures were summarized by these two instructions.

Loving another the way we would want to be loved is consistent with willing what would truly be good for them. This dovetails nicely with the concept of love affirming differentness, since only when we truly see somebody can we really *will* their good. In this regard, I have personally found it useful to call affirmation a "love *of* the beloved" and benevolence a "love *for* the beloved."

The latter is important to the concept of generosity. Love is a gift—from a lover to a beloved. If I give a gift to someone, that gift is *for them*; I have *their* best interest in mind. Many times, though, we "give" to others based upon subtle assumptions of what would be best for *us*. This seems to be a curious modification of the Golden Rule, where we do unto others as we would have them do unto us *without awareness of difference* and differentness. Often, we inadvertently insist on our own way.

Jesus seems to anticipate this way we can mistakenly, though likely with good intentions, "love" those around us, including

---

84  Matthew 22:40

85  Mark 12:29-31

396 | MAYBE THE WHOLE OCEAN

our enemies. For example, prior to teaching the Golden Rule, Jesus warns of how a person can attempt to remove a splinter from another's eye without first extracting the beam from their own. He thereby emphasizes how important it is to "see clearly" before trying to help, which in this case, particularly traces back to the overarching instruction to refrain from judging other people.[86]

In a word, Jesus is both literally and figuratively addressing the ways we can "project" our own material, so to speak, onto others, which can be at odds with truly willing their good. In fact, rigid practice of such behavior will likely be called narcissistic. In this regard, projection of our own agenda may be like operating as though we are seeing mirrors wherever we look. Like Ovid's self-infatuated Narcissus, we will be mesmerized by our own reflection, ultimately to our own demise.[87]

In our chapter on communication, we noted that we can all project our own assumptions onto others and that a useful principle is: *The answer to projection is reflection.* A good follow-up to keep in mind, then, is that if we can become so attuned to others that we effectively hold up a mirror to them, we will be better positioned to truly will their good. We will see them for their sake and on their terms, convey this to them, and thus be so much more aware of what will bless them.

This is the essence of love: blessing. Like rains from heaven that fall to the ground, love refreshes and nourishes and rejuvenates. In the end, the blessing of rain or any other gift, carries a kind of restorative gentleness. Even if the showers begin as harsh, torrential downpours, the effects of the water seeping into the soil and hydrating the earth are always to bring life, and the new shoots of vegetation are always tender.

And so it is with love—the goal is always the betterment, the well-being, the life and thriving of the beloved. Often far from easy, this can call for significant effort and attentiveness, faith and hope. As the apostle Paul reminds us, love is "patient and

---

86   see Matthew 7:5

87   For additional information, see https://www.cornellcollege.edu/classical_studies/cla216-2-a/narcissus-echo/ (retrieved January 6, 2018).

kind."[88]

In addition to and consistent with affirming others, by truly seeing a person for who they are, love continues to persevere even when difficulties arise. As an example, love as benevolence will wisely discern how the beloved's offenses are largely their own projections, their own misguided and ineffective ways of willing the good. Again, offenses are primarily unnecessary reactions, and benevolence is just one more way that love gently responds to such reactions. Let us now look at one additional way in which love affirms, blesses, and courageously gives of itself—sacrifice.

*Sacrifice*

It has been said that we can give without loving but we cannot love without giving. Truly we can agree, since love is itself a gift, and as a gift, its highest, most sublime expression is made when the lover gives *of self* to the beloved. Here I distinguish between giving of oneself and giving from oneself. Giving *from* implies a source, whereas, giving *of* implies a cost. The miracle of love, however, is that the cost of giving *of* oneself also always implies a greater reward and ends up being a giving *to* oneself. While it is true that we cannot love without giving, we also cannot "outgive" love.

This is the driving force behind both the courage and the generosity of love—the endless river and bottomless pool that feed the formidable waterfall. This is the surface tension that magically buoys us up if we venture *out of the boat*—a self-giving, sacrificial heart to bless another and the confidence and joy in knowing that such giving is never in vain.

This power is, of course, not without risk, and the risks are like two sides of a double-edged blade. To truly understand sacrifice, to accurately experience the tip of the sword, so to speak, it is important to briefly revisit the importance of two concepts: individuality and mutuality.

As indicated, these principles have already informed our discussion and are rather interwoven into the fabric of this book. Individuality reminds us of the importance of each

---

88   I Corinthians 13:4

person's self, and mutuality reminds us of how we are all intricately interconnected. The fact remains, however, that we are looking for an almost precarious balance between the two. If too individualistic, we will miss out on freely giving love to others. If too self-effacing, we will miss out on the goodness of receiving when we love others. If we are at either extreme, we will burn out, because imbalances between self and others cannot ultimately be sustained.

The bottom line is love presupposes that we have a *self* to give and that *individual and collective vitality* are inextricable. Love as sacrifice understands this, but most of our conflicts suggest that we often operate otherwise.

Broadly speaking, when there is strain in a relationship, specific patterns are frequently at work. Though we may be committed to the relationship, we think we are doing enough, so we also assume that if the other person was more committed, they would make a change—back down, confess an error, or even better, "convert" to our position. As a result, we can often arrive at what seems like an insurmountable impasse.

The operative word here is that it *seems* to be an impasse. Love as sacrifice recognizes this, so the blocks need only be *apparent*. Besides, the truth is that resolving certain differences by simple conversion is too easy anyway. The things worth fighting for may call for an even deeper struggle, and sometimes it can even feel as though both people are fighting for their lives. It is worth emphasizing that nothing is more precious than each person's life. However, here is where the precious becomes precarious, since, to the extent that we are against another, we are also against ourselves. By contrast, any affirmations or acceptances of the other for *who they are* will be indispensable to preserving the balance. It is a fragile balance for sure, but with every move one makes to *bless* the other, it is retained.

### Flesh and Spirit

Love as sacrifice knows that there is a part of us that can masquerade as caring even though such a charade is detrimental, especially when we consider the importance of *both* individuality and mutuality. This part of us tends to equate surrender with defeat and vies for a kind of egoism that is more burdensome than freeing.

In the Bible, this part of us is often regarded as "the flesh" and distinguishing it from our true "self," or what we might also call our spirit, is a matter of life and death.[89] In fact, when love involves sacrifice, the death of the flesh means life for the spirit.[90]

---

## "Where people love, people thrive, and when people thrive, they are truly alive."

---

To truly love others and ourselves, yes, *to truly love others as ourselves*, involves both honoring the treasure of each person's individuality as well as relinquishing, indeed, vanquishing the flesh. The two are mutually exclusive, and we ignore either or both to our peril. What our spirit aspires to give, our flesh will call taken; what our flesh would call loss, our spirit regards as gain.

Love, being inextricably related to one's spirit, can graciously yield to another. Love trusts that things will be good, because, again, where love is involved, another's gain is, to reiterate the words of Dr. Martin Luther King, Jr., a "double victory."[91]

---

89  See Romans 8:5-9. Here we are primarily using "flesh" to describe an exclusively autonomous way of being and acting that insists on remaining in full control and refuses help from others, including God. Indeed, this passage makes clear that if we want to avoid living by the flesh, it is necessary to set our minds on what God (the Spirit) desires. However, it is important to note that in the Bible, "flesh" (from the Greek *sarx*) is not always problematic or evil. For example, important, favorable uses of it include references to marital sex (Ephesians 5:31), physical, embodied living (Galatians 2:20), and the miraculous way in which Jesus, while eternally divine, became a human being (John 1:14). Retrieved January 6, 2018, from http://biblehub.com/greek/4561.htm

90  Again, I appreciate Dallas Willard, who distinguishes between the spirit and the soul where the spirit is the will or heart of a person and the soul is the "whole person" or integration of body, mind, and spirit. See Dallas' explanation in his book, Renovation of the Heart (Willard, D. (2002). Renovation of the heart: Putting on the character of Christ. Colorado Springs, CO: NavPress. For a helpful summary of definitions suggested by Dallas Willard, see Bill Gaultiere's SoulShepherding blog. Retrieved July 13, 2020, from https://www.soulshepherding.org/dallas-willards-definitions/

91  Rev. Dr. Martin Luther King, Jr.'s 1963 speech to the faculty and students of Western Michigan University on December 18, 1963 as reproduced at https://libguides.wmich.edu/mlkatwmu/speech, retrieved December 16, 2019.

This is the essence of the esteemed win/win; there is again no fear because there is no threat. And being open to all outcomes, love can give these lasting gifts: the option for people to truly live *their* lives and the opportunity for people to *truly live*. Where people love, people thrive, and when people thrive, they are truly alive.

Is it any wonder, then, that the apostle Paul completes his description of love by declaring its unparalleled, unlimited ways? Thus, he writes, *"Love always protects, always trusts, always hopes, always perseveres. Love never fails."*[92]

This is generosity in all its fullness, pulling out all the stops, no holds barred, with no reservations and no discriminations. *Nowhere is this more evident than in the extravagant love of God in the person of Jesus.*

And so, the "beloved" apostle John effectively connects the highest love with the highest generosity when, referring to a conversation between Jesus and an interested follower (Nicodemus), he writes, "For God so loved the world that he *gave . . .*"[93] In this account, Jesus is portrayed as the ultimate gift—for the salvation of the world. If that is not enough, John later records Jesus teaching that sacrifice, namely His sacrifice, is the strongest form of love saying, "Greater love has no one than this, that someone lays down his life for his friends."[94]

These references are an acquired taste. For those yet unfamiliar with the story, they can seem barbaric, since, as we have seen, the context of such sacrifice is Jesus' horrific death on a cross. To those more familiar, the thought of God graciously giving Himself to rescue humanity is hope itself—the "romance of the ages!"[95] We have touched on this story throughout this book, but one last mention of it is fitting for this final topic, perhaps this time in a more symbolic, poetic way:

92   I Corinthians 13:7-8 (NIV)

93   John 3:16, italics added

94   John 15:13

95   I am grateful to theologian and author, Francois du Toit, for this description of the biblical story. Retrieved September 24, 2018, from http://www.mirrorword.net/about-us

*God. Triune King*
*of the universe.*
*Bears with the*
*people who had*
*essentially declared*
*war on Him,*
*because He had*
*purposed to adopt them*
*from the beginning.*
*Eternally patient and kind, God sets into motion a plan to*
*ultimately outsmart, destroy, and undo the treason. He graciously*
*makes an ancient promise to covenant with a man and all his*
*descendants, to be their God and to have them be His people, under*
*penalty of death should the promise be broken.*
*Time after time,*
*the promise is*
*broken, by people*
*after people, through*
*sin upon sin,*
*bringing death upon*
*death. Until finally*
*this God, who*
*is Himself Love,*
*declares war upon*
*death once and*
*for all, and enters*
*the brokenness,*
*takes mortality and*
*despair upon Himself,*
*and dies,*
*though innocent,*
*for the sins of*
*the world.*
*Absorbs*
*the penalty*
*of death*
*and gives His life.*
*But three days later,*
*death will yield to*
*Resurrection*
*and faith and hope and love*
*will shine forever with new and inextinguishable light.*
*Given, not taken. Gaining through loss and ultimately rising.*
*Affording all who will trust Him the opportunity*
*to love, to thrive, and to live truly alive.*

John, the Beloved, possibly the only male disciple who remained with Jesus to the end, over and over reminds us that love is a person, and love is cross-shaped. Further, John, on multiple occasions, documents that Jesus had one singular instruction for his followers—to love one another as He Himself had loved them.[96] On one hand, this might seem abstract or even impossible. Apart from martyrdom, how are we to live a life characterized by the same Love that gave Himself for friends and in a profoundly real way, for enemies as well? Even more practically, how are we to ward off our fears, in their various forms when, these theories notwithstanding, differences still loom or we just don't feel up to the task?

In such instances and in any other circumstances, when we find ourselves at some sort of a loss to love or otherwise engage others on the ocean of relationships, let us return to the towering truth tucked away in John's first letter: *"We love because He first loved us."* [97]

We are ourselves already loved and nothing will ever change this. In fact, we can look forward to each new day deepening our understanding of this truth, for, to borrow again from N. T. Wright, love is our "destiny."[98] As we increasingly arrive at an acceptance of this love, it will also become our identity. And, since love is the basis and ground of our identity, we will find again, that we are truly safe.

Courageous Generosity. This is the lifeblood of love and indeed the bloodline we are from. For the word courage is quite literally "from the heart," and historically, generosity referred to one being "of noble birth."[99]

To the extent that the beloved apostle is accurate, we are, as beloved children, heirs of God, who is both a Father and a King. What's more, whenever we do love with even the slightest courage or even the faintest hint of generosity, we demonstrate

---

96   John 13:34-35

97   I John 4:19

98   See Wright, N. T. (2007). Surprised by hope. London, United Kingdom: SPCK.

99   See entries for "courage" and "generosity" in the English Oxford Dictionary online: https://en.oxforddictionaries.com/definition/courage and https://en.oxforddictionaries.com/definition/generosity (retrieved January 6, 2018).

our "family" resemblance and point others back to the prospect of freedom and joy. For we are never more joyfully free than when God's love makes sense to our heart, and we are never more like God than when we give.

## Postscript

This concludes our exploration of the Triangle and our navigation of this journey. We began with risk and we have ended with even more risk. For as already noted, we set out to primarily consider the ocean, the metaphor which has stood for the horizontal dimensions of relationships which, like the seas, make up most of the surface area of our lives. In every chapter, I have sought to also add brief observations from the spiritual or vertical dimension, especially influenced by my personal reflections on certain Judeo-Christian teachings. Admittedly as the journey has progressed, I have given more latitude to this discussion of the sky, so to speak, until this final chapter which has rather boldly landed on the stars of faith, hope, and love. I trust that this has not been too indulgent or overbearing, though I also trust that my own passion for these spiritual considerations has also been evident.

There remains one last reference to the seas that seems too precious not to mention, and in this case, it might be one final bridge between the earthly ocean and the heavenly sky of our journey.

In this book, the ocean has been referenced primarily as a positive entity. Relationships have been depicted as not only what comprise most of our lives but also the primary ways in which we can influence the quality of our lives. However, in Judeo-Christian culture and history, the ocean was usually not regarded as a positive place but rather as a symbol of negativity and even evil.[1] The seas often represented chaos and turmoil and strife.

---

1  For example, consider these summaries by Bible teacher Ray Vander Laan: https://www.thattheworldmayknow.com/the-sea-and-the-abyss and https://www.thattheworldmay-know.com/jesus-power-over-the-sea (retrieved July 13, 2020).

Against this backdrop, we find a prophecy, a promise about how one day "the earth will be filled with the knowledge of the glory of the Lord, *as the waters cover the sea.*"[2] If we would like one more reason to take heart, this seems an exceptional candidate. For, like the language of Ecclesiastes, it can often seem like the ocean of relationships is "below" the sky of faith, hope, and love. It can seem like certain relationships are beyond any kind of help, natural or supernatural, so emotional or cognitive strategies can seem futile and even prayer can seem powerless. Faith can flag, hope can fade, and love can be so lacking.

However, this passage points to a time when not only the ocean but the whole earth will be filled with the knowledge of God's glory. Moreover, the earth will be filled with this knowledge as the waters cover the sea, which is interesting since, as N. T. Wright points out, "the waters *are* the sea."[3] At that time, the supernatural will be natural and all our experiences will be permeated by the knowledge of God's glory.

Returning to the apostle John's counsel, if we can "set our hearts at rest" in God's presence because God both knows everything and is greater than our hearts, how much more will we be able to rest if the knowledge of His glory saturates the earth just as the waters make up the sea? As we live by faith, hope, and love and draw our strength from God, we can again rest in knowing that we are safe, and the future will be good.

Faith as confident belief. Hope as joyful anticipation. Love as courageous generosity. One word, maybe two . . .

And one day, all will know God's glory. As all the waters in the sea. Someday. One day. One word. Just a drop, maybe two, and then the whole ocean, the whole earth, and all of heaven will be one.[4]

---

2  Isaiah 11:9; Habakkuk 2:14

3  Again, I'm indebted to N. T. Wright and grateful for his reflections on this prophecy. See the following link: http://spu.edu/depts/uc/response/summer2k5/features/imagination.asp (retrieved January 6, 2018).

4  Consider the last line of Maltbie Babcock's hymn "This is My Father's World." I am grateful again to the teachings of Dr. N. T. Wright for this insight.

## Gratefully Dedicated, With Love, To

*Mrs. Kerilee L. Lim*
*Dr. Francis T. O. Lim and Mrs. Diana J. Lim*
*Mr. Jerome L. Ching and Mrs. Katherine A. Ching*
*Reverend Robert L. Paris and Mrs. Kendis L. Paris*

I am honored, humbled, and blessed to first acknowledge the love of my life and my best friend, Keri. Ever patient and kind, she gently told me for the first time, "I think your book is taking too long" in the tenth year of my writing! Those who know Ker will immediately recognize such reticence as an anomaly since she is usually quick to light a fire and put in a good word for efficiency as soon as anything is "taking too long." In this case, though, she has suffered long with me and trusted the process even when I wavered. I am greatly indebted to her for bearing with me, cheering me on, praying for me, and inspiring me. She's done all these things in addition to being a phenomenal mom, loving family member, faithful friend, dedicated contributor to our church and two boards of directors, and co-founder/administrative "chief of staff"/team coordinator for our professional practice, to name just a few ways she serves so many! She is a model of courageous and generous love, and though we have now been together for 30 years (married for 24), I still marvel daily that God providentially granted me the unbelievable favor of being in her life. This book exists largely because of you, Beautiful, and it is joyfully dedicated to you. "Many women do noble things, but you surpass them all..." I love you with all that I am, Keri.

I am grateful for my parents, Frank and Diana Lim, who gave me life and who continue to demonstrate to me, by their lives and their actions, the values of integrity and hard work and the virtues of bold faith, tenacious hope, and sacrificial love. I am fortunate to have grown up with their mentoring and to continue to benefit from their wisdom. I appreciate you, Dad, for always reminding me of the Lord's faithfulness, listening to my ideas, and being a fountain of wisdom for me and our family. You are a constant model of kindness, commitment, and character. And Mom, I appreciate you for your friendship, your open heart of compassion, and for encouraging me to persevere with writing, especially when it was such a slog, and it seemed no headway was being made. I love you both and hope that this book in some way gives back a little of the much that you have lavished upon me and our family.

I am likewise so thankful for my parents by marriage, Jerome and Kathy Ching. From the day I met them (before I had even met Keri), I have experienced their constant, gracious support and kindness. I owe an equal debt to them as I do to my birth parents for the priceless treasure I have received in Keri and the equally precious opportunity of now being family. Dad, I continue to enjoy learning from you and "talking story" about all facets of life and faith, including many of the principles in this book. And Mom, I continue to appreciate all the ways you give of yourself to Keri and me and how your endless availability to Jessie, Ella, Zoe, and Jakey has afforded me time to rest and to write. You both continue to give so much of yourselves to our family and to me, and I love you.

I finally hope this book honors my late, dear brother in Christ, Rob Paris and his beloved wife, Kendis. Next to my parents, Rob, you were my greatest mentor in life and faith, and for nearly three decades you shaped my heart, mind, and spirit with your encouragement and counsel. I'll always be grateful, Robby, for your investment in me and in my family and for your leadership and partnership in the Gospel. With Kendis and your amazing family, you fought the good fight, kept the faith, and finished your race. Even as I miss you greatly, I am strengthened by your reverberating encouragement to make our home in the Father's love as His very children! I love you and am so, so thankful for your life.

# Acknowledgements

I want to acknowledge and extend my heartfelt thanks to so many who have encouraged me in life as well as the journey that has unfolded with this writing process. The fact that it has spanned nearly a quarter of my life means words are especially inadequate and individual contributions impossible to quantify. Nonetheless, please know that I am indebted to each of you, and I thank each of you for helping me in so many vital ways.

To my editor, Joan Phillips, thank you for being such a godsend to me. I am so grateful for how our Lord provided you as an expert who took the time to hear my heart even as you refined and elevated my message. You exemplify what it means to have both a tough mind and tender heart, and it has been a joy and honor to work with you.

To my friends Pam and Neu-Wa O'Neill, what can I say? Pam, your graciousness and generosity, and Neu-Wa, your persistent encouragement are such blessings! Thank you both so much for being such a clear and tangible representation of the gospel to Keri and me!

To my friends, Pat and Tammy McLeod, thank you for believing in me. I cannot tell you how much it meant to me, Pat, when you took time on your road trip through Wyoming to talk with me and share the experiences you and Tammy had with writing and publishing your own book, *Hit Hard*, not to mention your gracious willingness to share my manuscript with your contacts. I respect you and your family and testimony and am so blessed by your generosity toward me.

To my sailing consultant, Pastor Julie Olson, I am so grateful for the time you took to read these ideas and offer your expertise as a seasoned sailor! I have so much respect for how you have participated in *actual oceanic crossings*, and even more, for the ways you live so deeply and continue to bless this world with faith, hope, and love. It is truly an honor for me to share this journey with you!

To my children, Jessalyn, Michela, Zoe, and Jacob, you all mean the absolute world to me, and I am always proud of you and always love you. Specifically, thank you Jessie, for being my amazing Publishing Assistant and Public Relations Manager; Ella, for all your creative encouragements, especially for writing your song which particularly helped me to persevere; Zoe, for your phenomenal job of drawing the cover illustration and logo; and Jakey, for keeping us all laughing and for playing a game of catch whenever I needed a break! I know how patient you all have been with Daddy, and I am looking forward to more time with each of you and Mommy. I hope that somehow you will be blessed by all the sacrifices we have made as a family during this writing season. Mommy and I pray that you will increasingly thrive in your journeys as you navigate your own oceans, individually and collectively, with our Lord as your constant Captain and Companion. Always remember that He loves and delights in you, and we live and move and have our being *in Him*!

To my siblings and their spouses and families—Eric and Gess, Jonathan and Jill, Jeremy and Megan, JoAnna and Tim, and Kristine—I am so thankful for each of you, for your willingness to be such helpful sounding boards throughout this process and for your encouragement to persevere. And Jer, thank you especially for taking the time to read these pages and offer your insight, feedback, and invaluable assistance with editing—your help in these ways as my brother means so much to me! All of you continue to inspire me by your lives and by the ways you invest in your own relationships. I cannot state too strongly how much each of you has contributed to who I am, and I hope that this book will also be a blessing to you. I respect and love all of you more than I can say.

To my beloved, late family members: Russell H. and Ruth W. Bill, Francis K. B. and Margaret H. N. Lim, J. S. Goh, James P. O. Lim, and Jerry A. Y. and Henrietta M. Ching. I am so grateful for each of you and miss you so much. I trust that you are all more alive than ever, experiencing pure joy and perfect relationship in the company of our Lord. Thank you for sharing the gift of your lives and for all your love.

And to each member of the Lim, Bill, Ching, Goh, Lim, Hayashi, Lum, and Ming families, please know how much you mean to me and how thankful and proud I am to be a part of your 'ohana. I pray you each increasingly know and grow in the grace of our Heavenly Father "from whom every family in heaven and on earth is named." I especially want to thank Dr. Jean Goh for her encouragement over the years to persevere as well as Nyla Fujii-Babb for graciously sharing her expertise and suggestions.

Also, I want to acknowledge the mentors, teachers, and key encouragers who have contributed to my own personal and spiritual growth by their lives, their counsel, and time spent together—many beginning their influence on my life long before I ever began writing. You all have given of yourselves, empowered me, and spoken words of healing and hope into my life, and I am truly grateful. I am particularly indebted to Dr. Richard Butman and Dr. Mark McMinn who both inspired and empowered me when I was first beginning my journey into the field of psychology. I want to especially acknowledge and thank Pastor Warren and Alane Aihara for pouring your time, talent, and love into me and my family and for teaching us the preciousness of worship and Reverend Dr. Siang-Yang and Angela Tan for all your time, example, encouragement, and prayers over the years, both towards me and my family.

To colleagues and families, I am (and have been) privileged to work alongside at Paradigm, I want to thank you for how you stand with and bless every individual, couple, and family we have been entrusted with. It is a great honor for me to partner with you in our mission to bring "grace to heal, change, and rest" to our community. I pray that this book will be useful to each of you as you continue to help others and navigate your own relationship journeys.

Likewise, I want to thank each person who has given me the opportunity to work with them as their personal counselor.

Thank you to each one of you for sharing so courageously, for trusting me with your lives and with your loved ones, and for showing me the power of grace and love over every kind of adversity. I have learned so much from you and count it a privilege of the highest honor to have shared the dialogues and conversations that you have afforded me. I pray that this book will also be a blessing to you as you continue to face fears, pursue dreams, and grow in truly living and truly loving. I am deeply grateful for each of you.

To dear and cherished friends and family members who have particularly journeyed with Keri and me and our family during this writing season, I am more than grateful for you, and again, I owe so much of who I am to you. I want to thank Pastor Matt and Cyndi Dirks and the community of Harbor Church Honolulu and the Kailua Community Group, Pastors Siang-Yang Tan and John Lo and First Evangelical Church Glendale/Epicentre, and Pastors Brad Barshaw, Rick Stinton, Darryl Keane and the ʻohana of (former) Faith Baptist Church. I also especially want to recognize and appreciate Kawika Haglund, Wally and Pam Holzapfel, Aaron and Maris Jones, Rick Kobayashi, Steve Smith, Matt and Tim Stevens, Jim and Nita Straayer, Damian Wyman, and Owen Yamamura for particularly entering into this journey with me and for your committed friendship, prayers, encouragements, and listening ears. And a huge *mahalo* to Kawika and Jenny and Makana and Pastor Jon and Jeri Rawlings for their generosity, expertise, patience, and gracious hospitality during the initial publishing process.

And finally, to You, Lord—Father, Son, and Holy Spirit—I am eternally grateful. You who created and sustain the universe, You, who gave Yourself for us all, You, who are Love and the Source of all relationships—thank you for every relationship You have given and continue to give and for the precious gift of eternal life through relationship with You. Thank you for adopting us as Your own, uniting us to Yourself, and for being our very life. To You alone be all thanksgiving and praise, glory and worship. I pray that this book honors You and ask You now to do with it as You please.

*Winter 2022*
*Kailua, Oʻahu*

# About the Author

**Brian R. K. B. Lim** completed his B.A. in Psychology from Wheaton College and his Ph.D. in Clinical Psychology from Fuller Theological Seminary. He is co-founder together with his amazing wife, Keri, of Paradigm Hawaii Counseling in Kailua, Hawai`i.

They have four delightful children—
Jessalyn, Michela, Zoe, and Jacob.

Thank you for joining the journey!
To continue the adventure, please visit

*maybethewholeocean.com*
*instagram.com/maybethewholeocean*
*facebook.com/maybethewholeocean*

www.ingramcontent.com/pod-product-compliance
Lightning Source LLC
Chambersburg PA
CBHW060833280326
41934CB00007B/771